Early Intervention for Special Populations of Infants and Toddlers

Early Intervention for Special Populations of Infants and Toddlers

Edited By:
Louis M. Rossetti, Ph.D.
Jack E. Kile, Ph.D.
Center for Communicative Disorders
University of Wisconsin–Oshkosh

SINGULAR PUBLISHING GROUP, INC.
SAN DIEGO • LONDON

Allen County Public Library
900 Webster Street
PO Box 2270
Fort Wayne, IN 46801-2270

Singular Publishing Group, Inc.
401 West A Street, Suite 325
San Diego, California 92101-7904

19 Compton Terrace
London N1 2UN, U.K.

e-mail: singpub@mail.cerfnet.com
Website: http://www.singpub.com

© 1997 by Singular Publishing Group, Inc.

Typeset in 10/12 Souvenir® by CFW Graphics and So Cal Graphics
Printed in the United States of America by McNaughton & Gunn

All rights, including that of translation, reserved. No part of this publication may be reproduced, stored in a retrieval system or transmitted in any form or by any means, electronic, mechanical, recording, or otherwise, without the prior written permission of the publisher.

Library of Congress Cataloging-in-Publication Data

Rossetti, Louis Michael.
    Early intervention for special populations of infants and toddlers
  / Louis M. Rossetti, Jack E. Kile.
       p.   cm.
    Includes bibliographical references and index.
    ISBN 1-56593-798-8
    1. Communicative disorders in children—Treatment.
    2. Communicative disorders in infants—Treatment. I. Kile, Jack E.
II. Title.
RJ496.C67R685   1997
618.92—dc21

96-49788
CIP

Contents

From the Editors   vii
Louis M. Rossetti, Ph.D., and Jack E. Kile, Ph.D.

Part I: Identification, Assessment, and Management of Hearing Impairment   1

Seizing the Moment, Setting the Stage, and Serving the Future: Toward Collaborative Models of Early Identification and Early Intervention Services for Children Born with Hearing Loss and Their Families
Part 1: Early Identification of Hearing Loss   3
Gary W. Mauk, M.A., CAGS,NCSP, Donald G. Barringer, Ph.D., and Pamela P. Mauk, M.A.

Seizing the Moment, Setting the Stage, and Serving the Future: Toward Collaborative Models of Early Identification and Early Intervention Services for Children Born with Hearing Loss and Their Families
Part II: Follow-up and Early Intervention   31
Gary W. Mauk, M.A., CAGS, NCSP, Donald G. Barringer, Ph.D., and Pamela P. Mauk, M.A.

Preface to Identification, Assessment, and Management of Hearing Impairment in Infants and Toddlers   53
Jack E. Kile, Ph.D., and Kathryn Laudin Beauchaine, M.A.

Identification, Assessment, and Management of Hearing Impairment in Infants and Toddlers   55
Jack E. Kile, Ph.D., and Kathryn Laudin Beauchaine, M.A.

The Effects of Mild Hearing Loss on Infant Auditory Function   77
Robert J. Nozza, Ph.D.

Issues in Amplification for Infants and Toddlers   91
Kathryn Laudin Beauchaine, M.A., CCC-A, and Kris Donaughy, M.A., CCC-A

Encouraging Intelligible Spoken Language Development in Infants and Toddlers with Hearing Loss   109
Elizabeth B. Cole, Ed.D.

Part II: Enhancing the Overall Performance of Children with Physical Limitations   131

The Relationship Between Powered Mobility and Early Learning in Young Children with Physical Disabilities   133
Richard A. Neeley, Ph.D., and Phyllis A. Neeley, M.S.P.

Development of Communicative Intent in Young Children
with Cerebral Palsy: A Treatment Efficacy Study **141**
Gay Lloyd Pinder, Ph.D., Lesley B. Olswang, Ph.D.

The Development of Communicative Intent in a Physically Disabled Child **161**
Gay Lloyd Pinder, M.Ed., Lesley Olswang, Ph.D., and Kathleen Coggins, M.S.

Part III: Effects of Cocaine and Drug Exposure   **179**

Interactions of Neonates and Infants with Prenatal Cocaine Exposure **181**
Shirley N. Sparks, M.S., and Colette Gushurst, M.D.

Service Patterns and Educational Experiences Between Two Groups Who
Work with Young Children Prenatally Exposed to Cocaine:
A Study Across Four States **195**
*J. Keith Chapman, Ph.D., Phyllis K. Mayfield, Ph.D.,
Martha J. Cook, Ed.D., and Brad S. Chissom, Ed.D.*

Cognitive Performance of Prenatally Drug-Exposed Infants **215**
Delmont Morrison, Ph.D., and Sylvia Villarreal, M.D.

Part IV: Tracheostomy, Vocalizations, and Communicative Intentions   **225**

The Role of Vocalizations on Social Behaviors of a Tracheostomized Toddler **227**
Laura A. Fus, M.A., and David P. Wacker, Ph.D.

Communicative Intentions of Three Prelinguistic Children with a
History of Long-term Tracheostomy **235**
Marilyn K. Kertoy, Ph.D., and Robert J. Waters, M.Cl.Sc.

Part V: Development of Premature and Low Birthweight Children   **249**

Effects of Prematurity on the Language Development of Hispanic Infants **251**
*Gary Montgomery, Ph.D., Donald Fucci, Ph.D., Maria Diana Gonzales, M.Ed.,
Ramesh Bettagere, M.S., Mary E. Reynolds, M.A., and Linda Petrosino, Ph.D.*

Differences in the Early Social Interaction Between Jaundiced Neonates
Treated with Phototherapy and Their Nonjaundiced Counterparts **265**
Shahrokh M. Shafaie, Ph.D., and Patricia A. Self, Ph.D.

Preverbal Communicative Abilities of High-Risk Infants **281**
Marcia J. Brown, Ph.D., CCC-SLP, and Kenneth F. Ruder, Ph.D., CCC-SLP

Index **301**

From the Editors

One of the most significant challenges early interventionists faced over the past decade related to changes in the populations they served. The emergence of new diagnostic techniques, advances in medical technology, changing family composition, the development of more effective intervention procedures, health care modifications, and new models of service delivery have all combined to present early interventionists with a fresh set of demands. Professionals are expected, to an ever-increasing degree, to be adept at meeting the needs of all infants and toddlers who are at risk or handicapped, regardless of the circumstances surrounding their developmental delays.

In our interactions with audiences of early intervention specialists, representing a wide array of professional disciplines throughout the United States and Canada, fewer than 10% reported having taken any course dedicated to children (birth to 3 years) and their families during their undergraduate or graduate preparation. Thus, they now seek this training on their own through personal investigation, attendance at inservice sessions, and reviewing professional literature dealing with early intervention services.

Early intervention professionals' needs for timely and relevant information regarding services for infants and toddlers have been met, to a large degree, by *Infant-Toddler Intervention: The Transdisciplinary Journal*. In reviewing articles published in the journal since its inception 7 years ago, a compilation of articles dealing with issues at the cutting edge of early intervention have been selected for inclusion in this volume, *Early Intervention for Special Populations of Infants and Toddlers*.

Part I consists of a series of six articles written by experienced professionals on a wide array of topics and issues which center around identification, assessment, and management of hearing impairments in infants and toddlers. In combination, these articles should provide early interventionists with insights into the unique demands faced by children with hearing impairment and their families. Mauk, Barringer, and Mauk have contributed a two-part series. Part I documents the need for early detection of hearing impairment, and Part II addresses issues related to follow-up and early intervention. Kile and Beauchaine report information regarding identification and assessment aimed at helping early intervention specialists manage hearing impairments in infants and toddlers. Nozza summarizes contemporary research dealing with the effects of mild hearing impairment on infant speech perception and its implications for management. Amplification issues relating to educational management of infants and toddlers who are hearing impaired are described by Beauchaine and Donaughy. Finally, Cole presents information for professional educators to assist infants and toddlers with hearing impairments in learning spoken language.

Part II provides information on enhancing the overall performance of children with physical limitations. Neeley and Neeley discuss the concept of powered mobility and how independent locomotion can enable children to explore and manipulate their environments to a greater degree, thus enhancing development. The next two articles (Pinder and Olswang and Pinder, Olswang, and Coggins) present information on the efficacy of intervention programs designed to enhance the communicative intent of young children with cerebral palsy.

A more recent population of children in need of early intervention services are those who were prenatally exposed to drugs. These children present even the most seasoned early intervention specialists with a unique set of challenges. The following series of articles, Part III, should enhance service provision and facilitate a better understanding of this special population of children and their families: Interactions of Neonates and Infants with Prenatal Cocaine Exposure by Sparks and Gushurst; Service Patterns and Educational Experiences Between Two Groups Who Work With Young Children Prenatally Exposed to Cocaine: A Study Across Four States by Chapman, Mayfield, Cook, and Chissom; and Cognitive Performance of Prenatally Drug-Exposed Infants by Morrison and Villarreal.

The next two articles which make up Part IV, deal with tracheostomized children. Fus and Wacker present information regarding overall impact of tracheostomy on children and provide practical suggestions for enhancing communicative skills in this population. Kertoy and Waters discuss the communicative intentions and social interactive behaviors of three prelinguistic children with histories of long-term tracheostomy.

Part V of the book provides information on the development of premature and low birthweight infants. The first article by Montgomery, Fucci, Gonzales, Bettagere, Reynolds, and Petrosino discusses the effects of prematurity on the communication and development of Hispanic infants whose mothers are known to have decreased access to prenatal care. A consideration of the social interaction skills by Shafaie and Self and preverbal communication abilities by Brown and Ruder comprise the final two articles.

In total, the content of this book represents current practice and information regarding effective strategies for special populations of infants and toddlers. Our goal in placing these articles in one volume is to provide the entire early intervention team with valuable insights into the unique and singular needs of all infants, toddlers, and their families. We are indebted to a wide array of scholar-clinicians for providing the manuscripts that make up this book. We trust that these articles will serve to sharpen our understanding and clinical skills for all populations of children and families we serve.

Louis M. Rossetti, Ph.D.
Jack E. Kile, Ph.D.
Oshkosh, Wisconsin

Part I:
Identification, Assessment, and Management of Hearing Impairment

Seizing the Moment, Setting the Stage, and Serving the Future: Toward Collaborative Models of Early Identification and Early Intervention Services for Children Born with Hearing Loss and Their Families

Part I: Early Identification of Hearing Loss

Gary W. Mauk, M.A., CAGS, NCSP
Donald G. Barringer, Ph.D.
SKI*HI Institute
Utah State University, Logan

Pamela P. Mauk, M.A.
Box Elder School District
Brigham City, Utah

As a result of the emergence and practical utility of transient evoked otoacoustic emissions (TEOAE) and automated auditory brainstem response (AABR) hearing screening technology in conjunction with a recent national recommendation and endorsements by influential professional organizations, it is now possible and recommended that every live birth be screened for auditory impairment prior to hospital discharge. However, screening every live birth for hearing loss presents a double-edged sword. Widespread implementation of hospital-based universal hearing screening programs is needed and is welcomed by the majority of professionals. However, lack of planning and proactive action on the part of hospitals, Part H early intervention program coordinators, and related professionals and agencies pertaining to appropriate pediatric audiological diagnosis and subsequent habilitative follow-up for infants identified with a variety of hearing disabilities could serve as landmines along the yellow-brick road to the emerald city of OS (optimum services), wherein young children with hearing losses and their families should dwell. This first article in a series of two articles will (a) discuss the importance of early identification and the scope of the problem of hearing loss in children and highlight some of the consequences of delay of identification, and (b) review the current status of and recommendations and practices related to early identification of hearing loss in the United States. The second article (to be published in a future issue) will explicate the rationale for and the importance of early intervention for infants and young children identified with a hearing loss, and examine issues related to the design and implementation of collaborative early identification and intervention services for children born with hearing loss and their families.

Hearing is perhaps our most versatile and valuable sense . . . [I]t personalizes or decodes much of the world in which we live. It reaches behind, under, above, around corners, through walls, and over hills, bringing in the crackling of a distant campfire, the bubbling of a nearby stream, the closing of a door, the message of a voice, the myriad of sound which identifies much of our experience. Hearing (decoding) the sounds of his environment enables an individual to spin a web of language during his early childhood. (Berg, 1976, p. 7)

Education commences at birth (Diener, 1993), and many early impairments, such as hearing loss and deficits in the ability to communicate (i.e., to have an effective language system) hold substantial morbidity for the individual economically and socially and for society in its productivity and socialization (Baumeister, 1992; Moore, 1991; Robins, 1990; Robinshaw, 1994; Ruben, 1991, 1993; U.S. Preventive Services Task Force, 1989). There is general agreement that the period between birth and the discovery of the hearing loss is a most valuable time for language development and that unrecoverable time is lost if there is late identification of the hearing loss (Goldstein & Tait, 1971; Ruben et al., 1982; Stewart, 1984). Although early-onset hearing loss negatively affects linguistic and communication skill development during the critical language-learning time between birth and 2 years of age, early-onset childhood hearing loss frequently is not detected until much beyond this period, and delays between confirmation of hearing loss and provision of intervention services are much too long and developmentally deleterious (Allen & Schubert-Sudia, 1990; Barringer, Strong, Blair, Clark, & Watkins, 1993; Calogero, Giannini, & Marciano, 1987; Davis, 1992; de Villiers, 1992; Diefendorf & Weber, 1994; Kile, 1993; Mauk, White, Mortensen, & Behrens, 1991; Ruben et al., 1982; Stewart, 1984; Strong, Clark, & Walden, 1994; Thornton, 1992; Yoshinaga-Itano, 1995).

The Developmental Importance of Language and Communication

Clark and Terry (1995) observe that, "At all times, language and communication connect children with their world and with the people in their lives" (p. 170). Because hearing, speech, language, and communication are the means by which a child conceives, classifies, and manipulates the world, an early onset hearing loss can negatively impact psychological and social processes (Allen, 1969; Berg, 1976; Boothroyd, 1982; Schum, 1987; Seyfried, Hutchinson, & Smith, 1989).

Although hearing is vital in the development of speech communication skills, it also allows a child to acquire cognitive and social-emotional information about the world, as well as to monitor his or her physical and social environment (Diener, 1993). Thus, early identification of hearing loss and subsequent early intervention for affected children holds the promise of optimizing children's language, speech, intellectual and psychosocial development, and occupational/economic opportunity (Brackett, 1993; Buttross, Gearhart, & Peck, 1995; Downs, 1993, 1994; Hall, Kripal, & Hepp, 1988; Mace, Wallace, Whan, & Steimachowicz, 1991; Marlowe, 1993; Mauk & White, 1995; Ruben, 1993; Scanlon & Bamford, 1990; Strong et al., 1994; Yoshinaga-Itano, 1995). Schum (1987) remarks that children with significant sensorineural hearing loss (SNHL) or deafness may be delayed in social growth, because they have two experiential deficits: (1) These children have no common communication method via which to receive information from other people in their life, especially their family in the early stages of development; and (2) these children have no fully developed language system to enable them to encode, process, and manipulate experiential information.

Hence, audiologist Judy Marlowe (1994) has stated that auditory deprivation, regardless of type or degree, during the first 3 years of life may exert a lifelong impact on the level of language function achieved. Neonatologist Betty Vohr (1994) recently stated that it is imperative for professionals in the health care field to advocate for infants and children with hearing losses and to endeavor to provide for them the best possible care through universal hearing screening, habilitation, and early intervention services. Finally, early detection and habilitation of all infants with hearing losses must continue to be a major goal for health care systems and, "as advocates for children with hearing loss, we must improve our strategies for early identification and intervention" (Northern & Hayes, 1994, p. 13).

Toward Universal Newborn Screening for Hearing Loss

Downs (1986) has asserted that no other group has more to gain from early identification than do those with a hearing disability. The economic benefits resulting from early identification of hearing disabilities are better documented than those among any other disability group (Downs, 1994; Ross, 1990). This importance is recognized in the *Healthy People 2000 Goals* (U.S. Department of Health and Human Services, 1990), which establish as a priority the identification of infants with a hearing disability by 1 year of age. The achievement of the foregoing goal is dependent on finding better ways to identify hearing impairment in young children. Toward that end, a recently convened National Institutes of Health (NIH) Consensus Panel concluded, among other things, that (a) all newborns (both high and low risk) be screened for hearing loss prior to discharge from the newborn nursery, (b) the preferred model of screening should begin with an evoked otoacoustic emissions (EOAE) test (described below) and should be followed by an auditory brainstem response test for all infants who fail the evoked otoacoustic emissions test, and (c) comprehensive intervention and management programs must be an integral part of a universal screening program (National Institutes of Health [NIH], 1993; see Figure 1).

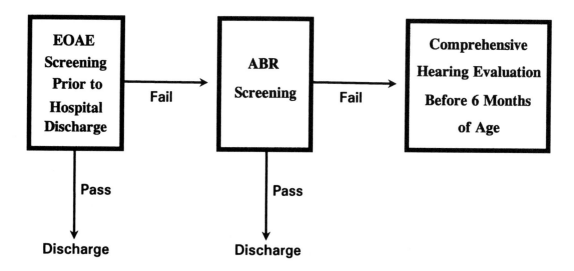

Figure 1. National Institutes of Health (NIH) recommended protocol for universal newborn hearing screening. (Adapted from *NIH Consensus Statement: Early Identification of Hearing Impairment in Infants and Young Children, 11*(1), 1–25, 1993.)

Hayes (1994) recently observed that, "Early, appropriate, beneficial, and effective intervention can only occur in the presence of early identification" (p. 955), and that, "Implementation of universal infant hearing screening is an important first step toward improving outcomes for infants with hearing loss" (p. 955). Finally, Northern (1994) has noted that screening for SNHL in infants is justified because (a) the condition of early childhood hearing loss is developmentally consequential; (b) currently available neonatal hearing screening procedures are safe, effective, simple, reliable, valid, reasonably low cost, and practicable: and (c) treatment and habilitation practices for early hearing impairment are effective.

The Scope of the Problem of Hearing Loss

A sensorineural hearing loss (SNHL) is a hearing loss that is "due to pathology in the inner ear, or along the nerve pathway from the inner ear to the brainstem" (Roeser & Price, 1981, p. 81). Although severe to profound (71 to 91+ dB HL) (Sweitzer, 1977) SNHL is thought to be present in about 1 out of every 1,000 normal live births, the prevalence of mild or moderate hearing impairment in the general newborn population is unknown (American Speech-Language-Hearing Association [ASHA], 1989; Hall, 1992).

The American Academy of Audiology (AAA) (as cited in Bess & Hall, 1992, Appendix 2, p. 507), in its vision/mission statement on screening children for auditory function, stated (a) that each year in the United States, about 4,000 children are born deaf or with a profound and permanent SNHL and (b) that approximately 37,000 additional children are born with milder degrees of permanent SNHL (> 35 dB HL), which can still interfere with development of communication. A recent cohort study of hearing loss in Rhode Island (White, Vohr, & Behrens, 1993) reported a prevalence rate for both unilateral and bilateral SNHL of 6 per 1,000 children. Northern (1994) has supported this higher prevalence: "Based on results from infant hearing screening studies, 5.5 to 6 per 1000 is a more accurate estimate of moderate, severe, and profound sensorineural hearing loss in infants" (p. 955).

A Brief Review of the Consequences of Delay in Identification of Sensorineural Hearing Loss

The following section will review briefly the developmental consequences of delayed identification of bilateral and unilateral sensorineural hearing loss (SNHL). Readers interested in the early identification and consequences of and intervention for conductive hearing loss are referred to Feagans (1986); Feagans, Hannan, and Manlove (1992); Grievink, Peters, van Bon, & Schilder (1993); Maxon, White, Vohr, and Behrens (1993); Peters, Grievink, van Bon, & Schilder (1994); Stewart and Downs (1993); and Teele, Klein, Chase, Menyuk, Rosner, and the Greater Boston Otitis Media Study Group (1990).

Bilateral SNHL

The negative consequences of bilateral (two ears) SNHL include cognitive, perceptual, speech, language, and academic factors (de Villiers, 1992; Ross, 1990). Furthermore, research by Markides (1986) and Ramkala-wan and Davis (1992) has indicated that the earlier identification and habilitation occur, the greater the level of speech production and linguistic competence achieved by children during their early years of life.

Although the negative consequences of severe to profound hearing loss have long been recognized, researchers have reported that early identification and habilitation are also critical for those with mild or moderate SNHL (AAA, 1988; Davis, Elfenbein, Schum, & Bentler, 1986; Downs, 1994; Tharpe & Bess, 1991). In a review of selected language and learning studies, Matkin (1986) concluded that even mild SNHL creates significant psychoeducational deficits for affected children. Similarly, Bullerdeick (1987) has noted that research is challenging, and changing, the long-held assumption that minimal hearing loss in children is harmless. Marlowe (1994) has observed that, presently, all severities of hearing loss (from mild to moderate) are appreciated as a source of significant delay in the acquisition of communication skills. Recently, Nozza (1994) observed that, unlike the conspicuous effects of moderate to profound hearing impairments, the impact of mild hearing loss on infants and toddlers is not well understood. It has become clear only recently that mild (or even unilateral) hearing loss has an effect on affected children's levels of scholastic achievement (e.g., Bess, 1985; Blair, Peterson, & Viehweg, 1985; Davis et al., 1986; Montgomery & Matkin, 1992; Tharpe & Bess, 1991). Such research findings have "caused us to revise our thinking on what constitutes hearing impairment in children" (Nozza, 1994, p. 285)

Unilateral SNHL

The potential impact of unilateral (one ear) SNHL is frequently misunderstood and should not be underestimated (Gjerdingen, 1992; Zarrella, 1995). Historically, it has been thought that unilateral hearing loss is not a disabling condition for children (Northern & Downs, 1978; Oyler, Oyler, & Matkin,

1987, 1988). However, past and current research have demonstrated the serious negative consequences of unilateral hearing loss in areas of auditory and psycholinguistic skills, educational progress, communication, and classroom behavior (Bess & Tharpe, 1984, 1986; Bovo et al., 1988; Brookhouser, Worthington, & Kelly, 1991; Culbertson & Gilbert, 1986; Oyler et al., 1987, 1988; Stein, 1983; Zarrella, 1995).

For example, with regard to academic failure, Bess and Tharpe (1986) found that 35% of children with unilateral hearing losses had repeated a grade, in contrast to a normal failure rate of about 3½%. Klee and Davis-Dansky (1986) found that 32% of children with unilateral hearing losses failed a grade in school, whereas none of the children in the matched normal-hearing group failed. Oyler et al. (1988) reported similar rates of grade retention among children with unilateral hearing losses in their research and noted that the chance of repeating a grade was 10 times greater for children with a unilateral hearing loss than for the general school population. Further exacerbating the problem is the fact that, according to Bess, Klee, and Culbertson (1986), "many of our current approaches to screening neonates and infants are insensitive to unilateral hearing loss" (p. 43).

The History and Status of Early Screening for Hearing Loss

National Level

The federal government has been involved for almost 40 years in the quest to identify hearing loss at an early age in the form of conferences, advisory groups, and research projects and has sought to lower the age of identification of significant hearing loss and thereby forestall the deleterious developmental effects of reduced hearing acuity during a child's early years of life (Mauk & Behrens, 1993). Federal governmental interest in initiatives related to early identification of hearing loss dates back to at least 1965, when a report to the Secretary of Health, Education, and Welfare recommended the development and nationwide implementation of "universally applied procedures for early identification and evaluation of hearing impairment" (Babbidge, 1965, p. C-10). Two years later, the Report of the National Conference on Education of the Deaf (U.S. Department of Health, Education, and Welfare, 1967) recommended that (a) a high-risk register to expedite identification of young children with hearing losses be adopted immediately, (b) the public information media should be used to make hearing loss as common a concern as cancer and heart disease, and (c) testing of newborn infants and children 6 to 12 months old should be investigated with particular attention paid to the question of cost-effectiveness.

According to a report released in 1988 by the Commission on Education of the Deaf to the President and Congress of the United States, "more than 20 years [after the Babbidge Report], the average age of identification for profoundly deaf children in the United States is reported as 2 and 1/2 years" (p. 3). The Commission's report went on to recommend that the U.S. Department of Education, in cooperation with the Department of Health and Human Services, should issue federal guidelines to assist individual states in implementing improved screening procedures for all newborns (Commission on Education of the Deaf, 1988).

In response to the Commission's report, the Office of the Assistant Secretary of Special Education and Rehabilitative Services of the U.S. Department of Education in collaboration with the Office of Maternal and Child Health of the U.S. Department of Health and Human Services convened an advisory group of national experts in April, 1988 to advise the federal government about the feasibility of developing guidelines for early identification of hearing loss, the content to be included in the guidelines, and the process that should be used in implementing such guidelines (Advisory Group on the Early Identification of Children with Hearing Impairments, 1988). The advisory group concluded that the federal government could promote early identification of children who are hearing-impaired most effectively by funding demonstration projects to expand and to document systematically the cost efficiency of the proven techniques already in existence but infrequently used.

In 1988, C. Everett Koop, then Surgeon General of the United States, issued a challenge that by the Year 2000, 90% of all children with significant hearing loss should be identified by 12 months of age. Simultaneously, the Public Health Service initiated a campaign to make parents aware of behavioral indicators of childhood hearing loss. At about the same time, the U.S. Department of Health and Human Services (1990) was involved in a massive project to focus existing knowledge, resources, and commitment to exploit opportunities to prevent needless disease and disability. The result was a report, *Healthy People 2000: National Health Promotion and Disease Prevention Objectives*, released in 1990, which committed the federal government to work toward the accomplishment of a series of objective, specific, attainable goals designed to improve the health of our country's citizens by the Year 2000. It is noteworthy that a goal was included to "reduce the average age at which children with significant hearing impairment are identified to no more than 12 months" by the year 2000 (U.S Department of Health and Human Services, 1990, p. 460).

Most recently, in March of 1993, the federal government organized a National Institutes of Health Consensus Development Conference on Identification of Hearing Impairments in Infants and Young Children in March of 1993 (NIH, 1993). The conclusions and recommendations of that conference were reported earlier in this article.

State Level

Individual states have been involved in efforts to screen for hearing loss at an early age for the past three decades (Blake & Hall, 1990). However, although there is professional consensus that early identification of hearing disability is critical to the optimization of a child's potential (Marlowe, 1993), only 3–5% of all newborns in the United States are screened for hearing impairment (Bess & Hall, 1992). States simply have not moved ahead in a committed and aggressive manner to implement infant hearing screening programs even for at-risk children.

Welsh and Slater (1993) recently reported the results of a survey conducted by ASHA on the status of infant hearing impairment identification programs (IHIIPs) as of December, 1992. Three groups of IHIIPs were delineated from the survey: (1) statewide programs that were legislatively mandated, (2) statewide programs that were *not* legislatively mandated (identified in the study as "statewide programs"), and (3) states with individual birthing sites (e.g., hospitals) which operate IHIIPs. Representatives from 45 states (90%) responded to the survey.

Only 40% of states in this survey (Welsh & Slater, 1993) reported having legislatively mandated infant hearing impairment identification programs (IHIIPs). Additionally, 89% of these states target *high-risk infants only* (e.g., that high-risk registries be maintained, high-risk screenings be conducted, and/or only infants flagged as high-risk receive a hearing screening). Even in those states with nonlegislatively mandated "statewide" programs and nonstatewide "individually operated" programs, many are implemented only in large population centers and target only high-risk infants. Finally, the relationship between screening programs, follow-up care, and early intervention service systems is frequently not strong (J. Johnson et al., 1993; Mahoney, Eichwald, & Fronberg, 1992; Welsh & Slater, 1993). Welsh and Slater (1993) report that, even for legislatively mandated IHIIPs, "Follow-up care is not required" (p. 51). Aspects and limitations of high-risk registries for early identification of hearing loss are discussed later in this article.

Pros and Cons of Various Approaches to Early Screening for Hearing Loss

Although a number of different methods have been tried over the past 40 years, we have made very little progress in reducing the average age at which significant hearing loss is identified (Mauk & Behrens, 1993; Mauk & White, 1995). Some of these methods are delineated briefly below.

Public Awareness Campaigns

Public awareness campaigns are relatively inexpensive to implement and can provide broad coverage, but are not very effective for many reasons (e.g., uncertain yield for hearing losses identified; parental suspicions are often ignored).

Behavioral Screening

Behavioral screening for hearing loss can take a variety of forms, depending on the age and accessibility of the child. For very young children, the most frequently used approaches include behavioral observation audiometry in the hospital, home health visitors, and Crib-O-Grams.

Behavioral Observation Audiometry (BOA) and Visual Reinforcement Audiometry (VRA)

Behavioral observation audiometry (BOA) procedures are used with infants who are less than 6 months old (Hodgson, 1987). One frequently utilized BOA procedure involves a high-intensity, narrow band noise presented by a hand-held instrument positioned near the infant (Diefendorf, 1992). One of the earliest efforts was by Downs and Sterritt (1964), in which testing was completed in the nursery following a specific protocol. The advantages of this form of BOA are that the equipment is relatively inexpensive and maintenance-free; it is time-efficient (screening accomplished in less than 5 minutes); the testing is straightforward, and it tests frequency-specific, behavioral responses to hearing (Hall, 1992; Hodgson, 1987; Northern & Gerkin, 1989). However, this form of BOA has produced many critics because of the high number of false-positive and false-negative results (e.g., Alberti, Hyde, Riko, Corbin, & Abramovich, 1983; Durieux-Smith & Jacobson, 1985). Further, the determination of whether a response has occurred is highly subjective, the test requires a sound-treated room, and there is a dearth of personnel trained to observe the often very subtle physical responses to sound (Hall, 1992; Northern & Gerkin, 1989).

In some countries, behavioral testing of infants' hearing by home health visitors has become established practice (Bentzen & Jensen, 1981; Johnson & Ashurst, 1990; McCormick, 1983). This BOA procedure employs what is known as the "distraction test" (first described by Ewing & Ewing 1944, 1947). In this procedure, a trained home visitor employs simple behavioral testing techniques and observes whether the infant responds to various noises generated by such items as rattles and bells. However, in recent years, an electronic warble tone device for screening hearing at 500Hz, 2 kHz, and 4 kHz at two screening levels of 25 dB HL and 35 dB HL has been introduced (McCormick, 1986). In countries such as England where universal home visits to check on children's health status are conducted, this approach is quite economical (McCormick, 1983). In countries without universal home visiting, such as the United States, the costs would be prohibitive (Mauk & Behrens, 1993).

In the Crib-O-Gram (COG) hearing screening procedure, a 90 dB SPL, 3 kHz sound stimulus is presented to the infant in a crib. Underneath the child's crib, a photoelectric transducer sensor records movements. If, with repeated stimuli, simultaneous changes in activity are recorded within 2.6 seconds, it is concluded that the child can hear. Advantages of the Crib-O-Gram include the following: (a) a relatively untrained individual can administer it (Fritsch & Sommer, 1991), (b) it is automated, (c) it does not require a sound-treated room, (d) it does not interrupt the nursery routine, and (e) it is an objective procedure (Hall, 1992; Northern & Gerkin, 1989).

A major disadvantage of the COG procedure is that many false positives and false negatives occur, leading to serious questions about reliability and validity, particularly in the NICU population (Diefendorf & Weber, 1994; Durieux-Smith, Picton, Edwards, Goodman, & MacMurray, 1985).[1] Durieux-Smith et al. (1985) found that 32% of the babies tested with COG shifted from pass to fail, or vice versa, when they were retested within 48 hours. Another problem with the COG is that it is difficult to determine threshold versus habituation. Also, because high stimulus intensities are needed to elicit a detectable behavioral response, COG, like BOA, may miss mild-moderate and unilateral hearing losses (Gravel, 1993; Hall, 1992; Shimizu et al., 1990; Weber, 1988). Because of these limitations, in recent years there has been a reduction in the use of the COG procedure (Diefendorf & Weber, 1994; Markowitz, 1990).

Although not applicable to neonatal hearing screening, from 6 months of age through well into the second year of life, visual reinforcement audiometry (VRA; Liden & Kankkunen, 1969) can be used successfully to screen the frequency-specific auditory sensitivity of infants and toddlers (Frye-Osier, 1993; Hodgson, 1987; Moore, Wilson, & Thompson, 1977). Frye-Osier (1993) explains that the VRA procedure depends on the child learning the contingent relationship between "a very rewarding and motivating visual display [e.g., an animated toy] and the presence of carefully chosen, frequency-specific auditory stimuli" (Frye-Osier, 1993, p. 31). The stimuli used in VRA are generally warble tones or narrow bands of noise (Hodgson, 1987), and single syllable speech sounds such as *"buh"* (Frye-Osier, 1993). VRA screening is most likely to be successful when conducted in the sound field using loudspeakers at a specific distance from the

---

[1] A "false-positive" identification occurs when an infant fails the screening test, but does not have a hearing loss. A "false-negative" identification occurs when an infant passes the screening test, but actually has a hearing loss.

child (Primus, 1992). However, although sound field localization VRA may provide "a quick and easy method of substantiating functionally normal hearing sensitivity in situations where an infant's hearing is suspect" (Hodgson, 1987, p. 203), Frye-Osier (1993) points out that VRA sound field screening can rule out all but mild hearing loss in the *better* ear only. Unilateral hearing losses may not be detected at all (Hodgson, 1987). For additional information on VRA protocols and procedures, the reader is referred to Primus (1988) and Primus and Thompson (1985).

High-Risk Registries

High-risk registries (HRR; both maternal questionnaire-based and birth certificate-based) are relatively inexpensive, and some, such as the Utah birth certificate-based registry have demonstrated success in identifying large numbers of children with SNHL (Mahoney & Eichwald, 1987; Mahoney, 1989, 1993). In 1982, the Joint Committee on Infant Hearing (JCIH) recommended the identification of infants at risk for hearing impairment by means of the following seven criteria: (1) a family history of childhood hearing impairment; (2) congenital perinatal infection (e.g., cytomegalovirus [CMV], rubella, herpes, toxoplasmosis, syphilis); (3) anatomical malformations involving the head or neck (e.g., dysmorphic appearance including syndromal and nonsyndromal abnormalities, overt or submucous cleft palate, morphologic abnormalities of the pinna); (4) birthweight less than 1500 grams; (5) hyperbilirubinemia at level exceeding indications for exchange transfusion; (6) bacterial meningitis, especially Haemophilus influenzae; and (7) severe asphyxia (often measured with Apgar scores between 0 and 3 or infants who fail to institute spontaneous respiration by 10 minutes and those with hypotonia persisting to 2 hours of age). In 1989, ASHA, utilizing the JCIH 1982 risk criteria, released "guidelines for the establishment of auditory screening programs for newborn infants who are at risk for hearing impairment" (ASHA, 1989, p. 89).

In 1990, the JCIH released another position statement (JCIH, 1991), which clarified some of the original seven risk criteria and expanded the list of risk criteria to a total of 10: (8) ototoxic medications used for more than 5 days and loop diuretics used in combination with aminoglycosides, (9) stigmata associated with syndromes known to include SNHL, and (10) prolonged mechanical ventilation ($\geq$10 days) were added to the risk criteria list. The JCIH 1990 Position Statement (JCIH, 1991) also differentiated between neonates (birth through 28 days) and infants (29 days through 2 years), and recommended a specific screening protocol. The 10 risk criteria discussed above applied to neonates. The 8 risk criteria for infants were: (1) parent/caregiver concern regarding hearing, speech, language, and/or developmental delay; (2) bacterial meningitis; (3) neonatal risk factors that may be associated with progressive SNHL (e.g., CMV); (4) head trauma; (5) stigmata associated with syndromes known to include SNHL; (6) ototoxic medications used for more than 5 days and loop diuretics used in combination with aminoglycosides; (7) children with neurodegenerative disorders (e.g., neurofibromatosis, Tay-Sach's disease); and (8) childhood infectious diseases known to be associated with SNHL (e.g., mumps, measles).

Although infants with the high-risk variables proffered for more than a decade by the JCIH (1982, 1991) are much more likely to have a hearing loss, published data collected over the past decade by several researchers and clinicians have clearly demonstrated that only about 50% of the children with severe to profound bilateral SNHL will manifest at least one of the high-risk criteria generated by the JCIH (American Academy of Pediatrics [AAP], 1995; Eichwald & Mahoney, 1993; Elssmann, Matkin, & Sabo, 1987; Epstein & Reilly, 1989; Fowler & Fowler, 1994; Mauk et al., 1991; Todd, 1994). The 1994 Position Statement acknowledged this problem: "risk factor screening identifies only 50% of infants with significant hearing loss . . . Failure to identify the remaining 50% of children with hearing loss results in diagnosis and intervention at an unacceptably late age" (AAP, 1995, p. 152).

Thus, the 1994 JCIH Position Statement addressed the need to identify *all* infants with hearing loss, not just those who manifested one of the risk factors. The 1994 JCIH Position Statement "endorses the goal of universal detection of infants with hearing loss as early as possible" (AAP, 1995, p. 152), but still "maintains a role for the high-risk factors" (p. 152) contained in the previous JCIH Position Statement (JCIH, 1991) "for use with neonates (birth through age 28 days) when universal screening is not available" (p. 153). However, as Kile (1993) recently observed, "much is still not known about the relationship between accepted risk factors and hearing impairment" (p. 155). Only time will tell whether the modified neonatal and infant risk criteria contained within the JCIH 1994 Position Statement are more sensitive and detect more than 50% of children ultimately identified specifically with SNHL. The JCIH 1994 Position Statement (AAP, 1995) also recognized that some neonates and infants may pass initial hearing screening, but may have indicators that would require periodic monitoring of hearing to detect delayed-onset SNHL and/or conductive hearing loss (CHL). Indicators identified in the JCIH 1994 Position Statement as associated with delayed-onset SNHL include (a) family history of hereditary childhood hearing loss, (b) in utero infection (e.g., CMV, rubella), and (c) neurofibromatosis Type II and neurodegenerative disorders. Indicators identified by the JCIH 1994 Position Statement as associated with conductive hearing loss include (a) recurrent or persistent otitis media with effusion, (b) anatomic deformities and other disorders that affect eustachian tube function, and (c) neurodegenerative disorders (AAP, 1995).

Auditory Brainstem Response Audiometry

Auditory brainstem response (ABR) audiometry is a technique "to investigate the response of the inner ear and the various relays of the acoustic pathway to auditory stimuli (clicks)" (Francois, Bonfils, & Narcy, 1995, p. 176). In this test, a computer is used to make recordings of brainstem electrical activity of the newborn in response to the auditory stimuli. *Conventional ABR* has been generally recognized as the technique of choice for identifying hearing loss among newborns, but it is usually performed only on neonates at-risk for hearing loss (Hyde, Riko, & Malizia, 1990; Jacobson, Jacobson, & Spahr, 1990), is time-consuming (Fritsch & Sommer, 1991), and is too expensive to use with all babies (Fritsch & Sommer, 1991; Hall, 1993; Sininger, 1993). Recently, *automated ABR* (AABR) (Hall, 1992; Jacobson et al., 1990; Kileny & Magathan, 1987; Peters, 1986; Weber, 1988), although reducing the cost of both equipment and operation somewhat, can still prove to be quite expensive especially in small institutional settings and settings in which only at-risk newborns are screened (Mahoney, 1993).

As the techniques that have been used in the past are considered, it becomes evident that significant progress in early identification of hearing loss, ideally during the neonatal period, is unlikely unless we can find screening techniques that are practicable, valid, and cost-efficient (Mauk & Behrens, 1993; Mauk & White, 1995; Turner & Cone-Wesson, 1992). Although they each have various advantages and disadvantages (Martin, Schwegler, Gleeson, & Shi, 1994; Mauk & Behrens, 1993), two of the more promising approaches for much earlier identification of hearing loss, ABR and transient evoked otoacoustic emissions (TEOAEs), are discussed in greater detail.

ABR and Neonatal Hearing Screening

Conventional ABR (sometimes referred to as brainstem auditory evoked response [BAER]) has been used in newborn hearing screening for many years (Hall et al., 1988; Jacobson et al., 1990; Jacobson & Morehouse, 1984; Schulman-Galambos & Galambos, 1979; Shimizu et al., 1990), has been implemented successfully in both HRR-based and universal newborn hearing screening programs (AAP, 1995, p. 153), and continues to be regarded by many audiologists as the "gold standard of neonatal screening" (Mauk & Behrens, 1993, p. 11).

However, in recent years, advances in technology have led to the development of equipment that makes possible automated detection of the presence or absence of ABR activity in neonates (Hall, 1992; Jacobson et al., 1990; Peters, 1986). Automated ABR (AABR) screeners, such as the ALGO-1 Plus™ Infant Hearing Screener (manufactured by Natus Medical, Inc. of Foster City, CA) "were developed as a faster, less expensive alternative for hearing loss identification in newborns" (Maxon, White, Vohr, & Behrens, 1993, p. 77). AABR screeners provide a "pass" or "refer" outcome, comparing/matching an individual newborn's ABR signal (or waveform) with a pattern (template) derived from a composite signal from a sample of normally hearing newborns (Hall, 1992; Peters, 1986). Hall (1994) stated that, from his clinical experience with infant hearing screening during the past 8 years, AABR "is a feasible and effective procedure for hearing screening of all newborn infants" (p. 949). Many states and individual programs are currently operating successful neonatal hearing screening programs using AABR (Davis, 1994; Folsom, 1990; Hall & Chase, 1993; Joseph, Herrmann, Thornton, & Pye, 1993; Marlowe, 1993; Stewart, Bibb, & Pearlman, 1993; Welsh & Slater, 1993).

Transient Evoked Otoacoustic Emissions (TEOAEs) and Neonatal Hearing Screening

Most hearing impairments, including severe congenital or early onset hearing loss, can be attributed to the absence or loss of function of the delicate hair cells in the inner ear. These hair cells, located in the inner ear (cochlea), are specialized nerve cells that convert sound energy into electrically coded signals which the brain can interpret. The health of these hair cells, and hence their ability to convert sound into interpretable signals, can be assessed via a relatively new technique called otoacoustic emission (OAE) screening.

What Are OAEs?

Otoacoustic emissions (OAEs), first discovered in 1978 by Dr. David Kemp of Great Britain, "are defined as acoustic energy produced in the cochlea and recorded in the outer ear canal . . . OAEs are vibrational energy that is generated in the cochlea and travels all the way through the middle ear structures, to be transduced as sound at the tympanic membrane; this is the reversed course of the normal sound conduction into the inner ear" (Martin et al., 1994, p. 488). Transient evoked otoacoustic emissions (TEOAEs) are externally produced acoustic responses emitted by the cochlea across the sound frequencies of 500-6000 Hz in response to brief acoustic stimuli, such as sound clicks or tone pips (Francois et al., 1995; Gorga, Stover, Bergman, Beauchaine, & Kaminski, 1995; Hanley & Becker, 1993; Kile, Schaffmeyer, & Kuba, 1994; Lonsbury-Martin, Martin, McCoy, & Whitehead, 1995; Probst, Lonsbury-Martin, & Martin, 1991). Although the process by which TEOAEs are emitted is not completely understood (Martin et al., 1994), it is believed that they come from the activities of the outer hair cells (OHCs) of the cochlea (Brownell, 1990; Radcliffe, 1993). Kemp's work showed that the OHCs, when stimulated externally by sound clicks, simultaneously emit sound or an "echo," called the otoacoustic emission, back through the middle ear. This "echo" can be recorded in the external ear canal using a small microphone.

The ease with which EOAEs can be measured led to the development of one commercial device that is presently available for measuring TEOAEs, the Otodynamic Analyzer (Bray & Kemp, 1987; Kemp, Bray, Alexander, & Brown, 1986). This equipment consists of a self-contained probe/microphone assembly connected to a computerized analyzer. The probe is inserted into the infant's external ear canal and a series of soft clicks is emitted. OAEs generated by the infant's cochlea in response to these clicks are picked by the microphone contained in the probe and sent to the computer for analysis and visual display of the infant's cochlear response (Kemp & Ryan, 1993). Kile et al. (1994) have stated that, "For those children having greater than mild sensorineural hearing impairment, or any conductive hearing loss [e.g., a hearing loss associated with debris in the external ear canal and/or fluid in the middle ear cavity], OAEs are generally absent" (pp. 300–301).

Research and Application of TEOAEs in Newborn Hearing Screening

An expanding body of research with infants has demonstrated the value and accuracy of TEOAEs in assessing auditory function (Bonfils, Uziel, & Pujol, 1988a, 1988b; Elberling, Parbo, Johnsen, & Bagi, 1985; Engdahl, Arnesen, & Mair, 1994; Johnsen, Bagi, & Elberling, 1983; Kemp, 1978, 1988; Kemp et al., 1986; Lutman, Mason, Sheppard, & Gibbin, 1989; Maxon, White, Behrens, & Vohr, 1995; Meredith, Stephens, Hogan, Cartlidge, & Drayton, 1994; Norton, 1994; Richardson, Williamson, Lenton, Tarlow, & Rudd, 1995; White & Behrens, 1993; White, Behrens, & Strickland, 1995; White et al., 1994). Probst et al. (1991) in their review of the literature on the use of TEOAEs with infants stated that "TEOAEs may represent an ideal means for screening hearing and infants compose the primary subject group in which such objective testing is most desirable" (p. 2049).

The state of Rhode Island has been conducting a legislatively mandated statewide system of universal newborn hearing screening since July, 1993 in eight maternity hospitals. This system, known as the Rhode Island Hearing Assessment Program (RIHAP), utilizes the TEOAE screening technique and includes a follow-up program for families whose children have been identified as having a hearing loss. RIHAP was implemented in February of 1990 at Women and Infants Hospital in Providence, Rhode Island, as the first large-scale, clinical trial of TEOAE-based neonatal hearing screening (White & Behrens, 1993). Aspects of the RIHAP have been described in detail elsewhere (Maxon et al., 1995; White & Behrens, 1993; White et al., 1994, 1995), and the reader is referred to these sources for additional information.

Prior to the inception of RIHAP, adequate clinical studies had not been conducted in the United States to examine the feasibility, validity, and cost-efficiency of large-scale TEOAE-based newborn hearing screening (Maxon et al., 1995). The results of RIHAP have shown that use of the TEOAE procedure in universal newborn hearing screening is indeed feasible, valid, and cost-efficient (Maxon et al., 1995; White & Behrens, 1993; White et al., 1994, 1995). The data and practical experience of RIHAP also provide additional information on which successful neonatal hearing screening programs can be planned and implemented (Maxon et al., 1995). Recently, Lonsbury-Martin et al. (1995), in a current analysis of the use of OAEs to evaluate the auditory system, asserted that, "Overall, the initial findings from ongoing clinical trials of newborn screening with evoked OAEs have been successful. Thus it appears to be logistically and economically feasible to screen every newborn child with TEOAEs for the purpose of detecting hearing impairment" (p. 54). However, neither TEOAE or AABR should be viewed strictly as tests of hearing, "but rather as measurements of physiological events associated with hearing" (Francois et al., 1995, p. 176).

For further information on the performance and estimated and actual costs associated with various models of protocols for early identification of hearing loss, the reader is referred to Bess and Paradise (1994), Maxon et al. (1995), Raffin and Matz (1994), Robinette (1994), Thornton (1992), Turner (1990, 1991, 1992a, 1992b, 1993), and Turner and Cone-Wesson (1992).

Early Identification: Only the Beginning of the Adventure

After more than 50 years of work and advocacy (Ewing & Ewing, 1944), *universal screening* for hearing impairment prior to hospital discharge is our ultimate and attainable goal (Mauk & White, 1995). Frye-Osier (1993) recently observed that, "Quality hearing screening programs for infants and children, delivered as early in life as possible, are essential to limiting or eliminating the negative developmental and social consequences of hearing loss" (p. 41). Although the commitment to technology for neonatal and infant hearing screening in this country has come a long way and is evolving rapidly, the average age of 18–30 months, at which young children with auditory disabilities are identified, is still unacceptable. The promise of earlier detection, diagnosis, and habilitation of hearing loss is within reach (a) if we have appropriate understanding of the magnitude and consequences of the problem, (b) if we are able to learn from past efforts, (c) if we are able to evaluate and to use emerging technologies appropriately, and (d) if we are willing to develop collaborative uses of resources and agencies already in place.

The time is prime for states to move toward integrated and collaborative universal systems of newborn hearing screening, diagnosis, and early intervention. Recent advances in hearing screening technology, such as TEOAE and AABR, combined with current emphasis and concern to identify and serve children with disabilities, bring together necessary components to move ahead. As Maxon et al. (1995) observed recently, "Universal newborn hearing screening is not only feasible, but the relatively low associated costs make it very practical. We believe it is now time to move forward in implementing universal newborn hearing screening" (p. 275). However, for readers of this article, it is important that we note that, although universal screening for infant hearing impairment has been recommended by a multidisciplinary panel convened by the National Institutes of Health (1993) and endorsed by the prominent Joint Committee on Infant Hearing (AAP, 1995), universal screening for infant hearing impairment does have some vocal critics and opponents (e.g., Bess & Paradise, 1994).

Specifically of note is a critical commentary published by Dr. Fred Bess, an audiologist, and Dr. Jack Paradise, a pediatrician, in the February 1994 issue of Pediatrics in response to the Consensus Statement "Early Identification of Hearing Impairment in Infants and Young Children" issued in March 1993 by the National Institutes of Health (1993). They argued that universal screening for infant hearing impairment was not simple, not free of risk, not necessarily beneficial, and not currently justified for implementation in the United States. At risk of understatement, the professional response to this commentary of Drs. Bess and Paradise (1994) has consisted of plaudits (e.g., Miller, 1994) and resistance (e.g., White & Maxon, 1995).

Because the commentary by Drs. Bess and Paradise on implementation of universal newborn hearing screening in the United States has been welcomed by some professionals and assailed by other professionals, we feel that it is necessary to outline briefly the major concerns and perspectives regarding the NIH Consensus Statement proffered by Bess and Paradise (1994). While acknowledging the fact that "early childhood hearing loss can impose burdens on the affected child and on the child's family, and on society" (Bess & Paradise, 1994, p. 332), Bess and Paradise (1994) state that the Consensus Statement "falls short of being justified on grounds of practicability, effectiveness, cost, and harm-benefit ratio" (p. 330). Specifically, they assert the following.

1. Universal hearing screening of newborns is not practicable in all hospitals for sundry reasons (e.g., the large number of newborns who are discharged within 24–48 hours; the logistics and costs associated with hospitals in rural or remote areas), the two-stage EOAE-ABR screening protocol recommended in the Consensus Statement would result in a high over-referral (false-positive) rate, and "the direct monetary costs alone of the proposed program, assuming ideal conditions, would approximate $200,000,000 annually" (Bess & Paradise, 1994, p. 332).

2. Admonitions and concerns expressed in the Consensus Statement regarding the long-term developmental effects of early-onset hearing impairment "do not discriminate sufficiently between the acknowledged adverse effects of moderate to severe, persistent hearing loss, and the entirely speculative and perhaps nonexistent effects of mild or moderate temporary hearing loss" (Bess & Paradise, 1994, p. 330).

3. Regarding efficacy of early treatment of hearing loss in young infants and citing critical limitations in research studies' designs or methodologies which complicate interpretation of research findings, Bess and Paradise (1994) observe that "no direct evidence demonstrates conclusively that intervention appropriate by current standards results in more good than harm to the child and the family" (p. 332).

4. With respect to concerns about availability of follow-up care for infants identified with hearing loss, Bess and Paradise (1994) note that, "It is improper to screen for a disorder without certainty that facilities for suitable follow-up care of individuals who fail the screen are both available and accessible" (p. 332), and this is not always possible in rural or remote areas of the United States.

5. Although the issue of parental noncompliance was not addressed in the Consensus Statement, "It seems reasonable to anticipate that noncompliance would constitute a problem os substantial magnitude in any universal screening pro-

gram, and that substantial effort and resources would be required to minimize its effects" (Bess & Paradise, 1994, p. 333).

6. Regarding early versus later treatment or intervention for infants with congenital hearing loss, Bess and Paradise (1994) assert that, "Although supported by theory and belief, no empirical evidence, to our knowledge, supports the proposition that outcomes in children with congenital hearing loss are more favorable if treatment is begun early in infancy rather than later in childhood (e.g., 6 months vs 18 months)" (p. 333).

Although we may not concur with all of the concerns expressed by Bess and Paradise (1994) regarding the NIH Consensus Statement (NIH, 1993), their commentary has focused a spotlight on several relevant issues pertaining to universal newborn hearing screening and has caused many professionals, including ourselves, to pause and to consider, if you will, the "environmental impact" of widespread implementation of universal newborn hearing screening. Although it may indeed be time to move forward in our efforts to detect hearing loss in all infants as early as possible, ideally before 3 months of age, and provide them (and their families) with appropriate intervention by 6 months of age (AAP, 1995), we must be professionally discerning. As with many new technologies and approaches that are sometimes advocated and sold with the assistance of government entities and proclamations, we must be prudent and contemplative.

In the specific case of the NIH Consensus Statement (NIH, 1993) which recommends universal newborn hearing screening prior to hospital discharge, we may find ourselves walking a fine line between (a) well-informed professional zeal, which may indeed lead to positive "systems change" and improved outcomes for young children with hearing losses, their families, and society at large, and (b) ill-advised professional impetuosity, which may indeed result in a substantial increase in the number of hospital-based universal newborn hearing screening programs, but which likely may be programs that have high-false positive rates, inadequate follow-up processes and care, and that are linked poorly, if at all, to early intervention systems for children identified with hearing loss and their families.

As a result of the recent NIH Consensus Statement (1993), there is new or renewed interest in many states, to implement hospital-based screening of all newborns for hearing loss (Mauk & White, 1995). However, in their zeal to implement such programs, many hospitals may not give enough thought not only to the implementation of valid screening protocols, but they may fail to design and institute an adequate follow-up system for those infants who are identified with various types and degrees of hearing loss. Also, there may not be effective, or even any, tracking mechanisms or requisite coordination or collaboration between agencies involved with providing an array of services for very young children with hearing loss and their families.

We cannot afford to forget, for the sake of children with hearing loss and their families, the words of audiologist John Jacobson (1990) regarding the vital necessity of a solid follow-up component in newborn hearing screening: "Without an active follow-up, the initiation of a screening program is indefensible" (p. 123). Thus, in our zeal for attainment of our long-sought goal of very early identification of hearing loss in children, if we fail to plan for the follow-up and early intervention needs of those children we identify before we invest in and implement universal newborn hearing screening programs, we will be planning to fail.

Also, in the realm of early identification of hearing loss, it is important to note that *screening* and *diagnosis* have fundamentally different goals. The goal of early screening for hearing loss is to select from the targeted population of infants a smaller number of infants at greatest risk of having a hearing loss. If the hearing screening (e.g., TEOAE or AABR) indicates that the child is at risk for a hearing loss, further *diagnosis* will need to be conducted to confirm or refute the existence of a hearing loss (Galambos, Wilson, & Silva, 1994). The goal of early diagnosis of hearing loss is to confirm whether a child actually has a hearing loss and to ascertain and to clarify the exact nature and severity of the confirmed hearing loss (i.e., is the hearing loss a result of fluid or debris in the ear canal, nerve damage, or both?) (Diener, 1993; Galambos et al., 1994).

As MacCarthy and Connell (1984) noted more than a decade ago, early identification and habilitative service provision to children with hearing losses "requires an extension of regular screening, a development of the referral system with the necessary collaboration between professionals, and direct work with more disadvantaged parents" (p. 85). Therefore, universal newborn hearing screening efforts must interface with educational strategies to form a comprehensive system of identifying, tracking, referring, and intervening with children with hearing loss. There can be unfortunate psychosocial consequences for children and their families if these processes are not brought into a comprehensive system of services: Children born with hearing loss and their families are sentenced to doing time within an uncoordinated, noncollaborative array of services. In 1987, former Surgeon General C. Everett Koop issued a call to action for this country to develop services for children with disabilities that were family-centered, community-based, and coordinated across relevant agencies (U.S. Department of Health and Human Services, 1987). Successful universal newborn hearing screening programs often create new early intervention challenges (Brackett, Maxon, & Blackwell, 1993), hence the attributes of family-centered, community-based, coordinated, as well as transdisciplinary, are particularly important (Apuzzo & Yoshinaga-Itano, 1995; M. Johnson, Maxon, White, & Vohr, 1993; Mauk & White, 1995).

Clearly, for universal newborn hearing screening programs to be successful, multidisciplinary cooperation and professional persistence across multiple agencies is needed (AAP, 1995; Brown, Thurman, & Pearl, 1993; Buttross et al., 1995; Diefendorf & Weber, 1994; Frye-Osier, 1993; Matkin, 1994; M. Johnson et al., 1993; Mauk & White, 1995; Pugh & Hicks, 1995; Rittenhouse & Dancer, 1992; Rushmer, 1994; see Figure 2). In the second article in this series, we will discuss the individual and societal benefits of early detection of and intervention for hearing loss, emphasize the imperative nature of aggressive and appropriate audiological and medical follow-up and early intervention for children identified with hearing loss and their families, and explore issues related to implementation of collaborative early identification and intervention services for this population.

Acknowledgment

The authors extend great appreciation to Dr. Karl R. White, Director of the National Consortium for Universal Newborn Hearing Screening at Utah State University, for providing current data and state-of-the-art technical information on universal newborn hearing screening using evoked otoacoustic emissions.

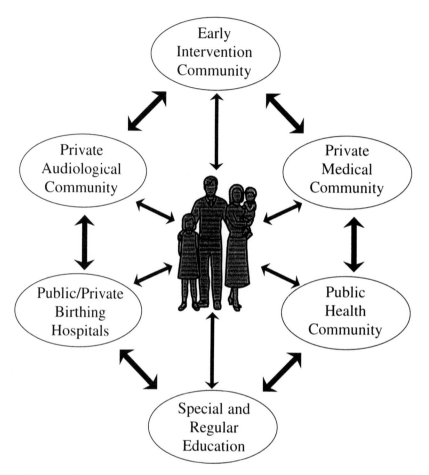

Figure 2. Universal newborn hearing screening and family-centered, community-based, coordinated services.

References

Advisory Group on the Early Identification of Children with Hearing Impairments. (1988, April). *Minutes of the Bureau of Maternal and Child Health/Office of Special Education and Rehabilitative Services Advisory Group on the Early Identification of Children with Hearing Impairments*. Washington, DC: Bureau of Maternal and Child Health.

Alberti, P. W., Hyde, M. L., Riko, K., Corbin, H., & Abramovich, S. (1983). An evaluation of BERA for hearing screening in high-risk neonates. *Laryngoscope, 93,* 1115–1121.

Allen, D. V. (1969). *Modality aspect of mediation in children with normal and impaired hearing ability* [Final Report, U.S. Bureau of Education for the Handicapped, Project No. 7-0837]. Detroit, MI: Wayne State University.

Allen, M. C., & Schubert-Sudia, S. E. (1990). Prevention of prelingual hearing impairment. *Seminars in Hearing, 11,* 134–149.

American Academy of Audiology (AAA). (1988). Proposed position statement on early identification of hearing loss in infants and children. *Audiology Today, 1*(2), 8–9.

American Academy of Pediatrics (AAP). (1995). Joint Committee on Infant Hearing 1994 Position Statement. *Pediatrics, 95*(1), 152–156.

American Speech-Language-Hearing Association (ASHA). (1989). Audiologic screening of newborn infants who are at risk for hearing impairment. *ASHA, 31*(3), 89–92.

Apuzzo, M. L., & Yoshinaga-Itano, C. (1995). Early identification of infants with significant hearing loss and the Minnesota Child Development Inventory. *Seminars in Hearing, 16*, 124–139.

Babbidge, H. (1965). *Education of the deaf in the United States: Report of the Advisory Committee on Education of the Deaf.* Washington, DC: U.S. Government Printing Office.

Barringer, D., Strong, C., Blair, J., Clark, T., & Watkins, S. (1993). Screening procedures used to identify children with hearing loss. *American Annals of the Deaf, 138*(5), 420–426.

Baumeister, A. A. (1992). Policy formulation: A real world view. In F. H. Bess & J. W. Hall, III (Eds.), *Screening children for auditory function* (pp. 111–123). Nashville, TN: Bill Wilkerson Center Press.

Bentzen, O., & Jensen, J. H. (1981). Early detection and treatment of deaf children: A European concept. In G. T. Mencher & S. E. Gerber (Eds.), *Early management of hearing loss* (pp. 85–103). New York: Grune & Stratton.

Berg, F. S. (1976). *Educational audiology: Hearing and speech management.* New York: Grune & Stratton.

Bess, F. H. (1985). The minimally hearing-impaired child. *Ear and Hearing, 6*, 43–47.

Bess, F. H., & Hall, J. W., III. (Eds.). (1992). *Screening children for auditory function.* Nashville, TN: Bill Wilkerson Center Press.

Bess, F. H., Klee, T., & Culbertson, J. L. (1986). Identification, assessment, and management of children with unilateral sensorineural hearing loss. *Ear and Hearing, 7*, 43–51.

Bess, F. H., & Paradise, J. L. (1994). Universal screening for infant hearing impairment: Not simple, not risk-free, not necessarily beneficial, and not presently justified. *Pediatrics, 93*(2), 330–334.

Bess, F. H., & Tharpe, A. M. (1984). Unilateral hearing impairment in children. *Pediatrics, 74*, 206–216.

Bess, F. H., & Tharpe, A. M. (1986). Case history data on unilaterally hearing-impaired children. *Ear and Hearing, 7*, 14–19.

Blair, J. C., Peterson, M. E., & Viehweg, S. H. (1985). The effects of mild sensorineural hearing loss on academic performance of young school-age children. *The Volta Review, 87*(2), 87–93.

Blake, P. E., & Hall, J. W., III. (1990). The status of state-wide policies for neonatal hearing screening. *Journal of the American Academy of Audiology, 1*, 67–74.

Bonfils, P., Uziel, A., & Pujol, R. (1988a). Evoked oto-acoustic emissions from adults and infants: Clinical applications. *Acta Otolaryngolica (Stockholm), 105*, 445–449.

Bonfils, P., Uziel, A., & Pujol, R. (1988b). Evoked otoacoustic emissions: A fundamental and clinical survey. *Journal of Otorhinolaryngology and Related Specialties, 50*, 212–218.

Boothroyd, A. (1982). *Hearing impairments in young children.* Englewood Cliffs, NJ: Prentice-Hall.

Bovo, R., Martini, A., Agnoletto, M., Beghi, A., Carmignoto, D., Milani, M., & Zangaglia, A. M. (1988). Auditory and academic performance of children with unilateral hearing loss. *Scandinavian Audiology, 30*(Suppl.), 71–74.

Brackett, D. (1993). Social/emotional and academic consequences of hearing loss. In *Program and Abstracts of the NIH Consensus Development Conference: Early Identifi-cation of Hearing Impairment in Infants and Young Children* (pp. 57-61). Bethesda, MD: National Institutes of Health, National Institute on Deafness and Other Communication Disorders.

Brackett, D., Maxon, A. B., & Blackwell, P. M. (1993). Intervention issues created by successful newborn hearing screening. *Seminars in Hearing, 14*(1), 88–104.

Bray, P. J., & Kemp, D. T. (1987). An advanced cochlear echo technique suitable for infant screening. *British Journal of Audiology, 21*, 191–204.

Brookhouser, P. E., Worthington, D. W., & Kelly, W. J. (1991). Unilateral hearing loss in children. *Laryngoscope, 101*, 1264–1272.

Brown, W., Thurman, S. K., & Pearl, L. F. (Eds.). (1993). *Family-centered early intervention with infants and toddlers: Innovative cross-disciplinary approaches.* Baltimore: Paul H. Brookes.

Brownell, W. E. (1990). Outer hair cell electromotility and otoacoustic emissions. *Ear and Hearing, 11,* 82–92.

Bullerdeick, K. M. (1987). Minimal hearing loss may not be benign. *American Journal of Nursing, 87,* 904, 906.

Buttross, S. L., Gearhart, J. G., & Peck, J. E. (1995). Early identification and management of hearing impairment. *American Family Physician, 51,* 1437–1446.

Calogero, B., Giannini, P., & Marciano, E. (1987). Recent advances in hearing screening. *Advances in Otorhinolaryngology, 37,* 60–78.

Clark, K. A., & Terry, D. L. (1995). A collaborative framework for intervention. In R. J. Roeser & M. P. Downs (Eds.), *Auditory disorders in school children: The law, identification, and remediation* (3rd ed., pp. 169–187). New York: Thieme Medical Publishers.

Commission on Education of the Deaf. (1988). *Toward equality: Education of the deaf.* Washington, DC: Author.

Culbertson, J. L., & Gilbert, L. E. (1986). Children with unilateral sensorineural hearing loss: Cognitive, academic, and social development. *Ear and Hearing, 7,* 38–42.

Davis, J. M. (1992). Signing and total communication. In R. D. Eavey & J. O. Klein (Eds.), *Hearing loss in childhood: A primer. Report of the 102nd Ross Conference on Pediatric Research* (pp. 141–148). Columbus, OH: Ross Laboratories.

Davis, J. M., Elfenbein, J., Schum, R., & Bentler, R. A. (1986). Effects of mild and moderate hearing impairments on language, educational, and psychosocial behavior of children. *Journal of Speech and Hearing Disorders, 51,* 53–62.

Davis, S. (1994, November). *Hearing screening at Baptist Memorial Hospital.* Paper presented at the National Seminar on Universal Infant Hearing Screening, Nashville, TN.

de Villiers, P. A. (1992). Educational implications of deafness: Language and literacy. In R. D. Eavey & J. O. Klein (Eds.), *Hearing loss in childhood: A primer. Report of the 102nd Ross Conference on Pediatric Research* (pp. 127-135). Columbus, OH: Ross Laboratories.

Diefendorf, A. O. (1992). Screening for hearing loss: Behavioral options. In F. H. Bess & J. W. Hall, III (Eds.), *Screening for auditory function* (pp. 243-260). Nashville, TN: Bill Wilkerson Center Press.

Diefendorf, A. O., & Weber, B. A. (1994). Identification of hearing loss: Programmatic and procedural considerations. In J. Roush & N. D. Matkin (Eds.), *Infants and toddlers with hearing loss: Family-centered assessment and intervention* (pp. 43–64). Baltimore: York Press.

Diener, P. L. (1993). *Resources for teaching children with diverse abilities: Birth through eight* (2nd ed.). Fort Worth, TX: Harcourt Brace Jovanovich.

Downs, M. P. (1986). The rationale for neonatal hearing screening. In E. T. Swigart (Ed.), *Neonatal hearing screening* (pp. 3–19). San Diego: College-Hill Press.

Downs, M. P. (1993). Benefits of screening at birth: Economic, educational, and functional factors. In *Program and Abstracts of the NIH Consensus Development Conference on Early Identification of Hearing Impairment in Infants and Young Children* (pp. 63–66). Bethesda, MD: National Institutes of Health, National Institute on Deafness and Other Communication Disorders.

Downs, M. P. (1994). The case for detection and intervention at birth. *Seminars in Hearing, 15*(2), 76–84.

Downs, M. P., & Sterritt, G. M. (1964). Identification audiometry for infants: A preliminary report. *Journal of Audiological Research, 4,* 69-80.

Durieux-Smith, A., & Jacobson, J. T. (1985). Comparison of auditory brainstem response and behavioral screening in neonates. *Journal of Otolaryngology, 14,* 47–52.

Durieux-Smith, A., Picton, T., Edwards, C., Goodman, J. T., & MacMurray, B. (1985). The Crib-O-Gram in the NICU: An evaluation based on brain stem electric response audiometry. *Ear and Hearing, 6,* 20–24.

Eichwald, J., & Mahoney, T. (1993). Apgar scores in the identification of sensorineural hearing loss. *Journal of the American Academy of Audiology, 4*(3), 133–138.

Elberling, C., Parbo, J., Johnsen, J., & Bagi, P. (1985). Evoked otoacoustic emissions: Clinical applications. *Acta Otolaryngolica* (Stockholm), 421 (Suppl.), 77–85.

Elssmann, S., Matkin, N., & Sabo, M. (1987). Early identification of congenital sensorineural hearing loss. *The Hearing Journal, 40*, 13–17.

Engdahl, B., Arnesen, A. R., & Mair, I. W. S. (1994). Otoacoustic emissions in the first year of life. *Scandinavian Audiology, 23*, 195–200.

Epstein, S., & Reilly, J. S. (1989). Sensorineural hearing loss. *Pediatric Clinics of North America, 36*, 1501–1519.

Ewing, I. R., & Ewing, A. W. G. (1944). The ascertainment of deafness in infancy and early childhood. *The Journal of Laryngology and Otology, 59*, 309–333.

Ewing, I. R., & Ewing, A. W. G. (1947). *Opportunity and the deaf child.* London: University of London Press.

Feagans, L. V. (1986). Otitis media: A model for long-term effects with implications for intervention. In J. F. Kavanagh (Ed.), *Otitis media and child development* (pp. 192–208). Parkton, MD: York Press.

Feagans, L. V., Hannan, K., & Manlove, E. (1992). An ecological and developmental/contextual approach to intervention with children with chronic otitis media. In F. H. Bess & J. W. Hall, III (Eds.), *Screening children for auditory function* (pp. 435–461). Nashville, TN: Bill Wilkerson Center Press.

Folsom, R. C. (1990). Identification of hearing loss in infants using auditory brainstem response: Strategies and program choices. *Seminars in Hearing, 11*(4), 333–341.

Fowler, B. A., & Fowler, S. M. (1994). Infant hearing screening: A practical approach. *Seminars in Hearing, 15*(2), 85–99.

Francois, M., Bonfils, P., & Narcy, P. (1995). Screening for neonatal and infant deafness in Europe in 1992. *International Journal of Pediatric Otorhinolaryngology, 31*, 175–182.

Fritsch, M. H., & Sommer, A. (1991). *Handbook of congenital and early onset hearing loss.* New York: Igaku-Shoin.

Frye-Osier, J. (1993). *The Wisconsin guide to childhood hearing screening.* Madison: Wisconsin Department of Public Instruction.

Galambos, R., Wilson, M. J., & Silva, P. D. (1994). Identifying hearing loss in the intensive care nursery: A 20-year summary. *Journal of the American Academy of Audiology, 5*(3), 151–162.

Gjerdingen, D. (1992). Evaluation, and then what? What pediatricians should know about hearing loss in young children. In R. D. Eavey & J. O. Klein (Eds.), *Hearing loss in childhood: A primer. Report of the 102nd Ross Conference on Pediatric Research* (pp. 88–94). Columbus, OH: Ross Laboratories.

Goldstein, R., & Tait, C. (1971). Critique of neonatal hearing evaluation. *Journal of Speech and Hearing Disorders, 26*, 3–18.

Gorga, M. P., Stover, L., Bergman, B. M., Beauchaine, K. L., & Kaminski, J. R. (1995). The application of otoacoustic emissions in the assessment of developmentally delayed patients. *Scandinavian Audiology, 24*(Suppl. 41), 8–17.

Gravel, J. S. (1993). Behavioral measures. In *Program and Abstracts of the NIH Consensus Development Conference: Early Identification of Hearing Impairment in Infants and Young Children* (pp. 71–73). Bethesda, MD: National Institutes of Health, National Institute on Deafness and Other Communication Disorders.

Grievink, E. H., Peters, S. A. F., van Bon, W. H. J., & Schilder, A. G. M. (1993). The effects of early bilateral otitis media with effusion on language ability: A prospective cohort study. *Journal of Speech and Hearing Research, 36*, 1004–1012.

Hall, J. W., III. (1992). *Handbook of auditory evoked responses.* Needham Heights, MA: Allyn & Bacon.

Hall, J. W., III. (1993). Hearing screening of infants with auditory brainstem response: Protocols, personnel, and price. In *Program and Abstracts of the NIH Consensus Development Conference: Early Identification of Hearing Impairment in Infants and Young Children* (pp. 99–102). Bethesda, MD: National Institutes of Health, National Institute on Deafness and Other Communication Disorders.

Hall, J. W., III. (1994). Universal screening for infant hearing impairment [Letter to the editor]. *Pediatrics, 94*(6), 949.

Hall, J. W., III, & Chase, P. (1993). Answers to 10 common clinical questions about otoacoustic emissions today. *The Hearing Journal, 46*, 29–34.

Hall, J. W., III, Kripal, J. P., & Hepp, T. (1988). Newborn hearing screening with auditory brainstem response: Measurement problems and solutions. *Seminars in Hearing, 9*(1), 15–33.

Hanley, J., & Becker, T. (1993). Otoacoustic emissions: A new tool in diagnosing childhood hearing loss. *Infant-Toddler Intervention: The Transdisciplinary Journal, 3*(3), 165–170.

Hayes, D. (1994). Universal screening for infant hearing impairment [Letter to the editor]. *Pediatrics, 94*(6), 954–955.

Hodgson, W. R. (1987). Tests of hearing—The infant. In F. N. Martin (Ed.), *Hearing disorders in children* (pp. 185–216). Austin, TX: PRO-ED.

Hyde, M. L., Riko, K., & Malizia, K. (1990). Audiometric accuracy of the click ABR in infants at risk for hearing loss. *Journal of the American Academy of Audiology, 1*(2), 59–66.

Jacobson, J. T. (1990). Issues in newborn ABR screening. *Journal of the American Academy of Audiology, 1*(3), 121–124.

Jacobson, J. T., Jacobson, C. A., & Spahr, R. C. (1990). Automated and conventional ABR screening techniques in high-risk infants. *Journal of the American Academy of Audiology, 1*(4), 187–195.

Jacobson, J. T., & Morehouse, C. R. (1984). A comparison of auditory brainstem response and behavioral screening in high risk and normal newborn infants. *Ear and Hearing, 5,* 247–253.

Johnsen, N. J., Bagi, P., & Elberling, C. (1983). Evoked acoustic emissions from the human ear. III. Findings in neonates. *Scandinavian Audiology, 12,* 17–24.

Johnson, A., & Ashurst, H. (1990). Screening for sensorineural deafness by health visitors. *Archives of Disease in Childhood, 65,* 841–845.

Johnson, J. L., Mauk, G. W., Takekawa, K. M., Simon, P. R., Sia, C. C. J., & Blackwell, P. M. (1993). Implementing a statewide system of services for infants and toddlers with hearing disabilities. *Seminars in Hearing, 14*(1), 105–119.

Johnson, M. J., Maxon, A. B., White, K. R., & Vohr, B. R. (1993). Operating a hospital-based universal newborn hearing screening program using transient evoked otoacoustic emissions. *Seminars in Hearing, 14*(1), 46–56.

Joint Committee on Infant Hearing (JCIH). (1982). Position statement. *ASHA, 24,* 1017–1018.

Joint Committee on Infant Hearing (JCIH). (1991). 1990 position statement. *ASHA, 33*(Suppl. 5), 3–6.

Joseph, J. M., Herrmann, B. S., Thornton, A. R., & Pye, R. K. (1993, November). *Well-baby hearing screening using automated ABR.* Paper presented at the annual convention of the American Speech-Language-Hearing Association, Anaheim, CA.

Kemp, D. T. (1978). Stimulated otoacoustic emissions from within the human auditory system. *Journal of the Acoustical Society of America, 64,* 1386–1391.

Kemp, D. T. (1988). Developments in cochlear mechanics and techniques for non-invasive evaluation. *Advances in Audiology, 5,* 27–45.

Kemp, D. T., & Ryan, S. (1993). The use of transient evoked otoacoustic emissions in neonatal hearing screening programs. *Seminars in Hearing, 14*(1), 30–45.

Kemp, D. T., Bray, P., Alexander, L., & Brown, A. M. (1986). Acoustic emission cochleography—Practical aspects. *Scandinavian Audiology, 25* (Suppl.), 71–95.

Kile, J. E. (1993). Identification of hearing impairment in children: A 25-year review. *Infant-Toddler Intervention: The Transdisciplinary Journal, 3*(3), 155–164.

Kile, J. E., Schaffmeyer, M. J., & Kuba, J. (1994). Assessment and management of unusual auditory behavior in infants and toddlers. *Infant-Toddler Intervention: The Transdisciplinary Journal, 4*(4), 299–318.

Kileny, P., & Magathan, M. (1987). Predictive value of ABR in infants and children with moderate to profound hearing impairment. *Ear and Hearing, 8,* 217–221.

Klee, T. M., & Davis-Dansky, E. (1986). A comparison of unilaterally hearing-impaired children and normal-hearing children on a battery of standardized language tests. *Ear and Hearing, 7,* 27–37.

Liden, G., & Kankkunen, A. (1969). Visual reinforcement audiometry in the management of young deaf children. *International Audiology, 8,* 99–106.

Lonsbury-Martin, B. L., Martin, G. K., McCoy, M. J., & Whitehead, M. L. (1995). New approaches to the evaluation of the auditory system and a current analysis of otoacoustic emissions. *Otolaryngology-Head and Neck Surgery, 112*, 50–63.

Lutman, M. E., Mason, S. M., Sheppard, S., & Gibbin, K. P. (1989). Differential diagnostic potential of otoacoustic emissions: A case study. *Audiology, 28*, 205–2110.

MacCarthy, A., & Connell, J. (1984). Audiological screening and assessment. In G. Lindsay (Ed.), *Screening for children with special needs: Multidisciplinary approaches* (pp. 63–85). London: Croom Helm.

Mace, A. L., Wallace, K. L., Whan, M. Q., & Steimachowicz, P. G. (1991). Relevant factors in the identification of hearing loss. *Ear and Hearing, 12*, 287–293.

Mahoney, T. M. (1989). Screening infants and children for hearing loss. In G. M. English (Ed.), *Otolaryngology* (Vol. 1, Chapter 7, pp. 1-18). Philadelphia: J. B. Lippincott.

Mahoney, T. M. (1993). U.S.A. models. In *Program and Abstracts of the NIH Consensus Development Conference: Early Identification of Hearing Impairment in Infants and Young Children* (pp. 123–128). Bethesda, MD: National Institutes of Health, National Institute on Deafness and Other Communication Disorders.

Mahoney, T. M., & Eichwald, J. G. (1987). The ups and "Downs" of high-risk hearing screening: The Utah statewide program. *Seminars in Hearing, 8*, 155–163.

Mahoney, T. M., Eichwald, J. G., & Fronberg, R. (1992). Utah Bureau of Communicative Disorders high risk registry non-respondent survey. *Audiology Today, 4*(1), 16–17.

Markides, A. (1986). Age at fitting of hearing aids and speech intelligibility. *British Journal of Audiology, 20*, 165–168.

Markowitz, R. K. (1990). Cost-effectiveness comparison of hearing screening in the neonatal intensive care unit. *Seminars in Hearing, 11*, 161–166.

Marlowe, J. A. (1993). Screening all newborns for hearing impairment in a community hospital. *American Journal of Audiology, 2*(1), 22–25.

Marlowe, J. A. (1994). Amplification and audiological management of infants. *Seminars in Hearing, 15*(2), 114–127.

Martin, W. H., Schwegler, J. W., Gleeson, A. L., & Shi, Y. B. (1994). New techniques of hearing assessment. *Otolaryngologic Clinics of North America, 27*(3), 487–510.

Matkin, N. D. (1986). The role of hearing in language development. In J. F. Kavanagh (Ed.), *Otitis media and child development* (pp. 3–11). Parkton, MD: York Press.

Matkin, N. D. (1994). Strategies for enhancing interdisciplinary collaboration. In J. Roush & N. D. Matkin (Eds.), *Infants and toddlers with hearing loss: Family-centered assessment and intervention* (pp. 83–97). Baltimore: York Press.

Mauk, G. W., & Behrens, T. R. (1993). Historical, political, and technological context associated with early identification of hearing loss. *Seminars in Hearing, 14*(1), 1–17.

Mauk, G. W., & White, K. R. (1995). Giving children a sound beginning: The promise of universal newborn hearing screening. *The Volta Review, 97*(1), 5–32.

Mauk, G. W., White, K. R., Mortensen, L. B., & Behrens, T. R. (1991). The effectiveness of screening programs based on high-risk characteristics in early identification of hearing loss. *Ear and Hearing, 12*, 312–319.

Maxon, A. B., White, K. R., Behrens, T. R., & Vohr, B. R. (1995). Referral rates and cost efficiency in a universal newborn hearing screening program using evoked otoacoustic emissions. *Journal of the American Academy of Audiology, 6*(4), 271–277.

Maxon, A. B., White, K. R., Vohr, B. R., & Behrens, T. R. (1993). Feasibility of identifying risk for conductive hearing loss in a newborn universal hearing screening program. *Seminars in Hearing, 14*(1), 73–87.

McCormick, B. (1983). Hearing screening by health visitors: A critical appraisal of the Distraction Test. *Health Visitor, 56*, 449–451.

McCormick, B. (1986). Screening for hearing impairment in the first year of life. *Midwife, Health Visitor, and Community Nurse, 22*, 199–202.

Meredith, R., Stephens, D., Hogan, S., Cartlidge, P. H. T., & Drayton, M. (1994). Screening for hearing loss in an at-risk neonatal population using evoked otoacoustic emissions. *Scandinavian Audiology, 23*, 187–193.

Miller, A. R. (1994). Universal screening for infant hearing impairment [Letter to the editor]. *Pediatrics, 94*(6), 949–950.

Montgomery, P. E., & Matkin, N. D. (1992). Hearing-impaired children in the schools: Integrated or isolated? In F. H. Bess & J. W. Hall, III (Eds.), *Screening children for auditory function* (pp. 477-492). Nashville: Bill Wilkerson Center Press.

Moore, J. M., Wilson, W. R., & Thompson, G. (1977). Visual reinforcement of head-turn responses in infants under 12 months of age. *Journal of Speech and Hearing Disorders, 42*, 328–334.

Moore, W. (1991). Managing the infant hearing impairment problem: The contributions of industry. *Seminars in Hearing, 12*, 175–181.

National Institutes of Health (NIH). (1993). *NIH Consensus Statement: Early Identification of Hearing Impairment in Infants and Young Children, 11*(1), 1–25.

Northern, J. L. (1994). Universal screening for infant hearing impairment [Letter to the editor]. *Pediatrics, 94*(6), 955.

Northern, J. L., & Downs, M. P. (1978). *Hearing in children* (2nd ed.). Baltimore: Williams & Wilkins.

Northern, J. L., & Gerkin, K. P. (1989). New technology in infant hearing screening. *Otolaryngologic Clinics of North America, 22*, 75–87.

Northern, J. L., & Hayes, D. (1994). Universal screening for infant hearing impairment: Necessary, beneficial, and justifiable. *Audiology Today, 6*(2), 10–13.

Norton, S. J. (1994). Emerging role of otoacoustic emissions in neonatal hearing screening. *American Journal of Otology, 15*(1), 4–12.

Nozza, R. J. (1994). The effects of mild hearing loss on infant auditory function. *Infant-Toddler Intervention: The Transdisciplinary Journal, 4*(4), 285–298.

Oyler, R. F., Oyler, A. L., & Matkin, N. D. (1987). Warning: A unilateral hearing loss may be detrimental to a child's academic career. *The Hearing Journal, 40*, 18, 20–22.

Oyler, R. F., Oyler, A. L., & Matkin, N. D. (1988). Unilateral hearing loss: Demographics and educational impact. *Language, Speech, and Hearing Services in the Schools, 19*, 191–200.

Peters, J. G. (1986). An automated infant screener using advanced evoked response technology. *The Hearing Journal, 39*, 25–30.

Peters, S. A. F., Grievink, E. H., van Bon, W. H. J., & Schilder, A. G. M. (1994). The effects of early bilateral otitis media with effusion on educational attainment: A prospective cohort study. *Journal of Learning Disabilities, 27*, 111–122.

Primus, M. A. (1988). Infant thresholds with enhanced attention to the signal in visual reinforcement audiometry. *Journal of Speech and Hearing Research, 31*, 480–484.

Primus, M. A. (1992). The role of localization in visual reinforcement audiometry. *Journal of Speech and Hearing Research, 35*, 1137–1141.

Primus, M. A., & Thompson, G. (1985). Response strength of young children in operant audiometry. *Journal of Speech and Hearing Research, 28*, 539–547.

Probst, R., Lonsbury-Martin, B. L., & Martin, G. K. (1991). A review of otoacoustic emissions. *Journal of the Acoustical Society of America, 89*, 2027–2067.

Pugh, G. S., & Hicks, D. (1995). Deaf Education Initiatives Project: A response to the challenge. *Journal of Childhood Communication Disorders, 17*(1), 5–8.

Radcliffe, D. (1993). In identifying hearing loss in infants, time is of the essence. *The Hearing Journal, 46*(4), 13–22.

Raffin, M. J. M., & Matz, G. J. (1994). Universal screening for infant hearing impairment [Letter to the Editor]. *Pediatrics, 94*(6), 950–952.

Ramkalawan, T. W., & Davis, A. C. (1992). The effects of hearing loss and age of intervention on some language metrics in young hearing-impaired children. *British Journal of Audiology, 26*, 97–107.

Richardson, M. P., Williamson, T. J., Lenton, S. W., Tarlow, M. J., & Rudd, P. T. (1995). Otoacoustic emissions as a screening test for hearing impairment in children. *Archives of Disease in Childhood, 72,* 294–297.

Rittenhouse, R. K., & Dancer, J. E. (1992). Educational and legislative issues in students with hearing loss: Inter-disciplinary considerations. *The Volta Review, 94,* 9–17.

Robinette, M. S. (1994). Universal screening for infant hearing impairment [Letter to the Editor]. *Pediatrics, 94*(6), 952–954.

Robins, D. S. (1990). A case for infant hearing screening. *Neonatal Intensive Care, 3,* 24–26, 29, 42.

Robinshaw, H. M. (1994). Deaf infants, early intervention and language acquisition. *Early Child Development and Care, 99,* 1–22.

Roeser, R. J., & Price, D. R. (1981). Audiometric and impedance measures: Principles and interpretation. In R. J. Roeser & M. P. Downs (Eds.), *Auditory disorders in school children: The law, identification, and remediation* (pp. 71-101). New York: Thieme-Stratton.

Ross, M. (1990). Implications of delay in detection and management of deafness. *The Volta Review, 92,* 69–79.

Ruben, R. J. (1991). Effectiveness and efficacy of early detection of hearing impairment in children. *Acta Otolaryngolica* (Stockholm), Suppl. 482, 127–131.

Ruben, R. J. (1993). Early identification of hearing impairment in infants and young children—Introduction and overview. In *Program and Abstracts of the NIH Consensus Development Conference: Early Identifica-tion of Hearing Impairment in Infants and Young Children* (pp. 17–19). Bethesda, MD: National Institutes of Health, National Institute on Deafness and Other Communication Disorders.

Ruben, R. J., Levine, R., Fishman, G., Baldinger, E., Feldman, W., Silver, M., Stein, M., Umano, H., & Kruger, B. (1982). Moderate to severe sensorineural hearing impaired child: Analysis of etiology, intervention, and outcome. *Laryngoscope, 92,* 38–46.

Rushmer, N. (1994). Supporting families of hearing-impaired infants and toddlers. *Seminars in Hearing, 15*(2), 160–172.

Scanlon, P. E., & Bamford, J. M. (1990). Early identification of hearing loss: Screening and surveillance methods. *Archives of Disease in Childhood, 65,* 479–485.

Schulman-Galambos, C., & Galambos, R. (1979). Brainstem evoked response audiometry in newborn hearing screening. *Archives of Otolaryngology, 105,* 86–90.

Schum, R. L. (1987). Communication and social growth: A development model of deaf social behavior. In M. S. Robinette & C. D. Bauch (Eds.), *Proceedings of a symposium in audiology* (pp. 1–25). Rochester, MN: Mayo Clinic-Mayo Foundation.

Seyfried, D. N., Hutchinson, J. M., & Smith, L. L. (1989). Language and speech of the hearing impaired. In R. L. Schow & M. A. Nerbonne (Eds.), *Introduction to aural habilitation* (2nd ed., pp. 181–239). Austin, TX: PRO-ED.

Shimizu, H., Walters, R. J., Proctor, L. R., Kennedy, D. W., Allen, M. C., & Markowitz, R. K. (1990). Identification of hearing impairment in the neonatal intensive care unit population: Outcome of a five-year project at the Johns Hopkins Hospital. *Seminars in Hearing, 11*(2), 150–160.

Sininger, Y. S. (1993). Evaluation of hearing in the neonate using the auditory brainstem response. In *Program and Abstracts of the NIH Consensus Development Conference: Early Identification of Hearing Impairment in Infants and Young Children* (pp. 95–97). Bethesda, MD: National Institutes of Health, National Institute on Deafness and Other Communication Disorders.

Stein, D. (1983). Psychosocial characteristics of school-age children with unilateral hearing losses. *Journal of the Academy of Rehabilitative Audiology, 16,* 12–22.

Stewart, D. L., Bibb, K. W., & Pearlman, A. (1993). Automated newborn hearing testing with the ALGO-1 screener. *Clinical Pediatrics, 32,* 308–311.

Stewart, I. F. (1984). After early identification — What follows? A study of some aspects of deaf education from an otolaryngological viewpoint. *Laryngoscope, 94,* 784–799.

Stewart, J. M., & Downs, M. P. (1993). Congenital conductive hearing loss: The need for early identification and intervention. *Pediatrics, 91,* 355–359.

Strong, C. J., Clark, T. C., Johnson, D., Watkins, S., Barringer, D. G., & Walden, B. E. (1994). SKI*HI home-based programming for children who are deaf or heard of hearing: Recent research findings. *Infant-Toddler Intervention: The Transdisciplinary Journal, 4*(1), 25–36.

Strong, C. J., Clark, T. C., & Walden, B. E. (1994). The relationship of hearing loss severity to demographic, age, treatment, and intervention effectiveness variables. *Ear and Hearing, 15*, 126–137.

Sweitzer, R. S. (1977). Audiologic evaluation of the infant and young child. In B. F. Jaffe (Ed.), *Hearing loss in children: A comprehensive text* (pp. 101–131). Baltimore, MD: University Park Press.

Teele, D. W., Klein, J. O., Chase, C., Menyuk, P., Rosner, B. A., and the Greater Boston Otitis Media Study Group. (1990). Otitis media in infancy and intellectual ability, school achievement, speech, and language at age 7 years. *Journal of Infectious Diseases, 162*, 685–694.

Tharpe, A. M., & Bess, F. H. (1991). Identification and management of children with minimal hearing loss. *International Journal of Pediatric Otorhinolaryngology, 21*, 41–50.

Thornton, A. (1992). Neonatal screening. In R. D. Eavey & J. O. Klein (Eds.), *Hearing loss in childhood: A primer. Report of the 102nd Ross Conference on Pediatric Research* (pp. 61–68). Columbus, OH: Ross Laboratories.

Todd, N. W. (1994). At-risk populations for hearing impairment in infants and young children. *International Journal of Pediatric Otorhinolaryngology, 29*, 11–21.

Turner, R. G. (1990). Recommended guidelines for infant hearing screening: Analysis. *ASHA, 32*(9), 57–61, 66.

Turner, R. G. (1991). Modeling cost and performance of early identification protocols. *Journal of the American Academy of Audiology, 2*(4), 195–205.

Turner, R. G. (1992a). Comparison of four hearing screening protocols. *Journal of the American Academy of Audiology, 3*(3), 200–207.

Turner, R. G. (1992b). Factors that determine the cost and performance of early identification protocols. *Journal of the American Academy of Audiology, 3*(4), 233–241.

Turner, R. G. (1993). Models for early identification and follow-up: An overview. In *Program and Abstracts of the NIH Consensus Development Conference: Early Identification of Hearing Impairment in Infants and Young Children* (pp. 119–122). Bethesda, MD: National Institutes of Health, National Institute on Deafness and Other Communication Disorders.

Turner, R. G., & Cone-Wesson, B. K. (1992). Prevalence rates and cost-effectiveness of risk factors. In F. H. Bess & J. W. Hall, III (Eds.), *Screening children for auditory function* (pp. 79–104). Nashville: Bill Wilkerson Center Press.

U.S. Department of Health and Human Services. (1987). *Surgeon General's Report on Children with Special Health Care Needs: Commitment to Family-Centered, Community-Based, Coordinated Care.* Washington, DC: Public Health Service.

U.S. Department of Health and Human Services. (1990). *Healthy People 2000: National Health Promotion and Disease Prevention Objectives.* Washington, DC: Public Health Service.

U.S. Department of Health, Education, and Welfare. (1967). *Education of the deaf: The challenge and the charge. A report of the National Conference on Education of the Deaf.* Washington, DC: Author.

U.S. Preventive Services Task Force. (1989). *Guide to clinical preventive services: An assessment of the effectiveness of 169 interventions.* Washington, DC: U.S. Department of Health and Human Services, Office of Disease Prevention and Health Promotion.

Vohr, B. R. (1994). Universal screening for infant hearing impairment [Letter to the editor]. *Pediatrics, 94*(6), 948–949.

Weber, B. A. (1988). Screening of high-risk infants using auditory brainstem response audiometry. In F. H. Bess (Ed.), *Hearing impairment in children* (pp. 112–132). Parkton, MD: York Press.

Welsh, R., & Slater, S. (1993). The state of infant hearing impairment identification programs. *ASHA, 35*, 49–52.

White, K. R., & Behrens, T. R. (Eds.). (1993). The Rhode Island Hearing Assessment Project: Implications for universal newborn hearing screening. *Seminars in Hearing, 14*(1), 1–119.

White, K. R., Behrens, T. R., & Strickland, B. (1995). Practicality, validity, and cost-efficiency of universal newborn hearing screening using transient evoked otoacoustic emissions. *Journal of Childhood Communication Disorders, 17*(1), 9–14.

White, K. R., & Maxon, A. B. (1995). Universal screening for infant hearing impairment: Simple, beneficial, and presently justified. *International Journal of Pediatric Otorhinolaryngology, 32*, 201–211.

White, K. R., Vohr, B. R., & Behrens, T. R. (1993). Universal newborn hearing screening using transient evoked otoacoustic emissions: Results of the Rhode Island hearing Assessment Project. *Seminars in Hearing, 14*(1), 18–29.

White, K. R., Vohr, B. R., Maxon, A. B., Behrens, T. R., McPherson, M. G., & Mauk, G. W. (1994). Screening all newborns for hearing loss using transient evoked otoacoustic emissions. *International Journal of Pediatric Otorhinolaryngology, 29*, 203–217.

Yoshinaga-Itano, C. (1995). Efficacy of early identification and early intervention. *Seminars in Hearing, 16*, 115–123.

Zarrella, S. (1995). Managing communication problems of unilateral hearing loss. *Advance for Speech-Language Pathologists and Audiologists, 5*(6), 12.

Address correspondence to:
Gary W. Mauk, Research Associate
SKI*HI Institute
Utah State University
809 North 800 East
Logan, UT 84322-1900

Seizing the Moment, Setting the Stage, and Serving the Future: Toward Collaborative Models of Early Identification and Early Intervention Services for Children Born with Hearing Loss and Their Families
Part II: Follow-up and Early Intervention

Gary W. Mauk, M.A., CAGS, NCSP
Donald G. Barringer, Ph.D.
SKI*HI Institute
Utah State University
Logan, Utah

Pamela P. Mauk, M.A.
Box Elder School District
Brigham City, Utah

It is recommended and we now have the capability to screen every live birth for auditory impairment cost-efficiently prior to hospital discharge. However, universal newborn hearing screening presents a double-edged sword. Although establishment of such hospital-based hearing screening programs is needed and is welcomed by the majority of professionals, lack of planning and proactive action on the part of hospitals, Part H early intervention program coordinators, and related professionals and agencies pertaining to appropriate pediatric audiological diagnosis and subsequent habilitative follow-up for infants identified with hearing losses could create service difficulties for affected families and responsible agencies. This article discusses the individual and societal benefits of early detection of and intervention for hearing loss and emphasizes the imperative nature of aggressive, appropriate, and coordinated audiological and medical follow-up and early intervention for children identified with hearing loss and their families.

The assessment of hearing loss in early infancy is a multifaceted process, combining identification, intervention, and continued assessment. The importance of this process cannot be overstated. The earlier in life that intervention can be initiated, the greater the opportunity to mitigate the impact of that impairment on speech, language, and learning. (Folsom, 1990, p. 333)

The seeds of educational success are sown in the early years of life and the ability to hear effectively is vital to optimum developmental growth. The challenge of early identification, diagnosis, and habilitation of hearing loss in children, whether the loss is unilateral or bilateral, sensorineural, mixed or conductive, or mild, moderate, severe, or profound, is a critical one. Identification of hearing loss at such an early age and initiation of habilitative management as indicated by the screening outcome minimizes the auditory deprivation which can interfere with speech, language, intellectual, and social development and offers the promise of significant favorable economic impact to both the individual and society (Buttross, Gearhart, & Peck, 1995; Diefendorf, 1996; Downs, 1993, 1994; Gravel, Wallace, & Ruben, 1995; Laughton, 1994; Marlowe, 1994; Nozza, 1996).

In the first article in this two-part series (Mauk, Barringer, & Mauk, 1995), we discussed a variety of issues relating to the identification of hearing loss in young children. The topics addressed in the first article included the importance of very early identification of hearing loss for the affected child and his or her family, the scope of the problem of sensorineural hearing loss, the developmental consequences of hearing loss for the child, the history and current status of early screening for hearing loss in the United States, the pros and cons of various early hearing screening approaches including transient evoked otoacoustic emissions (TEOAEs) and conventional and automated auditory brainstem response (AABR), and the conviction that universal newborn hearing screening (UNHS) is only the beginning of the service adventure for children with hearing loss and their families. In this article, we discuss the individual and societal benefits of early detection of and intervention for hearing loss and emphasize the imperative nature of aggressive and appropriate audiological and medical follow-up and early intervention for children identified with hearing loss and their families.

Follow-up and Early Intervention: Completing the Circle

Early screening for hearing loss during the neonatal period whether performed on groups of children "at-risk" for hearing loss (Joint Committee on Infant Hearing [JCIH],

1994) or on all newborns prior to hospital discharge (National Institutes of Health [NIH], 1993) requires aggressive and comprehensive follow-up for children identified by the screening protocol as needing further audiological assessment. In 1989, the U.S. Preventive Services Task Force, in its overview of the rationale and efficacy of early detection of hearing loss, noted that "abnormal [hearing] test results should be confirmed by repeat testing at appropriate intervals, and all confirmed cases identified through screening should be referred for ongoing audiological assessment, selection of hearing aids, family counseling, psychoeducational management, and periodic medical evaluation" (p. 198). A year later, Kenworthy (1990) observed that the identification process for hearing loss in infants and young children "can either streamline or overload any service-delivery system" (p. 315).

Because of the recent NIH Consensus Statement (NIH, 1993) on early identification of hearing loss in infants and young children, there is renewed interest in many states to begin testing newborns for hearing loss (Mauk & White, 1995; White & Maxon, 1995). However, far too few states and hospitals currently have validated and formalized plans and procedures for UNHS and follow-up activities (Finitzo, 1995a; Mauk et al., 1995; Mauk & White, 1995). Consequently, interested individuals and organizational entities are left to develop their own procedures for screening and diagnosis. Furthermore, because there is frequently no central coordination or collaboration between involved institutions and agencies, there are few or, usually, no follow-up processes in place.

Follow-up in Universal Newborn Hearing Screening Programs

Clearly, the buck does not stop with hearing screening. Adequate follow-up and early intervention services must be in place for children identified with hearing loss and their families (Diefendorf, 1996; Goldberg, 1996; Nozza, 1996; Pugh & Hicks, 1995; Mauk & White, 1995; Yoshinaga-Itano, 1995). Addressing the topic of pediatric hearing screening, Nozza (1996) recently asserted that

It is important that audiologic screening of children takes place in the context of a program that meets all of the basic principles of screening so there is a well-thought-out and organized sequence of events and available resources for the follow-up of those identified . . . Screening is only part of the early identification program. The involvement of the community, the families, the schools, and the professionals to whom referrals will be made is essential. (p. 112)

Brown and Taxman (1993) have noted that a major criticism of neonatal hearing screening programs has been that the programs do not incorporate a follow-up component for infants who pass the initial hearing screening. They observed that, "Without longitudinal audiological data on the group who passed unequivocally, it is impossible to ascertain if any of these infants subsequently presented with hearing sensitivity loss" (Brown & Taxman, 1993, p. 146). Some professionals (e.g., Jacobson & Jacobson, 1990; Penn & Gibson, 1994) have tackled this problem through the use of brief follow-up questionnaires completed by caregivers and based on caregivers' observations of their child's auditory-related behaviors and medical information (i.e., ear infections/treatment). Caregiver-completed questionnaires could also be used for those infants who failed the initial hearing screening but who did not return for follow-up audiological and/or medical assessment.

However, questionnaire-based follow-up approaches used by newborn hearing screening programs have met with varying degrees of success (Jacobson & Jacobson, 1990; Penn & Gibson, 1994), variability which stems from differences in types of hospitals (e.g., private vs. public), geographic and socioeconomic area, age of the child at follow-up contact, and method of inquiry (e.g., telephone contact vs. mailed questionaires). Brown and Taxman (1993) note that "although such follow-up is certainly preferable in any screening program" (p. 147), it is often not practical given the unique characteristics of a given screening program and its environment.

As Kenworthy (1990) has noted astutely, "Follow-up may represent the Achilles heel of birth-related [hearing screening] methods. . . . Therefore, what is required is a follow-up network dedicated to the singular purpose of early detection, confirmation, and management of hearing loss" (p. 324). Without aggressive follow-up policies and procedures, the ecumenical effectiveness of programs for early identification of infant hearing impairments will be reduced substantially. Even worse, without collaboration and coordination among professionals and agencies, audiologists and related professionals and constituencies may become disenchanted with the potential for screening all newborns. Diefendorf et al. (1990) assert that:

> Early assessment of hearing impairment must be followed up with a comprehensive plan of medical and educational management. Without such a plan any program of screening and assessment for hearing impairment by itself is incomplete. (p. 393)

Two of the major and extant "weak links" in follow-up activities related to UNHS are ineffective and inadequate data management and various complications and difficulties related to children's parents/guardians. Very often, data management and parent/guardian problems are intimately associated.

The Integral Link Between Data Management in UNHS Programs and Appropriate Follow-up

Without adequate planning, staff allocation, and data management and record-keeping technology, management of data from even a small hospital's UNHS program can be a Herculean task, one that is certain to involve substantial effort to maintain a high degree of accuracy and to maximize operational efficiency and accountability. Recordkeeping related to initial screening, rescreening, audiological follow-up, loss confirmation, management plans, and entry into early intervention services and programs for children identified with hearing losses may quickly overwhelm screening program and ancillary staff. In fact, Finitzo (1995a, 1995b) states that management of information generated by UNHS programs remains one of the major arguments proffered by critics against UNHS (e.g., Bess & Paradise, 1994).

In an effort to address some of the problematic follow-up issues in neonatal hearing screening programs, the state of Rhode Island (Johnson, Maxon, White, & Vohr, 1993) and, more recently, the National Center for Hearing Identification and Management [NCHIM] at Utah State University in Logan, as part of a project (the National Consortium for Universal Newborn Hearing Screening) funded by the U.S. Bureau of Maternal and Child Health to provide information on and training in UNHS using TEOAE (Mauk & White, 1995), have developed computer software to track infants and their families from initial hearing screening prior to discharge from the hospital to, if necessary, rescreening, audiological diagnosis, and development of an Individualized Family Service Plan (IFSP).[1]

---

[1]To obtain additional information regarding the mission, activities, services, and products of the National Center for Hearing Identification and Management (NCHIM) and, specifically, the infant tracking software developed by NCHIM for use in newborn hearing screening programs contact Dr. Karl R. White, Director, National Center for Hearing Identification and Management, Department of Psychology, Utah State University, Logan, Utah 84322-2810. [Phone: (801) 797-3589 and FAX: (801) 797-1448]

The Hearing Health Institute (HHI) in Fort Worth, Texas has also developed a neonatal hearing screening and information management software package (Finitzo, 1995b) for infant tracking and follow-up purposes.[2] Finitzo (1995a) describes effective data management in UNHS programs as "the transformation of data to information" (p. 25) and delineates two distinct roles for data management in UNHS programs: (1) assuring a strong link from infant assessment to infant benefit and (2) fostering programmatic evaluation and validation through documentation. She notes further that effective information management systems in UNHS should be accurate, timely, and achievable at minimal cost (Finitzo, 1995a). Finitzo (1995b) also notes that data management systems for UNHS programs must be designed to work on three important levels: (a) for the screener in the nursery (e.g., volunteer, screening technician, audiologist); (b) for the director of the screening program (e.g., the supervising audiologist); and (c) for the hospital administrator (or program sponsor) who reports screening program data and progress to hospital management and/or other entities (e.g., the state health or education department).

Finitzo (1995b) also states that the individuals who are actually performing hearing screening of neonates need at least three things from a data management system: (a) a quick response to the technical adequacy of their data collection, (b) a clear protocol, and (c) immediate interpretive feedback to minimize the number of infants who do not pass the initial hearing screening. Screeners also need to link test and ear data to a child's medical record, thereby enhancing referral management. With respect to the role of a UNHS management system in quality control, Finitzo (1995b) asserts that the audiologist who is directing or supervising the UNHS program must have access to data regarding screeners' proficiency (e.g., pass/refer rates, probe stability, intensity of stimulus, testing time).

Finitzo (1995a) describes adoption and maintenance of standards for data management in UNHS programs as "stewardship" (p. 25) activities of audiologists. She asserts that audiologists are the "stewards of infant hearing detection" (p. 25). Such stewardship requires that the UNHS programs initiated by audiologists "be of value to the infants and families" (p. 25), as well as practical and cost-efficient. Addressing the audiology community, Finitzo (1995a) notes that, "Stewardship of universal infant hearing detection programs is not only our most important role, but perhaps our most challenging" (p. 25).

The Parent/Guardian and Follow-up

Diefendorf et al. (1990) assert that, "Successful management of young hearing-impaired children requires the support and involvement of several different professionals, and most importantly parents" (p. 393). Because most D/HH children are born to parents who have normal hearing and who likely possess limited prior knowledge about hearing loss and its developmental effects, when the child's hearing loss is diagnosed, "the parents enter a world of confusion and controversy which can heighten their frustration as they begin the process of learning how to help their child" (Rushmer, 1994, p. 160).

Recently, the Joint Committee of ASHA and the Council on Education of the Deaf (1994) issued a report regarding services under the Individuals with Disabilities Education

---

[2]To obtain additional information about the Screening and Information Management System© for use in newborn hearing screening programs, contact the Hearing Health Institute (HHI) in Fort Worth, Texas at (817) 335-4443 or Optimization Zorn (OZ Enterprises) at (214) 922-9201 (Dr. Terese Finitzo, personal communication, December 13, 1995).

Act (IDEA), Part H, to D/HH children ages birth through 36 months. In establishing the framework for this report, the Committee noted the following:

Children who are deaf or hard of hearing and their families/caregivers constitute a unique group whose needs differ from those of other families. The variables that set children with hearing loss apart from those with other disabilities are related to the lack of full access to communication. This can have long-term effects on the child's cognitive, speech, language, and social-emotional development, as well as affect the family system. Early identfication, assessment, and management should: (a) be conducted by professionals who have the qualifications to meet the needs of children who are deaf or hard of hearing, particularly infants, toddlers, and their families; (b) be designed to meet the unique needs of the child and the family; and (c) include families in an active, collaborative role with professionals in the planning and provision of early intervention services. (Joint Committee of ASHA and the Council on Education of the Deaf, 1994, p. 308)

However, even professionals who are accomplished in working with D/HH children may not be prepared to meet the full challenge that awaits them (Atkins, 1995). To help a D/HH child reach his or her potential, professionals must address the child's most immediate environment: the family (Atkins, 1995; Diefendorf, 1996; Goldberg, 1996; Meadow-Orlans, 1995; Meyers, 1995). Emotions that may occur in family members (i.e., parents, siblings, etc.) in succession or, more likely, may appear and reappear for years after the confirmation of the child's hearing loss include shock, denial, anger, sadness, guilt, confession, jealousy, embarrassment, recognition, and constructive action (Atkins, 1995; Diefendorf, 1996; Fischgrund, Cohen, & Clarkson, 1987; Leigh, 1987; Luterman, 1979; Meadow-Orlans, 1995; Moses, 1985).

Atkins (1995) notes that professionals (e.g., audiologists, speech pathologists, school psychologists) are the link between the family of the child with a hearing loss and the world of people who are deaf or hard of hearing. She asserts that, because too few parents receive the benefits of regularly scheduled parents' group meetings that afford them the opportunity to share feelings, experiences, and information (Rushmer, 1994), the professional "is the main source of help for the parents, who must adapt to life with their deaf child" (Atkins, 1995, p. 14). As an integral part of the follow-up process in UNHS programs, "It is a professional's job to help parents rediscover their own strengths and resources that will help their children become independent, responsible, and successful" (Atkins, 1995, p. 14).

Also, although parents or guardians have the primary responsibility to arrange for and to secure a medical and audiologic evaluation, treatment, intervention, and follow-up services for their child, parents or guardians acting alone, for sundry reasons, are often not successful in these endeavors. Frye-Osier (1993, p. 20) has delineated some of the reasons for this lack of success in the follow-up and monitoring aspects of neonatal hearing screening programs:

1. Limited resources and stresses of families may prevent them from following through on recommendations made by hearing screening program staff;
2. Families may have no knowledge of the resources that are available;
3. Families may not receive accurate information from the hearing screening program about the potential significance of the hearing loss for their child;
4. Families may not receive accurate information from the hearing screening programs staff about the appropriate steps to take to ensure a satisfactory outcome of the follow-up process;
5. Medical providers may offer little or no guidance to families regarding appropriate nonmedical interventions;

6. Communication between hearing screening programs and medical providers may be poor, and either the hearing screening program and/or the medical provider may furnish inconsistent or conflicting information to the family;
7. Communication among hearing screening programs and early intervention programs may be poor;
8. Early interventionists may not understand the developmental and educational ramifications of the hearing loss; and
9. Families may believe that the existence of the hearing screening program means that "someone" is following through appropriately and adequately for their child when, in fact, no one is.

Setting the Stage: Early Intervention for Children with Hearing Loss

Currently, the opportunity exists to identify hearing loss at an early age, to establish high-quality services for young children with hearing losses, and to set the stage for future progress (Joint Committee on Infant Hearing, 1994). However, Johnson, Mauk, et al. (1993) observe that

Although there is a professional consensus that early identification of hearing disability is crucial to the optimization of a child's potential, there are very few examples of successful statewide systems that provide both early identification and appropriate early intervention services that children need to mitigate the deleterious effects of the hearing disability. (p. 116)

Laughton (1994) has asserted that, for infants and young children with hearing loss, "with early intervention our hope is to maximize prevention, capitalize on critical age, preserve developmental synchrony, and prevent the adverse impact on motor, perceptual, language, communication, and socioemotional development and academic achievement" (p. 150). As such, early identification of hearing loss followed by prompt intervention provided to affected children and their families holds the promise of considerable abatement of the economic burden of the hearing loss for the individual and society.

Early intervention may be described as "the provision of educational, therapeutic, preventive, and supportive services for young children with disabilities and their families" (Bailey, 1992, p. 385). Boothroyd (1982) has observed that the three immediate goals of intervention with young children who have SNHL are: (1) to reduce the primary impairment, (2) to prevent the development of secondary problems, and (3) to ensure that the needs of the child and family are met in spite of the hearing loss. Epstein and Reilly (1989) have stated that, "All children with SNHL [sensorineural hearing loss] must be started on a comprehensive and well-planned education program" (p. 1516). For an overview of family-centered early intervention programs for infants and toddlers with hearing loss and their families, readers are referred to the excellent edited text by Roush and Matkin (1994), and to a recent special issue of *The Volta Review* (Phillips & Cole, 1993).

Individual and Societal Benefits of Early Identification of and Early Intervention for Children with Hearing Loss

Early identification of hearing loss followed by early intervention holds the promise of optimizing language, speech, intellectual, psychosocial development, and occupational/economic opportunity for the affected child. Studies involving children who are deaf and hard of hearing show that intervention during the critical period from birth to 2½ or 3 years of age results in greater linguistic and academic gains than intervention after age 2½ or 3 years (Apuzzo & Yoshinaga-Itano, 1995; Glover, Watkins, Pittman, Johnson, & Barringer, 1994). Bailey (1992) states that

> From an historical perspective, early intervention grew out of the basic assumption that providing services at the earliest possible time would maximize the benefits that might accrue to the child, the family, and society. For example, it is assumed that early intervention will facilitate children's development, help support families in coping with the tasks associated with care of children with a disability, and reduce the need for costly specialized services in later years. (p. 385)

Individual Benefits

A quarter of a century ago, Moores (1970) stated that it is a psycholinguistic paradigm that language in a young child, rather than developing gradually, explodes. That is, "all children, given a linguistically 'normal' environment, learn the language of their society, in a consistent, relaxed, almost unconscious manner—and in a very short time" (Moores, 1982, p. 179). The earlier the onset of a sensorineural hearing loss, the more marked the speech, language, and communication disability (Markides, 1986; Nober & Nober, 1977; Ramkalawan & Davis, 1992; Schow & Nerbonne, 1989). Regarding the practice of neonatal screening for hearing loss, Stewart and Davis-Freeman (1994) state that, "hearing impairment affects an individual's entire life unlike most disorders that are screened for in this country" (p. 956). Gravel, Diefendorf, and Matkin (1994) have observed that "congenital or early-onset, sensory or neurologic disorders that result in long-term developmental disabilities are known to be more costly to society when such deficits are first detected at older ages" (p. 958).

"Early" Versus "Late" Intervention

Until recently, it was fairly common for professionals to wait until a child with hearing loss was 3 or 4 years old before providing language intervention (Davis, Elfenbein, Schum, & Bentler, 1986; Watkins & Schow, 1989). Thus, the child with a hearing loss typically became more educationally delayed than is warranted on the basis of his or her hearing loss alone, and, because of the parent's, and often the primary care physician's, failure to recognize and appreciate the impact of the hearing loss, the child was likely to be mismanaged in such a way as to impose additional impairments (Mauk, White, Mortensen, & Behrens, 1991; Stewart, 1984). Although clinicians have reported that early intervention frequently permits even children with severe to profound sensorineural hearing losses to progress through normal developmental sequences (Apuzzo & Yoshinaga-Itano, 1995; Ling, 1976), the benefits of early intervention for children with sensorineural hearing losses are often not evident in the published literature (U.S. Preventive Services Task Force, 1989).

However, there is a growing body of evidence that demonstrates dramatic enhancement of academic achievement, speech and language development, and life success for children with hearing loss if they are identified very early in life (Mauk & White, 1995). Glover et al. (1994) recently reviewed the conclusions of three research studies (Levitt, McGarr, & Geffner, 1987; Watkins, 1987; White & White, 1987) and the findings of a literature review (Meadow-Orlans, 1987) and reported that:

Concerning the importance of early intervention, studies involving children who are deaf and hard of hearing show that intervention during the critical period from birth to 2½ or 3 years of age results in greater linguistic and academic gains than intervention after age 2½ or 3 years.... Studies comparing "early" intervention for deaf and hard of hearing children (prior to about 30 months of age) to "late" intervention (after about 30 months of age) typically show greater progress for the children receiving "early" intervention on a variety of outcome variables. (Glover et al., 1994, p. 320)

A recent study from Colorado on children in the Colorado Home Intervention Program (CHIP) by Apuzzo and Yoshinaga-Itano (1995) support the "earlier is better" assumption. In their study, Apuzzo and Yoshinaga-Itano (1995) analyzed the general development of 69 hearing impaired infants with respect to their age of identification at the time of diagnosis of hearing loss. Children in the study were divided into four groups based on age of identification: Group A: birth to 2 months (14 subjects), Group B: 3 to 12 months (11 subjects), Group C: 13 to 24 months (30 subjects), and Group D: 25 months and older (14 subjects). Each category contained subjects of varying degrees of hearing loss.

All of the children in the study were between 24 and 60 months of age at time of testing and each identification category (A, B, C, D) had a mean age of approximately 40 months at the time of testing. All subjects' primary caregivers completed the 320-item Minnesota Child Development Inventory (MCDI; Ireton & Thwing, 1974). Subtests on the MCDI included gross motor, fine motor, expressive language, comprehension-conceptual, situation-comprehension, self-help, personal-social, and general development. MCDI Developmental quotients were used so that subjects' results could be compared irrespective of their age at the time of testing. Two major findings of the study were (a) that children in the earliest identification category (Group A) scored significantly higher than the other groups in expressive language and general development, and (b) that children with severe hearing loss demonstrated the greatest benefit from early identification during this age period.

Apuzzo and Yoshinaga-Itano (1995) remarked that the "striking performance of the earliest [identified] group supports the retention of current early identification practices and encourages the implementation of universal newborn hearing screening programs across the nation" (p. 124) and concluded that "significantly better performance [i.e., higher caregiver MCDI ratings] was associated with early intervention, the greatest benefit coming with intervention that was begun within two months of birth" (p. 134). Summarizing the recent experience of early identification of and early intervention for young children with diverse degrees of hearing losses in Colorado, Yoshinaga-Itano (1995) writes that:

Our data indicate that early identification of hearing loss, particularly at birth, not only minimizes the deleterious effect upon communication development, but can prevent delays in development from ever occurring.... It appears that when optimal early intervention services are provided from age of identification that the serious effects of sensorineural hearing loss upon communication skills can be avoided. (p. 13)

Societal Benefits

According to Downs (1993), identification of hearing loss at or near birth and immediate habilitative intervention for the congenitally deaf child would result in some approximation of the language skills of those children with onset of deafness at age 3. As a result, there would be "a marked improvement in earned income, approaching $129 million per year for the profoundly deaf group. The estimated total cost to society from deafness and hearing impairments stated above—$79 billion per year—might be reduced by 5 percent through newborn identification, that is, up to $3.9 billion per year" (Downs, 1993, p. 63). Comparison of this conservative annual monetary savings estimate from Downs (1993), $3.9 billion dollars, to both low ($144 million; Robinette, 1994) and high estimates ($200 million and $233 million; Bess & Paradise, 1994 and Raffin & Matz, 1994, respectively) of the annual cost of conducting UNHS of all live births (approximately 4 million per year) in the United States gives us some indication of how nationwide implementation of UNHS and appropriate and propitious early intervention can more than pay for itself.

Statements published by both NIH (1993) and the Joint Committee on Infant Hearing (1994) unequivocally recognize that "the failure to detect a hearing impairment—even a mild one—can cause both human suffering and economic loss" (Meister, 1993, p. 3). Ruben (1991) has commented that children with educationally significant hearing losses "will be economically disadvantaged unless they develop competent communication skills" (p. 129).

The "Aggregate Burden of Suffering"

Beitchman, Inglis, and Schacter (1992) have proffered an interesting perspective when they speak about the "aggregate burden of suffering" (p. 230) of a disorder or disability, such as educationally significant hearing loss. They state that the "aggregate burden of suffering varies with the disorder in question, based on its prevalence, severity, stability, and its impact on the individual, family, and community" (p. 230). Aside from the direct and indirect societal costs of the hearing loss, a major aspect of this "burden" involves the costs to the individual child and his or her "subjective sense of pain and suffering which result from the functional impairment of the [hearing] disorder" (Beitchman et al., 1992, p. 231) and how the problem affects, among other things, the child's progress in school (Hamburg, 1992).

Beitchman et al. (1992) have divided these costs into three areas: (1) *core costs* (the direct or indirect costs such as habilitation and resources to support training and research); (2) *non-core costs* (which result from the impact of the illness, etc. on institutions (e.g., schools) and other individuals (e.g., family members); and (3) *individual costs* (the child's subjective sense of pain and suffering as well as objective arresting of progress in school, social relationships, etc. which result from the functional impairment of the disorder). The Executive Board of the Educational Audiology Association (EBEAA, 1994) recently reminded the field of the following:

> [I]t is not possible to attach a monetary value to everything. The family stress and frustration that exists when communication between a child and the parents is impaired cannot be easily measured. Yet knowing a child's problems and needs as early as possible minimizes the anxiety that affects this relationship. (p. 957)

Early Intervention: Paying Now Versus Paying Later

Robinette (1994) recently provided an example of how educational cost savings might compensate for expenditures for UNHS. He states that

> By dividing the cost to identify each hearing-impaired child by the cost difference between education in a regular versus self-contained classroom and multiplying the quotient by 100, one can estimate the percent of early identified hearing-impaired children that would need to be educated in regular classrooms in place of self-contained classrooms for the universal screening/diagnostic program to pay for itself in educational savings. (p. 953)

For example, using the cumulative annual costs for 12 years of public school education for a child with a sensorineural hearing loss (1st through 12th grade) in a *resource room setting* (up to 20 hours/week of special education services; $6,397.55 per year × 12 years = $76,770.60) and the cumulative annual costs for 12 years of public school education for a child with a sensorineural hearing loss (1st through 12th grade) in a *self-contained classroom* (more than 20 hours/week of special education services; $12,389.75 per year × 12 years = $148,677.00) from recent data in Colorado (EBEAA, 1994), and the algorithm and the cost estimate of $6,045.00 per infant identified with a sensorineural hearing loss provided by Robinette (1994), we can estimate the percentage of children identified with a hearing loss at or near birth who would need to be educated in a resource room setting rather than a self-contained classroom environment for UNHS and diagnostic follow-up to recoup the costs.

As an example, the cost differential between a self-contained classroom setting and a resource room setting for a child with a sensorineural hearing loss is $71,906.40 [$148,677.00 − $76,770.60]. If we take the cost per infant identified with a sensorineural hearing loss of $6,045.00 and divide by the forgoing cost differential [$6,045.00 ÷ $71,906.40] and multiply by 100, we arrive at the inference that, if, as a consequence of UNHS finding children with sensorineural hearing loss at or near birth, 8.4% more children with sensorineural hearing losses could be educated in resource room settings instead of self-contained classrooms, the UNHS program would pay for itself.

From examination of the educational costs delineated by EBEAA (1994) and the cost estimates for UNHS provided by Robinette (1994), it becomes self-evident that education of youth who have sensorineural hearing loss in environments which require fewer specially trained personnel and special services (e.g., regular classrooms) costs less per year and saves tens of thousands of dollars per student over the course of their public school education. The more students with sensorineural hearing loss who can be educated toward the end of the educational services continuum that involves fewer specially trained personnel and special services, the fewer the dollars that will be spent on their educations.

The earlier the identification of hearing loss in a child, the earlier that child will receive intervention to avert or minimize the deleterious effects on and delays in communication and other developmental areas. The fewer and less severe the delays or problems in linguistic, cognitive, emotional, and social functioning, the less likely the child is to need special services, and the more likely he or she is to be served in educational settings in which special services and personnel are provided. Thus, the earlier children with hearing losses are identified, the more economical their education will be for society, because earlier identification of hearing loss and, thus, earlier intervention for children who have hearing loss can lower the probability of placement and services in more restrictive and more costly educational settings.

In summary, the identification of hearing loss, ideally at or near birth, and prompt initiation of appropriate, family-centered, community-based, coordinated intervention can both conserve our nation's fiscal resources *and* forestall the unconscionable loss of human potential caused by delayed identification and intervention. The message is clear: "we either pay a little bit on in a child's life (cost of screening and identification services) or pay more later (more intense educational services due to the child's delays)" (EBEAA, 1994, p. 957). The small costs associated with effective UNHS will more than be repaid in future years (National Commission on Children, 1991; Northern & Downs, 1991; Northern & Hayes, 1994; Robinette,

1994; Stewart & Davis-Freeman, 1994). Monies invested in early auditory screening, ideally at birth, will help to ensure early identification of hearing loss and, as such, will go a long way in preventing the emergence of developmental delays and in preparing each child to be "ready to learn" (U.S. Department of Education, 1991).

Early Identification/Early Intervention: Advocacy Efforts and Task Forces

Early identification and intervention efforts, being proactive, generally require substantive action on the part of interested members of local community members and professionals. Northern and Hayes (1994) assert that, "Early identification and habilitation of all infants with hearing impairment must continue to be a major goal for health care systems. As advocates for children with hearing loss, we must improve our strategies for early identification and intervention" (p. 13). Toward such an end, Baumeister (1992), Long (1992), and Mauk and White (1995) have recently offered various recommendations for ways in which citizens and professionals can impact human public service policies, especially those which involve (a) early screening to identify children with hearing impairments and (b) early intervention to mitigate the developmental consequences of auditory dysfunction.

Some states, including Arizona, California, Colorado, Connecticut, Iowa, Illinois, Kentucky, Louisiana, Maryland, New Jersey, Utah, and Vermont have established task forces or advisory committees to address earlier identification of hearing loss. The establishment of such groups is the often the first step in the process of UNHS implementation. Such a group could be, for example, composed of public agency and private practice audiologists, primary care physicians, otolaryngologists, public and private hospital administrators, private insurance and Medicaid representatives, nurses, university faculty, regular and special educators, public health personnel, administrators from Part H (P.L. 102-119) and Part B (619) of IDEA, representatives of the state school for the deaf, and parents of children with hearing disabilities.

Such collaborative and transdisciplinary endeavors by states represent bold steps and greatly needed efforts to bring together new technology for identifying newborns with hearing loss, methods of reimbursing hospitals for their screening efforts (American Medical Association, 1995, p. 322), and uniform statewide data systems (JCIH, 1994) so that children identified with hearing losses can be followed and served. Neonatal screening efforts must be integrally linked with educational policies and strategies to form a comprehensive system of identifying, tracking, referring, and intervening with children with hearing loss. There are unfortunate consequences if these processes are not brought into a comprehensive system of services. Children born with hearing loss and their families may be sentenced to doing time within an uncoordinated, noncollaborative array of services. Such a sentence simply is not justifiable given our current ability to do much more (Mauk et al., 1995; Mauk & White, 1995).

Otolaryngologist Irwin Stewart (1984) noted more than a decade ago that, as professionals dedicated to appropriate and effective services for children with hearing loss and their families, we must be aware of "the linguistic starvation a deaf infant is sentenced to when deprived of language in the first three years" (p. 797). However, in our zeal for earlier identification of hearing loss, we must go beyond being aware of this fact and convey this information to others in our communities, so they understand the developmental and linguistic urgency of early identification and so they will be allies in promoting infant hearing screening programs and follow-up networks (Mauk & White, 1995). For ourselves, the children, and our future, we cannot afford to take a position of non-involvement.

Accepting the Challenge: Seizing the Moment, Setting the Stage, and Serving the Future

Seizing the Moment

Buttross et al. (1995) recently stated that, "Childhood hearing loss is common and has life-long implications for communication, emotional well-being and achievement of educational-occupational skills" (p. 1445). Research has demonstrated that early identification of hearing loss, ideally at or near birth, and prompt initiation of appropriate, family-centered, community-based, coordinated early intervention can forestall this unconscionable loss of human potential. We must take this research to heart and establish UNHS programs across the nation. These UNHS programs must be grounded in sound and effective technology and serve as the foundation of an integrated and transdisciplinary amalgamation of strategies including parent education and involvement, appropriate diagnostic testing, aggressive follow-up, culminating in a comprehensive and well-planned early intervention/education program (Diefendorf & Weber, 1994; Matkin, 1994; Zipper, Hinton, Weil, & Rounds, 1993). We owe this to our children and we should do no less for them (Downs, 1994; Meister, 1993).

Although the commitment to technology for infant hearing screening in the United States has come a long way and is evolving rapidly, the average age of 18–30 months, at which young children with significant auditory disabilities are identified, is unacceptable.

Mauk et al. (1995) noted that the promise of earlier detection, diagnosis, and habilitation of hearing loss is within reach (a) if we have appropriate understanding of the magnitude and consequences of the problem of hearing loss in children, (b) if we are able to learn from professionals' past efforts in early detection of hearing loss, (c) if we are able to evaluate and to use emerging technologies appropriately to screen for hearing loss during the neonatal period, and (d) if we are willing to develop collaborative uses of resources and agencies already in place. Recent advances in hearing screening technology, such as TEOAE and AABR, combined with current emphasis and concern to identify and serve children with disabilities, bring together the necessary components for professionals and agencies to establish screening programs to detect hearing loss at a very early age.

Setting the Stage

Johnson, Mauk, et al. (1993) note that developing a successful statewide newborn hearing screening program requires at least seven critical components: (1) documenting the need, (2) generating constituency support, (3) securing legislation, (4) implementing the program, (5) refining the early intervention services system, (6) financing the system, and (7) identifying gaps in the system. They further assert that, "By following this plan, states committed to development of a comprehensive system for early identification of hearing disabilities would reduce substantially the average age at which children in the United States are identified and enrolled in early intervention services" (Johnson, Mauk, et al., 1993, p. 117).

As a complement to these seven critical components for a statewide newborn hearing screening program, Bailey and Wolery (1992) have delineated seven goals which have emerged as relevant for early intervention: (1) supporting families in achieving their own goals; (2) promoting child engagement, independence, and mastery; (3) promoting development in important domains; (4) building and supporting social competence; (5) facilitating the use of generalized skills; (6) providing and preparing for normalized life experiences; and (7) preventing the emergence of future problems or disabilities.

Bailey (1992) points out that the question, "Is early intervention effective for children with hearing loss?" can only be answered after determination is made of the goals for early intervention with this population. For those individuals engaged in the campaign to identify and provide services to children with hearing losses at an early age, the foregoing seven goals "represent an extraordinarily broad mandate for early intervention and constitute perhaps the most important issue facing early intervention professionals today: Why are we here, and what do we want to achieve as a result of these services?" (Bailey, 1992, p. 390).

For UNHS to be successful, multidisciplinary cooperation and professional persistence across multiple agencies is needed (Brown, Thurman, & Pearl, 1993; Frye-Osier, 1993; JCIH, 1994; Johnson, Maxon, et al., 1993; Matkin, 1994; Melaville & Blank, 1993; Pugh & Hicks, 1995; Rittenhouse & Dancer, 1992; Zipper et al., 1993; see Figure 1). As MacCarthy and Connell (1984) noted more than a decade ago, early identification and habilitative service provision to children with hearing losses "requires an extension of regular screening, a development of the referral system with the necessary collaboration between professionals, and direct work with more disadvantaged parents" (p. 85). Recently, Frye-Osier (1993) observed that

To ensure comprehensive, quality-driven, and valuable infant hearing screening services, leadership personnel in state-level health and human services and education must make a commitment to state-of-the-art screening methods; well-trained and well-supervised screening personnel; effective communications with families, medical providers, and educators; accurate recordkeeping; and persistent monitoring and follow-up. (p. 2).

Finitzo (1995a, 1995b) astutely reminds us that professionals involved in the establishment and operation of UNHS programs must be good stewards (Block, 1993) and must adopt and adhere to standards of accuracy, timeliness, and cost-efficiency with regard to management of information in UNHS programs. She notes that such standards apply to the end products of UNHS programs (i.e., early detection of hearing loss and child and family benefit), "not to the means or mechanisms" (Finitzo, 1995a, p. 25). Finitzo advises that such standards for information management in UNHS programs should not be synonymous with professional or systemic constraints or stagnation:

Indeed, local solutions which meet the standards should be encouraged, as it is through local, creative approaches that the field with thrive and improves. Standardization need not mean stagnation, but rather should foster communication and identify commonalities in our efforts. . . . Stewardship does not demand perfection, but if we operate out of control, or by greed, carelessness or insecurity, rather than in service, we will falter. (Finitzo, 1995a, p. 25)

Finally, infants and young children in the 1990s are served in a variety of educational settings and "the ultimate success of an audiologic screening effort will be determined by the extent to which the unique and individualized needs of each program can be identified, so that the procedures best suited for that program can be selected and implemented" (Roush, 1990, p. 369).

| **Early Identification** | **Early Intervention** |

 Universal Screening
*Well-baby nurseries
*Intensive care nurseries
*Public health agencies
*Statewide public awareness
*Professional education

 Referral Services
*Part H and private agencies
*Public health agencies
*Other public/private agencies
*Parent-infant programs
*Physicians and audiologists

 Diagnostic Services
*Hospitals/medical centers
*Audiologists
*University hearing clinics
*State/county health departments

 Intervention Services
*Part H home-based and/or
  center-based services
*SKI*HI programming
*Health intervention agencies
*Education intervention agencies

 Follow-up Services
*Complete computerized
  central tracking
*Pediatric/medical follow-up
*Public health agencies
*Audiological services
*Public awareness campaigns

 Follow-up Services
*Transition programming
  [home ---------> school]
*Ongoing audiological and
  medical follow-up
*IFSP to IEP process:
  community resources identified

 Outcomes
*Universal newborn hearing
  screening
*Efficacious statewide/national
  hearing screening/tracking system
*Confirmation of hearing loss and
  intervention/habilitation begun by
  no more than 6 months of age
  for all identified children

 Outcomes
*All children who are deaf or
  hard of hearing will enter
  school "ready to learn"
*Families of these children will
  be empowered to make
  informed educational choices
  for their children and will know
  where to obtain assistance
  and information

Figure 1. Aspects of a comprehensive system of early identification and early intervention for children with hearing loss and their families.

Serving the Future

National Education Goal #1 states that all children will enter school ready to learn (U.S. Department of Education, 1991). It is indeed a worthy and justified goal for all children, including children who are deaf or hard of hearing. This goal should and will be accomplished for deaf and hard of hearing children if they are identified early in their lives, if appropriate intervention strategies are implemented by their families and service providers, and if families and other caregivers accept the responsibility to help their children. Indeed, SKI*HI data collected for more than 12 years on more than 5,000 children demonstrate that children who are deaf or hard of hearing can and do make significant cognitive, social, communicative, and preacademic progress if early intervention strategies are implemented (Strong et al., 1994).

Cole (1994) has observed that, "Children with hearing loss are children, with all of the needs, curiosity, feelings, and delightfulness that children express. Consequently, children with hearing loss need all of the usual special attention that any child needs" (p. 263). However, unlike children with normal hearing, children with hearing loss possess a diminished auditory capacity that is invisible yet insidious and wreaks havoc with their linguistic and psychosocial development (Moore, 1991; National Institute on Deafness and Other Communication Disorders, 1989). Indeed, children with hearing loss *do* need all of the usual special attention that any child receives; but they also need more. They need to have their hearing losses identified at or near birth, and they and their families need to be provided with appropriate early intervention services (Joint Committee of ASHA and the Council on Education of the Deaf, 1994).

As otolaryngologist Burton Jaffe reported, "Deafness never killed anyone. But who can count the number of lives it has wasted?" (1977, p. xxi). Northern and Hayes (1994, p. 13) recently asserted that substantial data exist to support four irrefutable facts about hearing loss in early childhood: (1) sensorineural hearing loss in infants and young children is a serious condition which results in disabling difficulties across the life span (Downs, 1994); (2) continued reliance on the high-risk registry approach to screening infants will identify less than half of the infants with significant hearing loss (Elssmann, Matkin, & Sabo, 1987; Mauk et al., 1991; Todd, 1994); (3) valid hearing screening techniques, with proven acceptable sensitivity and specificity, are currently available to detect moderate, severe, and profound sensorineural hearing loss in neonates and infants (Hunter et al., 1994; Jacobson et al., 1990; Kileny & Magathan, 1987; White & Behrens, 1993; White, Behrens, & Strickland, 1995); and (4) early intervention is requisite for fostering language and communication skill development, cognitive ability, social-emotional development, and academic achievement (Brackett, 1993; First & Palfrey, 1994; Yoshinaga-Itano, 1995). Although adequate hearing alone does not determine an individual child's level academic attainment and general societal contribution, it does endow the child with enhanced opportunities to maximize his or her abilities in an increasingly varied and competitive society and validates the child's "right to become" (Marlowe, 1987, p. 339). Nozza (1996) recently noted that, "It is clear that early identification and intervention will minimize disability and that a child with a hearing impairment will achieve academically regardless of the academic path chosen" (p. 95).

To summarize, there currently exists (a) research and documentation regarding the feasibility, practicality, efficacy, and cost effectiveness of screening all newborns for hearing loss; (b) well-trained audiologists who can confirm the presence or absence of hearing loss and the degree of loss at very young ages; (c) the ability to computerize records and track children from the initial hearing screening to entry into early intervention; (d) effective early referral systems operating on statewide basis; (e) sound early intervention approaches and programs capable of meeting the needs presented by the young child who is deaf or hard of hearing; and (f) excellent preschools providing solid transition programming for children and families. Critically, what is still needed is a model that brings all of the foregoing elements together to provide a *comprehensive service system* for the child and the family. Such a model should incorporate (a) the latest technology available to screen all newborns for hearing loss; (b) the tremendous capacity of local and, ideally, statewide computerized data collection and tracking; (c) the abilities of the audiological profession to identify hearing loss in very young infants; (d) extant child find and referral systems that are part of mandated early intervention (P.L. 102-119); (e) the skills of the early interventionist, who is trained to address the unique psychoeducational aspects and family factors surrounding hearing loss; and (f) proactive transition programming so the child and family benefit from each new experience.

To provide the intervention and management strategies necessary to enable children with significant sensorineural hearing loss to make optimal developmental progress, a combination of strategies is needed including effective neonatal hearing screening based on sound and effective technology and criteria, parent education and involvement, appropriate diagnostic testing, aggressive follow-up, and education of health care professionals (Bess, 1993; Fowler & Fowler, 1994; JCIH, 1994; Pugh & Hicks, 1995). Attention to such strategies would substantially reduce the average age at which children with significant hearing losses are identified in the United States.

Diefendorf (1996) recently proclaimed that, "The goal for all children with hearing loss must be early detection followed immediately by appropriate intervention. . . . Through early detection and appropriate intervention we must work with children and their families to enable them to achieve their optimum personal development" (p. 18). Similarly, Clark and Terry (1995) have asserted that, "An ultimate goal for the education of young children who are deaf [and hard of hearing] is the development of their full potential as happy, healthy individuals, who are responsible members of society, confident and capable in their ability to communicate with others" (p. 169). Clearly, we need to set our sights on and begin to map our journey toward the following societal goal: All children born in the United States will be screened for hearing loss prior to hospital discharge, provided follow-up diagnostic audiological services, be included in statewide computerized data systems with appropriate safeguards for confidentiality, receive prompt and appropriate referral to early intervention programs which will assist them and families to transition from one educational placement to another, and, when they enter school, they will be prepared to learn alongside their peers with normal hearing.

Acknowledgement

The authors extend great appreciation to Dr. Karl R. White, Director of the National Center for Hearing Identification and Management (NCHIM) at Utah State University, for his personal and technical support in the completion of this manuscript.

References

American Medical Association. (1995). *Physicians' current procedural terminology codebook*. Chicago, IL: Author.

Apuzzo, M., & Yoshinaga-Itano, C. (1995). Early identification of infants with significant hearing loss and the Minnesota Child Development Inventory. *Seminars in Hearing, 16*(2), 4–139.

Atkins, D. V. (1995). Beyond the child: Hearing impairment and the family. *Volta Voices, 2*(5), 14–17, 22.

Bailey, D. B., Jr. (1992). Current issues in early intervention. In F. H. Bess & J. W. Hall, III (Eds.), *Screening children for auditory function* (pp. 385–398). Nashville, TN: Bill Wilkerson Center Press.

Bailey, D. B., & Wolery, M. (1992). *Teaching infants and preschoolers with disabilities* 2nd ed.). Columbus, OH: Macmillan.

Baumeister, A. A. (1992). Policy formulation: A real world view. In F. H. Bess & J. W. Hall, III (Eds.), *Screening children for auditory function* (pp. 111–123). Nashville, TN: Bill Wilkerson Center Press.

Beitchman, J. H., Inglis, A., & Schacter, D. (1992). Child psychiatry and early intervention: I. The aggregate burden of suffering. *Canadian Journal of Psychiatry, 37,* 230–233.

Bess, F. H. (1993). Early identification of hearing loss: A review of the whys, hows, and whens. *The Hearing Journal, 46*(6), 22–25.

Bess, F. H., & Paradise, J. L. (1994). Universal screening for hearing impairment: Not simple, not risk-free, not necessarily beneficial, and not presently justified. *Pediatrics, 93*(2), 330–334.

Block, P. (1993). *Stewardship: Choosing service over self-interest.* San Francisco: Borrell-Koehler.

Boothroyd, A. (1982). *Hearing impairments in young children.* Englewood Cliffs, NJ: Prentice-Hall.

Brackett, D. (1993). Social/emotional and academic consequences of hearing loss. In *Program and Abstracts of the NIH Consensus Development Conference: Early Identification of Hearing Impairment in Infants and Young Children* (pp. 57–61). Bethesda, MD: National Institutes of Health, National Institute on Deafness and Other Communication Disorders.

Brown, D. P., & Taxman, S. I. (1993). Five years of neonatal hearing screening: A summary. *Infant-Toddler Intervention: The Transdisciplinary Journal, 3,* 135–153.

Brown, W., Thurman, S. K., & Pearl, L. F. (Eds.). (1993). *Family-centered early intervention with infants and toddlers: Innovative cross-disciplinary approaches.* Baltimore: Brookes.

Buttross, S. L., Gearhart, J. G., & Peck, J. E. (1995). Early identification and management of hearing impairment. *American Family Physician, 51,* 1437–1446.

Clark, K. A., & Terry, D. L. (1995). A collaborative framework for intervention. In R. J. Roeser & M. P. Downs (Eds.), *Auditory disorders in school children: The law, identification, and remediation* (3rd ed., pp. 169–187). New York: Thieme Medical Publishers.

Cole, E. B. (1994). Encouraging intelligible spoken language development in infants and toddlers with hearing loss. *Infant-Toddler Intervention: The Transdisciplinary Journal, 4,* 263–284.

Davis, J. M., Elfenbein, J., Schum, R., & Bentler, R. A. (1986). Effects of mild and moderate hearing impairments on language, educational, and psychosocial behavior of children. *Journal of Speech and Hearing Disorders, 51,* 53–62.

Diefendorf, A. O. (1996). Hearing loss and its effects. In F. N. Martin & J. G. Clark (Eds.), *Hearing care for children* (pp. 3–19). Boston: Allyn and Bacon.

Diefendorf, A. O., Chaplin, R. G., Kessler, K. S., Miller, S. M., Miyamoto, R. T., Myres, W. A., Reitz, P. S., Renshaw, J. J., Steck, J. T., & Wagner, M. L. (1990). Follow-up and intervention: Completing the process. *Seminars in Hearing, 11*(4), 393–407.

Diefendorf, A. O., & Weber, B. A. (1994). Identification of hearing loss: Programmatic and procedural considerations. In J. Roush & N. D. Matkin (Eds.), *Infants and toddlers with hearing loss: Family-centered assessment and intervention* (pp. 43–64). Baltimore: York Press.

Downs, M. P. (1993). Benefits of screening at birth: Economic, educational, and functional factors. In *Program and Abstracts of the NIH Consensus Development Conference on Early Identification of Hearing Impairment in Infants and Young Children* (pp. 63–66). Bethesda, MD: National Institutes of Health, National Institute on Deafness and Other Communication Disorders.

Downs, M. P. (1994). The case for detection and intervention at birth. *Seminars in Hearing, 15*(2), 76–84.

Elssmann, S., Matkin, N., & Sabo, M. (1987). Early identification of congenital sensorineural hearing loss. *The Hearing Journal, 40,* 13–17.

Epstein, S., & Reilly, J. S. (1989). Sensorineural hearing loss. *Pediatric Clinics of North America, 36,* 1501–1519.

Executive Board of the Educational Audiology Association (EBEAA). (1994). Universal screening for infant hearing impairment [Letter to the editor]. *Pediatrics, 94*(6), 957.

Finitzo, T. (1995a). Stewardship in universal hearing detection programs. *Audiology Today, 7*(5), 25.

Finitzo, T. (1995b). Accountability in universal infant hearing detection. *The Hearing Review, 2*(8) 15–17.

First, L. R., & Palfrey, J. S. (1994). The infant or young child with developmental delay. *The New England Journal of Medicine, 330,* 478–483.

Fischgrund, J., Cohen, O., & Clarkson, R. (1987). Hearing impaired children in black and hispanic families. *The Volta Review, 89*(5), 59–67.

Folsom, R. C. (1990). Identification of hearing loss in infants using auditory brainstem response: Strategies and program choices. *Seminars in Hearing, 11*(4), 333–341.

Fowler, B. A., & Fowler, S. M. (1994). Infant hearing screening: A practical approach. *Seminars in Hearing, 15*(2), 85–99.

Frye-Osier, J. (1993). *The Wisconsin guide to childhood hearing screening.* Madison: Wisconsin Department of Public Instruction.

Glover, B., Watkins, S., Pittman, P., Johnson, D., & Barringer, D. (1994). SKI-HI home intervention for families with infants, toddlers, and preschool children who are deaf or hard of hearing. *Infant-Toddler Intervention: The Transdisciplinary Journal, 4,* 319–332.

Goldberg, D. M. (1996). Early intervention. In F. N. Martin & J. G. Clark (Eds.), *Hearing care for children* (pp. 287–302). Boston: Allyn and Bacon.

Gravel, J. S., Diefendorf, A. O., & Matkin, N. D. (1994). Universal screening for infant hearing impairment [Letter to the editor]. *Pediatrics, 94*(6), 957–959.

Gravel, J. S., Wallace, I. F., & Ruben, R. J. (1995). Early otitis media and later educational risk. *Acta Otolaryngolica, 115,* 279–281.

Hamburg, D. A. (1992). *Today's children: Creating a future for a generation in crisis.* New York: Random House.

Hunter, M. F., Kimm, L., Dees, D. C., Kennedy, C. R., & Thornton, A. R. D. (1994). Feasibility of otoacoustic emission detection followed by ABR as a universal neonatal screening test for hearing impairment. *British Journal of Audiology, 28,* 47–51.

Ireton, H., & Thwing, E. (1974). *Minnesota Child Development Inventory.* Minneapolis: Behavioral Science Systems.

Jacobson, C. A., & Jacobson, J. T. (1990). Follow-up services in newborn hearing screening programs. *Journal of the American Academy of Audiology, 1,* 181–186.

Jaffe, B. F. (1977). Introduction. In B. F. Jaffe (Ed.), *Hearing loss in children: A comprehensive text* (pp. xix–xxi). Baltimore: University Park Press.

Johnson, J. L., Mauk, G. W., Takekawa, K. M., Simon, P. R., Sia, C. C. J., & Blackwell, P. M. (1993). Implementing a statewide system of services for infants and toddlers with hearing disabilities. *Seminars in Hearing, 14*(1), 105–119.

Johnson, M. J., Maxon, A. B., White, K. R., & Vohr, B. R. (1993). Operating a hospital-based universal newborn hearing screening program using transient evoked otoacoustic emissions. *Seminars in Hearing, 14*(1), 46–56.

Joint Committee of ASHA and the Council on Education of the Deaf. (1994). Joint Committee of ASHA and the Council on Education of the Deaf regarding service provision under the Individuals with Disabilities Education Act—Part H, as amended (IDEA-Part H) to children who are deaf and hard of hearing ages birth to 36 months. *The Volta Review, 96*(4), 307–316.

Joint Committee on Infant Hearing (JCIH). (1994). 1994 position statement. *Audiology Today, 6*(6), 6–9.

Kenworthy, O. T. (1990). Screening for hearing impairment in infants and young children. *Seminars in Hearing, 11,* 315–332.

Kileny, P., & Magathan, M. (1987). Predictive value of ABR in infants and children with moderate to profound hearing impairment. *Ear and Hearing, 8,* 217–221.

Laughton, J. (1994). Models and current practices in early intervention with hearing-impaired infants. *Seminars in Hearing, 15*(2), 148–159.

Leigh, I. (1987). Parenting and the hearing impaired: Attachment and coping. *The Volta Review, 89*(5), 11–21.

Levitt, H., McGarr, N. S., & Geffner, D. (1987). Development of language and communication skills in hearing-impaired children. In H. Levitt, N. S. McGarr, & D. Geffner (Eds.), *Development of language and communication skills in hearing impaired children* (ASHA Monograph No. 26, pp. 1–8). Rockville, MD: American Speech-Language-Hearing Association.

Ling, D. (1976). *Speech and the hearing-impaired child: Theory and practice.* Washington, DC: Alexander Graham Bell Association for the Deaf.

Long, B. B. (1992). Developing a constituency for prevention. In M. Kessler, S. E. Goldston, & J. M. Joffe (Eds.), *The present and future of prevention* (pp. 69–77). Newbury Park, CA: Sage Publications.

Luterman, D. (1979). *Counseling parents of hearing impaired children.* Boston: Little, Brown, and Company.

MacCarthy, A., & Connell, J. (1984). Audiological screening and assessment. In G. Lindsay (Ed.), *Screening for children with special needs: Multidisciplinary approaches* (pp. 63–85). London: Croom Helm.

Markides, A. (1986). Age at fitting of hearing aids and speech intelligibility. *British Journal of Audiology, 20,* 165–168.

Marlowe, J. A. (1987). Early identification and the hearing impaired child's right to become. *American Annals of the Deaf, 132,* 337–339.

Marlowe, J. A. (1994). Amplification and audiological management of infants. *Seminars in Hearing, 15*(2), 114–127.

Matkin, N. D. (1994). Strategies for enhancing interdisciplinary collaboration. In J. Roush & N. D. Matkin (Eds.), *Infants and toddlers with hearing loss: Family-centered assessment and intervention* (pp. 83–97). Baltimore: York Press.

Mauk, G. W., Barringer, D. G., & Mauk, P. P. (1995). Seizing the moment, setting the stage, and serving the future: Toward collaborative models of early identification and early intervention services for children born with hearing loss and their families. Part I: Early identification of hearing loss. *Infant-Toddler Intervention: The Transdisciplinary Journal, 5,* 367–394.

Mauk, G. W., & Behrens, T. R. (1993). Historical, political, and technological context associated with early identification of hearing loss. *Seminars in Hearing, 14*(1), 1–17.

Mauk, G. W., & White, K. R. (1995). Giving children a sound beginning: The promise of universal newborn hearing screening. *The Volta Review, 97*(1), 5–32.

Mauk, G. W., White, K. R., Mortensen, L. B., & Behrens, T. R. (1991). The effectiveness of screening programs based on high-risk characteristics in early identification of hearing loss. *Ear and Hearing, 12,* 312–319.

Meadow-Orlans, K. P. (1987). An analysis of the effectiveness of early intervention programs for hearing-impaired children. In M. J. Guralnick & F. C. Bennett (Eds.), *The effectiveness of intervention for at-risk and handicapped children* (pp. 325–362). Orlando, FL: Academic Press.

Meadow-Orlans, K. P. (1995). Stress for mothers and fathers of deaf and hard of hearing infants. *American Annals of the Deaf, 140,* 352–357.

Meister, S. (1993). Emerging risk: Failure to detect hearing disability in newborns. The problem: Lack of screening programs for "normal" newborns. *Quality, Risk, and Cost [QRC] Advisor, 10*(2), 1–4.

Melaville, A.I., & Blank, M.J. (1993). *Together we can: A guide for crafting a profamily system of education and human services.* Washington, DC: U.S. Department of Education, Office of Educational Research and Improvement.

Meyers, K. (Ed.). (1995). *Your child's hearing loss: First steps for you and your family.* Minneapolis, MN: Miracle-Ear Children's Foundation.

Moore, W. (1991). Managing the infant hearing impairment problem: The contributions of industry. *Seminars in Hearing, 12,* 175–181.

Moores, D. F. (1970). Psycholinguistics and deafness. *American Annals of the Deaf, 15,* 37–48.

Moores, D. F. (1982). *Educating the deaf: Psychology, principles, and practices* (2nd ed.). Boston: Houghton Mifflin Company.

Moses, K. (1985). Infant deafness and parental grief: Psychosocial early intervention. In F. Powell, T. Finitzo-Heiber, S. Friel-Patti, & D. Henderson (Eds.), *Education of the hearing impaired child* (pp. 85–102). San Diego, CA: College-Hill Press.

National Commission on Children (NCC). (1991). *Beyond rhetoric: A new American agenda for children and families.* Washington, DC: U.S. Government Printing Office.

National Institutes of Health. (1993). *NIH Consensus Statement: Early Identification of Hearing Impairment in Infants and Young Children, 11*(1), 1–25.

National Institute on Deafness and Other Communication Disorders. (1989). *A report of the task force on the National Strategic Research Plan.* Bethesda, MD: National Institutes of Health.

Nober, E. H., & Nober, L. W. (1977). Effects of hearing loss on speech and language in the postbabbling stage. In B. F. Jaffe (Ed.), *Hearing loss in children: A comprehensive text* (pp. 630–639). Baltimore: University Park Press.

Northern, J. L., & Downs, M. P. (1991). *Hearing in children* (4th ed.). Baltimore: Williams & Wilkins.

Northern, J. L., & Hayes, D. (1994). Universal screening for infant hearing impairment: Necessary, beneficial, and justifiable. *Audiology Today, 6*(2), 10–13.

Norton, S. J. (1994). Emerging role of otoacoustic emissions in neonatal hearing screening. *American Journal of Otology, 15*(1), 4–12.

Nozza, R. J. (1996). Pediatric hearing screening. In F. N. Martin & J. G. Clark (Eds.), *Hearing care for children* (pp. 95–114). Boston: Allyn and Bacon.

Penn, T. O., & Gibson, B. (1994). Utilization of a questionnaire to provide follow-up services in an infant hearing screening program. *Journal of the American Academy of Audiology, 5,* 325–329.

Phillips, A. L., & Cole, E. B. (Eds.). (1993). Beginning with babies: A sharing of professional experience. *The Volta Review, 95*(5) [special issue].

Pugh, G. S., & Hicks, D. (1995). Deaf Education Initiatives Project: A response to the challenge. *Journal of Childhood Communication Disorders, 17*(1), 5–8.

Raffin, M. J. M., & Matz, G. J. (1994). Universal screening for infant hearing impairment [Letter to the editor]. *Pediatrics, 94*(6), 950–952.

Ramkalawan, T. W., & Davis, A. C. (1992). The effects of hearing loss and age of intervention on some language metrics in young hearing-impaired children. *British Journal of Audiology, 26,* 97–107.

Rittenhouse, R. K., & Dancer, J. E. (1992). Educational and legislative issues in students with hearing loss: Inter-disciplinary considerations. *The Volta Review, 94,* 9–17.

Robinette, M. S. (1994). Universal screening for infant hearing impairment [Letter to the editor]. *Pediatrics, 94*(6), 952–954.

Roush, J. (1990). Identification of hearing loss and middle ear disease in preschool and school-age children. *Seminars in Hearing, 11,* 357–371.

Roush, J., & Matkin, N. D. (Eds.). (1994). *Infants and toddlers with hearing loss: Family-centered assessment and intervention.* Baltimore: York Press.

Ruben, R. J. (1991). Effectiveness and efficacy of early detection of hearing impairment in children. *Acta Otolaryngolica* (Stockholm), Suppl. 482, 127–131.

Rushmer, N. (1994). Supporting the families of hearing-impaired infants and toddlers. *Seminars in Hearing, 15,* 160–172.

Schow, R. L., & Nerbonne, M. A. (1989). Overview of aural rehabilitation. In R. L. Schow & M. A. Nerbonne (Eds.), Introduction to aural habilitation (2nd ed., pp. 3–29). Austin, TX: PRO-ED.

Stewart, D. L., & Davis-Freeman, S. (1994). Universal screening for infant hearing impairment [Letter to the editor]. *Pediatrics, 94*(6), 956.

Stewart, I. F. (1984). After early identification — What follows? A study of some aspects of deaf education from an otolaryngological viewpoint. *Laryngoscope, 94,* 784–799.

Strong, C. J., Clark, T. C., Johnson, D., Watkins, S., Barringer, D. G., & Walden, B. E. (1994). SKI*HI home-based programming for children who are deaf or hard of hearing: Recent research findings. *Infant-Toddler Intervention: The Transdisciplinary Journal, 4*, 25–36.

Todd, N. W. (1994). At-risk populations for hearing impairment in infants and young children. *International Journal of Pediatric Otorhinolaryngology, 29*, 11–21.

U.S. Department of Education. (1991). *America 2000: An education strategy (sourcebook)*. Washington, DC: Author.

U.S. Preventive Services Task Force. (1989). *Guide to clinical preventive services: An assessment of the effectiveness of 169 interventions*. Baltimore: Williams & Wilkins.

Watkins, S. (1987). Long-term effects of home intervention with hearing-impaired children. *American Annals of the Deaf, 132*, 267–271.

Watkins, S., & Schow, R. L. (1989). Aural rehabilitation for children. In R. L. Schow & M. A. Nerbonne (Eds.), *Introduction to aural habilitation* (2nd ed., pp. 295–378). Austin, TX: PRO-ED.

White, S. J., & White, R. E. C. (1987). The effects of hearing status of the family and age of intervention on receptive and expressive oral language skills in hearing-impaired infants. In H. Levitt, N. S. McGarr, & D. Geffner (Eds.), *Development of language and communication skills in hearing impaired children* (ASHA Monograph No. 26, pp. 9–24). Rockville, MD: American Speech-Language-Hearing Association.

White, K. R., & Behrens, T. R. (Eds.). (1993). The Rhode Island Hearing Assessment Project: Implications for universal newborn hearing screening. *Seminars in Hearing, 14*(1), 1–119.

White, K. R., Behrens, T. R., & Strickland, B. (1995). Practicality, validity, and cost-efficiency of universal newborn hearing screening using transient evoked otoacoustic emissions. *Journal of Childhood Communication Disorders, 17*(1), 9–14.

White, K. R., & Maxon, A. B. (1995). Universal screening for infant hearing impairment: Simple, beneficial, and presently justified. *International Journal of Pediatric Otorhinolaryngology, 32*, 201–211.

Yoshinaga-Itano, C. (1995). Universal hearing screening for infants: Simple, risk-free, beneficial and justified. *Audiology Today, 7*(1), 13.

Zipper, I. N., Hinton, C., Weil, M., & Rounds, K. (1993). *Service coordination for early intervention: Parents and professionals*. Cambridge, MA: Brookline Books.

Address correspondence to:
Gary W. Mauk,
Research Associate,
SKI*HI Institute,
809 North 800 East,
Utah State University,
Logan, UT 84322-1900

Preface to Identification, Assessment, and Management of Hearing Impairment in Infants and Toddlers

Jack E. Kile, Ph.D.
Kathryn Laudin Beauchaine, M.A.

The Kile and Beauchaine article, Identififcation, Assessment, and Management of Hearing Impairment in Infants and Toddlers, appeared in a 1991 issue of *Infant-Toddler Intervention*. Although the information contained in the article remains pertinent, there have been significant developments in pediatric audiology since the article was published. These developments include the National Institutes of Health Consensus Statement on Early Identification of Hearing Impairment in Infants and Young Children (NIH, 1993); the updated Joint Committee on Infant Hearing Position Statement (JCIH, 1994); and the expanding use of otoacoustic emissions)OAE) in pediatric audiology for both hearing screening and assessment. Overviews of the NIH (1993) Statement and their application to infant hearing screening are included in the Mauk, Barringer, and Mauk article, Part I (1995).

The JCIH (1994) Position Statement supports universal detection of infants who have hearing loss. The high risk indicators from the 1990 Position Statement (JCIH, 1991) were maintained; however, additional indicators for infants age 29 days through 3 years who require periodic monitoring of hearing have been included. Indicators for late onset sensorineural hearing loss include: (1) family history of hereditary childhood hearing loss; (2) in utero infection, such as cytomegalovirus, rubella, syphilis, herpes, or toxoplasmosis; and (3) neurofibromatosis Type II and neurodegenerative disorders. Additionally, the detrimental effects resulting from conductive hearing loss were recognized and include: (1) recurrent or continued otitis media with effusion, (2) anatomic deformities and disorders that affect eustachian tube function, and (3) neurodegenerative disorders.

The use of OAEs in the pediatric audiologic test battery can be helpful in determining the status of the peripheral auditory system. To illustrate, an infant suspected of having normal hearing sensitivity, but with incomplete behavioral test results (e.g., visual reinforcement audiometry [VRA] in the sound field where ears are not isolated), may benefit from OAE testing. Assuming that the child has normal tympanograms,

OAE test results can provide useful information about the status of the peripheral auditory system. The presence of OAEs in each ear would be consistent with normal cochlear functioning which might support the behavioral findings. With specific OAE results, further audiologic assessments (e.g., ABR) might not be indicated. However, OAE testing does not preclude the need for doing behavioral testing to determine how the child responds to auditory stimuli (e.g., response latencies, response consistency, ability to localize).

Otoacoustic emissions can be used in an audiologic test battery as a differential diagnostic tool in determining whether the hearing impairment is due to involvement of the cochlea, or beyond at the level of the brainstem or above. To illustrate, a child was referred to the University of Wisconsin-Oshkosh Speech and Hearing Clinic for an audiologic assessment based on parental concerns. When seen initially at 14 months of age, the behavioral test results were equivocal. While demonstrating some response inconsistencies, the child occasionally responded to speech and frequency-specific stimuli at intensities well within conversational levels. The behavioral results were in contrast with ABR findings that suggested a profound hearing impairment.

Tympanograms were normal and OAEs were present. This combination of findings suggested a central auditory impairment. Although this child may be aware of some sounds, she functions as a person who is deaf (Kile, Schaffmeyer, & Kuba, 1994). Other similar articles have been reported (e.g., Sininger, Hood, Starr, Berlin, & Picton, 1995).

References

Joint Committee on Infant Hearing. (1991). 1990 Position statement. *Asha, 33*(Suppl. 5), 3–6.

Joint Committee on Infant Hearing. (1994). 1994 Position statement. *Audiology Today, 6*, 6–9.

Kile, J., Schaffmeyer, M. J., & Kuba, J. (1994). Assessment and management of unusual auditory behavior in infants and toddlers. *Infant-Toddler Intervention, 4*, 299–318.

National Institutes of Health. (1993). *Early identification of hearing impairment in infants and young children: Consensus development conference on early identification of hearing impairment in infants and young children.* Bethesda, MD: Author.

Sininger, Y. S., Hood, L. J., Starr, A., Berlin, C. I., & Picton, T. W. (1995). Hearing loss due to auditory neuropathy. *Audiology Today, 7*(2), 10, 12–13.

Identification, Assessment, and Management of Hearing Impairment in Infants and Toddlers

Jack E. Kile, Ph.D.
University of Wisconsin–Oshkosh
Oshkosh, Wisconsin

Kathryn Laudin Beauchaine, M.A.
Boys Town National Research Hospital
Omaha, Nebraska

Public Law 99-457 recognizes the audiologist as a provider of services. Focusing on this fact, this article presents information regarding identification and assessment which may assist early intervention specialists to better understand and manage the children they serve who are hearing-impaired.

Introduction

Public Law 99-457 (Part H) provides state funding for early intervention services for children with handicaps (birth through two years of age) and their families. Audiology is recognized as a provider of these services in areas of identification, assessment, and management of children with auditory impairment (Education of the Handicapped Act Amendments of 1986). As PL 99-457 is implemented, the audiologist will be challenged to provide these services and to communicate effectively with early intervention specialists who may have limited background and experience in working with infants and toddlers who are hearing impaired. (The term child/children will also be used in this article when referring to infants and toddlers.) The importance of open communication exchanges between the audiologist and early intervention specialist is recognized.

The intent of this article is to: (1) discuss identification of hearing impairment in infants and toddlers; (2) describe the wide range of test protocols used in assessing hearing of these children; (3) interpret audiologic results; (4) present a series of case studies illustrating a range of developmental levels and degrees of hearing loss; and (5) discuss audiologic follow-up.

Identification of Hearing Loss

Who Is At Risk for Hearing Loss?

In 1982 the Joint Committee on Infant Hearing (JCIH, 1982) identified seven risk factors for hearing loss. These were: severe asphyxia, a family history of hearing loss, congenital perinatal infection, craniofacial anomalies, birth weight under 1500 grams, hyperbilirubinemia exceeding levels requiring exchange transfusion, and bacterial meningitis, especially H. influenza. Although these factors may identify some of the neonates likely to have hearing loss, it has been estimated that up to 50% of children with hearing impairment would not be identified using these risk factors alone (Elssmann, Matkin, & Sabo, 1987). Subsequently, the JCIH revised the high-risk register (JCIH, in press), which may facilitate earlier identification of hearing loss. The revision includes recommendations for neonates (birth to 28 days old) and infants (29 days to 2 years old). None of the 1982 factors were eliminated for neonates, and three risk factors were added: (1) ototoxic medications and loop diuretics used in conjunction with aminoglycosides; (2) mechanical ventilation for ten or more days; and (3) stigmata or other physical findings associated with syndromes that include sensorineural hearing loss. In addition to these three potential causes of hearing loss, five risk factors were added for infants: (1) concerns for hearing, speech, language, or development expressed by the parent or caregiver; (2) factors associated with progressive hearing loss; (3) head trauma, especially longitudinal or transverse temporal bone fractures; (4) neurodegenerative disorders; and (5) infectious diseases that are associated with sensorineural hearing loss.

The American Speech-Language-Hearing Association (ASHA) has published "Guidelines for Audiologic Screening of Newborn Infants Who Are At Risk for Hearing Impairment" (ASHA, 1989). These recommendations support the JCIH goal to identify hearing loss and to initiate habilitation as early as feasible, at least within the first six months of life. A critical component of the recommendations from both JCIH and ASHA is the focus on parent/caregiver input in the process of early identification of hearing loss.

How Early Can Hearing Tests Be Done?

Estimates of the average age of identification of hearing loss vary substantially in the United States from as low as 7.6 months (Mahoney & Eichwald, 1986) to 19 months (Elssmann et al., 1987). It is technically possible to detect peripheral hearing loss very early in life using electrophysiologic procedures such as the auditory brainstem response (ABR) test. This test can be performed in the first hours of life (Adelman, Levi, Linder, & Sohmer, 1990).

How Does Hearing Loss Interact With Other Health or Educational Issues?

It is estimated that at least one-third of children who have hearing loss have additional educationally handicapping conditions (Karchmer, 1985). Thus, additional evaluations may be warranted to explore other factors that may be related to hearing loss, such as medical-genetics, otolaryngologic, ophthalmologic, developmental, and communication assessments.

After hearing loss is identified, parents often are interested in discovering why their child has hearing loss. Although it may not be possible to establish conclusively the etiology of hearing loss in all cases, it is a worthwhile pursuit. If etiology is not clearly established, a medical-genetics evaluation may yield information about the cause of the loss. This may uncover a syndrome or a related medical disorder that requires treatment, relieve the concerns of the parents, and/or be useful for family planning. In conjunction with the medical-genetics evaluation, an otologic evaluation should be completed. This evaluation has several purposes: a related disorder may be identified, the status of the middle ears can be assessed, and medical clearance for use of amplification can be obtained. These medical evaluations may generate recommendations for additional assessments or services, such as serologic and radiologic studies, vestibular and neurologic evaluations, and physical and occupational therapy.

Recently, it has been suggested that children who are congenitally deaf have an electrocardiogram (ECG) screening because of the high prevalence of deafness and abnormal ECG findings in children with Jervell and Lange-Nielsen syndrome (Jacobson, Jacobson, & Francis, 1990). This syndrome is associated with cardiac arrhythmias and fainting spells.

Ophthalmologic evaluation should also be considered a key assessment. The integrity of the visual system is critical because visual deficits can hamper language learning related to visual cues obtained from gesture, facial expression, speechreading, and the context provided by the visual environment. Adequate vision may be even more critical for a child with hearing loss for whom auditory information may be incomplete. A high incidence of visual deficits and ocular pathology has been reported in children who have hearing loss, with estimates ranging from 33% to 65% (Johnson & Caccamise, 1983; Pollard & Neumaier, 1974; Regenbogen & Godel, 1985; Rogers, Fillman, Bremer, & Leguire, 1988). Furthermore, both auditory and visual deficits are associated with some syndromes, and at least one of these, Usher syndrome, is associated with progressive loss of vision (Moller et al., 1989).

Developmental and communication evaluations are necessary to establish the child's current level of functioning and to plan goals and objectives for intervention. The communication goals and remediation plans for a child who has developmental delays must be adjusted to the appropriate developmental level with consideration for the effect hearing loss has on speech and language.

Audiologic Assessment

How Is Hearing Tested in Small Children?

Recently approved "Guidelines for the Audiologic Assessment of Children From Birth Through Thirty-Six Months of Age" (ASHA, in press) provide procedural recommendations for audiologic evaluation in this age group and serve as an excellent resource. For this article, four categories of test procedures used in pediatric audiologic assessment will be discussed: electrophysiologic assessment, behavioral techniques, speech audiometry, and acoustic immittance measurements.

Electrophysiologic Assessment

In the first category of test procedures, electrophysiologic evaluation of hearing, the discussion will be limited to *auditory brainstem response* (ABR) testing because it is the best predictor of hearing sensitivity in children under the chronological/developmental age of five months (Galambos, Hicks, & Wilson, 1984; Jacobson & Morehouse, 1984). The ABR is an objective test used to assess the sensitivity of each ear independently, and testing is accomplished with a child who is in a natural or sedated sleep. Thus, the active participation of the child is not required. The test can be used with children who are uncooperative or otherwise unable to give reliable responses to behavioral tests because of developmental, physical, or cognitive limitations.

During the test a sound is presented, typically via earphones, and the neural responses generated from the ear and auditory nerve are recorded by electrodes that are glued or taped to the child's head. These recordings are routed to a computer for storage and analysis. The intensity of the sound is varied and the lowest level at which a repeatable response is detected is called threshold. This threshold provides an estimate of the ear's sensitivity. When click stimuli are used, the ABR is a good indicator of high-frequency sensitivity (Hyde, Riko, & Malizia, 1990). Frequency-specific stimuli can be used to assess a wide range of frequencies (Stapells, Picton, Perez-Abalo, Read, & Smith, 1985). The ABR also can yield informaton about the integrity of the auditory brainstem pathways. To do so, components of the waveform are identified, and the time of occurrence (latency) of these components is calculated and compared to age-appropriate norms (Gorga, Kaminski, Beauchaine, Jesteadt, & Neely, 1989; Gorga, Reiland, Beauchaine, Worthington, & Jesteadt, 1987).

One limitation of the ABR is that it is not always an accurate indicator of auditory sensitivity if neuropathy or neuromaturational delay is affecting auditory brainstem pathways. Furthermore, it does not provide information about auditory processing ability. Even with these limitations, the ABR may be the best estimate of auditory sensitivity in very young or difficult-to-test children.

Behavioral Techniques

The second category of test procedures is behavioral techniques. The goal of these techniques is to obtain information about a child's ability to detect speech or tones. Several techniques are available to accommodate a range of developmental abilities. These techniques are: visual reinforcement audiometry, conditioned play audiometry, and tangible and visual reinforcement operant conditioning audiometry. Each of these techniques will be reviewed briefly. Signals can be presented via an earphone, a loudspeaker (sound field), a bone-conduction transducer, hearing aids, or other amplification devices.

Although behavioral observation is not a formal test technique and generally cannot be used to determine thresholds, observations about response latency, strength of response, and response mode can be used to facilitate formal testing.

Visual reinforcement audiometry (VRA) can be used successfully to elicit minimal response levels (MRLs) on children as young as 5 months of age using a conditioning paradigm to teach visually reinforced head-turn responses to auditory stimuli (Gravel, 1989; Thompson & Wilson, 1984). Because the response is a head turn, the child must have sufficient head control to turn to the reinforcer. Also the child must have visual acuity to see the reinforcer, which typically is some type of lighted and/or animated toy. Stimuli can be presented at various levels to search for MRLs.

Conditioned play audiometry (CPA) can be used to obtain thresholds on some children as young as 24 months (Thompson,

Thompson, & Vethivelu, 1989) and, as our clinic experience suggests, may be administered to children as young as 18 months. This technique requires a conditioned motor response to sound. The task is presented as a listening game and the child is taught a motor response, for example, to put a peg in a peg board or a block in a bucket, in response to a sound. This can be taught without verbal instruction by modeling the task. The game can be modified to accommodate the interest or motor ability of the child. The lowest level (in dB HL) where a response is observed 50% of the time is defined as threshold.

Tangible reinforcement operant conditioning audiometry (TROCA) and *visual reinforcement operant conditioning audiometry* (VROCA) can be used to elicit motor responses. For TROCA, the child performs a motor task (e.g., pushing a button) in response to the detection of sound, and then a tangible reinforcer, such as food or a token, is delivered (Fulton, Gorzycki, & Hull, 1975; Lloyd, Spradlin, & Reid, 1968). VROCA is like TROCA except a visual reinforcer, such as a lighted or animated toy, is given as a reward for the motor response (Wilson & Thompson, 1984).

Behavioral techniques depend on the child's developmental level and ability or willingness to participate in the task. When behavioral testing is precluded or inconclusive, ABR testing should be done.

Speech Audiometry

The third category, speech audiometry, attempts to describe the child's ability to detect and understand speech stimuli. For many young children, this testing is relegated to a *speech awareness or detection threshold* (SAT or SDT) which represents the lowest level at which speech (nonsense syllables, words, phrases, or sentences) can be detected. These thresholds can be elicited using the behavioral techniques previously described.

In an older child, the *speech recognition threshold* (SRT) may be obtained by determining the lowest level where 50% of two-syllable words (e.g., hotdog, baseball) are repeated correctly. This task can be modified by having the child point to pictures or objects representing familiar words. The SRT should generally agree with the *pure tone air conduction threshold average* (PTA) based on 500, 1000, and 2000 Hz. A comparison of the SRT and PTA often provides a validity check.

Standard word recognition tests are done by having the patient repeat one-syllable words presented at average conversational or optimal loudness levels. The results are expressed in percentage of correct responses. For children who are still developing speech, multiple choice picture-pointing tests (e.g., Word Intelligibility by Picture Identification [WIPI] [Ross & Lerman, 1971] and Northwestern University's Children's Perception of Speech [NU-CHIPS] [Elliot & Katz, 1980]) provide an alternative if the stimuli are part of their receptive vocabulary. Although some precocious 2-year-old children may be able to perform this task, standardized tests are not normed on children this young.

For other young children, informal assessments of word recognition often provide an alternative. For example, the child can point to familiar objects, pictures, or body parts (Matkin, 1979; Olsen & Matkin, 1979). The results from these informal tests are reported descriptively rather than as percentages. Although not predictive of real-world performance, word recognition scores reflect the child's use of residual hearing and may be useful in planning aural habilitation.

Acoustic Immittance Testing

The fourth category is accoustic immittance testing, two procedures of which are tympanometry and acoustic reflex testing. In both, the child is a passive participant.

Tympanometry, while not measuring hearing acuity, is used to assess the status of the tympanic membrane and middle ear. This procedure involves placing a probe into the ear canal and systematically altering the air pressure. A graph called a tympanogram is then generated that indirectly shows how the eardrum moves in response to pressure changes. A normal tympanogram often tends to rule out middle-ear dysfunction.

Acoustic reflex testing consists of introducing a high level tone or noise into the ear and monitoring the resultant change in sound transmission through the middle ear. In a healthy middle ear, the stapedius muscle contracts in response to loud signals; however, reflex thresholds may be elevated or absent in the presence of sensorineural hearing loss (> 65 dB HL). There is some debate on the accuracy of acoustic immittance tests in infants below 6 months (Margolis & Shanks, 1985; Sprague, Wiley, & Goldstein, 1985; Walters & Shimizu, 1990).

Interpretation of Audiologic Results

What Is Plotted on the Audiogram?

Minimal response levels (MRL) or thresholds for pure tones are obtained using the behavioral techniques described previously and are recorded on an audiogram, as shown in Figure 1. Frequency (in Hz) is shown on the horizontal axis. Frequency is related to pitch, with 125 Hz being the lowest frequency on the audiogram and 8,000 Hz the highest. Intensity in dB HL (Re: normal hearing) is shown on the vertical axis. Intensity is related to loudness, with 0 dB HL as

Figure 1

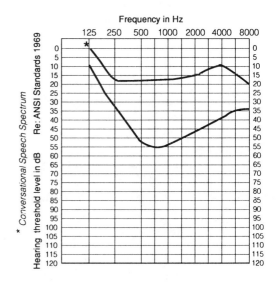

Conversational speech spectrum displayed on a pure tone audiogram. Adapted from Fletcher (1970) and Olsen, Hawkins, & Van Tassel (1987).

one of the softest levels on the audiogram and 120 dB one of the loudest. Optimally, pure tone thresholds under earphones (air conduction) are obtained in each ear at octave intervals between 250 and 8000 hz. If hearing loss is detected, bone conduction threshold testing is also required and frequently done at frequencies having octave intervals from 250 to 4000 Hz.

Because many young children have short attention spans, only a few frequencies may be tested during a single session. Both low and high frequencies should be used, preferably at octave frequencies from 500 to 4000 Hz (ASHA, in press). In some instances, children will not accept earphones or a bone conduction transducer, and behavioral testing must be done by presenting the auditory signals through loudspeakers (sound field), where the ears are not isolated. At a minimum, thresholds should be obtained at 500 Hz and 2000 Hz before the need for amplification is considered (ASHA, in press; Matkin, 1987).

How are the Degree and Type of Hearing Loss Classified?

Most classifications of the degree of hearing loss are based on adult norms (Clark, 1981). For purposes of discussion, the following classifications will be used: *mild* (26–40 dB HL), *moderate* (41–55 dB HL), *moderate-severe* (56–70 dB HL), *severe* (71–90 dB HL) and *profound* (91 + dB HL) (Goodman, 1965).

Classifications may not represent the effect a hearing loss will have on speech and language development or future academic performance for young children (Kenworthy, Bess, Stahlman, & Lindstrom, 1987). For example, it has been established that children with mild hearing loss and unilateral loss are at risk for academic problems (Bess, Klee, & Culbertson, 1986; Bess & Tharpe, 1986; Oyler, Oyler, & Matkin, 1988).

The three main types of hearing loss are conductive, sensorineural, and mixed. If a hearing loss exists by air conduction (under earphones or through loudspeakers), bone conduction testing is performed to determine the type of hearing loss. If a comparable degree of hearing loss is suggested by air and bone conduction, the loss is sensorineural. If a hearing loss is present by air conduction but not by bone conduction, a conductive loss is indicated. A mixed loss is a combination of conductive and sensorineural components.

A *conductive hearing loss* results from a dysfunction of the outer and/or middle ear and may or may not represent a pathological condition. For example, impacted cerumen, a perforated eardrum, or a middle ear infection (otitis media) could result in a conductive hearing loss. Otitis media is the most common cause of conductive hearing loss in young children. Conductive hearing losses are mechanical in nature and can often be corrected with medical intervention (e.g., medication, tympanostomy tubes). In some developmentally disabled populations such as children with Down syndrome, the incidence of hearing loss, often resulting from otitis media, has been reported to be as high as 80%. Further, it has been shown that these losses frequently are not being corrected with medical intervention (Kile, Kuba, Nellis, & Becker, 1990). For these children, as well as children with congenital middle-ear ossicular anomalies, where the hearing loss cannot be medically or surgically remediated, amplification may be warranted. Conductive hearing impairment ranges in severity from mild to moderate and results primarily in a reduction in the loudness of speech.

Sensorineural hearing loss, whether congenital or acquired, results from a dysfunction of the inner ear, which contains the delicate sensory structures for hearing, and/or the auditory nerve. Some risk factors were discussed previously. For children with sensorineural hearing loss, frequent hearing evaluations are necessary to determine if the loss is stable. Sensorineural hearing loss ranges in severity from mild to profound and frequently results in reduction of both loudness and clarity of speech. Because sensorineural loss is usually not medically or surgically treatable, the use of amplification may be warranted. An optimal fitting of amplification will often enable the child to hear conversational speech at a comfortable loudness level, at least when presented from short distances (< 6 feet). However, because of permanent damage to the inner ear, many speech sounds may be distorted and not identifiable. Some children with profound hearing loss, who do not benefit from amplification, may find the use of other devices, such as a vibrotactile unit or cochlear implant, to be helpful.

A *mixed hearing loss* is a combination of conductive and sensorineural components. If the conductive portion of the hearing loss can be corrected, the sensorineural component remains.

How Does the Pure Tone Audiogram Relate to Speech Perception?

Although very few sounds in a child's listening environment consist of pure tones, frequency-specific thresholds can provide information about the audibility of speech. Intonation, stress, and rhythm of speech, call suprasegmentals, are transmitted by the voiced components of speech, which are generally below 300 Hz. Therefore, a child with a profound hearing loss, but with residual low-frequency hearing, can often learn to identify and discriminate the suprasegmentals (Ling, 1976). The ability to discriminate vowels and consonants depends on the ability to perceive spectral peaks of energy called formants. If the frequencies between 250 and 6000 Hz are audible, all of these formants can be heard and speech sounds potentially identified.

For purposes of discussion, frequency regions between 250 and 500 Hz will be referred to as *low frequencies,* 500 to 1000 Hz as *mid frequencies,* and above 1000 Hz as *high frequencies.* Vowels have more power than consonants, and their audibility is not affected until there is a moderate hearing loss (> 50 dB). Vowels carry the power and consonants the intelligibility for speech. Problems with perception of consonants can occur even with mild hearing loss (26–40 dB). In order to perceive all vowels, signal audibility is needed from about 250 to 2000 Hz (e.g., /u/ as in boot—low frequency, /a/ as in not—mid frequency, /i/ as in beet—high frequency). Glides, semivowels (l, w, r, y), and some consonants (m, n, ng) can be identified with low frequency cues, while other consonants (e.g., s, sh, f, th) require high frequency cues to be identified. Thus, amplification devices that provide audibility of conversational speech over a broad frequency range are desirable.

The conversational speech spectrum is displayed on a pure tone audiogram in Figure 1 (see p. 60). Comparisons of thresholds to the speech spectrum provide a graphic representation of how hearing loss affects the audibility of speech. Frequency regions that may not be audible at conversational levels will be apparent from this type of display. Unaided and aided audiograms demonstrate which speech sounds the child may be capable of identifying. It should be stressed that audibility alone does not ensure that a clear speech signal will be perceived.

Informal assessments of speech audibility by frequency region can be made. One method uses five speech sounds (u, a, i, sh, s), which represent low, mid, and high frequencies (Ling & Ling, 1978). For example, if the child responds to all of the sounds with the exception of /sh/ and /s/, a high-frequency hearing loss may be present. Also, there are some indexes that weight frequencies according to their importance in discriminating speech in an attempt to predict the degree of auditory handicap from the pure tone audiogram (e.g., Mueller & Killion, 1990). Because the frequencies that contribute the most to speech understanding are in the frequency range 1000 to 3000 Hz, it follows that a high-frequency hearing loss would result in a greater handicapping condition than a low-frequency loss of the same severity.

Case Studies

The following case studies illustrate audiologic findings on children with conductive and sensorineural losses in three age groups: 6 months and under, 7 months old, and 2 years old. Referring back to the previous sections should assist in understanding why and how a particular test was done.

Conductive Hearing Loss

Introductory Comments and Background

When a conductive hearing loss cannot be medically or surgically corrected, such as in congenital ossicular defects, early fitting with amplification is recommended. If the loss is conductive, amplification should provide essentially normal hearing. This case describes a developmentally disabled 24-month-old child with a diagnosis of Trisomy 10. He was followed by an otologist and a cranio-facial disorders team for facial-maxillary anomalies, suspected congenital middle-ear deformities, and hearing loss. Exploratory middle-ear surgery will be performed when he is older. He has worn binaural ear-level hearing aids since 6 months of age, and he was enrolled in an early intervention program and was seen by a parent-infant specialist twice a week. In addition, he received speech and language and physical and occupational therapy weekly.

Audiologic Assessment

A speech-language pathologist, who had worked with the child on earphone acceptance and conditioning activities to prepare him for threshold testing, accompanied him to the test session. She assisted in testing the child using CPA. Pure tone thresholds suggested a bilateral, moderate, symmetrical hearing loss (PTA of 55 dB in the right ear and 58 dB HL in the left ear), as shown in Figure 2. SATs of 50 dB HL in each ear were in good agreement with the PTAs. Bone-conductions thresholds indicated a conductive hearing loss in at least one ear.

Figure 2

Behavioral thresholds obtained by air conduction in the left (x) and right (o) ears and by bone conduction (<) on a 2-year-old male using CPA. Results suggested a bilateral, moderate hearing loss, with a conductive impairment in at least one ear. Aided thresholds (A) for those tones assessed suggested amplification well within the conversational speech spectrum.

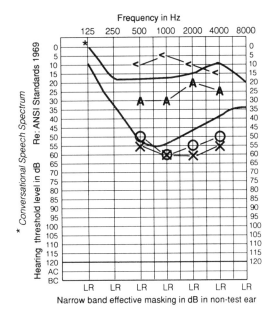

Tympanograms were flat, consistent with stiffened middle-ear systems. Acoustic reflexes were absent.

Hearing Aid Assessment

Aided results indicated an SAT at 20 dB HL and tone thresholds within the conversational speech spectrum for those frequencies assessed, as shown in Figure 2. Unsuccessful attempts were made to measure word recognition informally using a series of familiar pictures.

Interpretation and Recommendations

This child had a moderate bilateral hearing impairment that was conductive for at least one ear. Because no middle-ear surgery was contemplated in the near future, the continued use of hearing aids was recommended. With no inner-ear involvement, amplification should provide good fidelity signals. He should hear relatively normally when spoken to at distances within 6 feet. Audiologic re-evaluation was recommended in three months.

Comments

In addition to ossicular defects, other conductive losses warrant the use of amplification. For example, infants with atresia of the external auditory canals require fitting with amplification which can be done in the first month of life. Additionally, fluctuating mild conductive hearing loss resulting from otitis media might contribute to delays in a child's speech and language development (Garrard & Clark, 1985; Gravel, Wallace, & Abraham, 1990). Thus, some children with conductive losses who are not treated successfully with medical or surgical intervention might require amplification.

Mild-to-Moderate Sensorineural Loss: 6-Month-Old Child

Introductory Comments and Background

When performing audiologic testing it is important to consider the developmental level of a child and adjust the test method accordingly. Figure 3 displays ABR results from a 6-month-old female with delayed motor skills. She was referred for ABR testing by her school district after behavior observation suggested poor auditory responsiveness, and VRA was unsuccessful. Her mother reported concerns for poor response to sound. The only significant medical history was that the child had had three known ear infections.

Audiologic Assessment

ABR thresholds for clicks were observed down to 40 dB HLn in the left ear and to 50 dB HLn in the right ear. For 250 Hz tones, responses were noted down to 65 dB HL (30 dB above the mean for normal hearing subjects) in the left ear and 80 dB HL (45 dB above the mean) in the right ear. Both the otoscopic evaluation and tympanograms were normal.

Interpretation and Recommendations

ABR findings suggested bilateral, mild-to-moderate hearing loss, with slightly poorer hearing in the right ear. Normal tympanograms tended to rule out middle-ear dysfunction affecting the ABR thresholds. Without amplification, this child would miss much speech at conversational levels or softer. An additional finding from the ABR was that the interpeak latencies were somewhat prolonged for the child's age, reflecting neuropathy or neuromaturational delay affecting auditory brainstem pathways.

All test findings were discussed with the child's mother. Her observations of poor auditory responsiveness were confirmed. The recommendations were: fitting of amplification, follow-up for continued behavioral audiologic testing, and the other recommendations outlined in the Identification of Hearing Loss section of this article. Metabolic studies were already underway to deter-

Figure 3

ABR results showing mild-to-moderate hearing loss in a 6-month-old female. Wave V is denoted with a tick mark. Wave V thresholds for clicks were 40 dB HLn for the left ear and 50 dB HLn for the right ear. Thresholds were 65 dB HL for 250 Hz tones in the left ear and 80 dB HL for the right.

ABR - Mild-Moderate Sensorineural

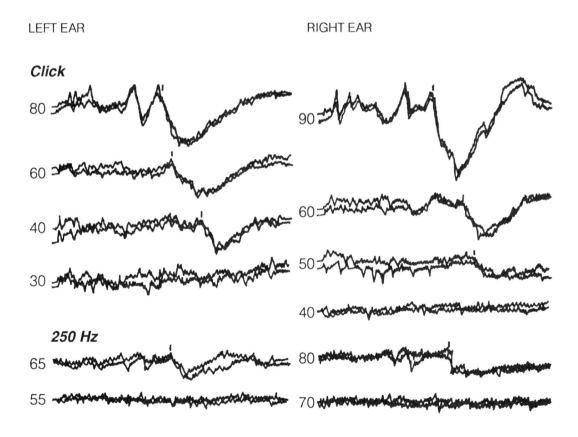

mine the etiology of the motor delays. Consideration also should be given for a neurologic evaluation given the prolonged interpeak latencies.

Moderate Sensorineural Hearing Loss: 7-Month-Old Child

Introductory Comments and Background

Because of the increasing number of children with multiple handicaps, more issues regarding case management need to be addressed. In particular, the demands placed on the parents/caregivers cannot be ignored. The case discussed here involves a child requiring 24-hour-a-day health monitoring. With a diagnosis of hearing loss, the addition of caring for and maintaining hearing aids and involvement in auditory training gives the parents more to do with little time to do it. Consequently, they may become overwhelmed and need support and respite.

This 7-month-old female with Charge Associated syndrome had choanal atresia for which she had multiple surgeries and tracheotomy tube. She also had hyperthyroidism and a seizure disorder for which she was taking medications. Tympanostomy tubes had been placed because of persistent otitis media. Due to poor coordination of oral and tongue musculature, she received all nourishment through a gastrostomy tube. She was seen by a parent-infant specialist weekly and for speech and language therapy and physical therapy twice a month. She had failed an ABR screening while hospitalized in a neonatal intensive care unit (NICU), but no follow-up testing was done until 7 months of age because of other health concerns. In spite of her fragile health, overall developmental performance was close to age expectations. She had an excellent home environment, and both parents were actively involved in her care.

Audiologic Assessment

This child did not have the head or neck control to perform a head-turn response for VRA; however, she consistently searched with her eyes toward the loudspeaker. MRLs to speech and a calibrated speech-like signal were obtained at 60 dB HL, as shown in Figure 4. She did not consistently respond to

Figure 4

Behavioral results obtained on a 7-month-old female, using modified VRA. Minimal response levels to a speech-like signal in the sound field (S) suggested a moderate hearing loss.

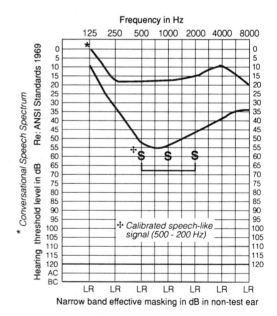

tonal stimuli. Testing under earphones or by bone conduction could not be accomplished because she refused to wear these devices. Because of limited behavioral test results, an ABR test was done. Those results confirmed a moderate-to-severe hearing loss at least in the high frequencies, with better hearing in the right ear (wave V thresholds for clicks were 55 dB HLn in the right ear and 75 dB HLn in the left ear). Tympanometry was consistent with patent tympanostomy tubes.

Interpretation and Recommendations

Behavioral and ABR test results indicated a moderate-to-severe hearing loss with better hearing in her right ear. The type of hearing loss, however, was not established definitely. These results suggested that this child will miss most conversational speech unless she uses amplification. Following medical clearance, she was fitted with an FM auditory trainer. With this device, the speaker wears a wireless microphone and transmitter. The child wears a receiver coupled to a headset or earmolds, and the signal is transmitted via radio waves. The loudness of the speech signal remains constant at the child's ear regardless of the distance between the child and the speaker. Following the introduction to amplification with the auditory trainer, a trial with binaural ear-level hearing aids will be initiated. The family was referred to a support group for parents who have children with multiple handicaps, and respite services were sought.

Moderate Sensorineural Hearing Loss: 24-Month-Old Child

Introductory Comments and Background

Many audiologists have not had extensive background in counseling families of children who are hearing impaired. Their counseling frequently consists of information-sharing with little attention given to the emotional impact the child's hearing loss may have on the family (Luterman, 1991). Often the audiologist is the first to confirm that a youngster has a permanent hearing loss and must communicate this to the family. As the mourning period begins, some parents/caregivers react to the initial diagnosis with denial, and second opinion evaluations should be encouraged. Little can be accomplished in an early intervention program until the family is convinced that their child has a hearing loss. Frequently their mourning does not cease with the acceptance, and many have feelings of guilt which they carry for a lifetime. At times, professionals communicate compassionately to the family that they understand their feelings, when in truth, they do not unless they have had a similar experience.

This case was one in which the parents initially did not accept the diagnosis of hearing loss. There were no risk factors for hearing loss or parental concerns for hearing loss or speech-language development. This 24-month-old female was referred for hearing evaluation by another clinic for a second-opinion. Previously, she had failed a hearing screening in her preschool nursery.

Audiologic Assessment

Threshold testing was accomplished easily under earphones and by bone conduction using CPA. Results suggested a bilateral, symmetrical, mild-to-moderate, sensorineural hearing loss. The PTA was 47 dB HL in the right ear and 52 dB HL in the left ear, as shown in Figure 5. SRTs of 40 dB HL in the left ear and 45 dB HL in the right ear were obtained using a picture-pointing response. These were in good agreement with the PTAs. Word recognition, measured with a multiple-choice picture test (WIPI), was

Figure 5

Behavioral thresholds from a 2-year-old female obtained using CPA, suggesting a bilateral, moderate, sensorineural hearing loss. Aided thresholds for tones were well within the conversational spectrum over a broad frequency range (250 to 6000 Hz).

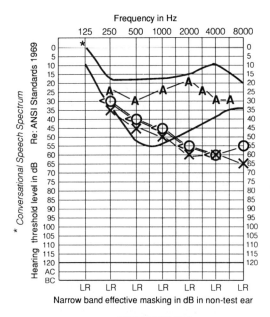

80% in each ear. Tympanograms were normal for both ears. Acoustic reflex thresholds were consistent with sensorineural hearing loss.

Interpretation and Recommendations

Test results were explained to the mother, stressing that the child had an educationally significant hearing loss, and that, depending on the listening situation, she would miss conversational speech or hear it only at a soft level. This was demonstrated on the audiogram with some pure tone thresholds falling outside of the conversational spectrum. Although the mother reluctantly accepted the results of the hearing test, she did not feel that the hearing loss caused a significant handicap for her daughter. In an attempt to demonstrate effects of the hearing loss, the child was tested in the sound field with her mother in the booth observing how loud sounds were before her daughter responded. Also, a simulation of how the child might be hearing conversational speech was presented. After the parents agreed to a trial with amplification and medical clearance was obtained from an otologist, the child was fitted with loaner hearing aids. Resources for parent counseling and parent support groups were given. It was recommended that the child have a diagnostic speech and language evaluation. Genetic and ophthalmologic evaluations also were recommended.

Hearing Aid Performance Check and Recommendations

After one month of hearing-aid use, the parents reported that their child had made an excellent adjustment to the hearing aids, and they observed substantial improvements in her auditory behavior. With the hearing aids in place, aided SRTs of 25 dB HL were obtained. Aided thresholds for tones were within the conversational spectrum over a broad frequency range (250 to 6000 Hz) (Figure 5). These results suggested that the child had the potential to identify all speech sounds. Word recognition, measured at an intensity level approximating conversational speech, was 84% in quiet and 60% in a background of noise. Subsequently, binaural ear-level hearing aids were recommended, and the child was enrolled in speech and language therapy with auditory training twice a week. A follow-up audiologic evaluation was scheduled in three months.

Severe-to-Profound Sensorineural Loss: 3-Month-Old Child

Introductory Comments and Background

Figure 6 shows ABR results for a 3-month-old female who was referred for testing by her pediatrician because of a family history of hearing loss and an outer ear abnormality. She was accompanied to the test by her parents, both normal hearing, who reported that the infant responded inconsistently to sound at home.

Audiologic Assessment

ABR testing for the left ear showed a click threshold to 60 dB HLn and down to 65 dB HL (30 dB above the mean for normal hearing subjects) for 250 Hz tones. For the right ear, a click threshold was observed at 80 dB HLn and a response to 250 Hz tones down to 80 dB HL (45 dB above the mean for normal hearing subjects). Tympanograms were attempted unsuccessfully because of the child's movement; however, the otologist who saw the child prior to the ABR test did not suspect middle-ear dysfunction.

Interpretation and Recommendations

These findings suggested severe-to-profound high-frequency hearing loss and mild-to-moderate low-frequency hearing loss. Interpeak latencies for the left ear were normal, tending to rule out neuropathy or neuromaturational delay affecting auditory brainstem pathways. No interpeak latencies could be calculated for the right ear, and a comment regarding the status of the auditory brainstem pathways could not be made for that side.

Following testing, all results were discussed with the parents. Earmold impressions were made in anticipation of fitting with amplification within one month. Follow-up testing was planned in the immediate future to confirm these initial test findings. Arrangements were made for initiation of habilitation services, a medical-genetics evaluation, and an ophthalmologic evaluation. It is highly unlikely that this child could develop normal speech or language without the intervention of amplification and habilitation, because most speech would be inaudible.

Severe Sensorineural Hearing Loss: 7-Month-Old Child

Introductory Comments and Background

Children with hearing loss whose parents are deaf require special management. As in the case reported here, some crucial management decisions are required. Because the parents/caregivers are actively involved in early intervention activities, some modifications in the service delivery system are warranted and must be considered when writing an Individualized Family Service Plan (IFSP) for deaf parents.

This 7-month-old male was referred by the maternal grandmother who had been an active and effective caretaker of the family. She accompanied the parents to the evaluation and served as the interpreter. She suspected the child of having a hearing loss but had difficulty getting the parents to agree to have the child's hearing evaluated. Although full-time hearing-aid users, both parents are functionally deaf and communicate exclusively using sign language. The

70 EARLY INTERVENTION FOR SPECIAL POPULATIONS OF INFANTS AND TODDLERS

Figure 6

ABR results for a 3-month-old female with severe-to-profound sensorineural hearing loss, following the convention of Figure 3. Wave V thresholds for clicks were 60 dB HLn for the left ear and 80 dB HLn for the right. Thresholds were 65 dB HL for 250 Hz tones in the left ear and 80 dB HL for the right.

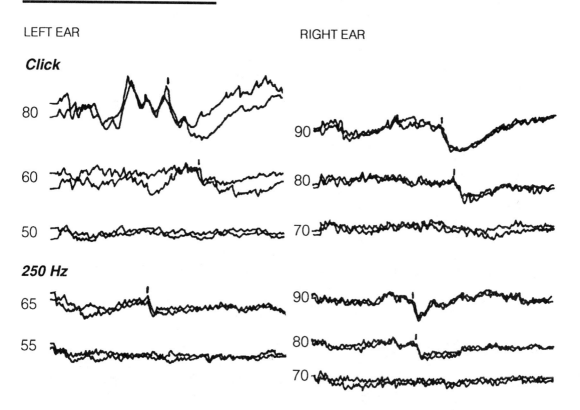

father's hearing loss was acquired in infancy due to meningitis and the mother's hearing loss was congenital, cause unknown. The child was the product of a normal, full-term pregnancy and an uneventful delivery. Developmental milestones were reported to be within normal limits. He had been healthy and did not have a history of middle-ear infections.

Audiologic Assessment

The child was alert and responsive to sensory stimulation, and testing was accomplished using VRA. Minimal response levels to speech were obtained at 80 dB HL in each ear using a hand-held earphone. After a short time, he rejected the earphone, and testing was completed in the sound field. Minimal response levels for tones were between 75 and 95 dB HL, as shown in Figure 7. Tympanograms showed normal eardrum movement in each ear with slight negative middle-ear pressure.

Interpretation and Recommendations

Results suggested a severe hearing loss, and indicated he was missing all speech at conversational levels. Residual hearing was suggested over a broad frequency range (250 to 4000 Hz). Tympanograms were essentially normal.

These results were explained to the parents. Although devastated by this news, they were anxious to have their child enrolled in an early intervention program and fitted with amplification. After enrollment in such a program, an itinerant teacher of the hearing impaired was scheduled to make weekly home visits. Following medical clearance, the child was fitted with a loaner auditory trainer with a modified headset. This device was chosen over hearing aids initially because the child's ears were too small to retain earmolds; however, hearing aids will be

Figure 7

Behavioral results from a 7-month-old male using VRA. Minimal response levels to tones in the sound field (S) and under earphones to speech stimuli suggested a severe hearing loss.

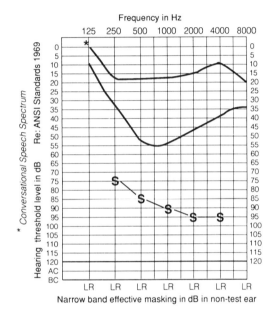

fitted in the future. Arrangements were made to have a deaf parent of a hearing-impaired preschool child visit with the parents to provide support and information. Recommendations were made for genetic and ophthalmologic evaluations.

Additional Comments

For children with little or no residual hearing who do not benefit from amplification, vibrotactile aids or cochlear implants may be useful (Osberger, et al., 1990). The vibrotactile units, which are about the size of a body-type hearing aid, can be clipped to the clothing. The vibrators, about the diameter of a nickel, are generally worn on the chest, in the sternum area, or on the wrist. Although not a substitute for hearing, vibrotactile training can facilitate the development of sound awareness and recognition of various aspects of speech including rhythm, duration, stress, phrasing, and intensity. Further, some deaf children may be more vocal when receiving vibrotactile cues.

Cochlear implants may be another option for some children with profound hearing impairment. Some parts of the implant are positioned externally; whereas other parts are implanted surgically within the mastoid bone and cochlea. Sound enters a microphone at ear level and is sent to a speech processor, which is about the size of a pocket radio. The speech processor does not amplify as does a hearing aid, but detects certain elements of sound useful in providing cues for identification. Electronic signals are sent to the transmitter through the skin to an implanted receiver-stimulator and to a series of electrodes that have been placed into the cochlea. The electrodes stimulate nerve fibers, and neural impulses are transmitted to the brain. The cochlear implant stimulates an irreversibly damaged ear, thus, normal hearing is not possible. Today, the best candidates for cochlear implants are people who became deaf after the acquisition of speech and language. They generally make better use of distorted auditory cues than do people born deaf. A rather conservative approach is generally taken with young children in determining candidacy for cochlear implants. It is important to know with certainty that a total hearing loss exists so that the implantation does not result in a loss of usable hearing. Even if a profound hearing loss is indicated, a lengthy trial with hearing aids is suggested (Tyler, Davis, & Lansing, 1987).

Follow-Up Audiologic Services

How Often Should a Child Have Hearing Tests?

Audiologic follow-up should occur frequently in infants and toddlers with known hearing loss; at least every three months after the loss is identified and confirmed. The purpose of frequent visits is to monitor unaided hearing sensitivity and the performance of hearing aids or other assistive devices. In some cases, such as in children with fluctuating or progressive losses, more frequent monitoring is necessary.

What Are Some Educational Resources for Children With Hearing Loss?

It is beyond the scope of this article to address the complicated issues of the choice of communication mode for a given child or habilitation techniques. These decisions involve many factors and are best addressed in ongoing diagnostic teaching parent-infant sessions. Such a program is described as the Diagnostic Early Intervention Project (DEIP), which specifically focuses on newly identified hearing-impaired children and their families (Moeller, Coufal, & Hixson, 1990).

Examples of three programs that focus on parent-infant training for children with hearing impairment are Beginnings, 1316 Broad Street, Durham, North Carolina, 27705, 919-286-9797; Infant Hearing Resources, Oregon Health Sciences University, 3930 S.W. Macadam Avenue, Portland, Oregon, 97201, 503-494-4206; and the John Tracy Clinic, 806 West Adams Boulevard, Los Angeles, California, 90007, 800-522-4582. There are too many national organizations that provide resources and support for children (and adults) with hearing loss to list here. A directory of these, the NICD Directory of National Organizations and Centers of and for Deaf and Hard of Hearing People, can be obtained from the National Information Center on Deafness, Gallaudet University, 800 Florida Avenue NE, Washington, DC, 20002-3625.

Acknowledgments

We would like to acknowledge Ann Dingman, Judy Gaines, Ann Karasek, and Patricia Stelmachowicz for their careful review of this manuscript and their many helpful editorial comments. We also acknowledge Betsy From and Linda Jahns for their assistance in the preparation of the manuscript.

References

Adelman, C., Levi, H., Linder, N., & Sohmer, H. (1990). Neonatal auditory brain-stem response threshold and latency: 1 hour to 5 months. *Electrocephalography and Clinical Neurophysiology, 77,* 77-80.

American Speech-Language-Hearing Association. (1989). Guidelines for audiologic screening of newborn infants who are at risk for hearing impairment. *ASHA, 31,* 89-92.

American Speech-Language-Hearing Association. (in press). Guidelines for the audiologic assessment of children from birth through thirty-six months of age. *ASHA.*

Bess, F. H., Klee, T., & Culbertson, J. L. (1986). Identification, assessment and management of children with unilateral sensorineural hearing loss. *Ear and Hearing, 7,* 43-51.

Bess, F. H., & Tharpe, A. M. (1986). Case history data on unilaterally hearing-impaired children. *Ear and Hearing, 7,* 14-19.

Clark, J. (1981). Uses and abuses of hearing loss classifications. *ASHA, 23,* 493-500.

Education of the Handicapped Act Amendments of 1986, Public Law 99-457, 34 CFR Part 303, Part H. *Federal Register, 54,* 119, 26306-26348, June 22, 1989.

Elliot, L. L., & Katz, D. R. (1980). *Northwestern University Children's Perception of Speech (NU-CHIPS).* St. Louis, MO: Auditec.

Elssmann, S. F., Matkin, N. D., & Sabo, M. (1987). Early identification of congenital sensorineural hearing impairment. *The Hearing Journal, 40,* 13-17.

Fletcher, S. G. (1970). Acoustic phonetics. In F. Berg, and S. Fletcher (Eds.), *The hard of hearing child* (pp. 57-84). New York: Grune & Stratton.

Fulton, R., Gorzycki, P., & Hull, W. (1975). Hearing assessment with young children. *Journal of Speech and Hearing Disorders, 40,* 397-404.

Galambos, R., Hicks, G. E., & Wilson, M. J. (1984). The auditory brain stem response reliably predicts hearing loss in graduates of a tertiary care nursery. *Ear and Hearing, 5,* 254-260.

Garrard, K. R., & Clark, B. Smith (1985). Otitis media: The role of speech-language pathologists. *ASHA, 27,* 35-39.

Goodman, A. (1965). Reference zero levels for pure-tone audiometer. *ASHA, 7,* 262-263.

Gorga, M. P., Kaminski, J. R., Beauchaine, K. L., Jesteadt, W., & Neely, S. T. (1989). Auditory brainstem responses from children three months to three years of age: Normal patterns of response II. *Journal of Speech and Hearing Research, 32,* 281-288.

Gorga, M. P., Reiland, J. K., Beauchaine, K. A., Worthington, D. W., & Jesteadt, W. (1987). Auditory brainstem responses from graduates of an intensive care nursery: Normal patterns of response. *Journal of Speech and Hearing Research, 30,* 311-318.

Gravel, J. S. (1989). Behavioral assessment of auditory function. *Seminars in Hearing, 10,* 216-228.

Gravel, J. S., Wallace, I. F., & Abraham, S. (1990, November). *Communicative sequelae of otitis media: Hearing, language and phonology.* Poster session presented at the American Speech-Language-Hearing Association Convention, Seattle, WA.

Hyde, M. L., Riko, K., & Malizia, K. (1990). Audiometric accuracy of the click ABR in infants at risk for hearing loss. *Journal of the American Academy of Audiology, 1,* 59–66.

Jacobson, J., Jacobson, C., & Francis, P. (1990). Congenital hearing loss in Jervell and Lange-Nielsen Syndrome. *Journal of the American Academy of Audiology, 1,* 171–173.

Jacobson, J. T., & Morehouse, C. R., (1984). A comparison of auditory brain stem response and behavioral screening in high risk and normal newborn infants. *Ear and Hearing, 5,* 247–253.

Johnson, D., & Caccamise, F. (1983). Rationale for performing visual assessments with hearing-impaired persons prior to conducting speech reading research and training. *Journal of the Academy of Rehabilitative Audiology, 16,* 128–142.

Joint Committee on Infant Hearing, Position statement (RE0011). (1982). *Pediatrics, 70,* 24–25.

Joint Committee on Infant Hearing, Position statement. (in press). *ASHA.*

Karchmer, M. A. (1985). A demographic perspective. In E. Cherow, N. D. Matkin, & R. J. Trybus (Eds.), *Hearing-impaired children and youth with developmental disabilities: An interdisciplinary foundation for service* (pp. 36–56). Washington, DC: Gallaudet College Press.

Kenworthy, O. T., Bess, F., Stahlman, M., Lindstrom, D. (1987). Hearing, speech and language outcome in infants with extreme immaturity. *American Journal of Otology, 8,* 419–425.

Kile, J. K., Kuba, J. M., Nellis, R. A., & Becker, T. (1990, November). *Children with Down Syndrome: Hearing, language, and speech issues.* Poster session presented at American Speech-Language-Hearing Association Convention, Seattle, WA.

Ling, D. (1976). *Speech and the hearing-impaired child: Theory and practice.* Washington, DC: The Alexander Graham Bell Association for the Deaf.

Ling, D., & Ling, A. L. (1978). *Aural habilitation: The foundations of verbal learning in hearing-impaired children.* Washington, DC: The Alexander Graham Bell Association for the Deaf.

Lloyd, L. L., Spradlin, J. E., & Reid, M. J. (1968). An operant audiometric procedure for difficult-to-test patients. *Journal of Speech and Hearing Disorders, 33,* 236–245.

Luterman, D. (1991). *Counseling the communicatively disordered and their families* (2nd ed.). Boston: Little, Brown and Company.

Mahoney, T. M., & Eichwald, J. G. (1986). Model program V: A high-risk register by computerized search of birth certificates. In E. T. Swigart (Ed.), *Neonatal hearing screening,* (pp. 223–240). San Diego, CA: College-Hill Press.

Margolis, R. H., & Shanks, J. E. (1985). Tympanometry. In J. Katz (Ed.), *The handbook of clinical audiology* (3rd ed., pp. 438–475). Baltimore, MD: Williams & Wilkins.

Matkin, N. (1979). The audiologic examination of young children at risk. *Ear, Nose, and Throat Journal, 58,* 29–38.

Matkin, N. (1987). Hearing instruments for children: Premises for selecting and fitting. *Hearing Instruments, 38,* 14–16.

Moeller, M. P., Coufal, K. L., & Hixson, P. K. (1990). The efficacy of speech-language pathology intervention: Hearing-impaired children. *Seminars in Hearing, 11,* 227–241.

Moller, C. G., Kimberling, W. J., Davenport, S. L. H., Priluck, I., White, V., Biscone-Halterman, K., Odkvist, L. M., Brookhouser, P. E., Lund, G., & Grissom, T. J. (1989). Usher syndrome: An otoneurologic study, *Laryngoscope, 99,* 73–79.

Mueller, H. G., & Killion, M. C. (1990). An easy method for calculating the articulation index. *The Hearing Journal, 43*(9), 14–17.

Olsen, W., Hawkins, D., & Van Tassell, D. (1987). Representations of the long-term spectra of speech. *Ear and Hearing, 8*(5), (Suppl. 5), 100S–108S.

Olsen, W., & Matkin, N. (1979). Speech audiometry. In W. Rintelmann (Ed.), *Hearing assessment.* Baltimore, MD: University Park Press.

Osberger, M. J., Miyamoto, R. T., Robbins, A. M., Renshaw, J. J., Berry, S. W., Myres, W. A., Kessler, K., & Pope, M. L. (1990). Performance of deaf children with cochlear implants and vibrotactile aids. *Journal of the American Academy of Audiology, 1,* 7–10.

Oyler, R. F., Oyler, A. L., & Matkin, N. D. (1988). Unilateral hearing loss: Demographics and educational impact. *Language, Speech, and*

Hearing Services in the Schools, 19, 201-209.

Pollard, G., & Neumaier, R. (1974). Vision characteristics of deaf students. *American Journal of Optometry and Physiological Optics, 51,* 839-846.

Regenbogen, L., & Godel, V. (1985). Ocular deficiencies in deaf children. *Journal of Pediatric Ophthalmology and Strabismus, 22,* 231-233.

Rogers, G. L., Fillman, R. D., Bremer, D. L., & Leguire, L. E. (1988). Screening of school-aged hearing impaired children. *Journal of Pediatric Ophthalmology and Strabismus, 25,* 230-232.

Ross, M., & Lerman, J. (1971). *Word intelligibility by picture identification-WIPI.* St. Louis, MO: Auditec.

Sprague, B. H., Wiley, T. L., & Goldstein, R. (1985). Tympanometric and acoustic-reflex studies in neonates. *Journal of Speech and Hearing Research, 28,* 265-272.

Stapells, D. R., Picton, T. W., Perez-Abalo, M., Read, D., & Smith, A. (1985). Frequency specificity in evoked potential audiometry. In J. T. Jacobson (Ed.), *The auditory brainstem response* (pp. 147-177). San Diego, CA: College-Hill Press.

Thompson, M., Thompson, G., & Vethivelu, S. (1989). A comparison of audiometric test methods for 2-year-old children. *Journal of Speech and Hearing Disorders, 54,* 174-179.

Thompson, G., & Wilson, W. R. (1984). Clinical application of visual reinforcement audiometry. *Seminars in Hearing, 5,* 85-99.

Tyler, R., Davis, J., & Lansing, C. (1987). Cochlear implants in young children. *ASHA, 29,* 41-49.

Walters, R. J., & Shimizu, H. (1990). Acoustic immittance screening of infants. *Seminars in Hearing, 11,* 177-185.

Wilson, W. R., & Thompson, G. (1984). Behavioral audiometry. In J. Jerger (Ed.), *Pediatric audiology,* (pp. 1-44). San Diego, CA: College-Hill Press.

Address Correspondence to Jack E. Kile, Ph.D., Center for Communicative Disorders, Arts and Communication Center, University of Wisconsin-Oshkosh, Oshkosh, WI 54901.

The Effects of Mild Hearing Loss on Infant Auditory Function

Robert J. Nozza, Ph.D.
University of Georgia
Athens, Georgia

The effects of mild hearing impairment on infants and young children have been difficult to determine. There is controversy over whether mild hearing impairment, especially transient hearing impairment such as accompanies episodes of otitis media with effusion, can cause long-lasting deficits or delays in speech and language development. This article summarizes laboratory work that was designed to estimate the effects of mild hearing impairment on infant speech perception abilities using normal hearing infants under conditions that simulate mild hearing loss. The findings are put into the context of research from other areas regarding the plasticity of the developing central nervous system, critical periods, and especially the vulnerability of developing perceptual systems to degraded sensory input during critical periods. Together, the data suggest that even mild alterations of the auditory input during infancy have the potential to cause significant developmental consequences. Identification, assessment, and management of mild hearing impairment in infants and toddlers is recommended until, and if, it can be shown that known deficits in auditory perception that result from mild hearing loss do not cause meaningful long-term changes in the development of speech, language, and cognition.

Unlike the obvious effects of moderate, severe, and profound hearing impairments, the impact of mild hearing loss on infants and toddlers is not well understood. Only in recent years has it become clear that mild (or even unilateral) hearing loss has an effect on a child's ability to achieve in school (Bess, 1985; Blair, Peterson, & Viehweg, 1985; Montgomery & Matkin, 1992). This realization has caused us to revise our thinking on what constitutes hearing impairment in children and has led Northern and Downs (1991) to suggest that for children the cutoff for impairment be set at 15 dB HL as opposed to the traditional 25 dB HL cutoff based on data from adults. The research supporting the notion that mild forms of hearing impairment can cause disabilities in school-age children includes data from studies of children with histories of chronic or recurrent otitis media with effusion. Although many of those studies have methodological flaws and have been criticized for lack of experimental rigor (see Bluestone et al., 1986 for a review), there are many indications that suggest that early otitis media can cause later language and learning problems and that the mediating variable is the hearing loss associated with the middle ear disease (e.g., Friel-Patti & Finitzo, 1990). The average hearing loss in children with middle ear effusion is about 25 to 30 dB HL (Fria, Cantekin, & Eichler, 1985) and is in the mild category by most definitions of impairment.

Paradise (1981; Bluestone et al., 1986), among others, has criticized the work that suggests long-term effects of the mild hearing impairment associated with early otitis media with effusion. His reviews detail many of the flaws in design and methodology in the research. His view is that, even if it is accepted that there are measurable consequences of early otitis, affected children "catch up" in the early elementary grades and suffer no long-standing developmental delays or deficits. Paradise, a pediatrician, is concerned that an exaggerated response to a self-limiting disease such as otitis media with effusion, namely placement of tympanostomy tubes in the ears of many children, is potentially more dangerous than the disease itself.

Whatever the viewpoint, the issue of the effects of mild hearing impairment is one that requires further investigation. Even if one accepts the skeptical view of Paradise, existing evidence is certainly strong enough to suggest the potential for problems, and such potential alone warrants attention. Furthermore, although it is a leading cause of mild hearing impairment, otitis media with effusion is not the only cause of mild hearing loss. Other causes of mild hearing impairment in children, unlike otitis media with effusion, are typically not temporary. Children with deficits in auditory information secondary to permanent hearing impairment may be less likely to have the opportunity to "catch up" unless there is intervention of some kind.

In this article, the issue of mild hearing impairment in infants is addressed. First, definitions of hearing impairment and hearing disability during infancy are considered. To discuss impairment, a definition of normal sensory function must be established. Disability relates to the effects of abnormal sensory function on the ability of the individual to function in a normal way. To understand such effects requires an understanding of the role that normal auditory input plays in the normal development of speech and language of the infant. Second, an experimental approach to the study of the effects of mild hearing impairment is presented. The data discussed are fairly narrow and focus on only certain dimensions of the auditory processes of infants. The goal is to present evidence that suggests that infants are affected by even small alterations in the auditory input, such as are imposed by a mild hearing loss, and that there is reason to believe that even mild hearing impairment can substantially alter the experiences of infants during crucial periods of language acquisition.

Impairment and Disability

The definition of a mild hearing impairment depends on a knowledge of what is normal and how it changes developmentally. In adults, the criterion for hearing impairment is often considered to be >25 dB HL in the better hearing ear. That is, using a test of the threshold for speech, or an average of pure tone thresholds for frequencies at 500, 1000, and 2000 Hz, a value greater than 25 dB HL places that individual in the category of impairment. Usually, beyond 40 dB HL is considered the moderately impaired category, so mild impairment for an adult would be thresholds in the 26 to 40 dB HL range. These values may vary among professionals, with some choosing 20 rather than 25 dB HL as the upper limit of normal. As mentioned, Northern and Downs (1991) have argued that 15 dB HL should be the upper limit for normal in young children.

The definitions are somewhat arbitrary. For adults the definition is based on the notion that with thresholds above 25 (or perhaps 20) dB HL, adults begin to demonstrate difficulty understanding speech under normal conversational conditions. That is, "impairment" is defined as the level of hearing at which a disability can be measured in the individual. The level chosen as the cutoff for impairment is based not on means and variances of hearing in individuals meeting criteria for normality, but rather on one's sense of when the individual is unable to perform in a normal way those functions that require use of the auditory system. How one measures hearing disability in adults has been a controversial question for many years. Is performance on a speech intelligibility test adequate to determine whether an individual with hearing loss is unable to function normally? Perhaps it should be speech intelligibility under unfavorable listening conditions; or should it be self-assessment of difficulties in normal daily activities? Even with adults, it has been difficult to decide how to determine when impairment of a system becomes a disability to the individual. Nonetheless, 25 dB HL seems to be a common cutoff for normal and seems to be based more on perceived loss of function than on objective criteria.

The World Health Organization (WHO, 1980) attempted to clarify definitions related to impairment and disability and, in a recent report, the American Speech-Language-Hearing Association (ASHA, 1993) adapted those definitions. According to ASHA (1993), an *impairment* is any loss or abnormality of psychological, physiological, or anatomical structure or function. Auditory impairment implies that there is a dimension of the auditory *system* that is outside the normal range, but does not imply necessarily that the level of performance of the individual in activities involving that dimension are restricted. *Disability* is any restriction or lack (resulting from an impairment) of ability to perform an activity in the manner or within the range considered normal for a human being. According to WHO, (1980), "disability represents a departure from the norm in terms of performance of the individual, as opposed to that of the organ or mechanism" (p. 28). That is, disability relates to performance of the *individual* and is considered to be the loss of function that results from an impairment.

For infants and young children, audiologists can measure hearing and determine a normal range, and they can define impairment as hearing outside of that range. However, the difficulty of determining when the effects of such impairment begin (i.e., when it becomes a disability) is greater even than it is with adults. To answer the question of the effects of mild hearing impairment during early life, some understanding of what role normal auditory input plays in the normal development of function is necessary. Also, the impact on the normal processes of various levels of hearing outside the normal range must be measured. If it is determined that even hearing thresholds slightly outside the normal range do not alter the infant's ability to perform the operations on auditory information that are needed to support language development at a given stage, then concern over mild hearing impairment might be diminished. On the other hand, if it were demonstrated that infants with mild hearing impairment cannot perform relevant auditory tasks in the same way as infants with hearing in the normal range, then it would be reasonable to hypothesize that development will be delayed or defective.

Normal Auditory Function in Infants

For many years, the view of the infant as a passive and reflexive organism, with poor vision and audition at birth, encouraged the notion that infants had great sensory deficits that were "normal" or natural, and, as such, did not constitute disabling conditions in the sense used here. The assumption was that the infant did not use sensory information in any meaningful way until much older, so the notion of impairment and disability were not considered. However, over the past 25 years or so, this view has changed. Current ideas about sensory function in infants are consistent with the view that the infant is an organism that is actively participating in the world around it and is incorporating sensory information into the development of cognition from the first days of life. Related to that view is evidence of critical periods during development during which sensory input has greater influence on long-term development than other periods. Research in the physiology and behavior of the visual system has shown, in both animals and in humans, that atypical, discordant or absent visual stimulation during certain developmental stages can cause lasting alterations to brain development (Barlow, 1975; Grobstein & Chow, 1975). A parallel in the auditory system has also been demonstrated, but the data are fewer than in the visual system (Clopton & Silverman, 1977; Webster, 1983, 1988; Webster & Webster, 1977, 1979).

It is believed that the developing nervous system is modifiable, or "plastic," during periods of developmental change (Gottlieb, 1981). It relies on normal input so that developmental changes can be properly guided. However, it seems that developing systems are more susceptible to abnormal input during such periods as well, with atypical or absent input slowing or misdirecting the developmental course. Therefore, when clinicians identify a period of developmental change for a given function, they must be aware that it may also be a period of heightened vulnerability to abnormal input. This has been discussed with respect to the question of otitis media. For example, there are normal developmental changes in electrophysiological measures of auditory brainstem function (Hecox & Burkard, 1982; Salamy, Mendelson, & Tooley, 1982; Teas, Klein, & Kramer, 1982) and electrophysiological evidence that brainstem function is different in children who have had chronic or recurrent otitis media early in life (Anteby, Hafner, Pratt, & Uri, 1986; Chambers, Rowan, Matthies, & Novak, 1989; Folsom, Weber, & Thompson, 1983; Gunnarson & Finitzo, 1991; Lenhardt, Shaia, & Abedi, 1985).

There is also psychoacoustic evidence of different binaural function, which is also mediated in the brainstem, in children with a history of otitis media. We have data that show that psychoacoustic phenomena, such as localization and release from masking, which are primarily dependent on binaural function, change normally during the first year of life (Morrongiello & Rocca, 1987a, 1987b; Nozza, 1987b; Nozza, Wagner, & Crandell, 1988). Given that this is a time of high prevalence of otitis media, it would seem that binaural function might be at risk for abnormal or delayed development secondary to mild hearing loss, especially if it is unilateral. In fact, the release from masking, which is the improvement in threshold for a binaural signal in binaural noise as a result of manipulation of the relative phases of the signal at the two ears, in children with a history of otitis media early in life, is inferior to that of children with no known history of otitis media (Moore, 1991; Moore, Hutchings, & Meyer, 1991).

The Normal Range of Hearing for Infants

The first task is to determine the limits of sensory function in infants and the range of normal values. With such information, clinicians can begin to define "mild" hearing impairment as a term to describe a level of functioning of a *sensory system*. There are many ways to measure auditory function in infants (Kile & Beauchaine, 1991). Objective measures of sensitivity, such as the auditory brainstem response (ABR) and otoacoustic emissions (OAE), can give audiologists information on certain aspects of auditory function. However, in determining degree of impairment and in developing intervention strategies, it is important also to have behavioral estimates of function. Behavioral estimates of auditory processing give audiologists information not only regarding the peripheral system, but whether the infant can process auditory information in a meaningful way, that is, transform auditory information into behavioral responses. Audiologists now have the ability to estimate behavioral thresholds in infants so that ear-specific and frequency-specific hearing information can be obtained reliably.

From the research laboratories, audiologists have learned that the audiogram of normal 6- to 12-month-old infants is different than that of normal adults. Although the normal adult audiogram is, by definition, the zero dB line on the audiogram, this is not the case for the infant. Using the best behavioral procedure available for assessing the hearing of infants, which is the computer-based head-turn with visual reinforcement procedure, commonly referred to as visual reinforcement audiometry (VRA), several laboratories have found that infant thresholds are poorer than those of adults and that infant thresholds diverge more from adult thresholds in the low frequencies than in the high frequencies (Nozza & Wilson, 1984; Schneider & Trehub, 1992; Werner, 1992). The differences between infants and adults range from 20 to 25 dB at 500 Hz to about 5 dB at 4000 Hz. Thresholds for speech are about 15 to 20 dB greater for infants than for adults when measured using a laboratory-based, conditioned head-turn procedure. There are a number of methodological issues that could be discussed related to these differences, but my opinion is that the differences reflect, by and large, real differences in sensory processing. It seems nonsensory factors, such as differences in attention, motivation, and others, may also play a role, but that it is not a major one (perhaps 5 dB) with respect to threshold differences between groups. Therefore, at best, the infants would have hearing in the high frequencies that is equivalent to that of adults, but in the low frequencies hearing that is less sensitive.

In summary, the behavioral thresholds of infants suggest that infants have different sensitivity as a function of frequency than adults and, as a result, the normal range for infants is different than that of adults. Therefore, criteria for describing hearing impairment (i.e., hearing outside the normal range) for infants, should be based on data for infants and not on data currently used to establish norms for adults. Because methods for determining thresholds in infants may vary from clinic to clinic, it is advisable for each clinic to evaluate age-representative groups of infants with no known otologic or auditory impairment to establish clinic norms. It is important to note also that, while infant sensitivity may be poorer than that of the adult, this should not be thought of as a deficit.

Speech Perception

Before infants can process linguistic information, they must be able not only to detect the presence of sound but also discriminate between different sounds. Of critical importance is the ability to discriminate between different phonemes in their language. Discrimination is a necessary prerequisite to identification of syllables and words and to identifying linguistic markers that signal tense, number, possession, and so on. Many studies have been done to demonstrate that infants can discriminate among most of the phonemes that are used in most languages (Aslin, Pisoni, & Jusczyk, 1983). That is, infants seem to be universalists with respect to their ability to distinguish between all of the phonemes that can be generated by humans, regardless of the language from which they come. It has also been shown that infants exhibit categorical perception and perceptual constancy in ways similar to adult listeners (Kuhl, 1992). One important question is whether infants can perform the complex task of phonetic perception based exclusively on peripheral auditory processes or whether there is a process that relates the acoustic information in the speech signal to the ultimate development of linguistic competence. That is, is the infant performing a simple discrimination based on only acoustic differences without analysis of the signals, in even a rudimentary way, as speech? This is an important issue because it relates to the second important question addressed in this article. How does the infant use the normal auditory input (speech) it receives and is that function compromised by a degraded input? Or, in other words, is there evidence that an impairment at the level of the auditory system could lead to a disability at the level of the individual?

With respect to speech perception in infants, there are recent studies that suggest that infants incorporate the auditory information they can extract from the speech signal into the formulation of a phonetic inventory that they will need to become competent in their native language; and they do this prior to the time they utter words. The studies of Werker and colleagues (Werker & Lalonde, 1988; Werker & Tees, 1984) and Kuhl, Williams, Lacerda, Stevens, and Lindblom (1992) are extremely important in this context. Werker and Tees (1984) and Werker and Lalonde (1988) demonstrated that by about 10 months of age, normally developing infants have selectively reduced their sensitivity to phonetic contrasts that are not linguistic in their native language. That is, although infants at very early ages can demonstrate almost universal discrimination of phonemes, by 10 months they have become less able to perform a discrimination task when speech sounds are tested that are not phonemic, that is, not used to contrast a linguistic distinction, in their native language. This finding was quite interesting, but because of the age at which the change in perception occurred, nearly coincident with the beginning of the use of words, it was interpreted as evidence that the fine-tuning of the phonetic inventory occurs with the onset of language. Kuhl et al. (1992), on the other hand, report evidence that exposure to a specific language early in life alters perception by the time the infant is 6 months of age, that is, *before* language. They looked at vowel perception in infants with exposure to either of two different languages (Swedish and English) and determined that their perception of vowels differed based on whether they were exposed to one or the other of the languages. This study provides very important evidence that infants, by the time they reach 6 months of age, demonstrate the effects of experience with the native language. They have already processed the acoustic stream we call speech and have made some language-specific developmental alterations to accommodate to it. It seems reasonable to argue that this is a biologically important process that is programmed to occur coincident with exposure to the language environment and that it is active during the first half of the first year of life.

With respect to the goal of determining whether mild hearing impairment can affect the development of speech, language, and cognition, the foregoing is critical information. These studies have established not only that infants have the auditory capabilities to detect and discriminate speech sounds, but that very early in life, prior to the use and understanding of words, phonetic information is being processed actively at some level. If infants by 6 months of age demonstrate that phonetic input is being used to categorize relevant speech sounds, then what happens when the phonetic input is degraded such as would occur with a mild peripheral hearing impairment? If infants with hearing only slightly outside our normal range of hearing were to demonstrate the ability to respond to the phonetic distinctions discussed above in the same way as those with hearing within the normal range, then the likelihood that such impairment is detrimental would be small. If, on the other hand, mild hearing impairment caused a breakdown of the infant's ability to make important phonetic discriminations, then it would be reasonable to assume that the infant would have difficulty making appropriate selections for the phonetic inventory it will need to learn the native language.

Modeling the Effects of Mild Hearing Impairment

To address infants' ability to tolerate mild degradation of auditory input, Nozza and colleagues investigated the effects of stimulus intensity (Nozza, 1987a; Nozza, Rossman, & Bond, 1991) and of noise (Nozza, Rossman, Bond & Miller, 1990; Nozza, Miller, Rossman, & Bond, 1991) on ability of infants to discriminate speech sounds. Both reduction of signal intensity and addition of masking noise have been used to simulate hearing loss in adult listeners. Also, in her dissertation research, Rossman (1992) investigated the effects of a simulated high frequency hearing loss, created by filtering acoustic information from the stimuli, on infant speech-sound discrimination.

The effects of reduced stimulus intensity, which can be considered a method of simulating a flat, conductive hearing loss because they both result in a simple attenuation of signal amplitude in the auditory system, were first reported in 1987 (Nozza, 1987a). In that study, infant ability to discriminate /ba/ from /da/ was measured at three different intensity levels (approximately 60, 50, and 40 dB HL). The two phonemes are quite similar acoustically and differ on only one distinctive feature, place of articulation. A head-turn with visual reinforcement procedure was used in which the infant was taught to respond to a change from a repeating background speech sound (/ba/) to the discriminative speech sound (/da/). With one speech sound repeated continuously in the background, the infants learned to respond only when they detected a change to the alternate speech sound. All three intensity levels were well above the level at which adults reach maximum performance on a speech discrimination task. The highest level used in the study, about 60 dB HL, is considered to be in the range for normal conversational speech (55 to 65 dB HL). The lowest level, about 40 dB HL, would be considered lower than normal speech in the environment. However, even the lowest level used in the study was sufficient for adults to achieve maximum performance on a task to discriminate between the speech sounds. On the other hand, for the infants, performance was optimal at the highest two intensities but was rather poor at the lowest intensity.

Figure 1 depicts the data from that study. Infants required considerably greater stimulus intensity to reach their maximum performance in the discrimination task than did the adults. The important feature of the two functions is their location with respect to the abscissa, or x-axis. That infant performance reaches maximum at only about .80 to .85 proportion correct is typical for the procedure used, even when easily distinguishable, acoustically dissimilar stimuli are used and probably relates to methodological limitations more than infant speech perception. That is, the fact that adults achieve nearly 1.0 and the infants achieve .85 correct responding is not the significant finding in the present context. What is important is that normal hearing infants require so much greater signal intensity before they reach maximum performance relative to the adults.

Figure 1 includes a shaded area that represents the approximate long-term average intensity level of conversational speech under quiet conditions. Infant speech-sound discrimination performance is optimal in that region. However, if a mild reduction of speech intensity level were imposed, say 15 or 20 dB, which is comparable to a shift in threshold and can be demonstrated by sliding the two functions 15 or 20 dB to the right, it is obvious that the conversational speech intensity will intersect the infant discrimination function in an area of greatly reduced performance (about .62, with chance performance in this task at .50). That is, infant speech sound discrimination performance, which is optimal at levels around normal conversational speech, are considerably reduced when the speech input is presented at intensity levels that are only 15 to 20 dB below conversational speech. Adult discrimination remains at the maximum level even with reductions in intensity of the speech sounds much greater than 20 dB.

The latter result was supported by another study (Nozza, Rossman, & Bond, 1991) in which a speech-sound discrimination threshold procedure was used. The threshold procedure is modeled after the traditional threshold procedure used in a detection task such as for thresholds on an audiogram (Kile & Beauchaine, 1991). In this adaptation, the speech sounds are varied in intensity in the same way that tones are varied in audiometry. An estimate of the intensity at which the infants can correctly discriminate the phonemes about 50% of the time is made with this technique. The speech-sound discrimination threshold procedure was shown to be reliable and valid in two studies of discrimination in noise (Nozza et al., 1990; Nozza, Miller, et al., 1991) and is a more efficient means of estimating differences in performance between groups. Rather than testing at many different intensity levels to develop functions such as shown in Figure 1, the adaptive threshold procedure is designed to estimate the inten-

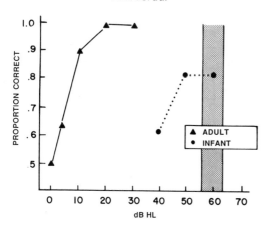

Figure 1. Performance versus intensity in a speech-sound discrimination task, /ba/ versus /da/, for infants and adults. The shaded bar approximates the long-term average amplitude, in dB HL, of typical conversational speech. Infant performance is below the maximum level within 20 dB of conversational speech, suggesting that even a shift in infant hearing of less than 20 dB could cause difficulties in the discrimination of simple speech sounds. (From Nozza, R. J. [1988]). Auditory deficit in infants with OME: More than a "mild" hearing loss. In D. J. Lim, C. D. Bluestone, J. O. Klein, & J. W. Nelson (Eds.), *Proceedings of the Fourth International Symposium on Recent Advances in Otitis Media* (pp. 376–379). Toronto: B.C. Decker.

sity level that corresponds to a predetermined performance level; in this case, 50% correct. In the discrimination threshold study, two speech sound contrasts were tested; /ba/ versus /ga/ and /ba/ versus /da/. The infant-adult differences in speech-sound discrimination thresholds were 25 and 28 dB, respectively (Table 1). The results were consistent with the earlier study in demonstrating that infants require considerably greater signal intensity to perform the task at the same level of accuracy as adults. Much of the difference between infants and adults could be attributed to differences in behavioral detection thresholds (about 15 to 20 dB) for the speech sounds (Nozza, 1988; Rossman, 1992). However, this does not account completely for infant-adult differences in threshold for discrimination, so the more complex process of discrimination requires even greater signal intensity relative to detection threshold for the infants to perform at the same level as the adults. It is apparent that infants can discriminate well when speech sounds are at conversational levels, but performance is poorer when the levels are reduced even by a small amount. It would be reasonable to assume, based on these data, that whatever processes are at work in the young infant to develop and narrow an appropriate phonetic inventory, they would have to be affected by even a small reduction in the input level of speech such as might accompany mild hearing loss.

Susceptibility to a simulated high frequency hearing impairment was demonstrated in a study of infant speech-sound discrimination by Rossman (1992). Infant performance was much poorer than adults when speech sound stimuli were filtered in a way that represented a mild-to-moderate, sloping high frequency hearing loss. The effects differed for two different stimuli pairs (/ba/ versus /ga/ and /da/ versus /ga/), depending on the acoustic cues underlying the phonetic distinctions, but in general, infant discrimination thresholds were elevated relative to those of adults in both the simulated hearing loss condition (filtered stimuli) and in the normal hearing condition (full stimuli).

The use of masking noise has also added to our understanding of the effects of hearing loss on auditory capabilities (e.g., Fabry & Van Tasell, 1986). In two studies of infant discrimination of /ba/ versus /ga/ in noise, it was demonstrated that infants required greater signal-to-noise ratio (S/N), which is greater stimulus intensity above the noise

Table 1. Thresholds for infants and thresholds for adults in a speech sound discrimination task (in dB SPL).

		Stimulus Pairs	
		/ba-da/	/ba-ga/
INFANTS	M	39.3	35.1
	(SD)	(6.5)	(5.6)
ADULTS	M	11.8	9.7
	(SD)	(5.1)	(3.7)
DIFFERENCE		27.5	25.4

Adapted from: Nozza, R. J., Rossman, R. N. F., & Bond, L. C. (1991). Infant-adult differences in unmasked thresholds for the discrimination of CV syllable pairs. *Audiology, 30,* 102–112.

level, than adults to perform optimally (Nozza, Miller, et al., 1990) or to reach speech-sound discrimination-in-noise threshold (Nozza et al., 1990; Nozza et al., 1991). By imposing the same masking noise on both infants and adults, the same degree of "hearing impairment" has been imposed on both groups. The infant-adult difference in threshold for discrimination of the speech sounds in noise, therefore, suggests that the infants are at a disadvantage relative to adults when performing the task of distinguishing one speech sound from the other under conditions that simulate the same degree of peripheral hearing loss.

Of course, the masking noise in this kind of simulation could affect the infants in a different way. It is possible that the masking noise served as a distraction to the infants and caused a reduction in performance unrelated to sensory processes. However, the effects of unfavorable (i.e., noisy) environments on infant speech perception abilities is a limitation to consider in it's own right. Consider the infant growing up in a noisy home environment. Our data (Nozza et al., 1990; Nozza, Miller, et al., 1991) suggest that noise causes greater interference with the process of phonetic discrimination in infants than would be predicted based on adult data. Combining a mild hearing loss, in which sounds are reduced in intensity, in an environment where there are high levels of background noise, could magnify this difficulty. The need for greater S/N was determined when speech sounds were presented at intensity levels shown to be optimal for normal hearing infants in a quiet environment. It is not difficult to speculate on the potential effects of the situation in which there is mild hearing impairment, pushing the infant performance down even under ideal circumstances, coupled with background noise for which infants require a better S/N.

The requirement for greater signal intensity and for greater S/N when a background noise is present indicates that infants cannot tolerate a degraded signal as well as adults when making simple speech sound discriminations. Given that infants are in the process of developing a phonetic code, learning the syntax of a language system that depends on discrimination of phonetic contrasts in initial and final syllable positions and so on, and trying to assign meaning to words, the breakdown of discrimination ability with only slight reductions in signal magnitude certainly is consistent with the hypothesis that mild hearing impairment can affect the development of speech and language in infants.

Summary

In this article, I have presented a case for the likelihood that mild hearing loss in infants could have long-lasting effects on the perception of speech and acquisition of language. The evidence that infants can demonstrate sophisticated abilities with regard to the analysis of speech sounds under normal conditions, but fare poorly under conditions that represent only mild degradation of the speech signal, has been offered as support for that case. Mild hearing loss, a sensory impairment, causes the infant to be unable to perform an activity, speech perception, in a manner considered normal. That is, mild hearing impairment, as modeled by stimulus manipulations, causes a disability, as defined by WHO (1980) and ASHA (1993), under laboratory conditions. Although the discrimination of speech sounds is a more complex task than detection, it probably is less complex than other processes that must be used to acquire language over the first few years of life. The possibility that the effects of simulated mild hearing loss would affect those processes at least as much as it affects simple phoneme discrimination must be considered. In other words, the effects of mild hearing loss on discrimination of two different phonemes

(Nozza, 1987a; Nozza et al., 1990; Nozza, Miller, et al., 1991; Nozza, Rossman, & Bond, 1991) would be equalled, or surpassed, when testing more sophisticated speech perception processes.

The importance of simple speech perception abilities early in life has been discussed by Menyuk (1980), Naremore (1979) and Strange (1986) in the context of the effects of the fluctuating hearing loss associated with otitis media with effusion. Speech is a stream of acoustic energy that must be segmented according to phonetic elements. In addition, the same phonetic elements may be acoustically different when spoken by different speakers or even when spoken by the same speaker in different syllabic contexts or with different stress and intonation patterns. This invariant characteristic of the speech signal, which is readily perceived by infants (Kuhl, 1992), may be disrupted or lost when speech input is degraded (Menyuk, 1980).

Not only are the infants charged with using phonetic cues to differentiate between syllables and words, but syntactic and semantic information must be derived as well. The structure of the native language typically is derived by the infant based on exposure to the language through the auditory channel. Strange (1986) suggests the possibility that with even mild hearing impairment such as accompanies otitis media, subtle acoustic differences that signal important phonetic information may be inaudible. This inaudibility of cues distorts the speech input and may lead to a delay or a deviation in the way the rules of language are inferred. Even though we may not totally understand how much of that signal is essential to the infant during early language acquisition, the data suggest that enough information is lost with only a "mild" hearing loss to cause a severe reduction in phoneme discrimination.

The implication of these findings is that infants listening in typical speech environments are operating near the limits of their ability, at least as can be determined using behavioral measures. Even small reductions or degradations of the speech signal, unimportant to adult listeners, appear to have the potential for large negative effects in infant speech perception. To the extent that the work of Kuhl et al. (1992) suggests that the infant is processing and building on acoustic-phonetic information during the first 6 months of life, the reduction in discrimination performance of young infants with only slightly reduced stimulus intensities should be taken seriously. The real effects can only be speculated upon, and the window, or critical period for fine-tuning the phonetic system, may be quite wide. However, even a delay in the acquisition of language could cause learning problems and/or psychosocial difficulties that will not be overcome later.

For the person involved in intervention with young infants and children, the data provided in this article do not give clear guidance or justification for specific therapies or extraordinary measures. The message, rather, is that the research data suggest two things that are relevant to the issue of the effects of mild hearing impairment. First, infants during the first year of life process and integrate the information in the speech signal into a basis for linguistic competence. Second, experimentally controlled simulation of mild hearing loss causes a breakdown in basic speech perception abilities among infants. It is likely that a prolonged period of time with distorted speech input could cause difficulty for the infants in abstracting the phonetic inventory of the language to which they are exposed and might even disrupt the development of syntax and semantics. Until, and if, it is shown that infants can overcome the effects of mild hearing impairment, whether temporary as in otitis media or permanent, efforts to identify infants with mild hearing impairment and to develop strategies for intervention should be encouraged. As Naremore (1979) simply, but quite appropriately, said, "If a child does not receive the entire auditory signal, then some information is being lost" (p. 59). Until someone proves that the lost information is irrelevant to the most important auditory task with which infants are charged, acquisition of language, clinicians must assume that the lost information is highly relevant and that infants with even a "mild" hearing impairment should be identified, monitored, and managed accordingly.

References

American Speech-Language-Hearing Association. (1993). *Report on audiologic screening.* The Ad Hoc Committee on Screening for Hearing Impairment, Handicap and Middle Ear Disorders. Rockville, MD: ASHA.

Anteby, I., Hafner, H., Pratt, H., & Uri, H. (1986). Auditory brainstem evoked potentials in evaluating the central effects of middle ear effusion. *Journal of Pediatric Otorhinolaryngology, 12,* 1–11.

Aslin R. N., Pisoni, D. B., & Jusczyk, P. W. (1983). Auditory development and speech perception in infancy. In M. M. Haith & J. J. Campos (Eds.), *Handbook of child psychology: Vol. II: Infancy and Developmental Psychology* (pp. 573–687). New York: Wiley and Sons.

Barlow, H. B. (1975). Visual experience and cortical development. *Nature, 258,* 199–204.

Bess, F. H. (1985). The minimally hearing-impaired child. *Ear and Hearing, 6,* 43–47.

Blair, J. C. Peterson, M. E., & Viehweg, S. H. (1985). The effects of mild sensorineural hearing loss on academic performance of young school-age children. *Volta Review, 87*(2), 87–93.

Bluestone, C. D., Fria, T. J., Arjona, S. K., Casselbrant, M. L., Schwartz, D. M., Ruben, R. J., Gates, G. A., Downs, M. P., Northern, J. L., Jerger, J. F., Paradise, J. L., Bess, F. H., Kenworthy, O. T., & Rogers, K. D. (1986). Controversies in screening for middle ear disease and hearing loss in children. *Pediatrics, 77,* 57–70.

Chambers, R. D., Rowan, L. E., Matthies, M. L., & Novak, M. A. (1989). Auditory brain-stem responses in children with previous otitis media. *Archives of Otolaryngology, 115,* 452–457.

Clopton, B. M., & Silverman, M. S. (1977). Plasticity of binaural interaction. II. Critical period and changes in midline response. *Journal of Neurophysiology, 40,* 1275–1280.

Fabry, D. A., & Van Tasell, D. J. (1986). Masked and filtered simulation of hearing loss: Effects on consonant recognition. *Journal of Speech and Hearing Research, 29,* 170–178.

Folsom, R. C., Weber, B. A., & Thompson, G. (1983). Auditory brainstem responses in children with early recurrent middle ear disease. *Annals of Otology Rhinology Laryngology, 92,* 249–253.

Fria, T. J., Cantekin, E. I., & Eichler, J. A. (1985). Hearing acuity of children with otitis media with effusion. *Archives of Otolaryngology, 111,* 10–16.

Friel-Patti, S., & Finitzo, T. (1990). Language learning in a prospective study of otitis media with effusion in the first two years of life. *Journal of Speech and Hearing Research, 33,* 188-194.

Gottlieb, G. (1981). The role of early experience in species-specific perceptual development. In R. M. Aslin, J. R. Alberts, & M. R. Peterson (Eds.), *Development of perception: Psychobiological perspectives* (Vol. I, pp. 5–44). New York: Academic Press.

Grobstein, P., & Chow, K. L. (1975). Receptive field development and individual experience. *Science, 190,* 352–358.

Gunnarson, A. D., & Finitzo, T. (1991). Conductive hearing loss during infancy: Effects on later auditory brain stem electrophysiology. *Journal of Speech and Hearing Research, 34,* 1207–1215.

Hecox, K., & Burkard, R. (1982). Developmental dependencies of the human brainstem auditory evoked response. *Annals of the New York Academy of Science, 388,* 538–556.

Kile, J. E., & Beauchaine, K. L. (1991). Identification, assessment, and management of hearing impairment in infants and toddlers. *Infant-Toddler Intervention, 1*(1), 61–81.

Kuhl, P. K. (1992). Psychoacoustics and speech perception: Internal standards, perceptual anchors, and prototypes. In L. A. Werner & E. W. Rubel (Eds.), *Developmental psychoacoustics* (pp. 293–332). Washington, DC: American Psychological Association.

Kuhl, P. K., Williams, K. A., Lacerda, F., Stevens, K. N., & Lindblom, B. (1992). Linguistic experience alters phonetic perception in infants by 6 months of age. *Science, 255,* 606–608.

Lenhardt, M. L., Shaia, F. T., & Abedi, E. (1985). Brain-stem evoked response waveform variation associated with recurrent otitis media. *Archives of Otolaryngology, 111,* 315–316.

Menyuk, P. (1980). Effect of persistent otitis media on language development. *Annals of Otorhinolaryngology, 89*(2) (Suppl. 68), 257–263.

Montgomery, P. E., & Matkin, N. D. (1992). Hearing-impaired children in the schools: Integrated or isolated? In F. H. Bess, & J. W. Hall, III (Eds.), *Screening children for auditory function* (pp. 477–492). Nashville: Bill Wilkerson Center Press.

Moore, D. R. (1991). Hearing loss and auditory brain stem development. In M. Hanson (Ed.), *The fetal and neonatal brainstem* (pp. 161–184). New York: Cambridge University Press.

Moore, D. R., Hutchings, M. E., & Meyer, S. E. (1991). Binaural masking level differences in children with a history of otitis media. *Audiology, 30,* 91–101.

Morrongiello, B. A., & Rocca, P. T. (1987a). Infants' localization of sounds in the median vertical plane: Estimates of minimum audible angle. *Journal of Exceptional Child Psychology, 43,* 181–193.

Morrongiello, B. A., & Rocca, P. T. (1987b). Infants' localization of sounds in the horizontal plane: Effects of auditory and visual cues. *Child Development, 58,* 918–927.

Naremore, R. C. (1979). Influences of hearing impairment on early language development. *Annals of Otorhinolaryngology, 88*(Suppl. 60), 5(1), 54–63.

Northern, J. L., & Downs, M. P. (1991). *Hearing in children* (4th ed.). Baltimore: Williams & Wilkins.

Nozza, R. J. (1987a). Infant speech-sound discrimination testing: Effects of stimulus intensity and procedural model on measures of performance. *Journal of the Acoustical Society of America, 81,* 1928–1939.

Nozza, R. J. (1987b). The binaural masking level difference in infants and adults: Developmental change in binaural hearing. *Infant Behavior and Development, 10,* 105–110.

Nozza, R. J. (1988). Auditory deficit in infants with OME: More than a "mild" hearing loss. In D. J. Lim, C. D. Bluestone, J. O. Klein, & J. W. Nelson (Eds.), *Proceedings of the Fourth International Symposium on Recent Advances in Otitis Media* (pp. 376–379). Toronto: B.C. Decker.

Nozza, R. J., Miller, S. L., Rossman, R. N. F., & Bond, L. C. (1991). Reliability and validity of the infant speech-sound discrimination-in-noise threshold test procedure. *Journal of Speech and Hearing Research, 34,* 643–650.

Nozza, R. J., Rossman, R. N. F., & Bond, L. C. (1991). Infant-adult differences in unmasked thresholds for the discrimination of CV syllable pairs. *Audiology, 30,* 102–112.

Nozza, R. J., Rossman, R. N. F., Bond, L. C., & Miller, S. L. (1990). Infant speech-sound discrimination in noise. *Journal of the Acoustical Society of America, 87,* 339–350.

Nozza, R. N, Wagner, E. F., & Crandell, M. A. (1988). Binaural release from masking for a speech sound in infants, preschoolers, and adults. *Journal of Speech and Hearing Research, 31,* 212–218.

Nozza, R. J., & Wilson, W. R. (1984). Masked and unmasked puretone thresholds of infants and adults: Development of auditory frequency selectivity and sensitivity. *Journal of Speech and Hearing Research, 27,* 613–622.

Paradise, J. L. (1981). Otitis media during early life: How hazardous to development? A critical review of the evidence. *Pediatrics, 68,* 869–873.

Rossman, R. N. F. (1992). The effect of simulated mild-to-moderate high-frequency hearing loss on the discrimination of speech sounds by infants. Unpublished doctoral dissertation, University of Pittsburgh.

Salamy, A., Mendelson, T., & Tooley, W. H. (1982). Developmental profiles for the brainstem auditory evoked potential. *Early Human Development, 6,* 331–339.

Schneider, B. A., & Trehub, S. E. (1992). Sources of developmental change in auditory sensitivity. In L. A. Werner & E. W. Rubel (Eds.), *Developmental psychoacoustics* (pp. 3–46). Washington, DC: American Psychological Association.

Silverman, M. S., & Clopton, B. M. (1977). Plasticity of binaural interaction. I. Effect of early deprivation. *Journal of Neurophysiology, 40*, 1266–1274.

Strange, W. (1986). Speech input and the development of speech perception. In J. F. Kavanagh (Ed.), *Otitis media and child development* (pp. 12–26). Parkton, MD: York Press.

Teas, D. C., Klein, A. J., & Kramer, S. J. (1982). An analysis of auditory brainstem responses in infants. *Hearing Research, 7*, 19–54.

Webster, D. B. (1983). Auditory neuronal sizes after a unilateral conductive hearing loss. *Experimental Neurology, 79*, 130–140.

Webster, D. B. (1988). Conductive hearing loss affects the growth of the cochlear nuclei over an extended period of time. *Journal of Hearing Research, 32*, 185–192.

Webster, D. B., & Webster, M. (1977). Neonatal sound deprivation affects brain stem auditory nuclei. *Archives of Otolaryngology, 103*, 392–396.

Webster, D. B., & Webster, M. (1979). Effects of neonatal conductive hearing loss on brain stem auditory nuclei. *Annals of Otorhinolaryngology, 88*, 684–688.

Werker, J. F., & Lalonde, S. C. (1988). Cross-language speech perception: Initial capabilities and developmental change. *Developmental Psychology, 24*, 672–683.

Werker, J. F., & Tees, R. C. (1984). Cross-language speech perception: Evidence for perceptual reorganization during the first year of life. *Infant Behavior and Development, 7*, 49–63.

Werner, L. A. (1992). Interpreting developmental psychoacoustics. In L. A. Werner & E. W. Rubel (Eds.), *Developmental psychoacoustics* (pp. 47–88). Washington, DC: American Psychological Association.

World Health Organization (WHO). (1980). International classification of impairments, disabilities, and handicaps: A manual of classification relating to the consequences of disease. *World Health Organization*, 25–43

Address correspondence to:
Robert J. Nozza, Ph.D.,
Department of Communication Sciences and Disorders,
565 Aderhold Hall,
University of Georgia,
Athens, GA 30602-7152

Issues in Amplification for Infants and Toddlers

Kathryn Laudin Beauchaine, M.A., CCC-A
Kris Donaughy, M.A., CCC-A

Boys Town National Research Hospital
Omaha, Nebraska

Use of amplification is a key component in the educational management of infants and toddlers who have hearing loss. Information is presented about auditory development, the goals of amplification, how amplification is selected and assessed, as well as practical pointers to enhance hearing-aid use and adjustment.

Physicists have developed intricate equations to describe and explain extraordinary phenomena that occur in our universe. There is no equation, however, to describe the complex interaction of hearing loss, developmental level, and environmental factors on the acquisition of an infant's speech and language skills. Our goal is not to attempt to provide such an equation. Our goal is to discuss some issues related to fitting amplification on infants and toddlers and how benefit from amplification is assessed. Case studies will be used to illustrate the discussion topics.

Although extensive efficacy studies are lacking, the notion that early identification and remediation of hearing loss facilitates the development of communication skills is well accepted (NIH, 1993; Ross, 1990). Technolnology exists to identify hearing loss within the first days of life. See Kile and Beauchaine (1991) for a review of the methods used to test infants and toddlers.

It is important to acknowledge that fitting amplification is only one aspect of care for children who have permanent hearing loss. Space does not permit a review of therapeutic techniques for remediation of hearing loss, generally called aural habilitation or rehabilitation. This discussion will focus on normal auditory development, effects of hearing loss on communication, amplification selection and fitting strategies, and a review of case studies.

Normal Auditory Development

The human ear is fully formed and functional during the third trimester of pregnancy. Auditory awareness has been demonstrated in infants during the first days of life (see Clifton, 1992, for an overview). As the infant matures and gains motor and cognitive skills, progressively more complex responses to sound can be observed.

A hearing infant should demonstrate an obvious response to environmental sounds and familiar voices, such as quieting, ceasing activity, or eye widening. It has been reported that the hearing infant with normal developmental milestones will orient to some sounds soon after birth. This behavior changes during the first 2 months of life and decreases at 6–8 weeks. Around 3–4 months of age head orienting reappears, and visual search to sound sources emerges by 2–3 months of age, and infants demonstrate slow head turns toward sound sources by 4–6 months (see Clifton, 1992). Also, by 4–6 months infants should demonstrate recognition of familiar voices by responding with generalized excitement. By 6–9 months they should begin to recognize their own name and familiar intonation patterns. At 9–12 months infants should develop emerging comprehension of familiar words and phrases, and attempt imitation of familiar speech sounds (e.g., bye-bye, ma-ma). By 1 year of age they should begin to recognize some familiar sounds, words, and phrases. Examples include excitement or anticipation in response to food preparation routines, lip puckering in response to a harsh voice (no-no), and anticipatory response to familiar phrases (i.e., want up, time to go bye-bye). Infants babble and coo, even in the presence of significant hearing loss. Depending on the degree of the hearing loss, differences in sound production have been observed (Cole, 1992; Oller, Eilers, Bull, & Carney, 1985). For an infant who has normal hearing, vocalization should increase in frequency and variety as the auditory feedback mechanism develops. A 1-year-old infant should imitate some common nonlinguistic sounds, such as laughter, raspberry sounds, and clicking. This is also the age when one-word sentences emerge.

Effects of Hearing Loss on Communication Skills and the Implications for Early Intervention Specialists

Parental Observations

Parental reports about how children respond to sound vary depending on the degree of hearing loss. Infants who have severe to profound hearing loss tend to be identified at younger ages than those who have milder losses. For example, Mace, Wallace, Whan, and Stelmachowicz (1991) reported that the median age of identification of severe to profound hearing loss was less than 18 months of age. Infants with less severe losses were identified at later ages.

Parents often describe infants who have severe to profound hearing loss as good babies, good sleepers, or sound sleepers. Many of these infants tend to be very visually alert, unless there is a concomitant vision problem.

A frequent comment by parents of children who have significant hearing loss is that the infant does not seem to be aware of sounds in the environment. For example, the infant does not notice when someone enters a room unless the baby sees the person, a light is turned on, or the crib is touched. As a toddler, the child may lean against a loudspeaker (to feel the vibrations) or turn a radio, TV, or stereo louder than anyone else can tolerate it. Of course, some of these behaviors also may occur when hearing is normal.

Speech Perception, Production, and Language Learning

Sometimes hearing loss is not suspected until a toddler is noticeably delayed in speech development. In general, the poorer the hearing, the more difficult it will be for the child to develop speech and language. Given a specific degree of hearing loss, however, there are many uncertainties as to the development of speech and language. Pure-tone thresholds do not predict the clarity of the speech signal. Two children with the same audiogram may have vastly different sound production or speech perception skills depending on the audibility of the speech spectrum in the unaided and aided conditions and their sound recognition skills. Audiological tests, completed with the child's hearing aid(s), delineate which speech sounds may be within the child's range of audibility and may provide some information about the clarity of the speech signal.

Hearing loss will also interact in an unpredictable way with the child's other disabilities. For example, if a child has oral-motor difficulties that affect speech production, it may be difficult for the clinician to sort out the interaction between auditory perceptual errors and the limitations of speech motor skills. Also, the child's gross motor skills may affect apparent auditory responsiveness. For example, an infant with limited head control or limb movement may not be physically able to demonstrate overt responses to sound.

Implications for Early Intervention Specialists

Incorporating the development of auditory skills into the Individual Family Service Plan (IFSP) and assisting in the management of amplification devices is a challenge to the early intervention specialist. Therapy goals and techniques must consider the child's cognitive, language, motor, and auditory status. Also, therapy goals should be considered within the context of the child's daily routine to take advantage of sounds and speech which occur in his or her environment.

There are few developmental assessment tools that provide normative data for children with impaired hearing or are not biased against those who have hearing loss (Diefendorf et al., 1990). With any assessment tool, it is important to distinguish verbal, listening-dependent tasks from other performance items. Audiologists and developmental specialists should consult with aural (re)habilitation support staff to select appropriate assessment tools and obtain guidance for appropriate services. Some early-intervention specialists are not specifically trained to provide services for hearing-impaired infants and toddlers and, therefore, they should also seek guidance from hearing support professionals.

Communication Alternatives

Primary choices in the mode of communication include: oral/aural, total communication, or augmentative communication. The oral/aural method uses speech for expression and audition and lip-reading only for reception. The total communication approach uses a combination of sign language, speech, and audition for both reception and expression. Augmentative communication uses other devices, such as communication boards or computers of varying complexity, for reception and/or expression.

There are other communication choices, such as cued speech, which are less commonly used. A basic discussion of communication options is available in Schwartz (1987).

Hearing Aids

Basic Components

Hearing aids are amplifiers. They can be selected or adjusted to amplify specific frequency regions depending on the degree of hearing loss. The basic components of hearing aids include: a microphone, a receiver, and a power source (battery). The style choices include: behind-the-ear (BTE) or ear-level, body-type, bone conduction (BC), in-the-canal (ITC), and in-the-ear (ITE).

Most children under the age of 5 years are fitted with BTE hearing aids (Martin & Gravel, 1989). These BTE aids are coupled to a child's ear with a soft earmold that can be re-made to ensure a good fit as the child grows. Some children may be fitted with a body-style aid if there are multihandicapping conditions or ear deformities that preclude use of a BTE aid. The major disadvantage of body-style aids is that the microphone typically is located on the chest which results in a poorer quality signal because of amplified clothing and body noise. If a child has atresia (congenital absence) of the ear canals or chronic problems with ear drainage, a BC hearing aid can be selected. Typically, ITC and ITE hearing aids are not recommended for very young children because of the need for frequent recasing with growth and because of the danger from the hard casings if a fall should occur. Additional detail about choosing amplification for young children is found in Roush and Gravel (1994).

The Goal of Amplification and Factors That Limit the Goal

The primary goal of amplification is to amplify speech signals and other important environmental sounds to within a comfortable listening range for the user. The degree of the hearing loss may make it difficult to meet this goal. Those who have profound hearing loss may hear only the louder components of speech or warning signals, such as alarms or car horns, even with powerful hearing aids. For those who have mild, moderate, or severe hearing loss, all or most of average conversational speech may be audible, at least under ideal listening conditions. High frequency components of speech may be difficult to amplify adequately. Audibility does not guarantee accurate perception, that is, there may be problems in the ear's ability to decipher a signal, even when the signal is audible. Thus, the comment frequently expressed by people who have hearing loss is: "I can hear you but I cannot understand you."

Typically, the long-term average speech spectrum (LTASS) contains energy in the frequency region between 125 and 8000 Hz (Olsen, Hawkins, & Van Tasell, 1987). Vowel sounds tend to have more low-frequency energy, and consonants have more high-frequency energy. The low frequencies also carry information about the suprasegmentals of speech, which are the temporal characteristics that communicate rhythm, intonation, and stress. The intensity and frequency content of speech fluctuates considerably in an individual speaker. Characteristics of the long-term average speech spectrum also vary from speaker to speaker. There may be gender effects, with male voices typically having lower fundamental frequencies than females. Overall, children's voices tend to have higher fundamental frequencies than those of male or female adults.

Distance, background noise, and room reverberation are three factors that can negatively impact one's ability to hear. Obviously, the closer the listener is to the sound source, the louder the sound. The effect of distance on the intensity of sound can be calculated mathematically. Furthermore, background noise and reverberation (Hawkins & Yacullo, 1984) also can interfere greatly with the quality or audibility of a signal. A child-care room with many children is a more difficult listening environment for the child who has hearing loss compared to a child with normal hearing.

Visual deficits and poor lighting can reduce the information that would otherwise be gained from observing the speaker's face. In addition to speech-reading cues, visual information includes indications of the mood of the speaker.

How Hearing Aids Are Selected and Tested

There is no universal, standard procedure for fitting hearing aids for any population. Most of the guidelines that have been developed and studied focus on adults (Byrne & Dillon, 1986; Cox, 1988; Humes & Hackett, 1990; Skinner, 1988; Sullivan, Levitt, Hwang, & Hennessey, 1988), and there remain many uncertainties as to what is the most appropriate fitting for any given individual or hearing loss. In most cases, hearing loss in both ears warrants that both ears should be fitted with hearing aids. A typical hearing aid evaluation should include electroacoustic analysis of the hearing aids, behavioral or real-ear hearing aid performance measures, and word recognition testing.

An electroacoustic analysis should be completed to determine if the hearing aid is working within manufacturer specifications and to document the gain and output characteristics of the device at use settings. The hearing aid is attached to a 2-cm^3 coupler in a test box. Analysis is performed according to a format prescribed by the American National Standards Institute (ANSI, 1987).

As stated previously, a general goal of fitting amplification is to make speech audible. The selection of hearing aids takes into account the required frequency-gain characteristics for a particular hearing loss, that is, which frequencies require amplification and how much. Another consideration is the maximum output (saturation response) beyond which sound will not be amplified further (Seewald, 1991; Skinner, 1988). Appropriate setting of the saturation response is critical to avoid loudness discomfort and/or potential damage to the auditory system. In addition, the availability of features, such as directional microphones, system flexibility, compatibility with assistive listening devices, and overall size also are considered.

An increasingly popular way to select frequency-gain characteristics and maximum output is the desired sensation level method (DSL) which was developed by Seewald and colleagues (Hawkins, Morrison, Halligan, & Cooper, 1989; Ross & Seewald, 1988; Seewald, 1992; Seewald, Ross, & Spiro, 1985; Seewald, Ross, & Stelmachowicz, 1987; Seewald, Zelisko, Ramji, & Jamieson, 1991; Stelmachowicz & Seewald, 1991). For this method, the audiologist enters the child's hearing threshold levels into a computer program (Seewald et al., 1991), and the program recommends target values on a frequency-by-frequency basis so that average conversational speech would most likely be audible and comfortable. A graph can be obtained which shows how well desired amplification levels are met and what portions of the long-term average speech spectrum would be audible. The DSL method also provides target values for the saturation response.

To assess aided compensation or to verify the hearing aid fitting, there are two primary test methods: behavioral, aided threshold tests and real-ear probe-tube microphone measures. For behavioral tests, the child's thresholds are obtained with hearing aids in place using a developmentally appropriate method. Once the sound-field aided thresholds are obtained, they are compared to the unaided thresholds and target values. The term functional gain is used to describe the difference between aided and unaided sound-field thresholds (Hawkins, Montgomery, Prosek, & Walden, 1987; Humes & Kirn, 1990; Stuart, Durieux-Smith, & Stenstrom, 1990). This information allows the audiologist to make some predictions about the levels at which the child can detect the presence of sound at certain frequencies. Sound-field aided testing does not provide measurement of the maximum sound pressure level (output) produced by the hearing aid in the child's ear.

Real-ear probe-tube microphone measures are not behavioral measures. Rather, a probe tube is placed in the ear and a stimulus (tone or complex noise) is delivered to the ear (see Hawkins & Northern, 1992). Output in the ear canal, after the input signal has been amplified by the hearing aid, is measured across frequencies. Probe-tube microphone measures allow the audiologist to demonstrate the audibility of average conversational speech and the real-ear saturation response (RESR). This method has numerous advantages over obtaining behavioral aided thresholds, not the least of which is that minimal patient cooperation and patient time is needed to complete the test.

Depending on the outcome of the aided tests, changes in hearing aid settings or volume-control settings may be recommended. Additionally, some alterations in the tone hook or earmold might be recommended.

The child's word recognition ability should be evaluated as soon as possible to estimate the clarity of the aided speech signal. Word recognition skills may be assessed in the sound field with the child's hearing aids at use settings. Typically, this testing is performed at the level of average conversational speech. Assessment tools include picture-pointing tasks such as the Northwestern University Children's Perception of Speech (NU-CHIPS) (Elliot & Katz, 1980) or the Word Intelligibility by Picture Identification (WIPI) (Ross & Lerman, 1971). If a child's speech is intelligble, the PB-K (phonetically balanced-kindergarten) word list may be used. The completion and interpretation of these tests is affected by the child's speech, language, and cognitive skills. Care should be taken to determine that the task is developmentally and language appropriate, and results need to be interpreted with caution. Further, single-word recognition tasks, completed in sound-treated rooms, may not predict the child's perception of connected speech in a typical listening environment.

Misconceptions About Hearing Aids

A hearing aid cannot cure or correct hearing loss, because it can only amplify sound. It cannot alter how the inner ear processes the speech signal. Misconceptions about hearing aids are:

1. *Hearing aids restore hearing to normal.* The danger of this misconception is that expectations may exceed performance, frustrating both the child and the parent (and the teacher). The child may be expected to perform as a child who has normal hearing in all situations.
2. *Hearing aids are not effective at all.* This misconception relegates the hearing aid to the level of a symbol of hearing loss, rather than as part of a solution. Persons who have this notion tend to shout at those who wear hearing aids. Parents may not be motivated to have their child use hearing aids because the hearing aids are not viewed as helpful. The danger is

that expectations of the child's performance with the hearing aids, if worn, will be low, and the child may not be sufficiently challenged.
3. *Hearing aids help, but will not always be needed.* Although hopeful, this notion creates a distorted view of the future and reflects poor understanding of the hearing aid's function. Hearing aids do not make hearing improve over time.
4. *The child will become dependent on the hearing aids and will not be able to go without them.* This statement is true only in the sense that children do tend to depend on their hearing aids to listen in the same way that many depend on glasses to see.

Initial Hearing-Aid Use

Parental acceptance of the hearing loss and their child's use of hearing aids may be the determining factor in the child's successful adjustment to hearing aids. The parents, after all, are the people who have to put the hearing aids on the child each day, troubleshoot the hearing aids on a daily basis and take the child to audiology appointments. Parents need to be educated about the function and value of the hearing aids. Only then can they feel responsible for hearing-aid use and have realistic expectations about the possible outcome. Parents also should be informed of the dangers of accidental ingestion of hearing-aid batteries.

Each family's and each child's response to hearing-aid use is unique. It often is difficult to distinguish between the child who will not wear hearing aids and the parent who wants to avoid having the child use hearing aids.

Hearing aids should be introduced to the child in a quiet, supervised, and pleasant situation, (e.g., during a favorite activity). The early intervention specialist should provide suggestions for parents that will encourage hearing-aid use. It is critical to avoid parent-child power struggles with the hearing aid that may lead to negative feelings toward the hearing aid by all. Often, support and encouragement from other parents of children with hearing impairment is of great benefit as hearing-aid use is initiated.

Hearing aids can include some features that may make them more child-friendly. These features include: small tone hooks, tamper-resistant battery compartments, volume control covers, battery covers and miniaturized hearing aid casings. In some cases, size is dictated by the power of the instrument; however, circuit miniaturization allows powerful devices to be housed in increasingly smaller cases.

There are some ways to facilitate keeping the hearing aid on the child; for example, a product called Huggie Aids™ helps to hold the hearing aid behind the ear and close to the head. Toupee tape or double-sided tape can be used for the same purpose when placed between the hearing aid and the side of the head. Ribbons or eyeglass straps can be attached to binaural hearing aids to hold them behind the ears. Fishing line or dental floss can be tied to the hearing aid and secured on the back of the shirt with diaper pins to prevent loss or damage should the hearing aid and earmold be removed from the ear.

Acoustic feedback is often a problem, especially with a powerful hearing aid in a small ear. When acoustic feedback is noted, earmold insertion should be checked. Feedback also can occur if the earmold is too small or has a leak around the perimeter. As a temporary solution, a product such as Otoferm™ can be applied to the earmold to help maintain an acoustic seal. Some earmold materials provide better acoustic seals than others; soft molds are preferable for use with children. Cracked tubing also can cause feedback, as can a cracked hearing-aid case.

When feedback occurs, a reduction in the volume-control setting can appear to eliminate the problem. Although this will reduce the feedback, it also will reduce the gain of the hearing aid and may result in inadequate amplification. Persistent feedback due to poorly fitting earmolds indicates that the earmolds must be re-made. Some children, especially new users of earmolds and hearing aids, may frequently require new earmolds.

Young children may show an initial decrease in vocalizations as they adjust to listening to new sounds. The child may be alert to softer sounds and may be startled by loud sounds. Unless the child has hearing aids for both ears, localization of sounds will be difficult.

When aided appropriately, an infant with hearing loss will gradually step through the stages of auditory development, from awareness of sound to discrimination of different sounds (Manolsen, 1985; Schuyler et al., 1985). Speech skills also tend to develop in an orderly fashion (Cole, 1992). Depending on the degree of hearing loss and the aided results, a plateau in auditory skill development might occur. Overall developmental level will contribute further to the child's acquisition of auditory skills.

For a developmentally delayed child who has hearing loss, there is a distinction between chronological, developmental, and listening age. A 2-year-old child who was fitted with hearing aids at 1 year of age has a listening age of 1 year. Developmental factors may further limit performance expectations.

A Daily Hearing-Aid Listening Check

To ensure adequate function of the hearing aids, a daily listening check should be completed. The listening check is best done in a quiet environment so that the listener is not surprised by unexpected, loud sounds. Special precautions are warranted when listening to a powerful device. The steps are outlined below for an ear-level hearing aid.

1. Test the battery.
2. Reduce the volume-control setting to a minimum (off). Using a listening tube or hearing-aid stethoscope, slowly increase the volume until a signal is heard. Listen to the device for clarity of the signal while talking in an average conversational voice.
3. While listening, turn the device on and off at a comfortable volume control setting. Also, manipulate the volume-control wheel and listen for a clear and undistorted signal that is without significant internal noise. Be sure there are no dead spots. A motorboat sound may occur when the battery needs to be replaced. Some hearing aid circuitry may sound slightly noisy when there is no input signal.
4. Inspect the earmold to assure that it is clean and not cracked, ripped, or damaged.

Recognize that the hearing aid is fitted for the child and that all hearing aids do not sound the same. Therefore, depending on the degree and configuration of the hearing loss, the signal may sound unusual to someone who has normal hearing. Subtler problems in the hearing aid could cause it to be out of manufacturer specifications and still sound adequate in the listening check. Thus, the hearing aid should undergo an electroacoustic analysis periodically by the managing audiologist. Also, the settings on the hearing aid should be re-set following any repairs according to recommendations from the managing audiologist.

There is some equipment that will assist in caring for the hearing aid: a small dehumidifier device, a stethoscope or listening tube, a battery tester, an earmold blower, and a moisture protector. Each hearing aid comes with an instruction booklet providing operating information specific to each device. (A jeweler's screwdriver is helpful for making alterations in the internal settings recommended by the managing audiologist.)

A Troubleshooting Guide: Four Major Problems

No output. The most common cause of this problem is a dead (or absent) battery. Other causes include: the earmold tubing is occluded with a water droplet or ear debris; the volume is turned down; or the aid is turned off.

Low output. There are several reasons for reduced output: the volume-control setting may be low; the microphone port may be blocked; the earmold may be plugged with debris; or the battery may be weak.

Intermittent output. Humidity, dirt, or dust can cause "shorts." Humidity can be reduced by using a hearing-aid dehumidifier overnight. (Batteries should not be placed in the dehumidifier.) Dirt-related or dust-related problems sometimes can be corrected with a cleaning by the audiologist.

Noisy output. A battery that is losing its charge may cause a motorboat sound. Be sure that the hearing aid is not in the T (tele-coil) or "MT" (microphone plus telecoil) mode during the listening check or there will be a static noise.

Not all hearing-aid problems are easily remedied. The source of the above problems could also be faulty circuitry, requiring technical repairs.

Alternatives to Hearing Aids

Some children who have hearing loss benefit from the use of amplification or assistive communication devices other than, or in addition to, hearing aids. These are summarized below according to the purpose of the device, who may benefit, and how the device differs from traditional hearing aids.

Auditory Trainer (AT) or FM System

The FM system transmits a frequency-modulated (FM) signal from a microphone/transmitter to a receiver, which may be at some distance (100–300 feet). FM systems can be adjusted to function for those with a wide range of hearing loss (Lewis, 1991). The FM system allows the presentation of a signal that goes from the microphone to the ear regardless of background noise, reverberation, or distance. This improves the signal-to-noise ratio and eliminates the distance factor.

Traditionally, FM systems were used primarily in classrooms, with the teacher wearing the microphone/transmitter and the student wearing the receiver. In recent years, use has expanded to environments beyond the classroom, including in the home (Benoit, 1989; Frisbie et al., 1991; Madell, 1992).

Vibrotactile Device (VT)

Rather than amplifying and transmitting sound, vibrotactile units transform sound into vibration, which then is transmitted to the body via a wrist-band transducer or a band of transducers on the chest. VT devices can provide an indication of the presence of some sounds and speech (Smith, 1991; Weisenberger & Miller, 1987). VT devices can be used in conjunction with auditory trainers. These devices are used in structured settings with children who have very little residual hearing and who get little to no benefit from even the most powerful hearing aids.

Cochlear Implant (CI)

The cochlear implant is a device that receives sound and transmits it as an electrical impulse to the ear. Part of the device is worn on the body, including the microphone and processor, and part is surgically implanted in the skull with an electrode, or electrode array, inserted in the cochlea. CIs can provide stimulation that allows sound detection and for some, recognition of sound that is not possible with traditional hearing aids.

Those who have shown limited benefit from traditional amplification and have met certain audiological, health, and psychological criteria could be candidates for a CI (Beiter, Staller, & Dowell, 1991; Carney et al., 1991). Because it is difficult and time-consuming to set the CI, some level of cooperation from the child is necessary. Currently, only one device is approved for use with children and they must be at least 2 years of age.

Case Presentations

The cases described below illustrate some of the management issues related to children who have hearing loss. The names have been changed, and in some cases, less pertinent history information has been deleted. These children and their families receive support services as requested by the family; however, information regarding family participation has not been included in these discussions. (See Condon, 1991 for additional comments pertinent to young children who have multiple handicaps including hearing loss.)

Note that audiological evaluations should occur at least every 3 months for infants and toddlers. In some cases, more frequent appointments are necessary, especially during the initial stages following the identification of the hearing loss when the degree and configuration of the hearing loss is being delineated. Often short attention spans and habituation to test stimuli combine to yield a small window of opportunity to obtain reliable test data in any given session.

Lilly

Lilly was the product of a normal, full-term pregnancy. She had a history of recurrent otitis media, bronchiolitis, and reactive airway disease. At 16 months of age, she was noted to have hypotonia with marked developmental and cognitive delays. Magnetic resonance imaging (MRI) was normal. She was enrolled in a parent-child (PC) intervention program that included occupational (OT) and physical (PT) therapy.

At 21 months of age, Lilly was diagnosed with muscular dystrophy (MD), middle ear dysfunction requiring tympanostomy tubes, and severe hearing loss. Initial behavioral testing suggested moderate to severe hearing loss, which was substantiated with auditory brainstem response (ABR) testing, and use of amplification was initiated. Her behavioral audiogram is shown in Figure 1. Note that not all thresholds have been obtained due to limited test reliability.

Lilly initially was fitted with a hearing aid with frequency-gain characteristics and output selected according to DSL 2-cm^3 targets. Because her home environment was very noisy due to 11 siblings, she also had a trial with an FM system. Each device had clear advantages and disadvantages. The hearing aid was easy and uncomplicated to use, but the signal-to-noise ratio was poor. Lilly frequently removed the hearing aid. The FM system afforded a better signal in her noisy environment, but was more cumbersome. Her oral communication was limited by her hearing loss and by oral-motor problems. Following the identification of hearing loss, her parent-child intervention program was supplemented with input from a speech-language pathologist who had extensive experience in aural rehabilitation.

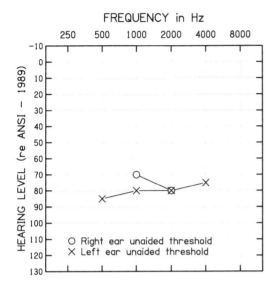

Figure 1. Unaided behavioral audiogram for Lilly, 21 months of age, with earphone thresholds (in dB HL) for selected frequencies. Right ear (o) and left ear (x) thresholds are plotted.

At 26 months of age, Lilly began to increase her sound production, and sign language was incorporated into her program. She demonstrated intentional and representational play.

Presently, Lilly continues to make slow progress with use of amplification. She alternates use of the FM system and hearing aid. She continues to be enrolled in an at-home PC intervention program with OT and PT services. Her audiological appointments focus on obtaining reliable behavioral thresholds for each ear.

Madison

Madison was the product of a full-term normal pregnancy. She had meconium aspiration at birth and remained in the hospital for 9 weeks after birth. There she required assisted ventilation, a gastrostomy tube, and extracorporeal membrane oxygenation (ECMO) therapy. She was noted to have high blood pressure (now resolving), only one functioning kidney, apnea, and a thyroid problem (resolved). During hospitalization, she was involved in a burn accident. By 10 weeks of age, she was receiving OT and PT. Just prior to hospital discharge an ABR test suggested significant, bilateral hearing loss. A follow-up test confirmed the presence of hearing loss with suspicion of a middle-ear (conductive) component to the loss. Following a month-long treatment with medication to resolve middle-ear dysfunction, a repeat ABR again suggested significant hearing loss. Subsequently, she was referred to her local education agency and enrolled in a PC intervention program. Madison was fitted with one hearing aid initially at 6 months of age and received two hearing aids after several months elapsed.

Because of health precautions, most of Madison's time after leaving the hospital was spent at home with her parents or in doctors' offices. Her specialty health visits included: pediatrics, feeding and growth (poor weight gain), neurology, endocrinology, urology, otolaryngology, plastic surgery (burns), and ophthalmology. At 18 months of age, she received tympanostomy tubes because of chronic otitis media.

An audiogram at 20 months of age, shown in Figure 2, revealed a severe hearing loss in both ears across frequencies. During a previous test session, it was apparent that the hearing loss was mixed (conductive and sensorineural components) even in the presence of patent tympanostomy tubes. Frequency gain characteristics and output for the hearing aid were chosen using the DSL method and recommended coupler values were matched. Because Madison was unwilling to have a probe placed in her ear, verification of target values was accomplished by using behavioral aided thresholds (also shown in Figure 2).

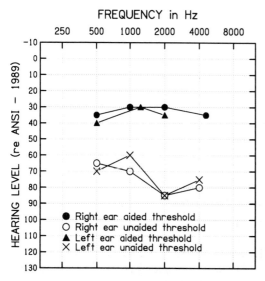

Figure 2. Unaided behavioral audiogram for Madison, 20 months of age, with earphone thresholds (in dB HL) for selected frequencies. Right ear (o) and left ear (x) thresholds are plotted, including right ear (filled triangles) and left ear (filled circles) aided thresholds.

At 18 months of age, a variety of communication-related tests were administered. These included the *MacArthur Communicative Development Inventory* (Dale & Thal, 1989), *(HELP)* (Parks, 1992), and *Parent-Infant Communication Scales* (Schuyler et al., 1985). Findings showed nonverbal communication, symbolic play, cognitive and social skills to be similar to a child 15–18 months without disabilities. Language abilities, both receptive and expressive, were at the 12–14 month level. Speech skills were at the 7–9 month level, with some concern that use of a pacifier was affecting speech production. Although Madison used some signs to communicate, she also showed improved listening skills. Motor skills, assessed at 18 months of age by an occupational therapist were at the 16-month level.

Currently, Madison is in a home-bound PC intervention program with a primary focus on aural habilitation. Improved speech skills is a continued focus of her therapy. She receives PT once a month for 1 hour, OT twice a month for a total of 2 hours, and PC intervention twice weekly for a total of 8 hours per month. Some joint sessions are planned to integrate strategies and activities. A transition into a toddler program is anticipated soon.

Elly

Elly was born 4 weeks prematurely. She was diagnosed with congenital heart disease requiring repeated surgeries, chronic (mild) renal failure, bronchopulmonary dysplasia (BPD), possible seizure disorder, microcephaly, a feeding disorder, amblyopia, and developmental delays. She was on assisted ventilation off and on for 6 months. A computerized tomography (CT) scan of the head showed cortical atrophy, possibly nutrition related. She was fed via a gastrostomy tube for almost the first 2 years of her life because of chronic aspiration.

She was first identified as having severe-profound hearing loss by ABR when she was 25 months old. The delay in identification was apparently related to her multiple primary health concerns. Initially she was fitted with a loaner hearing aid within 1 month following identification of hearing loss. Hearing-aid adjustment was good, and eventually she was fitted binaurally. A composite audiogram, obtained over several sessions, is shown in Figure 3. It reveals severe-profound hearing loss in both ears with the right ear poorer than the left. Normal tympanograms tend to rule out any conductive (middle-ear) component to the loss.

For amplification, Elly has two ear-level hearing aids for use at home and an auditory trainer for use at school. Verification of aided results using probe-tube microphone measures are shown for the left ear in Figure 4. Unaided left-ear thresholds, converted to dB SPL, are shown by the Xs. Target values

ISSUES IN AMPLIFICATION FOR INFANTS AND TODDLERS

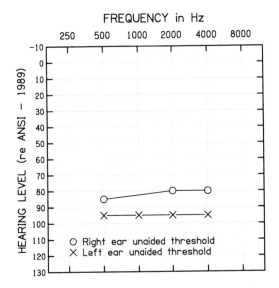

Figure 3. Unaided behavioral audiogram for Elly, 30 months of age, with earphone thresholds (in dB HL) for selected frequencies. Right ear (o) and left ear (x) thresholds are plotted.

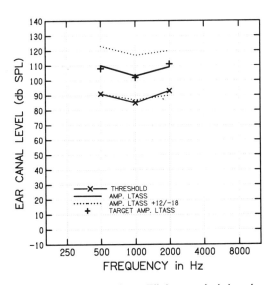

Figure 4. Plotted are Elly's unaided thresholds in SPL for the left ear; the amplified/aided long-term average speech spectrum (amp. LTASS); the amplified speech peaks for +12, −8; and the target amplified LTASS.

for the amplified (aided) long-term average speech spectrum (LTASS) are shown by the pluses (+). Actual aided values for the LTASS are shown by the solid line with the peaks and valleys of speech as the dotted lines. Thus, it appears that the targets for the LTASS have been met or approximated for the frequencies tested. This suggests that on the average the frequency components of loud speech would be audible to Elly at 1 meter.

Elly has difficulties in speech production related to unilateral true vocal cord paralysis identified at 26 months of age. She is in a developmental preschool where her communication is facilitated by use of total communication. Her audiological follow-up consists of monitoring aided and unaided responses to assure that hearing is stable and hearing-aid performance is acceptable.

Max

Max has a repaired unilateral cleft lip, a submucous cleft palate, chronic congestion, severe mixed hearing loss, middle-ear dysfunction with ventilation tubes, cochlear malformations, and gross motor delays. Hearing loss first was confirmed when he was 10 months old. The audiogram, shown in Figure 5, demonstrates bilateral mixed hearing loss, mostly in the severe range. Soon after the identification of the hearing loss, he was fitted with an ear-level hearing aid and now has two aids. At this time, hearing aid adjustment is good; however, repeated bouts of otitis media have limited full-time use of binaural amplification. Figure 6 displays the aided results for the right ear. DSL targets for the LTASS (+) and the real-ear saturation response (RESR) (*) were met or approached at most frequencies. In the high-frequencies, however, the louder components of these speech sounds would be audible only at lower sensation levels.

Neither Max's primary mode of communication nor full-time educational placement is fully determined at this time. Rather, Max

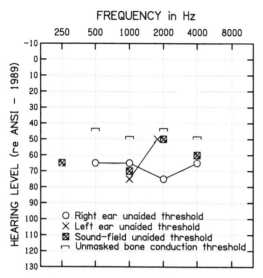

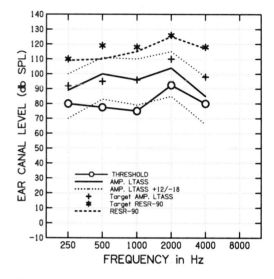

Figure 5. Unaided behavioral audiogram for Max, approximately 12 months of age, with earphone thresholds (in dB HL) for selected frequencies. Right ear (o) and left ear (x) thresholds are plotted, with the addition of sound-field unaided thresholds (squares) and unmasked bone conduction (⌐⌐).

Figure 6. Plotted are Max's unaided thresholds in SPL for the right ear; the amplified/aided long-term average speech spectrum (amp. LTASS); the amplified speech peaks for +12, −8; and the target amplified LTASS, with the addition of target amplified RESR-90 and obtained RESR-90.

continues in a diagnostic early intervention program while information is gathered. Beyond the audiology and educational components of his care, others involved in his care are day-care workers, allergists, geneticists, and a cranio-facial disorders team that includes an ear, nose, and throat (ENT) doctor.

Alex

Alex remained hospitalized until she was 19 months old. She had a severe lung disease of unknown etiology, bronchopulmonary dysplasia (BPD), and required assisted ventilation until she was 27 months old. During her hospital course, she received ototoxic medications. She continues on supplemental oxygen at almost 4 years of age.

She has a tracheostomy with a Passy-Muir speaking valve, requiring suctioning one or two times per day. Alex also has hypotonia and hip dysplasia. She has feeding problems and remains with a gastrostomy tube at almost 4 years of age. Although initially noted to have exotropia and amblyopia in her right eye, this has resolved.

Alex's first ABR was at 14 months of age and suggested moderate-severe hearing loss in both ears. Subsequently, she was fitted with an auditory trainer because of the background noise in her hospital room created by the alarms and the ventilator. A quieter ventilator and her move home allowed an opportunity to eventually use hearing aids more often. Now, she uses hearing aids at home and an auditory trainer at school. Her audiogram, shown in Figure 7, demonstrates

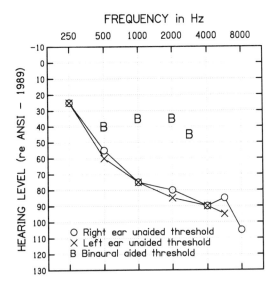

Figure 7. Unaided behavioral audiogram for Alex, 3 years, with earphone thresholds (in dB HL) for selected frequencies. Right ear (o) and left ear (x) thresholds are plotted, with the addition of binaural aided thresholds (B).

mild hearing loss in the low frequencies, which slopes into the profound hearing loss range. Also plotted are aided binaural sound-field thresholds for four frequencies. It is apparent that some high-frequency speech sounds will not be audible to her with her hearing aids.

At almost 4 years of age, Alex communicates expressively with gestures and total communication. Her receptive language is 22–24 months and her expressive language is 19–21 months. An OT evaluation suggests a 1 year delay in fine motor and motor/visual skills. Alex continues in PC therapy two times per week, supplemented with placement two times per week in a preschool program with other children who have hearing loss. Her hearing is monitored closely because she continues on a medication which is potentially ototoxic, with a recent increase in the dosage.

Summary

The field of amplification is constantly advancing. For example, circuit miniaturization and advances in signal processing have provided more fitting options. Also, test equipment, such as real-ear probe-tube microphone systems, has revolutionized hearing aid assessments. There continue, however, to be some questions and uncertainties regarding what is the best device for any given child, and research continues in this area. Even if it were technologically possible to determine and provide a device that functioned optimally for all listening requirements, the challenge of having the child wear the device would remain. Hearing aids alone do not fully compensate for hearing loss. The use of any assistive device must be integrated into the total service plan. Hearing aids and other listening devices are no exception.

Acknowledgments

We would like to acknowledge Dawna Lewis, Ann Kalberer, and Patricia Stelmachowicz for their careful review of this manuscript and their many helpful editorial comments. We also acknowledge Jeffrey Laudin, Paula Naikelis, and Linda Mace for their assistance in the preparation of the manuscript. This work was supported in part by NIDCD grant number P60 DC00982, Center for Hearing Loss for Children.

References

American National Standards Institute. (1987). *Specification of hearing aid characteristics: ANSI S3.22*. New York: ANSI.

Beiter, A. L., Staller, S. T., & Dowell, R. C. (1991). Evaluation and device programming in children. *Ear and Hearing, 12S*, 25S–33S.

Benoit, R. (1989). Home use of FM amplification systems during the early childhood years. *Hearing Instruments, 40,* 8–12.

Byrne, D., & Dillon, H. (1986). The National Acoustic Laboratories' (NAL) new procedure for selecting gain and frequency response of a hearing aid. *Ear and Hearing, 7,* 257–265.

Carney, A., Osberger, M. J., Miyamoto, R. T., Karasek, A., Dettman, D. L., & Johnson, D. L. (1991). Speech perception along the sensory aid continuum: From hearing aids to cochlear implants. In J. A. Feigin & P. G. Stelmachowicz (Eds.), *Pediatric Amplification: Proceedings of the 1991 National Conference* (pp. 93–114). Omaha, NE: Boys Town National Research Hospital.

Clifton, R. (1992). The development of spatial hearing in human infants. In L. A. Werner & E. W. Rubel (Eds.), *Developmental psychoacoustics* (pp. 135–157). Washington, DC: APA.

Cole, E. B. (1992). Promoting emerging speech in birth to 3 year-old hearing-impaired children. *The Volta Review, 94,* 63–77.

Condon, M. (1991). Unique challenges: Children with multiple handicaps. In J. A. Feigin & P. G. Stelmachowicz (Eds.), *Pediatric Amplification: Proceedings of the 1991 National Conference* (pp. 183–194). Omaha, NE: Boys Town National Research Hospital.

Cox, R. M. (1988). The MSU hearing instrument prescription procedure. *Hearing Instruments, 39,* 6–10.

Dale, P., & Thal, D. (1989). *MacArthur Communicative Development Inventory: Infants.* Developmental Psychology Laboratory. San Diego, CA: San Diego State University.

Diefendorf, A. O., Chaplin, R. G., Kessler, K. S., Miller, S. M., Miyamoto, R. T., Myres, W. A., Pope, M. L., Reitz, P. S., Renshaw, J. J., Steck, J. L., & Wagner, M. L. (1990). Follow-up and intervention: Completing the process. In A. O. Diefendorf (Ed.), *Pediatric audiology. Seminars in hearing* (pp. 393–411). New York: Thieme Medical Publishers, Inc.

Elliot, L. L., & Katz, D. R. (1980). *Northwestern University Children's Perception of Speech (NU-CHIPS).* St. Louis, MO: Auditec.

Frisbie, K., Beauchaine, K. L., Carney, A. E., Lewis, D. E., Moeller, M. P., & Stelmachowicz, P. G. (1991). Longitudinal study of FM use in non-academic settings. In J. A. Feigin & P. G. Stelmachowicz (Eds.), *Pediatric Amplification: Proceedings of the 1991 National Conference* (pp. 153–162). Omaha, NE: Boys Town National Research Hospital.

Hawkins, D. B., & Northern, J. L. (1992). Probe-microphone measurements with children. In H. G. Mueller, D. B. Hawkins, & J. L. Northern (Eds.), *Probe microphone measurements; Hearing aid selection and assessment* (pp. 159–181). San Diego: Singular Publishing Group, Inc.

Hawkins, D. B., & Yacullo, W. S. (1984). Signal-to-noise advantage of binaural hearing aids and directional microphones under different levels of reverberation. *Journal of Speech and Hearing Disorders, 49,* 278–286.

Hawkins, D. B., Montgomery, A. A., Prosek, R. A., & Walden, B. E. (1987). Examination of two issues concerning functional gain measurements. *Journal of Speech and Hearing Disorders, 52,* 56–63.

Hawkins, D. B., Morrison, T. M., Halligan, P. L. W., & Cooper, W. A. (1989). Use of probe tube microphone measurements in hearing aid selection for children: Some initial clinical experiences. *Ear and Hearing, 10,* 281–287.

Humes, L. E., & Hackett, T. (1990). Comparison of frequency response and aided speech-recognition performance for hearing aids selected by three different prescriptive methods. *Journal of the American Academy of Audiology, 1,* 101–108.

Humes, L. E., & Kirn, E. U. (1990). The reliability of functional gain. *Journal of Speech and Hearing Disorders, 55,* 193–197.

Kile, J. E., & Beauchaine, K. L. (1991). Identification, assessment and management of hearing impairment in infants and toddlers. *Infant-Toddler Intervention: The Transdisciplinary Journal, 1*(1), 61–81.

Lewis, D. (1991). FM systems and assistive devices: Selection and evaluation. In J. A. Feigin & P. G. Stelmachowicz (Eds.), *Pediatric Amplification: Proceedings of the 1991 National Conference* (pp. 115–138). Omaha, NE: Boys Town National Research Hospital.

Mace, A. L., Wallace, K. L., Whan, M. Q., & Stelmachowicz, P. G. (1991). Relevant factors in the identification of hearing loss. *Ear and Hearing, 12,* 287–293.

Madell, J. R. (1992). FM systems as primary amplification for children with profound hearing loss. *Ear and Hearing, 13*, 102–107.

Manolsen, A. (1985). *It takes two to talk: A Hanen early language parent guide book.* Toronto, Ontario: Hanen Early Language Resource Center.

Martin, F. N., & Gravel, K. L. (1989). Pediatric audiologic practices in the United States. *The Hearing Journal, 42*, 33–48.

National Institutes of Health Consensus Development Conference Statement. (1993, draft). *Early identification of hearing impairment in infants and young children.* Washington, DC: NIH.

Oller, D. K., Eilers, R. E., Bull, D. H., & Carney, A. E. (1985). Prespeech vocalizations of a deaf infant: A comparison with normal metaphonological development. *Journal of Speech and Hearing Research, 28*, 47–63.

Olsen, W. O., Hawkins, D. B., & Van Tasell, D. J. (1987). *Representations of the long-term spectra of speech. Ear and Hearing, 8*, 100S–108S.

Parks, S. (1992). *HELP Strands: Curriculum-based developmental assessment 0–3 years.* Adapted from the Hawaii Early Learning Profile. Palo Alto, CA: VORT Corporation.

Ross, M. (1990). Implications of delay in detection and management of deafness. *The Volta Review, 92*, 69–79.

Ross, M., & Lerman, J. (1971). *Word intelligibility by picture identification (WIPI).* St. Louis, MO: Auditec.

Ross, M., & Seewald, R. C. (1988). Hearing aid selection and evaluation with young children. In F. H. Bess (Ed.), *Hearing impairment in children* (pp. 190–213). Parkton, MD: York Press.

Roush, J., & Gravel, J. (1994). Acoustic amplification and sensory aids for infants and toddlers. In J. Roush & N. D. Matkin (Eds.), *Infants and toddlers with hearing loss: Family-centered assessment and intervention* (pp. 65–79). Baltimore: York Press.

Schuyler, V. S., Rushmer, N., Arpan, R. Melum, A., Sowers, J., & Kennedy, N. (1985). *Parent-infant communication: A program for parents and hearing impaired infants, 3rd Edition.* Portland, OR: Good Samaritan Hospital and Medical Center.

Schwartz, S. (1987). (Ed.). *Choices in deafness: A parent's guide.* Kensington, MD: Woodbine House, Inc.

Seewald, R. C. (1991). Hearing aid output limiting considerations for children. In J. A. Feigin & P. G. Stelmachowicz (Eds.), *Pediatric Amplification: Proceedings of the 1991 National Conference* (pp. 19–35). Omaha, NE: Boys Town National Research Hospital.

Seewald, R. C. (1992). The desired sensation level method for fitting children: Version 3.0. *The Hearing Journal, 45*, 36–42.

Seewald, R. C., Ross, M., & Stelmachowicz, P. G. (1987). Selecting and verifying hearing aid performance characteristics for young children. *Journal of the Academy of Rehabilitative Audiology, 20*, 25–37.

Seewald, R. C., Ross, M., & Spiro, M. K. (1985). Selecting amplification characteristics for young hearing-impaired children. *Ear and Hearing, 6*, 48–53.

Seewald, R. C., Zelisko, D. L. C., Ramji, K. V., & Jamieson, D. G. (1991). A computer-assisted implementation of the desired sensation level method for electroacoustic selection and fitting in children. *DSL 3.0 User's Manual.* London, Ontario: University of Western Ontario.

Skinner, M. W. (1988). *Hearing aid evaluation.* Englewood Cliffs, NJ: Prentice Hall.

Smith, D. (1991). Tactile aids. In J. A. Feigin & P. G. Stelmachowicz (Eds.), *Pediatric Amplification: Proceedings of the 1991 National Conference* (pp. 163–172). Omaha, NE: Boys Town National Research Hospital.

Stelmachowicz, P. G., & Seewald, R. (1991). Probe-tube microphone measures in young children. *Seminars in Hearing, 12*, 62–72.

Stuart, A., Durieux-Smith, A., & Stenstrom, R. (1990). Critical differences in aided sound field thresholds in children. *Journal of Speech and Hearing Research, 33*, 612–615.

Sullivan, J. A., Levitt, H., Hwang, J., & Hennessey, A., (1988). An experimental comparison of four hearing aid prescription methods. *Ear and Hearing, 9*, 22–32.

Weisenberger, J. M., & Miller, J. D. (1987). The role of tactile aids in providing information about acoustic stimuli. *Journal of the Acoustical Society of America, 82*, 906–915.

Address correspondence to:
Kathryn L. Beauchaine, M.A.,
Boys Town National Research Hospital,
555 North 30th Street,
Omaha, NE 68131

Encouraging Intelligible Spoken Language Development in Infants and Toddlers with Hearing Loss

Elizabeth B. Cole, Ed.D.
McGill University
Montreal, Quebec, Canada

This article describes what professional educators and parents can do to help hearing-impaired infants and toddlers learn intelligible spoken language. Since so much of any child's learning occurs in the course of normal, everyday interactions, it makes sense to target those times for the learning of intelligible spoken language by children with hearing loss. Adults in the child's life can subtlely, but consistently, embellish or "polish up" everyday playtime and routine events to make particular auditory, language, and/or speech aspects of the event more salient and to provide additional varied practice on those aspects. A 2-minute example is provided of an embellished interaction between a mother and her 13-month-old hearing-impaired daughter. Even in that short time, the event included a number of aspects where small changes were made to maximize the child's interest in listening, to promote her understanding of spoken language, and to encourage her to use her voice to communicate. The bulk of the article provides detail regarding specific reasons for and ways of encouraging the child's development of listening, spoken language, and clear speech. Practical information is provided for professional educators to implement immediately and wisely with hearing-impaired infants and toddlers.

Children with hearing loss are children, with all of the needs, curiosity, feelings, and delightfulness that children express. Consequently, children with hearing loss need all of the usual special attention that any child needs. In addition, when the parents, educators, and other related professionals determine that intelligible spoken language acquisition is one of the primary goals of the child's intervention program, certain areas of the child's daily existence and development require systematic and sustained special attention. These are the areas of audition, language, and speech. Luckily, much of the child's day-to-day intervention can be smoothly carried out in the course of normal, everyday play activities and routines which are slightly altered or "embellished" to emphasize or make more salient particular auditory, language, or speech aspects of the situation. With guidance, this kind of intervention is most appropriately carried out by the people who are most frequently with the child, which is most often the child's parents and preschool teachers. Guidance for the parents or preschool teachers could be provided by a knowledgeable speech-language pathologist, audiologist, aural habilitationist, auditory-verbal therapist, or teacher of the deaf.[1]

For an example of the kind of ordinary everyday spoken-language-promoting event being referred to, consider the following explicated scenario.

Thirteen-month-old Thea has been wearing hearing aids since she was 6 months old. She has a severe sensorineural hearing loss, and with her hearing aids on, can hear well within the speech spectrum.

This means that with her hearing aids on, Thea can hear conversational speech when it is of a normal loudness level, if it is being spoken within about 2 yards distance of Thea, and if it is relatively quiet (Ling, 1981). Whether Thea chooses to listen to a particular speaker in a particular instance is a different matter altogether, but she does have the capability of hearing speech under those conditions.

It is mid-afternoon, and Thea has been lying on the floor near her mother drinking a small bottle of milk, while her mother reads the newspaper headlines and absentmindedly strokes the cat in her lap. Thea's eyes have been on her mother while she has been drinking. When she finishes her bottle, Thea tosses it aside and crawls straight for her mother and the cat, vocalizing excitedly. "Oh—you see Shanti, eh? You want to pat Shanti? Okay, gently now. Paaat, paaat, paaat," says her mother.

Thea's mother responded immediately to Thea's vocalizing and her interest in the cat. She talked about the object of Thea's attention (Shanti), and she automatically extended the exchange by introducing the idea of patting the cat, which she knew quite well would be well-received. Then, when she demonstrated the patting, she paired the handstrokes with slightly stretching out the word "paaat." This may have made the word acoustically more interesting to Thea since it sounded a bit different and sort of rhythmic or singsongy. All of the mother's behaviors are supportive of Thea's spoken language and listening development.

The cat is nervous about the patting and soon runs off about 12 feet away. Thea sits back, watching the cat go. "Oh dear," says the mother, "I guess she had enough. Bye bye, Shanti."

Again the mother has talked about Thea's focus of attention. In addition, she has used a very clearly falling intonation and slightly stretched out the "oh dear" expression which makes that expression acoustically interesting. Assuming that she does this consistently in this sort of situation, "oh dear" with this intonational pattern is likely to be understood early and imitated by Thea. The mother is also using sentences and phrases of an appropriately short length and simple grammatical complexity in accordance with Thea's early language-learning level.

Thea turns to look carefully at her mother when she hears "Bye bye." Her mother waves at the cat now sitting and watching them, and

---

[1]This article is aimed at teachers and other professionals who may not have had training or experience with hearing-impaired children in the 0- to 5-year-old age range. It may also be of use to parents of young hearing-impaired children. One of the recurring themes in the article is that most of the learning needs of children in that age range can be best addressed in the course of normal, everyday events which are slightly "embellished." But it is also true that for children who are 3, 4, or 5 years of age, some systematic, adult-directed activities with prior-determined auditory, language, and speech goals may be useful. This semi-formal work is most appropriately carried out by a speech-language pathologist, audiologist, aural habilitationist, auditory-verbal therapist, or teacher of the deaf who has received specialized training in the content, sequence, and implementation of this kind of intervention. Details of this kind of work can be found in Cole, 1992a; Estabrooks, 1993, 1994; Northcott, 1977, 1978; Pollack, 1985; and Schuyler et al., 1985. Even when there are individual sessions of this nature being carried out usually by a therapist-parent-child triad, the vast majority of the day will still be spent in normal, everyday play and routines which need to be embellished in the ways described in this article.

ENCOURAGING INTELLIGIBLE SPOKEN LANGUAGE DEVELOPMENT

says, "Bye bye, Shanti." Thea starts to crawl after the cat. Her mother says, "Bye bye!" Apparently thinking that maybe her mother is leaving, Thea turns to look at her mother again. When she sees that her mother is not moving, Thea turns back to continue crawling after the cat. The mother again says, "Bye bye, Shanti" but Thea does not turn around this time while she is crawling.

Twice, Thea has demonstrated that she can hear her mother's voice a short distance away from her, and that she has some understanding of the expression "bye bye." This may actually be an example of the mother extending Thea's understanding of the expression by using it for a cat's leaving instead of a person's. Another important aspect of this part of the event is that several times Thea's mother talked when Thea was not watching her mother's face: The mother **expects** Thea to understand based on listening alone. It seems likely that the reason that Thea did not turn around the last time the mother said "Bye bye" was because Thea knew what the mother had said and to whom it was directed, and was simply more interested in catching the cat. One final important aspect of this part of the event is that the mother did not try to force Thea to imitate the expression here. The mother has noted that Thea heard it, was interested in it, and probably understood it. Opportunities for imitating "bye bye" were presented, since the mother paused in between her productions of it, but always to insist on imitation in normal everyday situations such as this one risks turning interactions into stilted and dreary **lessons**. The intention is for the child to experience many of these warm and friendly communicative exchanges, where the language is spontaneous, interesting, important, meaningful, and self-generated, since that is the kind of communicator one hopes for the child to become.

When Thea gets close to the cat, the cat again darts off, this time toward the front door. The mother says, "Oh dear, she ran off again." The mother moves beside Thea and says, "Let's call her. Here, Shanti. Shanti! Shanti!" Thea does not stay beside her mother as her mother is calling the cat, but immediately starts crawling toward Shanti again. To her mother's delight, as she is crawling Thea says something that sounds like "ah-ee" (with the mother's calling intonation). Partially imitating her, the mother says, "Shanti! Come back—we want to play with you!"

The mother has again taken advantage of an opportunity to use the "Oh dear" expression appropriately. She moved up close to Thea, partly to improve the likelihood of Thea's hearing her, but also to make the calling of the cat more meaningful. If she had called the cat from where she had been, it would have appeared that she wanted the cat to come to her, rather than to Thea. Thea did not stay with her mother and call the cat, but she must have heard her, since she then called the cat herself, and imitated the mother's intonation and rhythm in doing so. The mother then imitated Thea, using the same intonation and modeling the target word. Imitating the child's productions is a very important strategy to use, since it lets Thea know that she has been heard, and that what she said was appropriate. The mother did not produce Thea's "ah-ee" but used the actual word "Shanti." One reason for this is that this meant she could provide another example of the correct target. Another reason is that Thea undoubtedly thought she said "Shanti" and if the mother now says "ah-ee" she may very well be presenting an unnecessarily confusing element into the picture. It is also noteworthy that the mother did not say something like "Good talking! I like the way you called Shanti." This adult **praise** of the child's talk, well-intentioned though it may be, makes the child's talk appear to be something that the child did *for* the adult, rather than a normal part of the communicative event. It is also patronizing, and introduces a sidetrack to the real topic of the conversation.

Embellishments in this short scenario begin with the adult's raised level of awareness of the importance of taking advantage of all aspects of normal everyday events for their potential contribution to the child's auditory, language, and speech growth. The first auditory embellishment in this scene was that the child was wearing hearing aids. The mother was aware of what the child's optimal listening distance was and expected her to hear within that distance. That is, appropriately, she did not always draw the child's attention to her face before speaking. When the child moved away in chasing the cat, the mother moved closer to her (still not telling the child to watch her face while she spoke) in order to call the cat from close by the child, which not only made it appropriate for the situation, but made the calling acoustically more salient. Language embellishments include the mother's immediate responses to the child's apparent interests, the mother's use of complete sentences and phrases which were appropriately short and simple for a child of Thea's age and linguistic stage, and the mother's imitation of Thea's production with modeling of the target word. The mother also did not push the child to imitate her, but did pause between her own utterances to allow the child to make a contribution if she so chose. From a speech, auditory, and linguistic point of view, the consistent use of "Oh dear" with a characteristic falling intonation, as well as the slightly extended production of "paaat" paired with the hand motion are both quite significant. The consistent use of these expressions in the appropriate situations helps the child build up an understanding of the times when they can be used. The interesting intonation and rhythmic patterns used in their production add to the likelihood that the child will pay attention to them and perhaps will remember them.

The example also illustrates, however, that whether embellished or not, events in children's lives are "of a piece." All areas of development (including audition, language, and speech) in which growth may be stimulated in a particular play activity or routine are closely interwoven and interdependent. That is, the *language* used and/or modeled by the parent will be related to the child's *cognitive* and *linguistic* levels. The *speech* sounds selected for emphasis or repetition will be those important for some *language* item in the scene. The event will probably involve some age-appropriate *physical* activity on the part of the child, at least partly because little children are active, and partly because it will keep the child's *attention* and be *motivating*. The event is probably occurring within the context of a positive *affective relationship* with the adult, which is fundamental to the child's wanting to communicate and to listen. A positive affective relationship between adult and child is also fundamental to the adult's continued willingness to be vigilant for opportunities to help the child gain competence and confidence in his or her *auditory* and *linguistic* abilities.[2] From all of the areas important for a child's development, the following discussion will emphasize the areas of audition, language, and speech to consider carefully what might be appropriate targets for young hearing-impaired children who are learning spoken language.

---

[2]It is all very well to say that a positive affective relationship should be there for the child's spoken language to develop normally. But these early years of any child's life are sometimes emotionally and physically difficult for parents, and the added realities of having a child with a hearing loss are significant. There is often a great deal of emotional turmoil surrounding the discovery, as well as the continuing presence of hearing loss in one's child. This emotional turmoil needs to be addressed on an ongoing basis for the parents to be able to provide the kind of emotional, affective climate that is described in this article. At the very least, parents need supportive professionals around them; other more experienced parents are also sometimes invaluable; and often group, couple, or individual counseling or therapy are recommended. These issues are more fully addressed in Cole, 1992a; Klevans, 1988; Luterman, 1979, 1984; Moses and Van Hecke-Wulatin, 1981; Schuyler and Rushmer, 1987.

Encouraging the Child's Use of Residual Hearing

The Acoustic Basis of Speech

Approximately 90 to 95% of children with hearing loss have some residual hearing which the child can learn to use with the help of properly fit hearing aids. This is an immensely important factor to remember when attempting to teach spoken language to a hearing-impaired child, particularly in view of the additional fact that spoken language is acoustically or auditorally based. To illustrate, the primary acoustic dimensions and examples of their relatedness to various aspects of speech are listed below.

Speech Examples of Acoustic Dimensions

INTENSITY. **(1) The overall loudness or average intensity of speech is used as a guideline for fitting hearing aids.** The average overall loudness of conversational speech is generally described as approximately 55 dBHL[3] at a distance of about 6 feet from the speakers. Since the ability to hear speech is the primary goal of most hearing aid usage, it is not surprising that when selecting and fitting hearing aids for a child, the audiologist is aiming to have the child able to hear sound which is at 55 dB or (better still) even quieter.

Most hearing-impaired children can hear conversational speech *when they are wearing properly selected and well-maintained hearing aids, and when they are in quiet circumstances.* That is, assuming that the hearing aids are appropriate and functioning well, when the adult expects the child to use hearing for understanding speech, it is most likely to happen if the room is relatively quiet. Conversely, if the room is unavoidably noisy, the adult may need to draw the child's attention to the speaker's face (to allow the child access to speechreading cues in addition to the auditory cues), and/or to tap the child lightly on the shoulder to get his or her attention.

(2) Differences in typical loudness of particular speakers can help the child identify the speaker. Very early on, the child learns to tell whether it is mother or father speaking (a male versus female speaker). Clearly there is a difference in pitch of the two voices, but there are also likely to be intensity differences which aid in that discrimination.

(3) Loudness differences also accompany the expression of particular emotional states, so that the child quickly learns that a very loud voice may well be an angry one, that normal conversation has a medium loudness level, and that lullaby singing is usually in a soft, gentle voice.

(4) Differences in loudness occur as the speaker emphasizes particular words or syllables. This can be intensity or stress markings that signal differences in word meanings, such as *rebel* versus *rebel*. It can also be related to stress that occurs at phrase boundaries and accompanies intonational changes to help make phrases, sentences, questions, and exclamations all rhythmically appropriate for English (or for other languages).

(5) Variations in loudness (presence, absence, and gradations of intensity of sound) also exist in different individual speech sounds. For example, the major difference between voiced and unvoiced sound pairs such as /b/ and /p/ is the absence or presence respectively of a 20 millisecond "quiet space" between the produc-

---

[3]The abbreviation "dB" stands for "decibels" which are used as a measure of intensity, just as degrees are a measure of temperature. "HL" stands for "Hearing Level" which is one of the reference scales in hearing measurement (the other being "SPL" or "Sound Pressure Level"), analogous to the co-existence of Fahrenheit and centigrade scales. Additional information about basic audiological terms can be found in Kile and Beauchaine, 1991; Ling and Ling, 1978; Newby and Popelka, 1992; and Sanders, 1993.

tion of the /b/ or /p/ consonant and the vowel which follows it. This differentiation is usually not difficult for hearing-impaired children to learn to hear, as well as to produce.

FREQUENCY. **(1) The overall pitch of the speaker's voice generally falls within a certain range, and varies according to the speaker's age and sex.** That is, children's voices tend to be the highest, women's next highest, and men's voices the lowest in pitch. As mentioned above, most hearing-impaired children can easily learn to tell whether it is a man, woman, or child speaking by using pitch as one of the major cues.

(2) Within phrases and sentences, the voice goes up and down in a kind of intonational melody that is particular to each language as it is spoken in a region. These changes in intonation can signal the ends of thought groups, whether the intention is to ask a question or make a statement, or they can signal the emotional state of the speaker. Cues for intonation exist in the frequencies where most hearing-impaired people have usable residual hearing, which means that most hearing-impaired children can learn to make their voices go up and down in normal sorts of ways, and that they can learn to listen to intonational cues in others' speech as an aid to their own understanding.

(3) Each speech sound can be described in terms of the typical frequencies involved in its production. For example the vowel /a/ as in "father" has strong energy produced at about 800 and 1200 Hz; and the consonant /s/ has relatively weak energy produced in a wide band of frequencies from about 4000 to 8000 Hz. Knowing the typical frequency characteristics of speech sounds, it is possible to make predictions about which speech sounds a particular child with a particular audiogram is likely to learn to detect and/or produce using hearing alone, as well as which sounds the child will need to use additional visual and/or tactile means in order to learn to detect and produce them. An audiologist, speech-language pathologist, or teacher of the deaf should be able to interpret a particular child's audiogram in this manner for parents and educators who may not have been exposed to this information before.

DURATION. **(1) Duration (the length of the sound) is one of the easiest cues for a hearing-impaired child to learn to listen for and to produce.** This means that if the adult is saying a single syllable for a word such as "Hi!" and prolonging the word just a bit, then it will not be long before the child will be repeating or imitating a similar slightly prolonged sound. In the same way, if the adult consistently and frequently says a short "Pop!" in playing with bubbles, it is likely that the child will soon make a similarly brief sound in imitation or even spontaneously in observing or chasing the bubbles. Even if the speech is not precise, approximating the length of the speech segment is highly desirable listening-and-producing behavior on the part of the child. This is one of the reasons that it makes sense to speak to the young hearing-impaired child in phrases and sentences of a length and content consistent with that for any young child.

(2) The rate of speaking is a another duration-related item. Hearing-impaired people of all ages understand spoken messages when they are carefully articulated and spoken with some degree of deliberateness. Fortunately, most adults tend to slow their speech somewhat when speaking with young children, regardless of the child's hearing status. However, what is to be avoided is speech which is abnormally slow and consequently **over**-articulated. This kind of slowing distorts both the auditory and visual cues to the message, and it is harder to understand rather than easier. It is not, for example, doing a hearing-impaired child a favor to pronounce a word such as "ball" with an initial tucking in of the lips exploding into a gigantic "ba," followed by an "l" that exposes all of the veins underneath the tongue. Even if the child learns to decipher the meaning of this display performed by a particular speaker, he or she will certainly not connect that production with the same word produced by 99% of the rest of the population.

(3) **In addition to having typical intensity and frequency characteristics, all individual speech sounds have typical durational characteristics.** They can be long or short in usual duration (such as a /h/ versus a /t/), they can have a sudden or gradual onset (such as a /b/ versus a /w/, they can stay relatively constant throughout their production (like an /m/) or they can change during their production (like an /r/). Interestingly, when we measure the child's hearing audiometrically, we get information about the quietest level at which the child can hear sounds across the pitches or frequencies which are important for speech. But we do not have ways of measuring the child's ability to deal with timing or durational cues. The only way we can get an estimate of that area of the child's competence is to try to teach speech to the child auditorally, that is, to try to bring the timing differences to his or her attention and see how the child does.

(The entire preceding section on speech acoustics is based on Cole & Paterson, 1984; Erber, 1982; Fry, 1978; Kent and Reed, 1992; Ling, 1976, 1986, 1989; Sanders, 1977, 1993.)

The human ear is the most efficient of the sensory organs for perceiving and analyzing these essential (acoustic) dimensions of speech. Vision can provide some important information about speech sounds (lip rounding, spreading, closure; frontal tongue and teeth positioning and movement), as can the tactile sense (continuous versus explosive breathstream on some sounds; nasal versus oral breathstream; vibration of vocal chords; vibration of oral and/or nasal cavities). However, these bits of visual and tactile information are secondary correlates of the speech sounds. They acquire usefulness particularly when the acoustic part of the speech sounds is also present. Consequently, if the child has aided residual hearing that allows him or her to detect conversational speech, it makes sense to give the child a chance to learn spoken language primarily using the most efficient means possible: audition. On a practical level, using audition has at least four implications.

Embellishments to Enhance Listening

First, maximizing audition means that the child must be provided with hearing aids which are properly selected and well-maintained. Two of the simplest—and perhaps most important—things that any infant or preschool educator or therapist can do for a hearing-impaired child is to learn how to insert the child's hearing aids and how to check and replace the hearing aid batteries. If the hearing aids are not on the child's ears, or if the batteries are not functioning, then the child is being unfairly deprived of listening and language-learning time, as well as deprived of one source of a sense of connectedness to his or her surroundings. The adults in the child's life must be certain that this kind of neglect does not occur.

Second, it means that the best auditory and spoken language-learning environment for the child will be one which is sound-treated with carpeting on the floor, sound tiles on the ceiling, drapes on the windows, and without noisy fans, heaters, air conditioners, or traffic (human or automotive) close by. In a preschool setting, since the children themselves will be an unavoidable source of noise, the child's audiologist may recommend an FM system, which functions like a tiny radio station. For most FM systems in use today, the adult wears a microphone within about 4 to 6 inches of his or her mouth. The wire from the adult's microphone plugs into a small transmitter box worn on a belt. The child wears a small receiver box with a connecting wire to the hearing aid. When the adult speaks into the microphone, the child hears the adult's voice as loudly as if the adult were right next to him or her and speaking at a distance of 4 to 6 inches from the ear. This means that the signal is much louder than the surrounding noise, and it is a tremendous asset in noisy situations. A potential drawback is that the voices of the other children or adults in the room are likely to be much less audible to the hearing-impaired child, so the FM may be best used in situations where it is especially important to hear a single speaker. Another caution regarding the use of FM systems is for the adult to be sure that the system is not left in the "on" position when the adult is engaged in tasks unrelated to the child, such as carrying on conversations with other people or having coffee or bathroom breaks.

The third practical implication related to helping the child maximize his or her use of audition for spoken language-learning is adult use of particular strategies when interacting with the child (Cole, 1992a,b; Estabrooks, 1993, 1994; Pollack, 1985; Simser and Steacie, 1993). These strategies can be viewed as auditory "embellishments" of normal, everyday conversational events. A list of the strategies, with explanations of their importance, follows.

1. Sitting close by the child (behind or beside). This strategy results in the signal (the talk by the adult) being louder than the surrounding noise, in much the same way that an FM system does. When the child is wearing his or her regular hearing aids, the closer the speaker is to the microphone, the louder the message will be for the child. Fortunately, very young children **are** most often physically close to the adults who are speaking to them. (It is not like the situation an older child faces when the hockey coach is giving directions from halfway across the arena.) Infants are frequently talked to when they are in their parents arms or laps or when parents are squatting down or sitting down close by. This is definitely desirable from an auditory point of view.

2. Talking when the child is not watching the speaker's face. If the goal is to encourage the child to understand even when he or she is not watching the speaker's face, then the child must be given opportunities to do just that. This includes calling the child when his or her back is turned. If the child does not respond after several auditory-only attempts, then the speaker can move into the child's field of vision, or tap the child gently on the shoulder, or ask a nearby child to tell the child that someone is trying to get his or her attention.

3. Directing the child's attention toward an object or activity. When seated close beside the child with an object or activity in front of the child, the adult tries to keep the child's visual attention on the toys or materials when the adult is speaking rather than have the child's eyes glued to the speaker's face. If the child does not understand after two or three attempts (including paraphrasing), he or she can be allowed to watch the speaker's face, and/or the speaker can demonstrate what she or he is talking about. The next time that message is to be said, the speaker should again begin by trying to convey the message auditorally alone.

4. Obscuring your mouth. If the child persists in watching the speaker's face, the speaker's mouth can be covered with a piece of paper or with a hand. However, if this technique is used, the speaker must be sure to hold the hand or paper at a short distance from the mouth and on a slight angle so that the sound is not muffled.

5. Using an interesting, animated voice. This is acoustically important since an interesting, animated voice will model a range of loudnesses, frequencies, and durations for the child. The child must hear them to begin to produce them. Adults typically use an interesting, animated voice when talking to small children, and one theory is that the reason they do this is that it signals the children that they are being talked to. Thus, even if the child does not understand all parts of the message, the child will know that this is talk being directed to him or her, and it is time to pay particular attention.

6. Providing varied repetition. This is a strategy widely used to try to patch-up communication breakdowns in interactions between adults, as well as between adults and children, regardless of hearing status: If the listener does not understand, try saying it another way. The difference here is that rather than repeating the same message several times while the child is not watching, the adult might repeat the message once, and the next time (without waiting any longer) provide a different form of the same message. If this third sending of the message is unsuccessful, then the child's attention should be drawn to the face.

7. Interacting more frequently. This suggestion is offered in an attempt to make up for the child's decreased exposure to spoken language. The decreased exposure refers to the listening time lost before the child began wearing hearing aids, as well as to the fact that most hearing-impaired children hear less spoken language than their peers because of difficulty in over-hearing, particularly when there is noise in the environment. Normally hearing children can effortlessly learn from talk directed at others within earshot and from conversations between others. Children with hearing loss learn best from talk which is directed at them and from talk which occurs within 6 to 8 inches of their hearing aid microphone. If the speakers are across the room, if there is noise in the room, and/or if the hearing-impaired child is engaged in an activity, messages between others may be unnoticed. Consequently, adults in the hearing-impaired child's life tend to make a special effort to communicate with him or her very frequently to make up for missed listening opportunities.

Within the interacting that adults do with hearing-impaired children, certain auditory aspects of the situation or the message can be made more salient, which is the fourth major practical implication of the fact that speech is most efficiently perceived auditorally. Examples follow of some audition-related items that might be emphasized, pointed out, repeated, contrasted, or otherwise highlighted in the course of normal, everyday conversations with a hearing-impaired child.

- Different levels of loudness and pitch of the voice can be connected to different speakers (the wolf versus Little Red Riding Hood, or the papa, mama, and baby bears in "The Three Bears"; also, different speakers within the family have higher or lower voices, and that is a good cue to use in trying to identify who the speaker is).
- Emotion is expressed through differences in loudness, pitch, and tension of the voice. In addition, the child needs to learn that the use of a very loud voice generally is not acceptable inside, but is fine in the playground.
- The voice follows characteristic intonational and rhythmic patterns to convey that the speaker is making a statement, asking a question (several

types), making a request, making a list, or reading a poem.
- With young children who have just begun wearing hearing aids, it is an important achievement when a child imitates or approximates the length of the adult utterance. When the child imitates the adult's "Uh-oh" in connection with something falling off of the table, the child's two-syllable imitation (regardless of whether the sounds themselves were exactly correct) should be met with a positive response from the adult.
- The sounds in speech differ from each other in terms of their intensity, frequency, and durational characteristics. This topic will be discussed more fully in the section entitled "Encouraging Clear Speech Development." However, it is mentioned here since listening for fine differences in speech sounds may be some of the most sophisticated listening done by the human ear and brain.

All of the auditory embellishing must obviously be carried out as part of the communicating which is going on. The next section focuses on strategies adults can use which target spoken language learning.

Encouraging Spoken Language Development

One of the best ways to learn to play soccer, swim, read, play chess, use a computer, or communicate using spoken language is to **do** it. At the same time, for each of those endeavors, it is also important to have a more knowledgeable person engaged in the activity with the learner to act as a correct model of the target behavior, and as a coach to shape the learning experience and to provide encouragement. Ideally, all of the adults in the very young hearing-impaired child's acquaintance will be able and interested in acting in those capacities to best facilitate the child's spoken language learning. The following discussion centers around the conditions which seem to be most conducive to spoken language learning which is occurring in the course of normal, everyday play and interacting with the child. There are two underlying assumptions for the discussion. One assumption is that for a very young child, most of the language learning is likely to occur in ordinary interactions with adults, rather than in therapy sessions (even though the latter are vitally important). The other assumption is that if the auditory-linguistic input is available early enough and in sufficient quantity and quality, the child can be expected to follow a normal, although possibly somewhat delayed, developmental course for spoken language development (Kretschmer & Kretschmer, 1978; Ling, 1976, 1989; Ling & Milne, 1981; Markides, 1986; Ramkalawan & Davis, 1992). Given these two assumptions, it becomes critically important to make the most of interactions between the hearing-impaired child and all of the adults who are significant in the child's life. Much of what follows is important in interacting with any young child, but becomes even more so when one is trying to maximize time and/or make up for lost listening and language-learning time.

Embellishments to Enhance Spoken Language Acquisition

Sensitivity and Awareness

For optimal learning, the very young child needs to get the message that the adult feels positively toward him or her (loves or likes him or her), is interested in him or her, and enjoys spending time with him or her (Bromwich, 1981; Clarke-Stewart, 1973; Dore, 1986; Thoman, 1981). The adult can express this through simply sitting near the child, watching what the child is doing, and being available and alert for any communicating the child might want to do. The adult can also express positive feelings toward the child through the way that the child is handled, such as through appropriately timed patting, hugging, smiling, or holding the child's hand, as well as through using a gentle tone of voice and friendly words. When the adult waits and watches to see what the child is interested in or is looking at, and then talks about whatever the child's focus happens to be, this is also likely to add to the child's impression that the adult cares about him. The child's interests and abilities change rapidly and dramatically from birth to age 3, as well as from 3 to 5 years of age. One of the best ways for an adult to "hit" the correct topic and level is to carefully observe the child before talking and then to talk about the child's focus. In addition, there are multitudinous books that can be consulted in order to surround the child of any age with developmentally appropriate activities, games, toys, and objects.

The adult's talk is likely to be especially well-received when it is paced according to the child's tempo in terms of both the amount of information presented and the rate at which is is presented. Pausing frequently is also useful. This allows and encourages the child to take his or her turn (during the speaker's expectant pause). Sometimes adults tend to do too much talking around hearing-impaired children, to do non-stop narration of obvious events that have little interest to the child, or to ask questions and then answer them themselves (Cross, 1984; Schodorf, 1982). Making an effort to talk about what the child is doing or is looking at and making a particular effort to pause frequently for the child to contribute to the interaction are strategies which should counteract those tendencies.

Clearly, this sort of child-focused interacting is probably some of the most important interacting that a child can do with an adult from a psychosocial point of view, as well as from a cognitive-linguistic one. It cannot be the only kind of interacting that occurs with a child, since children rarely have much interest in or a sense of urgency about getting clothes on, meals finished, toys picked up, or seatbelts on. That is, the child certainly needs to learn to listen and respond to the adult's agenda, also. But the child is more likely to do that if he or she has frequently experienced the adult being sensitive to and interested in listening to his or her agenda.

Special Considerations in Responding

In research studies, many parents of normally hearing and hearing-impaired children have been observed to be very responsive to their very young children's attempts to communicate (Anderson, 1979; Blennerhasset, 1984; Brazelton, Koslowski, & Main, 1974; Newson, 1977; Snow, 1977; Stern, 1974; Trevarthan, 1977). The crucial point seems to be the adult's ability to recognize the behaviors that may be attempts to communicate on the child's part. When the child can talk, this is a simple task. But prior to the emergence of words, the adult needs to be alert for changes in the child's rate of body movement or tension, changes in the child's facial expression or in the direction that the child is looking, as well as being alert for gestures and vocalizations (Bates, Benigni, Bretherton, Camaioni, & Volterra, 1979; Bateson, 1979; Carpenter, Mastergeorge, & Coggins, 1983; Lasky & Klopp, 1982; Scaife & Bruner, 1975). For a very young child who cannot yet speak, any of these may be part of an attempt to send a message. Even if the behavior really was not a communicative attempt, it does not hurt to treat it as if it were. This is exactly what many parents of very young children do: They interpret every gurgle and burp as communicative—as if the gurgle or burp were the child's way of taking a conversational turn—and the parents respond accordingly (Harding, 1983; Kaye & Charney, 1980, 1981; Snow, 1977; Snow, deBlauw, & Van Roosmalen, 1979). Consider this example of an exchange between a mother and the 2-month-old in her arms:

Child: /gurgle/
Mom: /smiling and putting her face close to the baby's/"Oh—is that what you think? You're so . . . o right!"

As the child gets older, parents gradually require behaviors that are more and more communicative before they will respond to them, such as vocalizations and gestures accompanied by particular gaze patterns. But the level of responsiveness remains high and is probably instrumental in encouraging and shaping children's attempts to communicate and to be involved in conversations, as a kind of self-fulfilling prophecy. The type of adult response varies, but usually includes the parent looking toward the child, as well as moving closer (or at least leaning toward the child), and some sort of verbal comment or question. There may also be smiling, nodding, and gesturing. The important element seems to be that the adult should be sensitive to the child's attempts to communicate—even if they are not words initially—and to respond in some positive manner to them.

There are some specific verbal responses that parents and professionals often use in responding to young children. For some adults these types of responses are automatic; for others they can become so. The three response types are:

- imitating the child's productions,
- providing the child with the words for what he wants to express, and
- expanding the child's productions.

Imitating the child was discussed in the scenario with Thea and her mother at the beginning of this article. For a child under the age of 12 months, entire interactive sequences can be based on the child making some sort of vocalization and the adult smiling and imitating it, the child laughing and vocalizing again, and the adult imitating that also, and so on. For somewhat older children, the adult's imitation can serve to confirm (or disconfirm) the adult's understanding of the child's utterance. For any age child, imitation has some additional benefits, also. For the adult to be able to imitate the child, the adult must be observing the child carefully enough to recognize the child's behavior as communicative, and must be following the **child's** focus of attention, rather than the adult's own interests.

The next strategy is the one of providing the child with the words the child needs to say what he or she wants to express. This strategy is similar to imitating the child in that it requires that the adult be observing the child carefully, be an accurate reader and interpreter of the child's cues, and be following the child's interests. To be a meaningful technique, obviously the adult's words must accurately fit with what the child wants to say. Not so obviously, though, this is a technique that can become useless from overuse. That is, if the adult is constantly verbalizing guesses about what the child could say in every situation, the adult may end up mindlessly narrating the scene or the action—and the child may well tune out the adult. Judiciously used at times when the child is actually trying to say something for which he or she does not have the words, this technique is generally recognized as making a very significant link between the child's cognitive understanding of an event and the linguistic expression of it (MacNamara, 1972; Snow, Midkiff-Borunda, Small, & Proctor, 1984; Vygotsky, 1978).

When the adult repeats the child's utterance and also adds to the child's utterance, either with additional ideas or with grammatical changes, the adult's utterance is called an "expansion." This kind of adult response to a child's utterance is often automatic, as the adult tries to be certain she or he has understood and because most adults do automatically produce the adult (correct) form of the child's utterance, rather than the incorrect or immature form. An example follows.

Context: The child has been petting a cat which the adult had been holding.
Child: "kikae rrrrrr."
Adult: "Yes! The kittycat is purring."

The adult's expansion in this instance is fairly minimal, as the adult primarily added syntactic items (the, is, -ing) and a correct phonologic model for "kittycat" and "purr." This is perfectly acceptable as an expansion. If the adult had added anything new to the scene in the responding utterance, the utterance would have qualified as an extended expansion.

Adult: "Yes! The kittycat is purring. I think the kitty is happy."

Extended expansions go beyond phonological, semantic, or syntactic correcting of the child's utterance to add new ideas or information. Furthermore, if the adult's extended expansion had some sort of attempt to get the child to respond in return, it might be even more powerful from a conversation-promoting point of view.

Adult: "Yes! The kittycat is purring. Do you think the kitty's happy?"

With this extended expansion, the adult has provided the grammatically and phonologically correct words for the exact focus of the child's attention, has introduced a new idea into the scene (the cat's frame of mind), and made an attempt to elicit continued conversation from the child. So often this sort of adult responding is done without any conscious effort; yet adult expansions of child utterances have long been considered to have enormous importance for promoting the child's language development (Barnes, Gutfreund, Satterly, & Wells, 1983; Cross, 1977; Ellis & Wells, 1980; Folger & Chapman, 1978; Furrow, Nelson, & Benedict, 1979; Kaye & Charney, 1980, 1981; Nelson, 1973; Newport, Gleitman, & Gleitman, 1977; Scherer & Olswang, 1984).

Hopefully, the "normality" of all of the strategies that have been suggested for promoting spoken language development is apparent. What is different or embellished for the hearing-impaired child is that there is a heightened consciousness on the adult's part of the vital importance of frequently and consistently putting these strategies into practice: being particularly sensitive, positive, child-focused, child-paced, and responsive, as well as employing strategies such as imitation, providing needed words, and expanding the child's productions.

Encouraging Clear Speech Development

In this section, "speech" refers to the following aspects of vocal productions:

- **prosody:** the cumulative effect of a particular language's conventional ways of producing intonational change and rhythmic features; the melody of the voice in a particular language;

- **quality of the voice:** tense/relaxed, oral/nasal, weak/strong, breath support; and
- **articulation:** the production of individual speech sounds (although, in practice, speech sounds are nearly always produced in conjunction with each other, that is, in co-articulated syllables).

Although speech abilities continue to develop into the early school years, having a normal-sounding voice and relatively clear speech has some definite advantages even for the toddler and preschool groups. Being able to speak clearly allows others to understand the child easily, which means that the conversation can continue and can stay centered on the message being exchanged. Having the conversation continue also means that the child is potentially being exposed to even more language and more information. Speakers naturally seek out others who are easy and enjoyable to speak with; a small child who can speak clearly is often given the message that he or she is a clever and valued conversational partner. Conversely, the small child who cannot speak clearly may be ignored when he or she speaks, or even avoided by speakers who do not want to take the time to try to understand, are embarrassed by their own lack of understanding, or who may have decided that the whole process of communicating verbally is just too frustrating for the child. Conversations with these children are marked by too-frequent breakdowns in the flow of information, where everything stops while the listener tries to determine what it was the child was trying to say before the child gets too upset or gives up. Of course, conversational breakdowns occur between fluent speakers, also, but relatively infrequently.

Articulatory differences in the speech of young normally hearing children can be from a variety of causes (including the categories "normal development" and "unknown"). These same causes are possible for unclear speech in hearing-impaired children. But usually when the speech of a hearing-impaired child is very unclear, it is either because of the severity of the child's hearing loss or because the child has not experienced the kind of teaching which would promote good speech. Fortunately, most hearing-impaired children can hear a great deal of the essential parts of speech and have the potential for ultimately learning to speak clearly enough for most people to understand them. Even at the preschool level, many hearing-impaired children are easily understood by their families, teachers, and others familiar to them. Most of the following discussion addresses the kinds of things that adults who are frequently with the hearing-impaired child (parents, relatives, preschool teachers) can do as speech-related embellishments of everyday events. But first, a brief discussion of the essential parts of speech and their availability to hearing-impaired children.

The Child's Ability to Hear the Sounds of Speech

Earlier in this chapter, the three major acoustic dimensions of intensity, duration, and pitch were illustrated using examples from speech. The point was repeatedly made that, wearing properly selected and maintained hearing aids, most hearing-impaired children can hear most of those dimensions. This is important because whatever dimensions the child can hear in others' speech, the child can use as a model for his or her own speech productions.

Let us consider the speech aspects mentioned above (prosody, voice quality, and articulation) and see where they would fall relative to the audiogram of a child who has some residual hearing, but very little. Most hearing-impaired children (well over 80%) have more residual hearing than this child. With his hearing aids on, the child has thresholds in the speech "banana" only in the lower frequencies, 250 and 500 Hz. The prosodic features of duration, rhythm, and intonation all have major cues contained in the low frequencies so the child should be able to learn to listen for those prosodic features. In addition, even with only low frequency hearing, the child has access to the acoustic cues for the difference between an oral and a nasal-sounding voice, as well as for the cues to a voice that is strong and properly supported by the breathstream versus one that is not. And finally, a number of acoustic cues for specific speech sound contrasts are available in the low frequencies. These include the nasal murmur (for /m/, /n/, /ŋ/), the first formants of most vowels, and the primary cues for discriminating amongst semi-vowels, nasals, and plosives with mid- and back vowels. With more residual hearing, a child obviously has more and more of the acoustic cues important for speech perception available to him, particularly those related to articulation.

Ling (1989, pp. 64–75) has an excellent discussion of the relationship between the amount of residual hearing the child has and specific aspects of speech the child can be expected to hear and learn to use. Realistically, regular preschool teachers, child care workers, and some parents may not have the background or interest to deal with this level of technicality. But the professional who is guiding the intervention for this child needs to be conversant with the relationship between speech acoustic characteristics and this particular child's auditory abilities. If the child does have the auditory capacity to detect the salient characteristics of a sound, then other means (visual or tactile) need to be employed in individual work with the child and parents. What everyone involved needs to know is that:

1. It is possible to make fairly reliable estimates of what the child should be able to learn to listen for, and
2. Most hearing-impaired children have enough residual hearing to hear a great number of the important aspects of speech.

Embellishments to Enhance Speech Learning

Speech target embellishing can be divided according whether the focus is on some aspect of voice quality or prosody, or whether the focus is on a specific vowel or consonant sound. Some desirable speech behaviors and suggestions for embellishments follow.

Abundant Vocalizing

When the child's hearing loss is not detected until after the age of about 12 months, the child may have experienced a long period of time without the ability to listen to the speech of others. The result, for a child whose loss is of severe-to-profound degree, may be that the child has stopped vocalizing, or vocalizes very little, or vocalizes using a very limited number of sounds. Typically those sounds would be a few neutral-sounding vowels which could almost be produced simply by opening the mouth and vocalizing, rather than by placing the articulators in any particular position. Examples would be sounds such as the /ɛ/ sound as in "bed" or the /ʌ/ sound as in "mud." Consonants would generally be absent, with the exception of consonants such as /b/ or /m/ which are easily visible, and which provide a certain amount of orosensory feedback. Short, rough, growling, or grunting sounds are also possible.

If this is the case, the immediate goal is to encourage an abundance of varied vocalizing by the child. Sometimes this begins to occur spontaneously as soon as the child begins consistent wearing of hearing aids. In any case, the adults in the child's life need to "reinforce" whatever vocalizing the child does by using responsive techniques such as immediately imitating the child, moving closer, smiling, and saying something briefly and then waiting with an expectant expression for the child's next contribution. Variety in the child's vocalizing may be variety in the prosodic features or in vowels and consonants, all of which are discussed below.

Control of Voice Quality and Prosodic Features

A fluent speaker of English usually uses a voice which is oral in quality and has a certain amount of strength and breath support associated with it. Sometimes, however, fluent speakers need to be able to produce a nasal quality in the voice and to speak with variations of strength (intensity) and breathiness. Fluent speakers also frequently produce variations of high and low voicing, rhythmic patterns, and stress features on particular syllables within words or phrases. The hearing-impaired child who is acquiring spoken language also needs to acquire flexible control of these features, which, as mentioned above, are auditorally available even to children with minimal residual hearing. Often after a child has begun to wear hearing aids, adults notice that the child is "playing with his or her voice," making high and low sounds, loud and soft sounds, yells, screeches, and quiet babble, and that the vocalizing begins to sound more speech-like in rhythmic patterns. With the wearing of hearing aids, the child is now able to hear these features in the speech of others, and is trying out his or her own voice on them. All of the child's attempts of this nature should be responded to in positive ways, similar to the suggestions made for trying to increase the amount and variety of the child's vocalizing. Sometimes when the child has very little residual hearing, variations in prosodic features do not appear spontaneously for a long time. One of the things that can be done to help the process along is to try to make the features more salient. One idea is to pair a particular prosodic pattern with a frequently occurring expression and to use that exact intonation and rhythmic pattern every time it is possible and appropriate to do so. An example would be the use of "Uh-oh" with a falling intonation and a characteristic short/long rhythmic pattern. This could be used every time some small domestic crisis occurred such as toys falling on the floor, pets misbehaving, messes being made, things being forgotten, flowers being pulled off stems, or squirrels eating the tomatoes. Speaking close to the child's microphone, the adult would say the "Uh-oh" using a slightly exaggerated prosodic pattern and facial expression to match, and would then pause expectantly to leave space for the child to try to imitate or vocalize in response. The adult might then repeat the "Uh-oh" and carry on with "Look at this mess" /pause/. "Let's clean it up" /pause/. Other examples of possible expressions to use for targeting prosodic patterns are in the Appendix, although any frequently occurring words or phrases could be used.

Vowels and Consonants

When the child spontaneously begins to produce vowel-like or consonant-like babble or words that include correct vowels and consonants, the adult response should be positive to encourage the child to do even more of it. Similar to what was suggested for prosodic features, vowels and consonants that occur in particular words or expressions can be paired consistently to make them more salient. Examples of sound-toy and sound-event associations are in the Appendix, although these should be viewed as only a limited list of examples. The child's parents should probably compile their own list of words and expressions that they frequently use, and add to it to target the full variety of sounds.

Summary

In summary, then, the very young hearing-impaired child will be learning spoken language primarily through daily interactive encounters with the adults in his or her life. The child is likely to learn best if the following conditions exist at home, in parent-toddler or preschool settings, as well as in therapy.

1. The child is wearing appropriately selected and properly maintained hearing aids.
2. The adult is conscious of noise and distance conditions that exist in all interactive situations, in that the closer the adult is to the child's hearing aid microphone and the quieter the situation, the better for the child's auditory reception of the message.
3. The relationship between the child and the adult is warm and friendly, with the adult using an interesting and animated voice appropriate to conversing with children.
4. When possible and appropriate, the adult's talk is directly related to whatever the **child** is looking at, playing with, or interested in, rather than whatever the adult might find interesting.
5. The adult provides age-appropriate toys and activities for the child and takes the time to interact individually with the child as often as possible. Clearly, hearing-impaired children need to have opportunities to play by themselves as much as normally hearing children do. But for the hearing-impaired child who is learning spoken language, a special effort needs to be made to try to make up for listening time lost prior to wearing the hearing aids, as well as for the fact that most hearing-impaired children cannot easily overhear and learn from the spoken language of others.
6. The adult talks in accordance with the child's tempo in terms of the times when the adult inserts talk, the amount of information presented, the length and complexity of the language used, and the rate at which the information is presented.
7. The adult pauses frequently for the child to take a turn. This includes sometimes simply sitting quietly near the child and being available for whatever spontaneous communicating the child may want to do.
8. The adult is very responsive to the child's attempts to communicate, including early attempts that are not actual words or phrases. The adult's positive response may be smiling, nodding, moving closer, imitating the child, providing the child with the appropriate words, expanding the child's production, or some other response which gives the child the message that the adult is interested in continuing the exchange.
9. The adult is aware of desirable voice quality and prosodic features for the child to develop, as well as the variety of possible speech sounds. These aspects are consistently used by the adult in sound-toy and sound-event associations as frequently as possible in the course of normal events.
10. Until it is known that the child cannot hear speech, the adult assumes that he or she can, since the vast majority of

hearing-impaired children can hear conversational speech with their hearing aids on, if the distance and surrounding noise are not too great. Evidence that the adult is expecting the child to hear will be that the adult uses strategies such as talking when the child is not watching the adult's face, directing the child's attention toward an activity while talking, and occasionally covering her or his mouth.

References

Anderson, B. J. (1979). Parents' strategies for achieving conversational interactions with young hearing-impaired children. In A. Simmons-Martin & D. R. Calvert (Eds.), *Parent-infant intervention* (pp. 223–244). New York: Grune & Stratton.

Barnes, S., Gutfreund, M., Satterly, D., & Wells, G. (1983). Characteristics of adult speech which predict children's language development. *Journal of Child Language, 10*, 65–84.

Bates, E., Benigni, L., Bretherton, I., Camaioni, L., & Volterra, V. (1979). *The emergence of symbols: Cognition and communication in infancy.* New York: Academic Press.

Bateson, M. C. (1979). The epigenesis of conversational interaction: A personal account of research development. In M. Bullowa (Ed.), *Before speech: The beginnings of interpersonal communication* (pp. 63–77). Cambridge: Cambridge University Press.

Blennerhasset, L. (1984). Communication styles of a 13-month-old hearing-impaired child and her parents. *Volta Review, 86*(4), 217–228.

Brazelton, T. B., Koslowski, B., & Main, M. (1974). The origins of reciprocity. In M. L. Lewis & L. A. Rosenblum (Eds.), *The effect of the infant on its caregiver* (pp. 49–76). New York: John Wiley & Sons.

Bromwich, R. (1981). *Working with parents and infants: An inter-actional approach.* Baltimore: University Park Press.

Carpenter, R. L., Mastergeorge, A. M., & Coggins, T. E. (1983). The acquisition of communicative intentions in infants eight to fifteen months of age. *Language and Speech, 26*, 101–116.

Clarke-Stewart, K. A. (1973). Interactions between mothers and their young children: characteristics and consequences. *Monographs of the Society for Research in Child Development, 38* (Nos. 6 and 7, Serial No. 149).

Cole, E. B. (1992a). *Listening and talking: A guide to promoting spoken language in young hearing-impaired children.* Washington, DC: A. G. Bell Association for the Deaf.

Cole, E. B. (1992b). Promoting emerging speech in birth to 3 year-old hearing-impaired children. *Volta Review, 94*, 63–77.

Cole, E. B., & Paterson, M. M. (1984). Assessment and treatment of phonological disorders in the hearing-impaired. In J. Costello (Ed.), *Speech disorders in children* (pp. 93–127). San Diego, CA: College-Hill Press.

Cross, T. G. (1977). Mother's speech adjustments: The contribution of selected child listener variables. In C. E. Snow & C. A. Ferguson (Eds.), *Talking to children: Language Input and Acquisition* (pp. 151–188). Cambridge: Cambridge University Press.

Cross, T. G. (1984). Habilitating the language-impaired child: Ideas from studies of parent-infant interaction. *Topics in Language Disorders, 4*, 1–14.

Dore, J. (1986). The development of conversational competence. In R. L. Schiefelbusch (Ed.), *Language competence: Assessment and intervention* (pp. 3–60). San Diego, CA: College-Hill Press.

Ellis, R., & Wells, G. (1980). Enabling factors in adult-child discourse. *First Language, 1*, 46–82.

Erber, N. P. (1982). *Auditory training.* Washington, DC: A. G. Bell Association for the Deaf.

Estabrooks, W. (1993). Still listening . . . auditory-verbal therapy for "older" children. *Volta Review, 95*, 231–252.

Estabrooks, W. (1994). *Auditory-verbal therapy for parents and professionals.* Washington, DC: A. G. Bell Association for the Deaf.

Folger, J. P., & Chapman, R. S. (1978). A pragmatic analysis of spontaneous imitations. *Journal of Child Language, 5*, 25–38.

Fry, D. B. (1978). The role and primacy of the auditory channel in speech and language development. In M. Ross & T. G. Giolas (Eds.), *Auditory management of hearing-impaired children* (pp. 15–43). Baltimore: University Park Press.

Furrow, D., Nelson, K. E., & Benedict, H. (1979). Mothers' speech to children and syntactic development: Some simple relationships. *Journal of Child Language, 6,* 423–442.

Harding, C. G. (1983). Setting the stage for language acquisition: Communication development in the first year. In R. M. Golinkoff (Ed.), *The transition from prelinguistic to linguistic communication* (pp. 93–113). Hillsdale, NJ: Lawrence Erlbaum.

Kaye, K., & Charney, R. (1980). How mothers maintain "dialogue" with two-year-olds. In D. Olson (Ed.), *The social foundations of language and thought* (pp. 211–230). New York: Norton.

Kaye, K., & Charney, R. (1981). Conversational asymmetry between mothers and children. *Journal of Child Language, 8,* 35–50.

Kent, R. D., & Reed, C. (1992). *The acoustic analysis of speech.* San Diego, CA: Singular Publishing Group, Inc.

Kile, J. E., & Beauchaine, K. L. (1991). Identification, assessment, and management of hearing impairment in infants and toddlers. *Infant-Toddler Intervention, 1*(1), 61–81.

Klevans, D. R. (1988). Counseling strategies for communication disorders. In R. F. Curlee (Ed.), *Counseling in Speech, Language, Hearing. Seminars in Speech and Language, 9*(3), 185–208.

Kretschmer R. R. & Kretschmer, L. W. (1978). *Language development and intervention with the hearing-impaired.* Baltimore: University Park Press.

Lasky, E. Z., & Klopp, K. (1982). Parent-child interactions in normal and language-disordered children. *Journal of Speech and Hearing Disorders, 47,* 7–18.

Ling, D. (1976). *Speech and the hearing-impaired child: Theory and practice.* Washington, DC: A.G. Bell Association for the Deaf.

Ling, D. (1981). Keep your hearing-impaired child within earshot. *Newsounds, 6,* 5–6.

Ling, D. (1986). Devices and procedures for auditory learning. In E. B. Cole, & H. Gregory (Eds.), *Auditory learning* (pp. 19–28). Washington, DC: A. G. Bell Association for the Deaf.

Ling, D. (1989). *Foundations of spoken language for hearing-impaired children.* Washington, DC: A. G. Bell Association for the Deaf.

Ling, D., & Ling, A. (1978). *Aural habilitation: The foundations of verbal learning in hearing-impaired children.* Washington, DC: A. G. Bell Association for the Deaf.

Ling, D., & Milne, M. (1981). The development of speech in hearing-impaired children. In F. Bess, B. A. Freeman, & J. S. Sinclair (Eds.), *Amplification in education* (pp. 98–108). Washington, DC: A. G. Bell Association for the Deaf.

Luterman, D. (1979). *Counseling parents of hearing-impaired children.* Boston, MA: Little, Brown & Co.

Luterman, D. (1984). *Counseling the communicatively disordered and their families.* Boston, MA: Little, Brown & Co.

MacNamara, J. (1972). Cognitive basis of language learning in Infants. *Psychological Review, 77,* 282–293.

Markides, A. (1986). The use of residual hearing in the education of hearing-impaired children: A historical perspective. In E. B. Cole & H. Gregory (Eds.), *Auditory learning* (pp. 57–66). Washington, DC: A. G. Bell Association for the Deaf.

Moses, K., & Van Hecke-Wulatin, M. (1981). The socio-emotional impact of infant deafness: A counselling model. In G. T. Mencher & S. E. Gerber (Eds.), *Early management of hearing loss* (pp. 243–278). New York: Grune & Stratton.

Nelson, K. E. (1973). Structure and strategy in learning to talk. *Monographs of the Society for Research in Child Development, 38* (Serial No. 149).

Newby, H. A., & Popelka, G. R. (1992). *Audiology* (6th ed). Englewood Cliffs, NJ: Prentice Hall, Inc.

Newport, E. L., Gleitman, H., & Gleitman, L. R. (1977). Mother, I'd rather do it myself: Some effects and non-effects of maternal speech style. In C. E. Snow & C. A. Ferguson (Eds.), *Talking to children: Language input and acquisition* (pp. 109–149). Cambridge: Cambridge University Press.

Newson, J. (1977). The growth of shared understandings between infant and caregiver. In M. Bullowa (Ed.), *Before speech: The beginnings of interpersonal communication* (pp. 207–222). Cambridge: Cambridge University Press.

Northcott, W. H. (Ed.). (1977). *Curriculum guide for hearing-impaired children—Birth to three years—and their parents*. Washington, DC: A. G. Bell Association for the Deaf.

Northcott, W. H. (Ed.). (1978) *I heard that! A developmental sequence of listening activities for the young child*. Washington, DC: A. G. Bell Association for the Deaf.

Pollack, D. (1985). *Educational audiology for the limited-hearing infant and preschooler* (2nd ed.). Springfield, IL: Charles C Thomas.

Ramkalawan, T., & Davis, A. C. (1992). The effects of hearing loss and age of intervention on some language metrics in a population of young hearing-impaired children. *British Journal of Audiology, 26*, 97–107.

Sanders, D. A. (1977). *Auditory perception of speech*. Englewood Cliffs, NJ: Prentice-Hall.

Sanders, D. A. (1993). *Management of hearing handicap: Infants to elderly*. Englewood Cliffs, NJ: Prentice Hall.

Scaife, M., & Bruner, J. (1975). The capacity for joint visual attention in the infant. *Nature, 253*, 265–268.

Scherer, N., & Olswang, L. (1984). Role of mothers' expansions in stimulating children's language production. *Journal of Speech and Hearing Research, 27*, 387–396.

Schodorf, J. K. (1982). A comparative analysis of parent-child interactions of language-delayed and linguistically normal children. *Dissertation Abstracts International, 42*(5), 1838-B.

Schuyler, V. S., & Rushmer, N. (1987). *Parent-infant habilitation: A comprehensive approach to working with hearing-impaired infants and toddlers and their families*. Portland, OR: Infant Hearing Resource.

Schuyler, V. S., Rushmer, N., Arpan, R., Melum, A., Sowers, J., & Kennedy, N. (1985). *Parent-infant communication*. Portland, OR: Infant Hearing Resource.

Simser, J. I., & Steacie, P. (1993). A hospital clinic early intervention program. *The Volta Review, 95*(5) (monograph), 65–74.

Snow, C. E. (1977). The development of conversation between mothers and babies. *Journal of Child Language, 4*, 1–22.

Snow, C. E., deBlauw, S., & Van Roosmalen, G. (1979). Talking and playing with babies: The role of ideologies of child-rearing. In M. Bullowa (Ed.), *Before speech: The beginnings of interpersonal communication* (pp. 269–288). Cambridge: Cambridge University Press.

Snow, C. E., Midkiff-Borunda, S., Small, A., & Proctor, A. (1984). Therapy as social interaction: Analyzing the context of language remediation. *Topics in Language Disorders, 4*, 72–85.

Stern, D. N. (1974). Mother and infant at play: The dyadic interaction involving facial, vocal, and gaze behaviors. In M. L. Lewis & L. A. Rosenblum (Eds.), *The effects of the infant on its caregiver* (pp. 187–213). New York: John Wiley & Sons.

Thoman, E. B. (1981). Affective communication as the prelude and context for language learning. In R. L. Schiefelbusch & D. D. Bricker (Eds.), *Early language: Acquisition and intervention* (pp. 181–200). Baltimore: University Park Press.

Trevarthen, C. (1977). Descriptive analyses of infant communicative behavior. In H. R. Schaffer (Ed.), *Studies on mother-infant interaction* (pp. 227–270). London: Academic Press.

Vygotsky, L., (1978). *Mind in society*. Cambridge, MA: Harvard University Press.

Address correspondence to:
Elizabeth B. Cole, Ed.D.,
Associate Professor, Aural Habilitation,
School of Communication Sciences and Disorders,
McGill University
1266 Pine Avenue West
Montreal, Quebec, Canada H3G 1A8

Appendix

Sound-Toy and Sound-Event Associations[4]

Intonation: Use expressions such as "uh oh" (for things falling down), "all gone" (for food being finished), "oh no!" (for toys colliding or breaking; accidents of all kinds), "Wow!" (for delightful events), "mmmm" (for anything smelling or tasting good), /a/ or /ai/ of long duration (to signify flying of airplanes or birds). Produce the phrases with very marked high/low contrasts of the intonational contours.

Intensity: Use "Shhh!" and a whisper for any quiet events such as a baby or doll sleeping. Play the "Wake Up" game where one person closes their eyes and pretends to sleep ("Shhh! X is sleeping.") The other one shouts "Boo!" or the person's name to wake them up.

Duration: Use expressions that have interesting contrasts of rhythmic patterns such as "So . . . big!"; or "Drip, drip, drip" for a faucet or for rain falling off a flower; or "mmmm" for something smelling or tasting good; or "up up up—down" for a small doll climbing up a slide and then coming down; "Choo-choo" for a train.

Vowels	/a/	hop hop hop (a rabbit or a frog); hot!
	/i/	Peek a boo! or Peek! Go to sleep! Whee!
	/u/	Boo! moooo, ooooooooooo (train whistle)
	/au/	meow, bowwow, ow! round and round, mouth
	/ai/	bye-bye, boo
	/ɛ/	bed, wet!
	/ʊ/	push, woof woof
	/æ/	quack quack, Daddy
	/ʌ/	up, cut
	/o/	nose, no no!, It broke./It's broken.
Consonants	/b/	bye-bye, boo
	/p/	/pʌpʌpʌ/ (boat sound), pop! (bubbles)
	/w/	walk walk walk (any toy or person walking)
	/m/	mmmm (for something smelling or tasting good)
	/h/	hi! hohoho (Santa Claus)
	/ʃ/	Shhh
	/f/	off! foot
	/tʃ/	ch-ch-ch (train sound)
	/r/	Errrrrrr (siren sound)
	/l/	hello

---

[4]*Source:* Reprinted with permission from "Promoting Emerging Speech in Birth to 3-Year-Old Hearing-Impaired Children," Elizabeth B. Cole, Ed.D., *The Volta Review*, Vol. 94 No. 5, p. 77. Copyright © 1992 by the Alexander Graham Bell Association for the Deaf, 3417 Volta Place, NW, Washington, DC 20007.

Part II:
Enhancing the Overall Performance of Children with Physical Limitations

The Relationship Between Powered Mobility and Early Learning in Young Children with Physical Disabilities

Richard A. Neeley, Ph.D.
Arkansas State University
Jonesboro, Arkansas

Phyllis A. Neeley, M.S.P.
Northeast Arkansas Comprehensive Learning Center
Jonesboro, Arkansas

The purpose of this article is to inform the reader of the importance of independent locomotion as it pertains to early learning. Because of restricted mobility, young children with physical disabilities in the first 3 years of life are at a disadvantage in the areas of learning, socialization, and independence. Restricted mobility may have a lasting, negative influence on the overall development of the child. Powered mobility is one form of technology that has been shown through clinical experience and research projects to be safe and effective in providing independent locomotion. Children as young as 17 months can be taught to use powered mobility. Through the use of this technology, some children with physical disabilities are better able to explore and manipulate their environment.

Theoretical Basis for Early Learning

How do young children learn? How do they become active participants in their world? Developmental theorists such as Bruner (1983), Piaget (1959), and Vygotsky (1978) believe that experiences with objects and people form the foundation for future learning. It is through these experiences that children develop an array of concepts and meanings while they build an understanding of their world. Therefore, children learn by making sense of their experiences (Genishi, 1988).

The casual observer can witness a variety of learning behaviors normally exhibited by developing young children. Children are curious by nature and seem to move constantly in their environment. They look, listen, and physically manipulate objects. They throw, bang, ride, roll, rattle, and "mouth" toys. It is this interaction with objects and people that forms the basis of learning.

Children initially learn from experience. These routine experiences occur naturally in their everyday lives and are embedded in their appropriate social contexts. From these experiences, children begin to expand their learning to include concepts and words. Developmental theorists argue that this experience-based learning continues beyond the preschool years (Genishi, 1988).

Negative Impact of Restricted Mobility

Developmental disabilities interfere with normal development by reducing the child's ability to experience the variety of stimuli in the world. The child may well become a passive recipient instead of an active initiator or participant of experience (Butler, 1988).

Efficient mobility is an important skill that many physically disabled children may never completely master. For even those children with the poorest prognosis for ambulation, much attention is given to promoting efficient movement. This attention can be manifested through a variety of means, including a number of invasive and expensive techniques such as surgery, braces, splints, and casts (Butler, Okamoto, & McKay, 1983). One rationale for promoting efficient movement in children with poor prognosis for individual mobility is that movement fosters exploration. Without exploration, the child misses vitally important experiences that will influence subsequent behavior and development (Butler, 1988).

Ambulation and mobility promote exploration of the environment, enhance social interaction, and foster communication (Porto & Lipka, 1992). Locomotion and other motor skills develop quickly early in a child's life. During the first 3 years of life, children use locomotion for learning socialization, independence, and competence (Butler, Okamoto, & McKay, 1983).

Without actively exploring and learning, the child becomes a passive recipient of life rather than an active participant. Active learning is essential for toddlers. They need to explore with their senses and discover for themselves the relationships between objects and persons. They need to make choices, interact directly, and manipulate not only objects but people (Muilenburg-Wilson & Nygard, 1992).

Lastly, when a disability diminishes the ability to speak and/or communicate, the child becomes a passive member of society instead of a productive, interactive one. The inability to influence the environment or manipulate it can lead to learned helplessness. Repeated failures to explore, interact, or communicate decreases the probability of further attempts (Butler, 1988).

Assistive Technology and Powered Mobility

Using assistive technology, children can overcome problems associated with intellectual, communicative, and physical disabilities. *Assistive technology* is defined as anything that allows or enables a disabled person to exercise some control over his or her life or environment so that he or she is, or may become, more fully integrated into society (Staff, 1991). Assistive technology offers opportunities for the physically disabled child to overcome some of the obstacles that interfere with his or her normal development. Technological advances in powered mobility are allowing children with physical disabilities to participate in a child's occupation — namely play. It is the hope that assistive technology can take the handicap out of disabilities (Butler, 1988).

Powered wheelchairs, adapted toys, microcomputers, augmentative communication devices, environmental control systems, and prosthetics now offer persons with disabilities the opportunity to experience learning, communicating, and socializing (United Cerebral Palsy Association, *Technology: The Future Is Today,* 1989). Assistive technology has the potential of eliminating the obvious differences in children's physical skills and abilities and giving the child with disabilities a more equal chance to achieve and learn in a normal environment (Haney, 1992).

Research projects that have dealt with powered mobility have focused on the earliest age at which children can successfully learn to safely and efficiently operate a powered device designed for independent locomotion. Most studies include children ranging in age from 30 to 60 months. However, it has been shown that children as young as 17 months can learn to operate the devices (Butler, 1988). These studies have also shown many positive benefits that were not initially anticipated. It was felt that powered mobility could have a negative effect on motor development. By enabling the child to move about in his environment, it was felt that he would not be motivated to continue working on skills for independent locomotion. But contrary to these thoughts, researchers found that the children with powered mobility exhibited improved head control, more hand-arm function, better trunk stability, and an increase in motivation for physical therapy or training (Butler, 1988). Perceptual development also improves because now the child who could not move has mobility. He or she can experience spatial relationships and the concepts related to body position in space. With powered mobility, children can propel themselves through space and increase their potential for perceptual growth (Trefler & Cook, 1992).

As mentioned before, powered mobility has the capability of assisting children in experiencing the world. They can control their environment, they can explore their environment, and like their normally developing peers they are empowered with the option of choosing to appropriately or inappropriately interact within that environment (Trefler & Cook, 1992).

Powered mobility does not have to be cost prohibitive. Devices such as a power scooter board that is switch driven can be purchased for approximately $350.00. Conversion kits are commercially available for do-it-yourself modifications usually for less than $200.00. Conversely, powered mobility can become quite sophisticated and expensive with prices ranging up to $10,000.00 (see the Appendix for selected manufacturers' descriptions obtained from Hyper-ABLEDATA, 1991, which is a database developed with funding from the National Institute on Disabilities and Rehabilitation Research).

Commercially available options for powered mobility devices include three- and four-wheel vehicles or chairs. They are all generally accessed or operated by fingertip controls, modified hand controls, joysticks, switches, or some combination of these. There are a variety of seating options that can be customized for the individual, such as adjustable head support, chest harnesses, lap belts, footrests, armrests, and elevated seating. Many of the devices offer automatic brakes, speed dampening, adjustable steering column, headlights, taillights, crutch holders, baskets for respiratory aids, and environmental control systems. Top speed is

4.5 miles per hour with a 20-mile limit between battery charges. Most of the powered mobility devices weigh up to 125 pounds. These can be dismantled without tools and usually fit in the trunk of an average size automobile. Supervisor override switches can be installed on most devices. These are used to minimize the potential for personal harm and property damage during the training stage.

Powered mobility must not be viewed solely as a means of transportation or training for powered wheelchairs. It is an opportunity to experience the world through independent movement (Porto & Lipka, 1992). Butler (1986) studied the benefits of powered mobility in six children who ranged in age from 24 to 39 months. All children became competent drivers of motorized wheelchairs as evidenced by their passing "driving tests" after practicing an average of 16 days. The competency test included driving in narrow hallways, making turns, and maneuvering around people and objects. An additional child (18 months of age) also learned to drive skillfully in a 3-week period. None of the children suffered any harm, and many positive responses were cited by parents in the areas of motor behavior, emotional maturity, and social interactions. Other behaviors analyzed in this study included frequency of self-initiated exploration in space, object interaction, and communication with parents and caregivers. Based on the results of this portion of the study, Butler (1986) concluded the following:

Three children showed increases in all three behaviors; one increased in communication and exploration; and two increased in spatial exploration only. The decreased communication for the last two children was regarded as positive, however, because they had been quite verbal and demanding. Independence through locomotion may have reduced their need for control through speech. (p. 68)

Further investigation of the benefits of powered mobility was conducted by Porto and Lipka (1992). These researchers investigated the responses of young children (13 months to 48 months of age) with physical disabilities to early powered mobility. Some of these subjects had a positive prognosis for walking either independently or with a walker. The onset of independent ambulation was predicted to occur much later for these subjects than for their normally developing peers. The remainder of the subject group had a poor prognosis for walking and would require a wheelchair of some kind. All the children were given a powered riding toy. Examples of these toys include Big Foot, Classic Convertible, Lil' Suzuki, Power Ride Honda ATC, and Armstrong Mobile Command Poweride. All the toys were modified to accommodate the size of the child and some round steering wheels were converted to tiller-style handle bars. Formal analysis of all research data is not yet available, however, one general trend was readily observed. All children learned to make the toy move regardless of his or her cognitive ability. Even with more significant motor delays, children with higher cognitive functioning levels became more proficient with their toy.

Studies such as these demonstrate the benefits of powered mobility for preschool children with physical disabilities. These devices afford these children the opportunity to experience independent movement, the ability to participate more equally with nondisabled children, and the opportunity to interact with their peers.

Summary

Powered mobility appears to be a powerful tool for enhancing overall child development. It can be used as a strategy for teaching communication, promoting social interaction, and, most important, introducing environmental exploration that will lead to later learning.

References

Bruner, J. (1983). *Child's talk*. New York: Norton.

Butler, C. (1986). Effects of powered mobility on self-initiated behaviors of very young children with locomotor disability. *Developmental Medicine and Child Neurology, 28,* 325–332.

Butler, C. (1988). High tech tots: Technology for mobility, manipulation, communication, and learning in early childhood. *Infants and Young Children, 1*(2), 66–73.

Butler, C., Okamoto, G., & McKay, T. (1983). Powered mobility for very young disabled children. *Developmental Medicine and Child Neurology, 25,* 472–474.

Genishi, C. G. (1988, November). Children's language: Learning words from experience. *Young Children,* 16–23.

Haney, C. A. (1992). The place for assistive technology. *Asha, 34,* 47–49.

Hyper-ABLEDATA — Fourth Edition. (1991). [Computer Data Base of Assistive Technology and Devices]. Madison, WI: Trace Research and Development Center.

Muilenburg-Wilson, D., & Nygard, J. (1992). Tech for tots — "A trip to the farm." *Closing the Gap, 11*(11), 18–19, 61.

Piaget, J. (1959). *The language and thought of the child* (M. Gabain & R. Gabain, Trans.). London: Routledge & Kegan Paul. (Original work published 1926)

Porto, M., & Lipka, D. (1992, June). Toy power. *TeamRehab Report,* 35–40.

Staff. (1991, July). Technology: Removing the shroud of mystery. *S.M.A.R.T. Moves.*

Trefler, E., & Cook, H. (1992, August). *Powered mobility for children.* Workshop conducted at the meeting of the Technology & Language Collaboration, West Memphis, AR.

United Cerebral Palsy Associations. (1989). *Technology: The future is today.* Washington, DC: Author.

Vygotsky, L. S. (1978). *Mind in society: The development of higher psychological processes.* Cambridge, MA: Harvard University Press.

Address correspondence to:
Richard A. Neeley, Ph.D.,
Special Education and Communicative Disorders,
Arkansas State University, P.O. Box 940, State University, AR 72467-0940.

Appendix

Brand Name: Motorized Scooter Board

Generic Name: Scooter board

Description: Motorized scooter board. Switch closure makes board go slowly in a circle. Control jack will accommodate a variety of switches. Adjustable wedge and abduction block for legs, block positioners for torso. Board accommodates seats and other inserts on platform, or parapodium, long leg and other braces. Custom modifications possible.

Comments: Scooter board lets children who cannot move independently learn to control their bodies in space, to stop at obstacles, and to reinforce learning of cause and effect relationships.

Cost: $350.00, 1993 price

Manufacturer: Toys For Special Children, Steven Kanor, Ph.D., Inc. 385 Warburton Ave., Hastings-on-the-Hudson, NY 10706. (914) 478-0960.

Brand Name: The Cooper Car

Generic Name: Powered Cart, Powered Wheelchair

Description: The Cooper Car is a low cost alternative to powered wheelchairs for children from 2 to 10 years of age. The Cooper Car is a conversion kit added to a commercially available powered cart called the BOSS (available from Toys "R" Us for $179.00, 1993 price). *Option A:* Purchase the conversion kit from R. J. Cooper and convert your own BOSS vehicle. You use your own seating, switch (joystick is recommended), and switch mounting mechanism (Ablenet Universal Mounting is recommended). *Option B:* For people who do not want to do-it-yourself, the entire system or just the Cooper Car can be purchased from Danmar (800-783-1998). Several safeguards have been built into the system to provide supervisory control over the car.

Comment: R. J. Cooper will talk with family or service providers about the limitations of the car.

Cost: $595.00 conversion kit, 1993 price

Manufacturer: R. J. Cooper & Associates, 24843 Del Prado, Suite 283, Dana Point, CA 92629. (714) 240-1912.

Brand Name: Bigfoot

Generic Name: Powered Wheelchair Alternative, Powered Cart.

Description: Hand-operated motorized truck for children from 2.5 years old and up to 65 pounds in weight. Stainless steel back support. Chest harness. Lap belt. Foot straps. Adjustable head support. Adjustable torso support. Hand control provides forward and reverse motion. Vehicle stops when hand is removed from control or placed in the center of the steering controls. Kit available to adapt the Bigfoot truck purchased locally from a Toys "R" Us or other toy store. Approximate speed is 2 miles per hour. Joystick control is in development.

Cost: $1,550.00 with vehicle, $795.00 kit without vehicle, 1993 price

Manufacturer: T M Innovative Products Inc, 830 South 48th Street, Grand Forks, ND 58201. (701) 772-5185

Brand Name: Power 9000

Generic Name: Powered Wheelchair

Description: Powered wheelchair for children or adults. Steel frame with aluminum cross braces. 14-, 16-, or 18-inch seat width. 16- or 18-inch seat depth. 20-inch seat height. Optional seat sizes available. Adjustable back height from 14- to 18-inches. 12-inch rear wheels. 8-inch semipneumatic front casters. Direct drive motors. Proportional joystick control. Dynamic braking. Flip-up armrests, full or desk length. Removable swingaway footrests. Batteries remove to allow frame to fold for transport. *Options:* elevating footrests, footboard, solid seat, solid back, heel loops, toe loops, seat cushion, seat belt. Maximum speed 4 miles per hour. Weight including batteries 123 pounds.

Cost: $3,324.00 base price, 1993 price

Manufacturer: Invacare Corporation, PO Box 4028, 899 Cleveland St, Elyria, OH 44036-2125. (800) 333-6900 or (216) 329-6000

Brand Name: Youthmobile Jaguar, Jaguar XC.

Generic Name: Powered Wheelchair

Description: Powered wheelchair for children. Vinyl upholstery. Seat width, adjustable to 12, 14, or 16 inches. Seat depth, adjustable to 12 or 14 inches. Back height 12 to 15 inches independent of seat dimensions. 16-inch rear wheels with pneumatic tires. 8-inch semipneumatic front casters. Adjustable height armrests, desk or full length. Three footrest assembly options. Proportional joystick. Adjustable speed, braking and tremor dampening controls. Slide out battery holder. Seat belt. *Options:* powered reclining backrest, heavy duty joystick, sip and puff control, environmental control interface, seat wedge, abductor, pneumatic casters. Maximum weight capacity 150 pounds. Weight including batteries 133 pounds.

Cost: $6,303.00 base price, 1993 price

Manufacturer: Invacare Corporation, PO Box 4028, 899 Cleveland St, Elyria, OH 44036-2125. (800) 333-6900 or (216) 329-6000

Brand Name: Meyra 2472

Generic Name: Powered Wheelchair

Description: Powered wheelchair for children. 13-inch seat width. 16-inch seat depth. 16-inch back height. 25-inch overall width. 20-inch pneumatic rear wheels. 8-inch pneumatic front casters. 24-volt motors. Proportional joystick control. *Other control options:* sip and puff, chin, foot or multiple switch control. Adjustable control parameters. Electromechanical and drum braking systems armrests. Swingaway or elevating legrests. Powered seat tilt or recliner models. Batteries disconnect and remove to allow frame to fold. Maximum speed, 4 miles per hour. Range, miles. Weight including batteries, 187 pounds.

Cost: $8,135.00, 1993 price

Manufacturer: Meyra Inc, 12 McCullough Drive, Suite 3, New Castle, DE 19720. (800) 833-9962 or (302) 324-4400.

Brand Name: Turbo

Generic Name: Powered Wheelchair, Powered Wheelchair Alternative

Description: Powered wheelchair for children. Base unit has two large front wheels and two rear casters. The seat is attached over the chassis and can be converted to a standing frame that also elevates. The chair has a joystick control which can be placed on either side or in midline. The chair has several control options for speed, dampening, and so on; these are changed by replacing modules in the drive system. Self jacking system for changing indoor and outdoor wheels. Uses 12-volt sealed lead acid gel battery. *Options:* outdoor wheels, standing frame, driver controlled on/off switch, special adaptations to controls. Overall width 23.5 inches. Overall length excluding seat 31.5 inches. Height folded flat 19 inches. Seat Widths: 10, 11, 12, 13 inches. Driver weight: up to 85 pounds without stabilizer unit, up to 110 pounds with stabilizer unit. *Controls:* programmable, proportional, variable sensitivity and operating force, variable acceleration, variable top speed up to 4 miles per hour, optional athetoid dampening. Total weight of wheelchair 138 pounds.

Cost: $9,995.00, 1993 price

Manufacturer: Electric Mobility Corp, #1 Mobility Plaza, Sewell, NJ 08080. (900) 662-4548 or (609) 468-0270.

Development of Communicative Intent in Young Children With Cerebral Palsy: A Treatment Efficacy Study

Gay Lloyd Pinder, Ph.D.
Children's Therapy Center of Kent
Kent, Washington

Lesley B. Olswang, Ph.D.
University of Washington
Seattle, Washington

The purpose of this study was to determine the effectiveness of treatment on the development of communicative intent in young children with cerebral palsy. The study investigated whether communicative intent, as signaled through looking, reaching, and looking from object to adult, could be taught to young children with moderate to severe physical disabilities. Four children with cerebral palsy, ages 11.5 to 13.5 months, participated in this single subject, time series design treatment study. Treatment sessions included structured communication opportunities and also physically facilitated exploration of toys. At least one session a week involved both the speech-language pathologist and the physical therapist in a co-treatment service delivery approach. The results indicated significant changes for all four children in their use of communicative signals during play and snack situations. The signals appeared to be related to context, with looking from object to adult being produced frequently when the children were attempting to request actions or objects. These results support early intervention for the development of intentional communication with cerebral palsy. Specific implications for treatment are suggested.

Cerebral palsy is one of the most common causes of motor handicap in young children and occurs in approximately 2 to 3 of every 1,000 live births (Batshaw, Perret, & Handyman, 1981; Harris, 1987; McDonald & Chance, 1964). There are an estimated half million children in the United States with cerebral palsy. By definition, cerebral palsy is a nonprogressive disorder of movement or posture resulting from brain damage before the age of 6 years (Bobath, 1966). While the physical disability associated with cerebral palsy may be the sole handicapping condition for a child, development in other areas is often compromised because of the motor problems (Bobath & Bobath, 1972). This is particularly true for infants and toddlers. Considering the importance of movement as a tool for learning and interacting during the first 2 years of life, children with cerebral palsy are especially vulnerable to delays in the area of early communication. Given this high-risk feature of the disorder, the need for early intervention seems critical. This study was designed to examine the effectiveness of early communication intervention for young children with cerebral palsy.

Research in child development offers a theoretical basis for understanding the developmental challenges that confront a child with a physical disability. The research also suggests possible reasons for delays in the development of prelinguistic communication and communicative intent in the child with a physical disability. The infant's early communicative attempts (prior to 10 months) are motor based in terms of eye movement, head movement, facial expression, and arm movement (Brazelton, 1982; Fogel, Diamond, Langhorst, & Demos, 1982; Stern, 1981). The communicative function of these signals is determined by the adult's abilities to recognize and respond to these behaviors, shaping them into increasingly clear and conventional forms (Bruner, 1985; Kaye, 1982). If the child's signals are not recognized by the adult as a communicative attempt, as is often the case for an infant with a physical disability, the adult-infant interaction will be negatively impacted (Als, 1979, 1989; Pinder, Olswang, & Coggins, 1993). This breakdown in interaction, created by the physical disability, may slow continued communication development, and perhaps development in other domains.

Although there has been some research regarding the early motor development of children with cerebral palsy (Allen & Alexander, 1992; Bower & McLellan, 1992; Eliasson, Gordon, & Frossberg, 1991; Harris, 1991), there has been little research on the early communication development of these children; only one study has explored the effectiveness of early treatment (Pinder et al., 1993). From a holistic perspective, early intervention must focus on cross-domain development, taking into consideration how motor skills influence the emergence of communication signals. Based on the work of Bates and others (Bates, Benigni, Bretherton, Camaioni, & Volterra, 1977; Bretherton, 1988; Harding, 1983; Sugarman-Bell, 1978; Sugarman, 1984), a child's early signals of communication involve eye gaze and reaching. At first the child uses these signals to focus solely on objects of interest or desire. Later (after approximately 10 months), the signals are used to intentionally attract and direct the adult's attention to the objects. Thus the developmental hierarchy in emerging communicative behaviors is looking at objects of interest, reaching toward these objects, and finally looking at/reaching for objects while engaging the adult in the interaction.

Early intervention for children with physical disabilities would begin with the identification of signals that can be communicative; this, of course, becomes an increasingly difficult task depending upon the degree of motor impairment. Intervention would be designed to shape the child's signals to focus on objects and then objects and adults, systematically demonstrating their intentional communicative value. A successful intervention would need to recognize a child's physical abilities, as they are needed to support the production of communicative signals. And, further, the intervention would need to incorporate opportunities to play with objects in adult-guided activities so that the communicative value of the signals could be shaped. In the Pinder et al. study (1993), intervention was provided to a young child with cerebral palsy; the treatment was designed to shape behaviors of looking and reaching into intentional communicative signals. The outcome of this study revealed two findings. First, noncommunicative behaviors could be shaped into what appeared to be intentional, communicative signals. Second, the use of the separate communicative signals was context dependent; that is, some signals were used more readily in one context than another.

This current study was designed to expand on the Pinder et al. findings. Specifically, this research was designed to investigate whether treatment could effectively influence the development of intentional communicative signals produced by young children who demonstrated different degrees of motor disability. The study also examined whether the specific communicative signals being taught (looking at and reaching toward objects, and coordinated looking at objects and adults) were differentially learned and used in two distinct contexts, choice and request.

Method

Subjects

Four children with cerebral palsy participated in this study; they ranged in age from 11.5 to 13.5 months. Each child was involved in an individual physical therapy program at a birth to three developmental center. According to medical reports, the children were medically stable, had normal hearing, and vision corrected to within normal limits. None of the children sat independently when they entered the study. All of the children showed interest in toys; however, their primary means of exploration was limited to mouthing. Table 1 provides a summary of the subject characteristics.

While all four children were producing early behaviors of looking at and/or reaching for objects, they were doing so limitedly and not involving adults in the their focus of attention. While Lauren and Nicholas were able to reach for and grasp a toy, they were unable to release the toy. Of the other two children, Dorothie was able to reach for a toy, but could not grasp independently. Benjamin was unable to reach due to the severity of his cerebral palsy. All of the children were considered to be beyond the age when the intentional communicative signal of looking from object to adult would be expected.

Design

The design of the study was a within and between series single subject design with multiple measures. The within series component involved the ABA of baseline, treatment, and withdrawal. The between series feature included both a between subject and between context component. The between subject component established the experimental control between children. The between context component examined the effects of treatment procedures provided in two contexts. In this study, the term context refers to two specific communication interactions: choice (choosing one of two items) and request (requesting a desired item or requesting more). Multiple measures were used to monitor the use of three different communication signals, including active looking at an object, reaching toward an object, and coordinated looking from object to adult. The three communication signals were monitored in two separate situations. The term *situation* refers to the communication environment, represented in this study by the two environments of play with toys and snack.

Two children were taught concurrently, one in the choice context and one in the request context. The initial baseline phase was continued for 4 weeks (one probe session per week). Following baseline, treatment was introduced in one context. Two of the

Table 1. Summary of Information Regarding Children

	Benjamin	Lauren	Dorothie	Nicolas
Birthdate	6/25/91	9/3/91	9/25/91	9/30/91
C.A. at Baseline:	12.5 months	11.5 months	13.5 months	13.5 months
C.A. at Withdrawal:	17 months	15 months	18 months	18 months
Diagnosis:	Mixed Spastic-Athetoid Cerebral Palsy	Mixed Spastic-Athetoid Cerebral Palsy	Spastic Diplegia Cerebral Palsy	Spastic Diplegia Cerebral Palsy
Tone level (as assessed by physical therapist):	fluctuating tone (primary hypo)	fluctuating tone (primary hypo)	fluctuating tone	hypertonia
Functional limb involvement (as assessed by physical therapist):	quadriplegia	quadriplegia	quadriplegia	quadriplegia
Developmental Assessment: *Bayley Scales of Infant Development*	Motor: PDI<50 Mental: MDI<50	Motor: PDI<50 Mental: MDI<50	Motor: PDI<50 Mental: MDI<50	Motor: PDI<50 Mental: MDI<50
Primary Communication Signal	active looking	active looking reaching	active looking reaching	active looking reaching
Primary Toy Manipulation	mouthing	mouthing	mouthing	mouthing throwing

four children were taught in the request context and two were taught in the choice context. Treatment was continued until the co-ordinated look at object and adult signal (LA) was produced at 50% or more for five consecutive sessions or until 12 weeks of treatment were completed. At that point treatment was withdrawn and behaviors were monitored for 4 additional weeks (one probe session per week).

Procedure

General Procedure

During the research project, each of the four children was seen individually. Individual sessions were either treatment or probe sessions. Treatment sessions occurred two times per week during the treatment phase of the study for each child. Probe sessions occurred one time per week throughout the study. The basic schedule for each child was as follows: 4 weeks of baseline, with one probe session per week; up to 12 weeks of treatment, with two treatment sessions and one probe session per week; and 4 weeks of withdrawal, with one probe session per week. The treatment sessions were 50 to 60 minutes long. Each probe session was 40 to 50 minutes long.

Environment

The treatment sessions took place either in the home or at a therapy center. Two of the children were involved in a therapy program that had home-based therapy for infants. The other two children were involved in a program that was center-based. The probe sessions took place primarily in the homes for all children.

During the treatment phase, each child was seen for treatment sessions twice a week. For three of the four children, one treatment session per week utilized co-treatment with the speech-language pathologist (SLP) and the physical or occupational therapist (PT/OT). For the fourth child, both treatment sessions utilized the co-treatment. In the co-treatment sessions, the child's position and movement were facilitated by the physical or occupational therapist so the child's ability to reach and handle toys was maximized in the play situation. The SLP was then free to interact from the front, responding to the child's signals and encouraging increased quantity and clarity of signals as well as providing support in the play experience.

In the "independent" treatment sessions that involved only the SLP, the child was positioned in a high chair adapted with a foam insert to increase hip stability and trunk support and to inhibit extension as much as possible. The SLP sat facing the child, in midline and slightly below eye level to encourage better head position and control of the eyes. The SLP used her hands to help encourage the child's arms and shoulders forward for more precise manipulation of the toys.

All probe sessions were carried out by the SLP alone. In the probe sessions, each child was positioned in a high chair as described above, with the SLP seated in front and below eye level. From this position she offered toys and a snack and followed the child's lead as appropriate.

The parents were present at all treatment and probe seasons, except those occurring at the day care centers. The parents observed the sessions but rarely were actively involved. The most active involvement happened on three occasions when one child was upset and worked best on his mother's lap. Otherwise, the parents were primarily observers, sometimes raising questions or offering comments, but mostly watching. Although the mothers were present throughout their children's participation in the study, all four father's were present for at least four sessions of their child's program.

Treatment

Procedure

The goal of the intervention was to provide the children with the opportunity to intentionally use communicative signals to **choose** or **request** in a richly supported environment. Two children were taught in the choice context and two were taught in the request context. Beginning with the child's baseline behavior, either looking at the object or reaching, the goal was to increase the consistency and clarity of the signal used and then shape the signal to the more sophisticated form, that is, looking at the adult communication partner as a component of the signal.

Choice Context

In the choice context, the child was offered a choice of two toys held before him or her. Following the communication of choice, the child was then assisted as needed by the SLP to explore the chosen toy. Throughout the "exploration time" opportunities for choice that emerged spontaneously were utilized for continued encouragement to the child to signal choices. For example, if a child was exploring a jar of bubbles, the opportunity might arise for the SLP to offer the child a choice between the top and the wand.

In the beginning of the treatment program, each child required more support to use her or his signals to choose a toy. More animated facial expressions, more exaggerated excitement about the objects offered, or more demonstration was required to elicit the child's participation. In addition, it was sometimes difficult to interpret the early signals. For example, was the lean in the direction of that toy a choice or simply poor trunk control? In the beginning, a lean was accepted and interpreted as a communicative "reach" signal. As the child's experience with successful signals became more consistent, his or her use of those signals improved. The exaggerated support was then gradually faded and the child was given more responsibility for the clarity of her or his communication.

Request Context

In the request context, a play situation was first initiated with the child. Once the child was involved, the SLP stopped the activity and waited for the child to signal a desire to resume play. In addition, two or three toys were set up out of reach (4 to 6 feet away) but visibly available, so the child could also signal interest in a new toy. The SLP could then respond to whatever subtle signals the child offered, gradually shaping those early signals to the more sophisticated signal of looking from object to adult.

Similar to teaching in the choice context, the SLP began by building a rich environment that supported the child's request signals. Exaggerated gestures, facial expression, and body language were employed to provide the child with many leads and cues to elicit requesting. As the child began to initiate with more consistency, the volume and intensity of the SLP's involvement was decreased and the child was thus encouraged to take over the lead.

Communicative Signals

The ultimate goal of treatment was to teach the children the communicative signal of **looking at object and adult**. According to the extant literature, this signal develops after looking at and reaching for objects and is viewed as the landmark milestone in a child's acquisition of intentional communication. Treatment was designed to identify a child's baseline level of signaling and to shape the production of the signal indicating intentionality, that is, looking at object and adult. Three of the four children had some form of active reaching behavior at baseline. For one of the four, Benjamin, reaching had been blocked due to the severity of his physical disability. He used active looking at objects, but even this was dependent on positioning so he could hold his head and maintain gaze. None of the children used the joint focus signal of looking at object and adult. Given the baseline performances, treatment was initiated for the looking at object and adult signal for the three children who already had a reaching behavior. For the fourth child who was not yet reaching, treatment was first initiated for a reach and then the looking at object and adult signal.

Treatment Materials

A variety of toy types were used in treatment; the goal was to attract the children's attention and to provide new play experiences. These included toys with different surfaces that invited tactile and visual exploration, toys with parts for spatial exploration, toys with cause-effect properties, toys that had specific purposes (e.g., cars, hairbrush, cup), and sensory activities such as lentils in a box and play dough. The toys used in treatment were different from the toys used in the probe sessions.

Dependent Measures

Procedure

In the probe sessions, each child was provided eight choice opportunities and eight request opportunities with toys. In addition, a snack situation was constructed in which the child was offered eight choice opportunities and eight request opportunities with food and drink (Total = 32 opportunities). Each child had been taught in either choice or request context in the toy situation, but had not been taught use of those signals in the snack situation. This probe offered the opportunity to see if the use of the communicative signals generalized to the new situation.

In the choice context, two objects were held in front of the child. Once attention was established, the SLP asked "Which do you want?" If the child did not respond in 20 seconds, the SLP moved onto the next choice pair. If the child signaled a choice, time was allowed for play with the chosen toy before moving onto the next pair. The SLP always allowed sufficient time, up to 20 seconds, for the most sophisticated signal to be given. In the snack situation, a choice was offered between food and drink. The procedure was similar to that described above.

In the request context, the SLP modeled an action with a toy twice, pausing halfway through the second action, looking at the child expectantly and asking "More?" She held the pose with the toy, waiting for the child to signal an interest in more of the action. The wait was again 20 seconds before moving onto the next item. If the child signaled for more, time was allowed for exploration of that toy. In the snack situation, the child was offered more of whatever had just been chosen, for example a bite of cracker or a drink.

During the probe sessions minimal contextual support (i.e., extra animated facial expression, toy demonstration) was provided by the SLP. The probe sessions were videotaped for later coding of the communicative signals.

Measurement Materials

The toys used during the probe sessions were different from the toys used during the treatment sessions, but included the variety of properties such as textures, cause effect, different functions, and so on. They were arranged into three groups of toys in boxes, each group including the variety of toy types. The choice of boxes were counter balanced, one chosen for use at the beginning of each probe session.

Outcome Behaviors: Taxonomy of Communication Signals

Three specific behaviors were measured throughout the study, **active looking at object, reaching toward object, and looking at object and adult.** These behaviors were operationally defined as follows:

Active looking (AL)

1. Active Looking (AL): Looks at object for three seconds with some indication of interest or excitement shown in vocalization, body movement, or change in facial expression.

Reaching (R/RG)

1. Reaching (R): Leans forward in the direction of the object, but without forward arm movement. Arms may be up or down.
2. Reach-Grasp (RG): Leans forward and reaches with arm.
   For all reaching, the reach must be accompanied by looking at the object. If the child reaches but does not look, the reach is not accepted as communication of choice or request.

Looking at object and adult (LA)

1. Looks at object and then at adult, then possibly but not necessarily back to object again. One of the object looks must be for a minimum of 3 seconds.

Data Reduction and Analysis

All probe sessions were videotaped. The videotapes were coded for communicative intent according to the taxonomy of communication signals described above. Frequency of occurrence of each communication signal was calculated. There were eight choice and eight request opportunities with toys in each probe session. In addition there were eight choice and eight request opportunities in the snack situation in each probe session. The percent occurrence of the three different communication signals (i.e., active looking, reach/reach grasp, and looking at object and adult) was calculated and compared in the two contexts (choice/request) and two situations (toys/snack). The information was displayed visually in the form of line graphs to illustrate performance during baseline, treatment, and withdrawal phases of the study. Trends in performance, including rate and magnitude of change, were analyzed to examine the effectiveness of treatment.

Reliability

The primary investigator (SLP) coded all videotapes of the probe sessions for the occurrence of the individual communicative behaviors as defined in the taxonomy. A secondary observer was trained to identify those behaviors through sample probe videotape viewing. The secondary observer was trained separately on each child; she was introduced to the coding of each child by first learning generally about the child's gross motor/fine motor capabilities (e.g., muscle tone, abnormal patterns, asymmetries, associated reactions with stimulation). The primary investigator (SLP) and secondary observer then coded portions of tapes together. The secondary observer was instructed to code the most sophisticated level of communicative behavior occurring during each opportunity. Once the secondary observer was comfortable with the mechanics of the coding (practice together ranged from nine 8-minute segments for the first child, seven for the second child, seven for the third child, and five for the fourth child), a 20-minute segment of one session was coded separately and then immediately compared for percent agreement. Competence in this ability was judged to be demonstrated by 80% point-to-point agreement with the primary investigator (SLP). This step was repeated until the 80% agreement criterion was reached (two sessions for two of the children, and four sessions for the other two children). Once competency was demonstrated, the secondary observer independently coded videotapes of four probe sessions for each child. These videotapes were chosen randomly across all phases of the study and were different from the training tapes.

The two observers' coding of the different communicative behaviors were compared by calculating Kappa coefficients for each of the reliability sessions. Kappa coefficients are shown in Table 2. The Kappa coefficients are above the .60 cutoff for all four children and are an indication of adequate reliability (Shellen, 1985).

Results

Summary of Data Presentation

The probe data are presented in Figures 1 through 4, one figure for each of the four children. Each figure contains several graphs depicting different communicative signals in the choice and request contexts. The signals include active looking (AL) (Benjamin only), reach/reach grasp (R/RG) (all four children), and look at object and adult (LA) (all four children). The graphs are presented in the order of development of signals, beginning with AL, then R/RG, and ending with the last and most sophisticated signal to emerge, LA. Each signal is represented in two separate graphs, one for choice and one for request. Each graph illustrates the child's use of the signal in both the "treatment" situation with toys and the "control" situation of snack. The data that follow will present the results per child.

Benjamin

Benjamin (Figure 1) was the only child who did not have a strong reach signal at baseline as shown in Figures 1B and 1E. His clearest signal during baseline was active looking (AL). Figures 1A and 1D show that Benjamin was using the active look signal in both contexts of request and choice during baseline, but in less than 50% of the opportunities. The data also show that his AL signal was more frequent in the snack situation.

Benjamin's first treatment target signal was reach/reach grasp (R/RG) taught in the context of request (Figure 1B). During the first 6 weeks of treatment (weeks 4 through 9), some initial change in R/RG was seen, but the signal then faded. It became clear during the treatment that Benjamin's ability to reach was dependent on optimum positioning and tone management, prerequisites only present consistently in the co-treatment situation or with familiar handlers. After 6 weeks of treatment, continued work on this signal seemed inappropriate, and was terminated.

Although the R/RG signal was not consistently produced during treatment, the AL signal remained functional, as shown in Figures 1A and 1D. In addition, Benjamin's percentage of overall use of his active looking (AL) increased from generally below 50% during baseline to a more consistent 50% or above during the intervention phase (Figures 1A and 1D). This suggests that, even while Benjamin's R/RG was not emerging as a functional signal, he was developing more consistent use of his AL signal in both contexts and both situations.

Table 2. Reliability: Kappa Values

	Benjamin	Lauren	Dorothie	Nicholas
Baseline	.821	.838	.873	.698
Treatment	.7131 .775	1.0 1.0	1.0 .915	1.0 .834
Withdrawal	.964	.728	.870	.838

As illustrated in Figure 1C, training for the look at object and adult (LA) signal in the context of request began in week 10 of Benjamin's program. The signal emerged within the first 3 weeks of treatment for LA. It then remained above 50% in both situations with toys and snack during weeks 13 and 14 of the study, and then through the final 4 weeks of withdrawal, except in snack in week 16 (Figures 1C and 1F). This single drop was due to severe teething discomfort during that week. Generally, however, Figure 1C shows robust change in Benjamin's use of the LA signal in the treatment context of request, and Figure 1F shows that the signal then generalized across contexts to choice. Likewise, Figures 1C and 1F show that the development of the LA signal in the treatment situation with toys also generalized across situations to snack.

Lauren

Lauren (Figure 2) was taught in the context of choice. As illustrated in Figures 2A and 2C, Lauren had a strong reach/reach grasp (R/RG) at baseline and she used that signal actively in both contexts of choice and request. The more sophisticated signal of looking at object and adult (LA) was only minimally present during the baseline phase (Figures 2B and 2D).

Lauren's target signal LA, was taught in the context of choice. As illustrated in Figure 2B, intervention continued for a period of 8 weeks. Interestingly, while she was taught in the context of choice, Lauren's use of LA first began to emerge in the context of request, as shown in Figure 2D. By week 7, her LA was consistently at 50% or above in the context of request, and by week 10 it was at 75% or above, where it remained through withdrawal. In week 10 of the study, Lauren's LA emerged strongly into the context of choice, as shown in Figure 2B, and remained at 85% or above through withdrawal.

As her use of the LA signal generalized across contexts, Lauren's use of the signal also generalized across situations. Figures 2B and 2D show that Lauren's use of the LA was within 10% in the two situations from week 10 through withdrawal in both contexts.

Dorothie

Dorothie (Figure 3) was also taught in the context of choice. As illustrated in Figures 3A and 3C, Dorothie had a reach (R/RG)

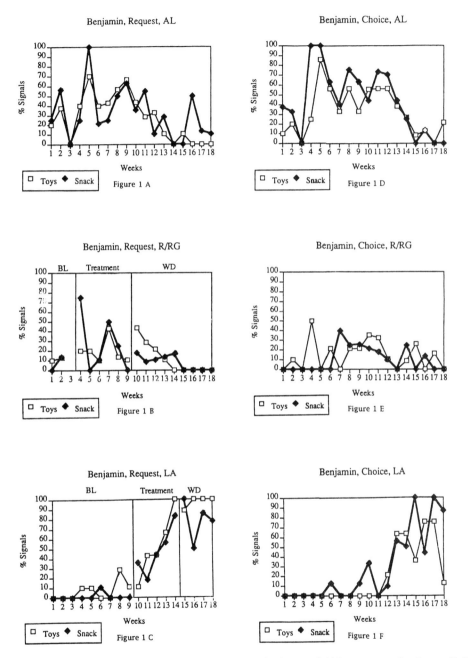

Figure 1. The percent occurrence of each individual signal (AL = active looking; R/RG = reach/reach grasp; and LA = look at object and adult) performed during each probe session in the situations of toys and snack for Benjamin. Each signal is illustrated first in the treated context of request and then in the context of choice during the baseline, treatment, and withdrawal phases of the study.

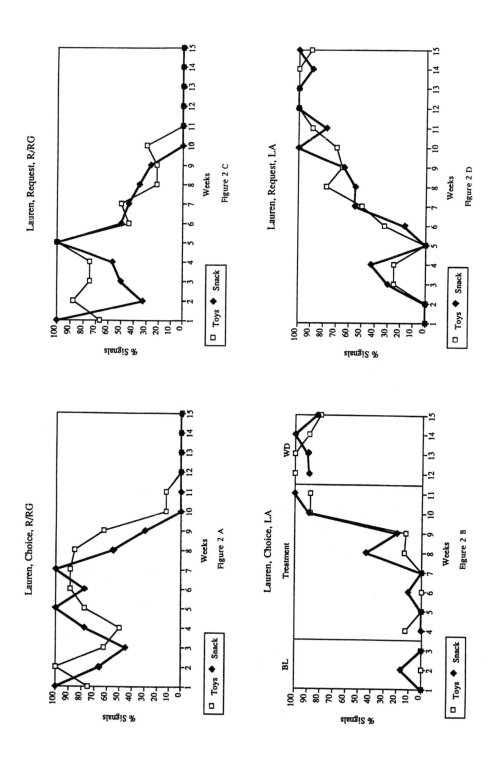

Figure 2. The percent occurrence of each individual signal (R/RG = reach/reach grasp; and LA = look at object and adult) performed during each probe session in the situations of toys and snack for Lauren. Each signal is illustrated first in the treated context of choice and then in the context of request during the baseline, treatment, and withdrawal phases of the study.

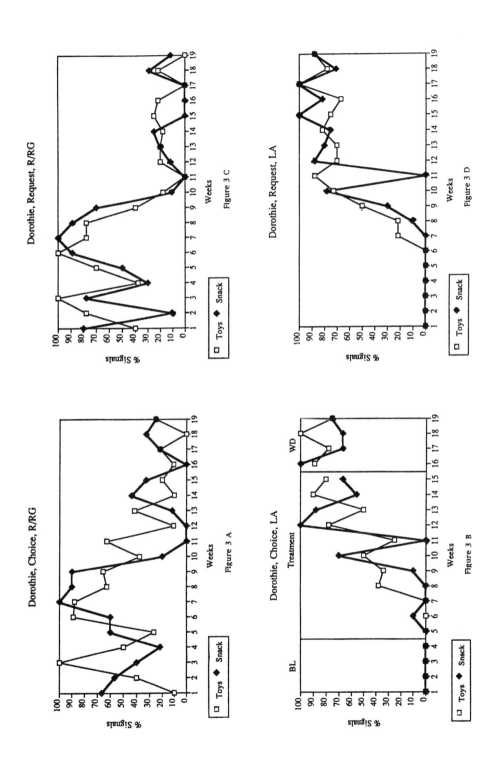

Figure 3. The percent occurrence of each individual signal (R/RG = reach/reach grasp; and LA = look at object and adult) performed during each probe session in the situations of toys and snack for Dorothie. Each signal is illustrated first in the treated context of choice and then in the context of request during the baseline, treatment, and withdrawal phases of the study.

signal during baseline, but her use of this signal was inconsistent from week to week. Furthermore, it seemed stronger in the snack situation. As illustrated in the baseline data in Figures 3B and 3D, Dorothie did not have the look at object and adult signal (LA) in her repertoire of baseline signals.

LA was Dorothie's target signal in the treatment phase of the study. Figures 3B and 3D show that, by week 8 of the study, the LA signal was present in both contexts of choice and request, and that it continued to increase at a steady rate. Once again, although Dorothie was taught in the context of choice, the increase in her use of LA was initially stronger in the request context, remaining at 75% or above in both play and snack situations from week 11 through withdrawal. In the context of choice, while the LA signal was definitely present, it was not consistent at 75% either with toys or in the snack situation until week 14.

As with the other children, Dorothie's use of the LA signal generalized across contexts, and also across situations as illustrated in Figures 3B and 3D. While the data in the two situations of toys and snack were not always as closely aligned for Dorothie as for Lauren, Dorothie's use of the LA in snack emerged at the same time it was becoming stronger in treatment with toys (week 10). As seen in Figure 3B, Dorothie's use of the LA in snack was at times even ahead of toys, particularly in the context of choice. Generally, Dorothie's robust change in signal with treatment generalized across both context and situation.

Nicholas

Nicholas (Figure 4) was taught in the context of request. As illustrated in Figures 4A and 4C, Nicholas was using the prelinguistic signal of reaching (R/RG) in both contexts of choice and request during baseline, and initially with strongest consistency in the snack situation. As seen in Figures 4B and 4D, during the entire 4 weeks of baseline, Nicholas used the look at object and adult signal (LA) only once. From these data, while the LA must be acknowledged as present, it certainly cannot be described as a significant tool in Nicholas's communication repertoire.

LA was the target signal for Nicholas in the treatment phase in the context of request. As illustrated in Figures 4B and 4D, Nicholas first showed a strong use of LA at week 7 of the study in request and by week 8 in choice, with steady increase from week 10 on in both contexts. Comparative use of the signal in the two situations of play and snack varied from week to week but the overall increase was steady in both situations. During the 4-week period of withdrawal, the LA signal remained at 60% or above in both contexts and both situations.

Discussion

The primary purpose of this study was to investigate the effectiveness of treatment for shaping intentional communicative signals in four infants with cerebral palsy and with different degrees of motor disability. In addition, the study was designed to explore the development and use of intentional communicative signals in two different contexts, choice and request.

The results yielded four major findings, as follows. First, the effectiveness of treatment was demonstrated by the robust increase in the target signal that occurred with the introduction of therapy in each of the four children. Second, the children's motor disability had a significant effect on the choice of behaviors to treat and in the shaping of intentional communicative signals. Third, the signals appeared to be tied to communicative contexts, as demonstrated by the consistent emergence of the **look at object**

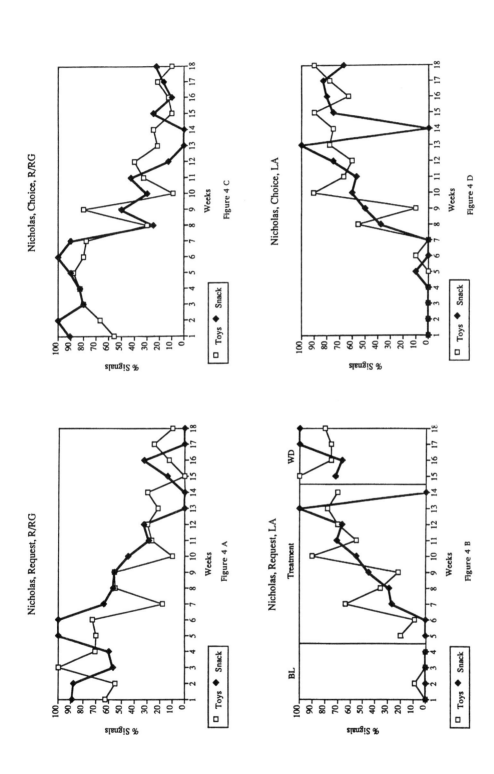

Figure 4. The percent occurrence of each individual signal (R/RG = reach/reach grasp; and LA = look at object and adult) performed during each probe session in the situations of toys and snack for Nicholas. Each signal is illustrated first in the treated context of request and then in the context of choice during the baseline, treatment, and withdrawal phases of the study.

and adult signal in the context of request, regardless of which context was taught. Fourth, in spite of the connection of signals to contexts, the generalization of the signals across contexts and situations revealed their potency as communicative behaviors.

Treatment Effectiveness

The results of this study indicate the benefits of early treatment in the area of prelinguistic communication development in young children with cerebral palsy. The data for all four children showed a robust change in the communication signals with the introduction of therapy. This offers exciting support to the idea that early intervention for these physically disabled children is effective and important for their development of early foundational communication skills.

The treatment utilized a holistic treatment approach in which the different disciplines (PT, OT, and SLP) worked together to bring about change in the connected areas of communication and motor development. Treatment involved providing the physical support through positioning and facilitation of movement to compensate for the motor disability. In this environment the child was given opportunities for successful communication and object exploration. The changes in each child demonstrate the effectiveness of the treatment.

Choice of Target Signal

The more severe the motor disability, the more it impacted the communicative signals. Benjamin's motor disability dictated which of the three prelinguistic signals emerged as a functional communicative tool for him. The reach signal, which in normal development gradually becomes pointing, was not a clear signal for Benjamin at baseline, though his effort to reach was clear in his increased tone and frustration. The treatment decision to change the target signal from reach to the look at adult signal was a serious decision for Benjamin. For a child who will likely become an augmentative communication system user, reaching is important. The ability to reach and point enables a person to make a direct selection from an array of objects and symbols, and is the clearest signal for the communication partner to read. In this sense, there were serious implications for Benjamin in the decision to drop the reach behavior as a goal. In short, his motor domain impacted his process of communication development.

In contrast, the other three children did not have as severe motor limitations. Each had an active reach at baseline that was shaped into the look at adult signal. Although these children were providing some evidence of potential speech production abilities, they are also candidates for early augmentative communication systems. The acquisition of intentional communication signals will serve as foundational skills for different systems of communication they encounter in the future.

Generalization Across Contexts

The use of the target signal (look at object and adult) generalized across contexts for all four children. Interestingly, for all four children the LA emerged first in the request context. This was true for Lauren and Dorothie, even though they were taught in the context of choice. The suggestion has been made by Pinder et al. (1993) that the signals are context-related as follows: active looking and reaching related to the choice context and looking at object and adult related to the request context. Perhaps the communicative demands of the two contexts are different, resulting in the signals being differentially effective. In the choice context, the adult is simply holding the objects at eye level and waiting and the child is object focused. In this context active looking (AL) and reaching (R/RG) for the object are clear and successful signals of choice.

In the request context, on the other hand, the adult's role is less clear and also potentially less focused. In the request context, the adult is involved in the play situation and therefore focused not only on the child but also on the toy. The adult could miss the child's signal or misinterpret the signal as being part of the child's play action. In the request context, the child may well need the stronger contact with the adult that the look at toy and adult (LA) provides in order to be understood.

The implications for treatment seem obvious. If the treatment goal is the development of the most sophisticated LA signal, in which the child is connecting with both object and adult, these data support treatment in the request context, which in itself is the more interactive of the two contexts. On the other hand, if the treatment goal is one of the earlier and more concrete signals, look at object or reach, the context of choice would better support those signals.

Generalization Across Situations

In viewing the results across children, the data indicated that the development of the LA signal also generalized from the toy play situation to the snack situation. Recall that the children were taught in the play situation with toys, but only experienced the opportunity to use the signal during the snack situation in the measurement probe sessions.

Interestingly, use of the baseline signals was initially stronger in the snack situation for three of the four children (Benjamin, Dorothie, and Nicholas). One possible explanation is that food activities are the most common interactions with adults. This is particularly true for young children with physical disabilities, where early interactions primarily focus on activities of daily living (feeding, diaper changing, dressing/undressing) leaving little time for object play. Furthermore, parents reported that play with objects had often been frustrating because of the children's physical difficulties with positioning and hand function. With the limited time available and the limited mutual satisfaction, the low priority of object play for family interaction was understandable. This, coupled with the children's inability to handle objects independently, would help explain why the children were initially using their signals to get food and drink, but showing less motivation to communicate to get toys.

The treatment program focused on use of signals in the toy situation and, as such, involved facilitated hands-on experience with the toys, as well as communication opportunities. Based on the systems view of development, gaps in one area (motor) could impact on the development in another areas (object exploration and communication). In this case, the treatment premise is that by encouraging successful experience exploring objects and making toys work, the child would become more motivated to communicate to get those objects. In fact, the change was robust and generalized across situations from the toys to snack. As the child's use of the communication signal LA emerged in the toy situation, it also increased in the snack situation. By the withdrawal phase, the data indicated that the children's use of LA in the two different situations was parallel and stable.

Conclusions

Based on these results, implications for treatment are interesting. First, these families' experiences suggest that parent scaffolding to encourage the child's use of communication signals at home occurs naturally in the feeding situation. Consequently, a treatment program designed to train parents to respond and shape their child's signals may begin most successfully in a snack or mealtime setting. Once established there, the program could then expand to include the more complex and less concrete situation with toys.

A different perspective and argument might be offered concerning the order of training in the two situations. If treatment occurs in the snack situation, with the toy situation serving as the control, the question arises as to whether generalization would occur across situations. The concern is that the toy situation is necessary to provide the children with the experience in treatment of supported object exploration and manipulation. Following the hypothesis that hands-on experience and success builds the motivation to communicate for more, the prediction would be that the children would learn in the snack situation, but there would be little or no generalization to the toy situation. Investigation of this question would be interesting, as the results could further strengthen the case for hands-on experience with objects in these early months of development.

In summary, the results of this study support the hypothesis that development within different domains, including motor, communication, and object exploration, appear to be interrelated so that gaps in one domain (motor) may impact on development in other domains (communication and object exploration). This has implication for treatment in that it supports the use of a team approach in which the PT/OT works closely with the SLP. In addition, the results of this study lead naturally to the involvement of parents as active team members. Parents may well be the most efficient trainers in contexts that fit with home interactions that are already occurring, that is, snack or mealtime. Finally, as the national health care system is being developed, there is a strong and even critical need to continue to document the effectiveness, effects, and efficiency of early treatment with children with motor disabilities. According to the research in prelinquistic communication development, the foundation for these children's later communication development is established during the first 12 months of life. Without effective early treatment, the developmental potential of these children will surely be compromised.

References

Allen, M. C., & Alexander, G. R. (1992). Using gross motor milestones to identify very preterm infants at risk for cerebral palsy. *Developmental Medicine and Child Neurology, 34*(3), 226–232.

Als, H. (1979). Social interaction: Dynamic matrix for developing behavioral organization. In I. C. Uzgiris (Ed.), *Social interaction and communication during infancy (New Directions for Child Development)* (pp. 21–41). San Francisco: Jossey Bass.

Als, H. (1989). Self regulation and motor development in preterm infants. In J. J. Lockman & N. L. Hazen (Eds.), *Action in social context: Perspectives on early development* (pp. 65-97). New York: Plenum Press.

Bates, E., Benigni, L., Bretherton, I., Camaioni, L., & Volterra, V. (1977). From gesture to first word: On cognitive prerequisites. In M. Lewis & L. Rosenblum (Eds.), *Interaction, conversation, and the development of language* (pp. 247–307). New York: Wiley.

Batshaw, M. L., Perret, Y. M., & Handyman, S. (1981). Cerebral Palsy. In M. L. Batshaw & Y. M. Perret (Eds.), *Children with Handicaps* (pp. 191–212). Baltimore: Paul H. Brookes.

Bobath, K. (1966). *The motor deficits in patients with cerebral palsy.* London: Spastics International Medical Publications/Heinemann.

Bobath, K., & Bobath, B. (1972). Cerebral palsy. In P. H. Pearson & C. E. Williams (Eds.), *Physical therapy services in the developmental disabilities* (pp. 28–185). Springfield, IL: Thomas.

Bower, E., & McLellan, D. L. (1992). Effects of increased exposure to physiotherapy on skill acquisition of children with cerebral palsy. *Developmental Medicine and Child Neurology, 34*(1), 25–31.

Brazelton, T. B. (1982). Joint regulation of neonate-parent behavior. In E. Z. Tronick (Ed.), *Social interchange in infancy: Affect, cognition and communication* (pp. 7–22). Baltimore: University Park Press.

Bretherton, I. (1988). How to do things with one word: The ontogenesis of intentional message making. In M. D. Smight & J. L. Locke (Eds.), *The emergent lexicon: The child's development of a linguistic vocabulary* (pp. 225–262). New York: Academic Press.

Bruner, J. S. (1985). Vygotsky: A historical and conceptual perspective. In J. E. Bruner (Ed.), *Culture, community, and cognition* (pp. 21–34). New York: Cambridge University Press.

Eliasson, A. C., Gordon, A. M., & Frossberg, H. (1991). Basic, coordination of manipulative forces with children with cerebral palsy. *Developmental Medicine and Child Neurology, 33*(8), 661 670.

Fogel, A., Diamond, G., Langhorst, B. H., & Demos, V. (1982). Affective and cognitive aspects of the two month old's participation in face to face interaction with the mother. In E. Z. Tronick (Ed.), *Social interchange in infancy: Affect, cognition, and communication* (pp. 37–58). Baltimore: University Park Press.

Harding, C. G. (1983). Setting the stage for language acquisition: Communication development in the first year. In R. M. Golinkoff (Ed.), *The transition from prelinguistic to linguistic communication* (pp. 93–114). Hillsdale, NJ: Lawrence Erlbaum Associates.

Harris, S. R. (1987). Early intervention for children with motor handicaps. In M. J. Bennett & F. C. Guralnick (Eds.), *The effectiveness of early intervention for at risk and handicapped children* (pp. 175–212). New York: Academic Press, Inc.

Harris, S. R. (1991). Movement analysis: An aid to early diagnosis of cerebral palsy. *Physical Therapy, 71*, 215–221.

Kaye, K. (1982). Organism, apprentice, and person. In E. Z. Tronick (Ed.), *Social interchange in infancy: Affect, cognition, and communication* (pp. 183–196). Baltimore: University Park Press.

McDonald, E. T., & Chance, B. (1964). *Cerebral Palsy.* Englewood Cliffs, NJ: Prentice-Hall.

Pinder, G. L., Olswang, L., & Coggins, K. (1993). The development of communicative intent in a physically disabled child. *Infant-Toddler Intervention: The Transdisciplinary Journal, 3*(1), 1–17.

Shellen, W. N. (1985, February). *A simple guide to reliability for quantitative coding of language samples.* Paper presented at the meeting of the Language Behavior Interest Group, Western Speech Communication Association convention, Fresno, CA.

Stern, D. N. (1981). The development of biologically determined signals of readiness to communicate which are language "resistant." In R. Stark (Ed.), *Language behavior in infancy and early childhood* (pp. 45–62). New York: Elsevier North Holland.

Sugarman-Bell, S. (1978). Some organizational aspects of preverbal communication. In I. Markova (Ed.), *The social context of language.* New York: Wiley and Sons.

Sugarman, S. (1984). The development of preverbal communication: Its contributions and limits in promoting the development of language. In R. Schiefelbusch & J. Pickar (Eds.), *Communicative competence: Acquisition and intervention* (pp. 23–67). Baltimore: University Park Press.

Address Correspondence to:
Gay Lloyd Pinder, Ph.D.,
116 N.E. 77th Street,
Seattle, WA 98115

The Development of Communicative Intent in a Physically Disabled Child

Gay Lloyd Pinder, M.Ed.
Lesley Olswang, Ph.D.
Kathleen Coggins, M.S.
University of Washington
Seattle, Washington

This single-subject study focused on teaching a young boy with cerebral palsy to use prelinguistic signals with communicative intent. The signals included looking, reaching, looking from object to adult, and negation for the purpose of choosing and requesting. The results indicated: (1) treatment was effective in increasing communicative signals during treatment; and (2) signals may be used differently in choice versus request contexts. Finally, the results supported a holistic view of development and treatment for physically disabled children.

An infant responds to her or his environment and physical state, smiling in comfort, crying in distress, wiggling with delight, and gazing with interest. All of these behaviors, and an array of others, may not be particularly directed at us, yet we delight in and respond to them as though they are. We are consistent in giving meaning to the infant's behaviors, following the infant's lead so that a pseudoconversation takes place between us (Bates, Camaioni, & Volterra, 1975; Harding, 1982; Wetherby & Prizant, 1989). However, not until the infant begins to knowingly direct her or his behaviors to another person for the purpose of influencing that person, is the infant said to be communicating with intentionality.

Theoretical Underpinnings

The development of communicative intent has been the focus of considerable research during the past 10 years. Elizabeth Bates and her colleagues have described three stages in the emergence of intentionality in communication: perlocutionary, illocutionary, and locutionary (Bates et al., 1975). The first two stages describe the prelinguistic infant and are the focus of this article. From birth to approximately 8 to 10 months, the infant is in the perlocutionary stage of development in which adults give meaning to the infant's behaviors, interpreting unintentional signals as intentional. Research has suggested that the earliest specific behaviors read by adults as having communicative significance include eye gaze, head orientation, vocalizations, and early gross movement sequences (Brazelton, 1982; Fogel, Diamond, Langhorst, & Demos, 1982; Stern, 1981). Gross movement sequences become increasingly more precise as motor control develops. Parents then respond with more frequency to those discrete signals and less frequently to the more global movements, thereby shaping the infant's motor signals. Through the systematic and consistent response of the adults, the infant begins to learn that her actions cause the adults to do something. At approximately 10 months, with this realization, the infant moves into the illocutionary stage of development and acts with the purposeful intention of causing the adult to act.

During the first 8 to 10 months, while the infant is in the perlocutionary period and prior to the shift to intentional communication, the infant is also experiencing many opportunities to explore and act on objects, gaining experience making things happen, and learning about her power to cause effects on objects. Bates and colleagues (1975) called this experience "tool use" and connected it to communication. Harding (1984) and Sugarman (1984) delineated several stages from reaching for the object, to using an object to get an object, and leading to the final stage when the infant uses the adult to get the object. This object experience coincides with the experience the infant is gaining through adults responding to her perlocutionary, unintentional signals. The coming together of the infant's knowledge of objects and the adult's responsiveness to her unintentional signals appear to be critical, shaping the infant's linking of people and objects and, thus, setting the stage for intentional communication.

As the infant moves into the illocutionary stage of communicative intent, the infant's signals remain the same but the focus changes so that the adult is included in the actions that involve objects. According to some researchers (Olswang & Carpenter, 1982; Sugarman, 1984; Trevarthen, 1986), there is a sequence in the development of focus, beginning with social focus in the first 4 to 5 months, which then shifts to object focus when the infant can reach and manipulate, and which finally shifts to a joint coordinated focus. In this joint focus, the infant uses the familiar eye gaze and looks from the object to the adult to signal that she wants the adult to either get the object (object focus) or to attend to the object with her (social focus) (Bruner, 1982; Harding, 1984). It is through such eye contact that the infant's focus becomes "joint" with the adult in either the object or social context, and it is this "joint focus" that appears to define intentionality.

Influence of Handicapping Conditions

Given this foundation, a number of powerful implications arise for the development of intentional communication in the physically disabled infant. The earliest area of concern appears in the parent-child interaction that provides the infant with experiential feedback about the effectiveness of her signals. The physical handicap affects not only the child, but the parent, in that the child's signals may not be recognizable or interpretable. Abnormal muscle tone can interfere with the infant's ability to direct and maintain eye gaze or to control head orientation in the direction of the focus of attention. Likewise the abnormal muscle tone can mask the infant's pleasure or excitement, which would normally be communicated by initial global movements and later by increasingly discrete and directed movements toward an object. The hypertonic infant may seem to pull away from the object of interest, while the hypotonic infant's affect may be so flat that she communicates disinterest when, in fact, she wants the object. In either case, the parent may be unable to ascertain whether the infant is responding or what the response is. This situation often leaves the parent simply guessing, assuming no signal and not responding, assuming intentionality when there may be none, or misreading a positive signal as a negative one.

The clarity of the infant's signals has been found to be extremely important for the mother to be able to fulfill her role in providing feedback (Brazelton, 1982; Bruner, 1985; Fogel et al., 1982; Harding, 1982). Without clear signals from the infants, mothers tend to become more directive and loud in their interaction style or to become less responsive and less sensitive to the infant's signals (Als, 1982; Buckhart, Rutherford, & Goldberg, 1978; Hanzlik & Stevenson, 1986; Murray & Trevarthen, 1986). In either case, the result is poor early experiential feedback for their infants about the effectiveness of signals for communication purposes.

Finally, in addition to the early disruption of the social/communicative interaction between infant and parent, the physically disabled infant's experience with objects in the environment is also impacted. For these infants, the important play activities of exploring objects and manipulating objects, either singularly or in relationship with another object is generally not available or is severely limited by the physical disability. Based on the research on normal developing infants, the disruption of this object play experience may place at risk the development of parallel intentional communication (Bates, Benigni, Bretherton, Camaioni, & Volterra 1979; Hanzlik & Stevenson, 1986; Kogan & Tyler, 1973; Sugarman, 1984).

Implications for Intervention

Following the above discussion, the implications for intervention for the physically disabled infant are both numerous and exciting. First, because of the early age at which the groundwork is being laid for the development of communicative intent, it is apparent that the intervention needs to begin early for a potentially disrupted system such as that of the physically disabled infant. With early training, parents can learn their infant's signals, however subtle, and respond with consistency and with the kind of confidence that is necessary for shaping intentional communication.

A second implication for intervention with the physically disabled infant is the need to view the infant from a holistic, developmental perspective. Although the motor area of development is generally addressed initially in such an infant, the previous discussion offers strong evidence that the area of communication is equally at risk in the early months. This fact argues for a coming together of disciplines, that is, co-treatment, in early intervention. In a co-treatment session, the occupational or physical therapist provides the stability in positioning and the normal movement experience transitioning from position to position, whereas the speech-language pathologist facilitates the interaction with toys and people, that is, focusing on communication. The result is a total approach to a total child. With this approach, the infant is enabled to bring all her potential to the experience at hand, be it successful play with toys, interaction with people, or simply experience with her body in a more normalized situation through the handling and interplay of the different therapy disciplines.

Finally, the literature supports an intervention that has an "object focus" and a "social focus." The object focus is provided through play experiences (i.e., toy manipulation), and the social focus is provided through communication experiences (i.e., choice and request situations with an adult). The essence of treatment is to shape clear, intentional communication signals. Based on the literature, a combination of eye gaze and reaching with and without vocalization would be targeted, but definitely adjusted to the physical abilities of the child. These signals, as they exist in object play and social contact, become shaped into intentional communication.

Given the theoretical information and its implications for intervention, a study was designed to investigate and to facilitate the development of communicative intent in a young boy with cerebral palsy.

Method

Subject

C, a 20-month-old boy diagnosed with moderate athetoid cerebral palsy and severe bilateral hearing loss, attended a preschool classroom for the hearing impaired at a university-sponsored special education facility. He received physical therapy twice weekly. He had never been involved in speech-language therapy.

At the time therapy was initiated, C was just beginning to sit independently, but was unable to use his hands in sitting because of poor balance reactions. He was beginning to roll independently but had not begun to use rolling as a means of mobility. C was unable to reach for a toy. If a toy was placed in his hands, he immediately brought it to his mouth in a pattern of total flexion. This was due, in part, to lack of stability and lack of experience with the manipulation of objects.

In oral motor function, C lacked overall jaw stability and was unable to maintain relaxed jaw or lip closure. He was being spoon-fed and was beginning to self-feed finger foods. He was bottle drinking and was beginning cup drinking. Vocalizations were primarily open vowel sounds, with few consonants, including no bilabials. The lack of consonants primarily was due to C's motor involvement, whereas the decreased quantity of sounds appeared to be caused by the hearing loss. Furthermore, when the study was initiated, C's vocalizations did not appear to be connected to his communicative intent.

Although exact level of cognitive functioning was not clear, C's level of play skills was observed to be restricted to mouthing toys and to emerging attempts at manipulation, limited by the cerebral palsy. His attention span was short and interest appeared to be quite narrow. He maintained eye gaze, but he did so inconsistently and often in such a passive manner that his motivation or interest in the toys was unclear. His overall activity level was inconsistent also. He had passive days when he showed no interest in toys or people, and he had active days when he responded to many communication opportunities.

In addition, C's communication signals lacked clarity. Maintaining eye gaze was often difficult because of the overall lack of stability. As a result, his looking was inconsistent as a signal. C did not yet have a consistent reach or reach-grasp, and his attempts to reach were blocked by increasing tone, as his excitement and interest increased. With his increase in tone, vocalization also was more difficult to initiate. Finally, C was not yet looking from toy to adult to indicate his desire.

C's signals were primitive and inconsistent enough that he could be described as operating in the perlocutionary stage. He was producing behaviors to which adults in his environment were inferring intent and responding accordingly. In addition the adults' responses to C's behaviors were inconsistent both in timing and message, so C was receiving an unclear response to his already unclear behaviors.

Although C also had a diagnosis of severe bilateral hearing loss, the cerebral palsy was judged to be the key to C's delayed communication development in this prelinguistic stage. According to the literature, during the perlocutionary and illocutionary periods, Deaf infants are developing similar signals on a similar timeline with their hearing counterparts (Bellugi & Klima, 1972). The signals include directed eye gaze as well as reaching and later pointing. Furthermore, as the infants move from the prelinguistic illocutionary period into the symbolic locutionary period, the timeline remains the same for Deaf infants in Deaf families where there is a common language, though in a different modality (Bellugi & Klima, 1972). Thus, without the cerebral palsy, C who has been exposed to sign language since early infancy would be expected to be communicating with intent by age 20 months (Bellugi & Klima, 1972).

Procedures

General Procedures

C was scheduled to be seen twice a week for 41 weeks. Approximately every third session was devoted to measurement. Each session lasted approximately 1 hour.

The design of the study was a multiple baseline across contexts. The contexts included structured choice between two items and requesting the continuation of an interrupted activity. The treatment attempted to facilitate the development of the specific communication behaviors across the two contexts, including looking at the object, reaching for the object, and looking at the object and at the adult.

Environment

The treatment and measurement took place in the clinic setting. C was positioned on a mat on a table with one therapist behind him. This therapist, not a trained physical therapist, provided support and facilitation as needed so C's overall stability was actively maintained, and his motor abilities were maximized for successful manipulation and exploration of the toys presented. A second therapist, a speech-language pathologist, was positioned in front and at midline, seated on a low chair so C's eyes were drawn down for better head position. This therapist interacted with the toys, often facilitating C's arm and hand function both in signaling and play. Communication with C included a combination of gestures, American Sign Language, and voice. C's mother was present at all therapy and measurement sessions and was often actively involved in the play and interaction.

Treatment

Treatment Materials

The toys used in treatment were different from the toys used in the measurement sessions. Toys and activities were used that were motivating to C, that he could have success manipulating with facilitation in spite of his motor disability, and that encouraged child-initiated communication/interaction with the therapist. The play was sequenced in small steps so C could experience it fully for himself. For example, bubble play included putting the top on and off the bottle, looking in the bottle for the wand, hooking the wand with a finger, pulling the wand in and out of the bottle, and finally removing the wand for the purpose of blowing. Other toys and activities included sending balls back and forth in a tube, making peanut butter play dough, and dressing and feeding a doll, to name a few. For C, each of those experiences was new, and he had the opportunity to direct the play through communication with his body movement, his eyes, and his facial expression.

Procedures

The purpose of the intervention was to provide C with opportunity to choose and request in a richly supported context. The goal was to sort out his signals and to increase their clarity and their consistency in the two communication contexts. An adjunct goal was to provide C the experience of manipulating toys and materials in play with another person.

During the choice training, C was offered a choice of two toys. During the play with the chosen toy or activity, every opportunity to offer a new choice within the play context was utilized. Initially, much support was provided; for example, the physical closeness of the toys was a form of support, in that the closeness encouraged an initial reach which could then be shaped; the praise, communicated through excited facial expression and clapping when he signaled, was also a form of support, which encouraged his continued effort. As C's signals came more quickly and more clearly, the therapist gradually withdrew the support.

The signals of looking at the object, reaching for the object, and looking from object to adult were introduced, in that order. As one became part of C's repertoire and was used consistently and clearly, the therapist taught the next in the sequence. As a new signal was being taught, the therapist would wait in a choice opportunity encouraging C to produce the most sophisicated signal available to him in his repertoire. If he did not reach, but continued to look, the therapist would respond after the initial wait. In this way, although he was encouraged to produce the most sophisticated signal, his earlier signals were still acceptable, and communication success was still available to him.

Following the teaching of each of these behaviors in the context of choice, they were taught sequentially in the context of requesting. Similar toys and materials were used during the requesting activities, again different from those used during the measurement sessions. They also were chosen specifically for the abundance of request opportunities they offered. Similar therapy techniques were used for requesting as for choice, including waiting for the most sophisticated signal and providing considerable contextual and reinforcement support to encourage C's attention and efforts.

Dependent Measures

Measurement Materials

The same group of toys were used during all measurement sessions. Toys were chosen according to Mother's report of favorite toys and C's ability to successfully manipulate the objects with some adult guidance and physical support. A minimum of seven opportunities was provided for each context, structured choice and requesting, but frequently more were given to ensure C's highest level of interest. For the seven choice opportunities, 14 toys were randomly paired during each session. Seven toys were selected from the pool of choice toys and were presented in random order for the seven request opportunities during each of the measurement sessions.

Procedures

In the choice situation, two objects were held in front of C, eye contact was obtained, and the question was signed and asked "Which?" After a 15-second waiting period, if C did not respond, the therapist moved to the next choice pair. In the request situation, the therapist performed an action with a toy twice then started the action, this time pausing in the middle and waiting for C to signal that he wanted it to happen again. Again the wait was for a maximum of 15 seconds before moving to the next item.

Items were presented to C, and the therapist waited 15 seconds for a response; the 15 seconds began from the time C made initial eye contact with the item. During the presentations, minimal support was provided by the therapist. When C produced a communication signal, the therapist responded to C either by giving the toy of choice or reactivating the activity. These sessions were videotaped for later coding of behaviors.

Outcome Behaviors

GENERAL DEFINITIONS. Four specific behaviors were measured: (1) looking at the object, (2) reaching, (3) looking from the object to the adult, and (4) negation. The first three behaviors were chosen, based on those universal behaviors reflected in the literature review as being used by all infants, hearing and Deaf, in the prelinguistic stages of developing communicative intent, and also on C's physical capabilities for clear and consistent use of those signals.

Negation was not specifically taught as a signal. It was, however, both part of C's natural communication repertoire, as well as a possible response in both the choice/request contexts. As such, the development of C's negation signals was analyzed as part of the data collected.

Vocalizations were not coded as a separate communicative behavior, because they were generally paired with one of C's other two signals, and C appeared to use the vocalization to augment other signals rather than to signal specific communicative intent on its own.

In addition to the explicit components of these behaviors, including visible movement and measurable time, there was also an implicit component seen in the assertiveness/activeness of some signals as opposed to a sense of passivity/disinterest of others. This was true for the eye gaze signal and the different negation signals. Implicit recognition rules for active/passive included judgments regarding variations in muscle tone, facial expression, vocalizing, body movement, and orientation.

TAXONOMY. *Looking*: (1) Passive Looking (PL): C looks at the object for 3 seconds with no change in facial expression or any indication of excitement or interest. (2) Active Looking (AL): C looks at the object for 3 seconds with some indication of excitement shown in vocalization, body movement, or change in facial expression. *Reaching*: (1) Reaching (R): C leans forward in the direction of the object, with his arms up or down. (2) Reach-Grasp (RG): C leans forward and reaches with his arm. For all reaching, the reach was accompanied by looking at the toy. If C reached but did not look, the reach was not accepted as communication of choice or request. *Looking at object and adult* (LA): C looks at the object and at the adult, and possibly back to the object again. One of the object looks had to be 3 seconds.

The final signal category involved *Negation*. Those signals that were accepted as communication of disinterest or rejection of the choices or toy for play were as follows: (1) No response (N): After initial eye contact with the toy, C looks around the room with no further attempt to focus on the items presented. This signal was also considered passive, in that C was not actively communicating NO, though this was the meaning inferred. (2) No Choice (NC): After making initial eye contact with the toys, C looks from one to the other, but without stopping on either. In addition, C shows little facial expression to indicate interest or excitement. (3) Fussing (NF): C continues to attend, but actively looks away or looks at and fusses at the examiner. This was considered the "active" form of the three negation behaviors.

DATA COLLECTION AND ANALYSIS. The video tapes of the measurement sessions were reviewed and behaviors coded according to the taxonomy of signals described previously.

The behaviors were grouped into passive (N, NC, PL) and active (AL, NF, R, RG, LA) and were figured as percentages of the total number of opportunities. The percentages were plotted and examined to evaluate the rate and level of change of the behaviors as a function of session/weeks and as related to the different contexts (see Figures 1 and 2). The percent occurrence of the three different behaviors taught, that is, looking, reaching, and looking at toy and adult, was also plotted and compared within and across contexts (see Figures 3 and 4).

Reliability

The primary observer scored all of the video tapes of the 16 measurement sessions. A second observer was trained to identify the behaviors defined in the taxonomy. The second observer was instructed to code the highest level of communicative behavior occurring during each opportunity. Competence in this ability was demonstrated by 80% agreement with the primary observer. This was achieved after five sample sessions. The two observers' coding of the different communicative behaviors were compared by calculating Kappa coeffients for each of the reliability sessions. Four or 25% of the total measurement sessions were judged for reliability. Kappa coeffients ranged from .60% to .85%, falling at or above the .60 cutoff as an indication of adequate reliability (Shellen, 1985).

Results

Figures 1 and 2 refer to the change of the signals in the two contexts of choosing and requesting over the 41-week period. The signals have been grouped according to whether they are passive or active in their intent. The passive category includes no persistent attention to the items (N), no clear choice (NC), and passive looking with no indication of excitement or interest (PL). The active category includes active looking with a sense of excitement and persistence in the eye gaze (AL), negation but with active fussing (NF), leaning in the direction of the object (R), reaching with body and arm in the direction of the object (RG), and looking from object to adult (LA).

Figure 1 illustrates C's use of the communicative signals in the context of choice; note that triangles are active behaviors and circles are passive. The baseline scores give indication as to the inconsistency of C's responses. On some days C was active in his responses, actively looking to make the choices, whereas on other days he was much more passive, showing much less attention and less interest in the communicative opportunities.

From baseline, treatment was initiated in the choice context, and from week 4 to week 15 there is a steady increase in C's communicative intent as illustrated by the active signals. Weeks 20 and 22 show a drop in performance; this followed a relatively substantial absentee period. At week 23, C showed a strong increase in perform-

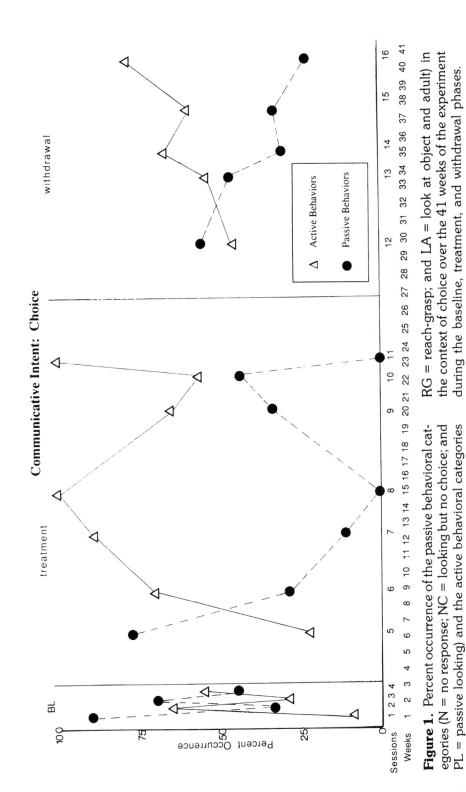

Figure 1. Percent occurrence of the passive behavioral categories (N = no response; NC = looking but no choice; PL = passive looking) and the active behavioral categories (AL = active looking; NF = active negation; R = reaching; RG = reach-grasp; and LA = look at object and adult) in the context of choice over the 41 weeks of the experiment during the baseline, treatment, and withdrawal phases.

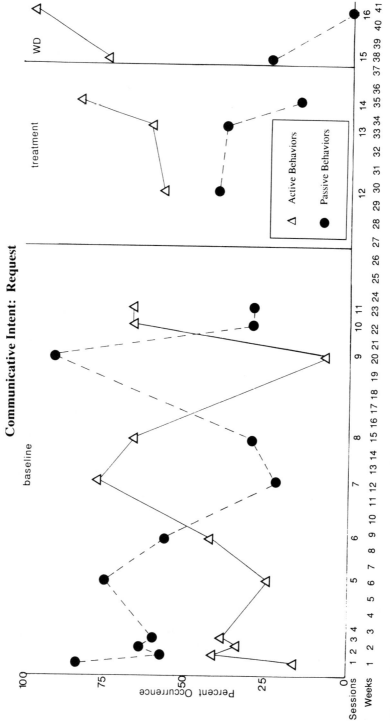

Figure 2. Percent occurrence of the passive behavioral categories (N = no response; NC = looking but no choice; PL = passive looking) and the active behavioral categories (AL = active looking; NF = active negation; R = reaching; RG = reach-grasp; and LA = look at object and adult) in the context of request over the 41 weeks of the experiment during the baseline, treatment, and withdrawal phases.

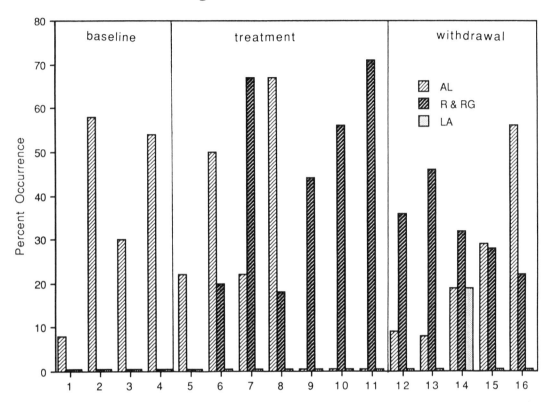

Figure 3. Percent occurrence of individual signals (AL = active looking; R/RG = reach-grasp; and LA = look at object and adult) performed during each measurement session in the choice context over the 41 weeks of the experiment during the baseline, treatment, and withdrawal phases.

ance. However, following another long break in treatment (weeks 23-26), the use of active communicative behaviors drops again. At this point, when therapy resumes, treatment has shifted to the request context and choice is being monitored. Note that even without the treatment focus, C's use of active communicative behaviors for choosing again rises steadily to the end of the project.

Figure 2 illustrates C's use of the communicative behaviors in the request context. As in the choice context, the behaviors were grouped for counting into the active and passive categories as listed. The patern of change was quite similar to that in the choice context, though the baseline inconsistency, while still present, was not as dramatic in the request context.

From week 4 to week 23, treatment was in the choice context, while the request context was being monitored. There was one "wildcard session" during this baseline phase in week 12 when C was active in his requesting. Otherwise, his signals remained under the 60% level during this monitoring period. After the holiday break from week

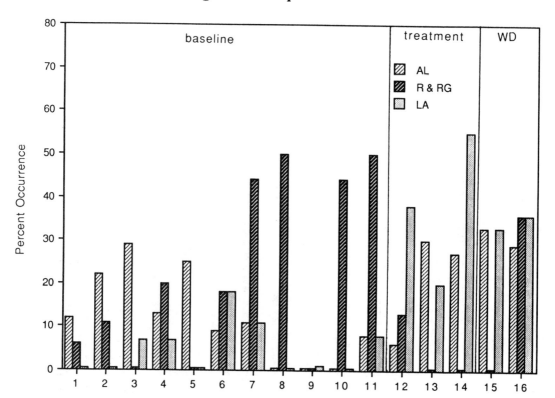

Figure 4. Percent occurrence of individual signals (AL = active looking; R/RG = reach-grasp; and LA = look at object and adult) performed during each measurement session in the request context over the 41 weeks of the experiment during the baseline, treatment, and withdrawal phases.

24 through 26, treatment in the request context was initiated in week 27, and C's use of signals in this context increased steadily to the end of the project in week 41.

As noted, there is a pattern of change in both Figures 1 and 2, the pattern of change indicating the increase of active signals used with intent, first in the choice context and later in the request context. The increase followed the training schedule and dropped off when training was not happening. It was interesting to note that active choosing dropped during a period of no training and picked up again when request training was initiated.

Figures 3 and 4 represent C's use of the specific behaviors in each measurement session, specifically those behaviors that were taught — looking (AL), reaching (R, RG), and looking at adult (LA). Recall that prior to treatment, C had both looking (AL) and leaning (R) in his repertoire. He was not yet reaching to grasp (RG), nor, as the baseline data show, was he using the more sophisticated signal looking from object to adult (LA) with communicative intent.

The results illustrate C's use of specific signals as they related to the two contexts, choice in Figure 3 and request in Figure 4. For example, the use of the most sophisticated signal, look at object and adult (LA), was more evident in the request context than in the choice context. LA only appeared once in the choice context, but it appeared in 11 of the 16 measurement sessions in the request context. Furthermore, it increased steadily during the request training and ranged from 20% to 55% in the last 5 sessions. Implications of this are discussed below.

On the other hand, C's use of reach grasp (RG), the most sophisticated and clear reach signal, was more evident in the choice context. It increased from zero in the first 5 sessions to a high of 56% in the 10th session and was consistently used for choice in the last 5 sessions. In the request context, on the other hand, C did not use the reach-grasp signal at all in 3 of the last 5 sessions. This adds support to the idea that certain signals may be more related to one context than another, suggesting interesting implications for intervention program planning, discussed below.

Discussion

This case study was designed to investigate and to facilitate the development of communicative intent in a physically disabled child. The results not only support the idea of early intervention in the area of communication with such infants, but also point out the critical role of the motor foundation in the development of communication signals. This has important implications for intervention strategies with this population and lends credence to the power of a multidisciplinary approach within a co-treatment situation. The results also raise some interesting questions regarding development that could have exciting implications for program planning.

Communicative Changes Reflected in Trends in the Data

At the end of the treatment program, C had not only made a number of exciting changes in his behaviors, but his rate of change followed the treatment schedule. First, he had shown a steady increase in his use of active signals and in his overall level of participation in the communication situations. This was true, not only in his affirmative choosing and requesting signals, but also in his negation signals. One might speculate that C's interest in communication was facilitated by therapy. One might speculate further that both components of therapy, (i.e., teaching signals and providing opportunities for play), contributed to the change required for C to put forth the extra effort necessary for him to play an active role in the process.

Although C was clearly learning to be more active in his communication, his actual timeline for beginning to use the different signals also implied a connection beween communication development and C's motor development and his play experience. The normally developing infant (Chronological Age [CA] 6 to 10 months) has approximately 2 to 4 months of experience, sitting with secure balance, with arms and hands free to manipulate and explore toys, prior to her development of strong communicative intent as represented in the illocutionary period. In addition to the independent play, the infant has also practiced moving her body in space and has experienced independent mobility, moving from sitting to crawling and beginning to pull to stand. It is only after that experience of independent motor control and manipulative play that she begins at 10 to 12 months to involve adults by requesting assistance in her play, signaling by looking from object to adult to communicate the request.

The child with cerebral palsy must, on the other hand, put forth extra effort to focus eyes and body movements either for play or for communication. It was interesting to note that C's development of the most sophisticated signal (look at toy and look at adult) came during the later phase of treatment in the request context, when his overall stability had increased to the point that he could hold his head steady, sit and reach for toys, and then play with them with some success. This suggests the possibility of needing to consider an experiential time line as well as a chronological age time line for physically involved children when we set out treatment goals and expectations.

In addition to the connection between C's motor development and use of the different signals, one must note that the data also implied a connection between the context and the specific signal being used. For example, in the choice context, the favored signals were looking and reaching, while the "look to toy and look to adult" signal only emerged with any consistency in the request context. Note that the two contexts are in themselves quite different, possibly resulting in one signal being more effective than another in different contexts. On the one hand, the choice context is quite clear in that the two toys are held at eye level and in midline, and the child signals which he wants. The communication partner's role is not only clear as the holder of the toys, but is also focused on the child in this context, as she waits for the child to choose. In this context the looking and the reaching are clear and are successful as signals of choice.

In the request context, on the other hand, the communication partner's role is less clear and also potentially less focused. The entire context is also less static than the choice context. In the request situation, the partner is involved in the play situation with the child and is therefore focused not only on the child but also on the toys or activity. Rather than simply sitting and looking as in the choice context, the child is using movements in play. In this context, the partner's dual focus could cause her to miss the child's looking signal, or could cause her to misinterpret the looking signal as the child's focus of interest on the activity. The child's increased overall movements in the play situation could also mask the reaching signal. If these speculations about the different qualities of the two contexts are valid, then C needed a stronger contact with the adult in the request context to make himself understood. The "look to toy and adult" signal provided that strong contact and clarity of intent in that context.

Implications for Treatment

The results of this case study have a number of implications for treatment of physically impaired infants and young children. First, the success of the co-treatment model in this situation supports the idea that the child's motor needs are a critical component of a treatment program for a child with cerebral palsy. The hands-on involvement of the second therapist provided flexible yet stable positioning throughout the sessions enabling C to actively participate to his maximum ability. Furthermore, because it was a therapist's hands providing the stability, she could change and grade her input, gradually allowing C to increase his active involvement as his motor abilities changed.

In addition to the use of the second therapist for positioning and movement, the toys and the communication therapist were set in middle and below eye level so that C's head position and direction of eye gaze were optimal. This also helped to maximize C's ability to use his body successfully for both communication and play. In addition, enabling C to handle the toys himself appeared to have two benefits. First, the experience allowed him to be in control of his environment in new ways. Second, the mere act of handling the toys slowed the activity sufficiently for C to track the toys with his eyes and process the information he was experiencing.

The effect of context on the selection and use of specific signals has definite and exciting implications for treatment. If there are specific signals that fit more naturally into certain contexts, knowledge of that pattern would enable the therapist to teach in the optimal situational context. This specifically relates to the use of looking and reaching to choose and looking from adult to toy to request. Likewise, if a child has had limited independent play experience, that child may be more interested in choosing and playing with the chosen toy "alone," before being interested in requesting more adult participation. Knowledge of such foundational precursors would enable therapists to prepare for later developing signals in the long-range therapy plan.

C's use of the signals followed the pattern from least to most complex in the level of motoric sophistication. Research has shown that in normal development, the earliest signal to develop and be used for interaction is the control and use of eye gaze (4 months), followed closely by head control, and then control of the upper trunk in leaning and then reaching in the direction of focus (6 to 9 months) (Stern, 1981). The signals were taught in that order in the treatment phase of this study, and as one signal was acquired, the next became the focus in treatment. Once C had several signals in his repertoire, for example, eye gaze, and lean/reach, it then became important for the therapist to wait for the most sophisticated signal to emerge in a communication opportunity. C would generally begin by using the most motor-simple signal, looking at the toy, and perhaps wiggling in excitement. Only after 5, 7, or even 10 seconds, would he move to a more complex motor signal and begin to lean and finally reach for the toy. Later, in the request context, the therapist again had to wait before C used his most sophisticated signal and looked from the toy to the therapist to request the activity.

Furthermore, as the more sophisticated signals entered C's repertoire, the data showed that his use of the earlier signals decreased, if he was given time to use the more sophisticated signals. Overall, this behavior pattern supports the concept that new skills are built on and incorporate familiar skills. This idea also follows Vygotsky's and Bruner's idea of scaffolding to support the change and maturation of a child's communication with the world (Bruner, 1985). C's communication behavior pattern is a strong reminder that, when working with a physically disabled child, the communication partner must wait to give the child time and reason to make the physical effort to move to her most sophisticated communication signal.

Appendix A

Taxonomy: Coding Communication Intent

Looking

Passive Looking (PL) Child looks at object for 3 seconds with no change in facial expression or any indication of excitement or interest.

Active Looking (AL) Child looks at object for 3 seconds with some indication of excitement shown in vocalization, body movement, or change in facial expression.

Looking at Object and at Adult (LA) Child looks at object and at adult, then maybe back to object. If the first look at object is sustained for 3 seconds, child may or may not return to object. If the initial look at object is less than 3 seconds, child must return to object and hold gaze for 3 seconds.

Reaching

Reaching (R) Child leans forward in direction of object; arms may be up but remain bent.

Reach-Grasp (RG) Child leans forward and reaches with arm; includes arm and hand movement out to object.

(Reaching is always accompanied by looking at toy, the look sustained through the reach.)

Negation Response

No Response (N) After initial joint attention, child looks around the room with no further attempt to focus on the toys or examiner.

No Choice (NC) After initial joint attention, child again looks from one to the other but without stopping on either. In addition, child shows little facial expression to indicate interest or excitement.

Fussing (NF) Child continues to attend, but actively looks away, or looks at examiner and fusses in negation.

References

Als, H. (1982). The unfolding of behavioral organization in the face of biological violation. In E. Tronick (Ed.), *Social interchange in infancy: Affect, cognition, and communication* (pp. 125-160). Baltimore: University Park Press.

Bates, E., Camaioni, L., & Volterra, V. (1975). The acquisition of performatives prior to speech. *Merrill-Palmer Quarterly, 21,* 205-226.

Bates, E., Benigni, L., Bretherton, J., Camaioni, L., & Volterra, V. (1979). *The emergence of symbols: Cognition and communication in infancy.* New York: Academic Press.

Bellugi, U., & Klima, E. (1972). The roots of language in the sign talk of the deaf. *Psychology Today, 6,* 61-76.

Brazelton, B. (1982). Joint regulation of neonate-parent behavior. In E. Z. Tronick (Ed.), *Social interchange in infancy: Affect, cognition, and communication* (pp. 7-22). Baltimore: University Park Press.

Bruner, J. (1982). The organization of action and the nature of the adult-infant transaction. In E. Tronick (Ed.), *Social interchange in infancy: Affect, cognition and communication,* (pp. 23-35). Baltimore: University Park Press.

Bruner, J. (1985). Vygotsky: A historical and conceptual perspective. In J. V. Wertsch (Ed.), *Culture, communication and cognition: Vygotskian perspective* (pp. 21-34). New York: Cambridge University Press.

Buckhart, J., Rutherford, R., & Goldberg, K. (1978). Verbal and nonverbal interaction of mothers with their Down syndrome and nonretarded infants. *American Journal of Mental Deficiency, 82*(4), 337-343.

Fogel, A., Diamond, G., Langhorst, B., & Demos, V. (1982). Affective and cognitive aspects of the two month old's participation in face to face interaction with the mother. In E. Z. Tronick (Ed.), *Social interchange in infancy: Affect, cognition, and communication* (pp. 37-58). Baltimore: University Park Press.

Hanzlik, J., & Stevenson, M. (1986). Interaction of mothers with their infants who are mentally retarded, retarded with cerebral palsy, or nonretarded. *American Journal of Mental Deficiency, 90*(5), 513-520.

Harding, C. G. (1982). The development of the intention to communicate. *Human Development, 25,* 140-151.

Harding, C. G. (1984). Acting with intention: A framework of examining the development of the intention to communicate. In C. Garvey, L. Feagans, & R. Golinkoff (Eds.), *The origins and growth of communication* (pp. 123-153). Norwood, NJ: Ablex.

Kogan, K. L., & Tyler, N. (1973). Mother-child interaction in young physically handicapped children. *American Journal of Mental Deficiency, 77*(5), 492-497.

Murray, L., & Trevarthen, C. (1986). The infant's role in mother-infant communication. *Journal of Child Language, 4*(1), 1-22.

Olswang, L., & Carpenter, R. (1982). Ontogenesis of agent: Cognitive notion. *Journal of Speech and Hearing Research, 25*, 297-305.

Shellen, W. N. (1985, February). *A simple guide to reliability for quantitative coding of language samples.* Paper presented at the meeting of the Language Behavior Interest Group, Western Speech Communication Association Convention, Fresno, CA.

Stern, D. N. (1981). The development of biologically determined signals of readiness to communicate which are language "resistant." In R. Stark (Ed.), *Language behavior in infancy and early childhood* (pp. 45-62). New York: Elsevier North Holland.

Sugarman, S. (1984). The development of preverbal communication: Its contribution and limits in promoting the development of language. In R. Schiefelbusch & J. Pikar (Eds.), *Communicative competence: Acquisition and intervention* (pp. 23-67). Baltimore: University Park Press.

Trevarthen, C. (1986). The development of intersubjective motor control in infants. In M. G. Wade & H. T. A. Whiting (Eds.), *Motor development in children: Aspects of coordination and control* (pp. 207-261). Dordrecht: Martinus Nijhoff.

Wetherby, A. M., & Prizant, B. M. (1989). The expression of communicative intent: Assessment guidelines. *Seminars of Speech and Language, 10*(1), 77-90.

Address correspondence to:
Gay Lloyd Pinder, M.Ed.,
Children's Therapy Center of Kent,
26461-104th Avenue S.E.,
Kent, WA 98031

Part III:
Effects of Cocaine and Drug Exposure

Interactions of Neonates and Infants with Prenatal Cocaine Exposure

Shirley N. Sparks, M.S.
Western Michigan University, Kalamazoo

Colette Gushurst, M.D.
Michigan State University–Kalamazoo Center for Medical Studies

Aberrant interactive gaze may affect later learning ability. This study evaluated the effect of prenatal cocaine exposure on gaze of neonates and recovery of gaze at 2 months. Eleven neonates exposed prenatally to cocaine and 13 matched nonexposed neonates were tested for length of interactive gaze under three levels of stimulus. Interactive gaze time was significantly different for the cocaine-exposed group (p < .04). Cocaine-exposed neonates had shorter gaze and 2-month-old exposed infants had longer gaze than controls. There was a significant interaction between age and treatment group (p < .007). It did not matter what level of stimulus was given to the neonate or infant (p < .59). The caution that cocaine-exposed infants can handle only one stimulus at a time to avoid gaze aversion is not supported by this study for all cocaine-exposed infants by 2 months of age.

Neonates who have been exposed to cocaine have been observed to react in aberrant ways when they receive natural stimuli from caregivers, that is, when they are engaged in mutual gaze, soothed by voice, and touched. Such newborns are hard to care for because they do not react as the caregiver expects, putting interactive communication and attachment with a caregiver at risk. Cocaine-exposed infants have been observed to differ from noncocaine exposed infants in responses to visual and auditory stimuli, but the effect of cocaine exposure has not been tested adequately. Cocaine is thought to suppress infant responses in infant-caregiver interaction. The present report uses a matched cohort study to determine the suppressor effect of prenatal cocaine exposure on gaze behavior under three levels of stimuli and recovery of gaze behavior as a function of age.

Mutual gaze occurs when the caregiver looks into the neonate's eyes and the neonate fixes that gaze and looks back at the caregiver. The mutual gaze is broken when the neonate looks away, which is termed gaze aversion. In this study, aberrant behavior refers to a neonate or infant's gaze aversion or inability to maintain mutual gaze so that communicative interaction may occur. Suppressor effect means that cocaine has reduced the length of time that an infant maintains mutual gaze. Mutual gaze is central to the interaction and may be interpreted as an indicator that interaction is taking place. Mutual gaze is the first communicative interaction that subsequently becomes the basis for infant-caregiver attachment, defined by Klaus and Kennell (1976) as a unique relationship between infant and caregiver that lasts a lifetime. Attachment is a foundation for optimal language development which, in turn, is the basis for cognitive skills development. This is not to say that language cannot be learned without attachment, but the positive effect of attachment has consistent theoretical bases.

There are several conclusions that can be drawn from the work to date. Infant characteristics shown to be related to subsequent attachment quality include irritability, sociability, and pleasure in close proximal contact. Infant differences in those characteristics alter the nature of the caregiver-infant interaction and thus indirectly affect the quality of attachment. Furthermore, infant behavior is more important as a predictor of later attachment behavior compared to maternal behavior (Lewis & Feiring, 1989). That language develops from early nonlinguistic conversations and joint activites between the child and his or her caregivers has been supported strongly in the theoretical and research literature in parent-child interactions (Bates, 1976; Dore, 1975; Lewis & Rosenblum, 1974; Moerk, 1977; Snow, 1972). Early assessments of mother-infant interaction are among the best predictors of language and IQ in older preschoolers, even better than measures of perinatal or infant physical status (Bee et al., 1982). Several authors underscore the importance of mutual gaze to attachment and readiness for learning (Ambrose, 1963; Robson & Moss 1970; Wolff, 1963). Conversely, gaze aversion is indicative of abnormality and is disturbing to adults (Robson, 1967; Hutt & Ounsted, 1966).

Normal infants are capable of maintaining mutual gaze in the presence of auditory and tactile stimuli. The Neonatal Behavior Assessment Scale (Brazelton, 1984) was developed to describe a range of behaviors that an infant may show. One item (orientation-animate visual) calls for the examiner to engage the neonate by using his or her face and gaze but to avoid talking. "The infant may turn the head to seek the examiner's face, and having found it, may rivet his or her attention and 'lock' on for long periods. No interest is unusual" (p. 31). Another item on the NBAS, (orientation-animate visual and auditory) is used to determine maintenance of mutual gaze in the presence of speech. The instructions to the examiner are, "speaking in a soft, high-pitched voice to the infant, with your face 12 to 18 inches in front of his or her face, move in horizontal rather than vertical arcs from the baby's midline. The voice should be continuous while the face is moving" (p. 33). A third maneuver includes tactile stimuli, where neonates are held while these items are administered and examiners are instructed to reproduce maneuvers commonly used by mothers.

Cocaine-exposed neonates typically display physical characteristics placing their developmental course at risk (Adler, 1989; Chasnoff, Burns, Schnoll, & Burns, 1985; Chasnoff, Lewis, Griffith, & Wiley, 1989;

Chouteau, Namerow, & Leppert, 1988; Hadeed & Siegel, 1989; Howard, 1989; Little, Snell, Klein, & Gilstrap, 1989). Furthermore, such infants are reported to have poor state control (Griffith, 1988), to be "irritable" and show "neurobehavioral disturbances" (Hume, O'Donnell, Stanger, Killam, & Gingras, 1989). Those characteristics of the cocaine-exposed infant reportedly interfere with the ability of the infant to interact with or respond to the caregiver. The caregiver may, in turn, become more passive in his or her attempts at interaction, thus setting up a cycle of decreasing interaction on the part of both infant and caregiver.

Figure 1 depicts very simply the theoretical linkages that were specified in the previous section. In this model, prenatal cocaine exposure is seen as a suppressor on gaze, thus diminishing the positive effect of gaze on attachment and the positive effect that attachment has on language learning.

Methods

Study Sample

All neonates born at Bronson Methodist Hospital, Kalamazoo, Michigan, from June 1, 1991 to June 1, 1992, who were placed in the well-baby nursery were potential candidates for the study. Subjects were free of conditions that would place them in the neonatal intensive care unit, thereby excluding very low birthweight and sick neonates.

The experimental group (n = 11) were neonates whom the hospital staff identified as "high risk." Either the mother or the neonate tested positive for cocaine exposure by positive urine assays. It was not the hospital's routine to screen all mothers for drug use. Therefore, only mothers or infants already identified by positive urine assays could be identified for the experimental group. One mother had two drug-exposed infants within the 1 year of the study, and both infants are included in the experimental group. One experimental infant died of SIDS at 4 months. The control group (n = 13) comprised a cohort selected from newborns matched to the experimental group for race, birthweight within 8 ounces., and socioeconomic group. Demographic data on the study population are provided in Table 1. There were no significant differences between the groups.

Four of the 15 mothers who were candidates for the experimental group declined to participate or did not keep appointments for videotaping, as did 16 of the 29 eligible control group mothers. Data were collected on those who were eligible but did not participate and are presented in Table 2. Neither group of nonparticipants differed significantly from the groups analyzed for the study.

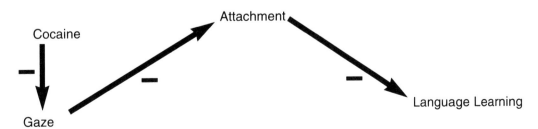

Figure 1. Theoretical suppressor effect of cocaine.

Table 1. Demographic Characteristics of the Study Population

	Cocaine Exposed	**Nonexposed**
Sample size	11	13
Race		
Black	10	12
White	1	1
Mean Birth Weight	6'4"	6'9"
Range	4'15"–8'1"	5'14"–8'7"
Mean Head Circumference: Birth	32.8 cm	34.7 cm
Range	31.25–34	33.5–36
Mean Gestational Age	38.2	39.8
Range	36–40	38–41
Gender		
Male	7	5
Female	5	8
Foster Care	2	0
Method of Delivery		
Vaginal	11	11
Caesarian	0	2

Table 2. Demographic Characteristics of Eligible Nonparticipants

	Cocaine Exposed	**Nonexposed**
Sample size	4	16
Race		
Black	2	15
White	1	1
Bi-racial	1	
Mean Birth Weight	6'3"	6'8"
Range	5'9"–7'5"	5'8¾"–8'4"
Mean Head Circumference	33.5 cm	33.4 cm
Range	33–34	31.75–35.5
Mean Gestational Age	38	38
Range	37–41	34–41
Gender		
Male	2	7
Female	2	9
Method of Delivery		
Vaginal	3	12
Caesarian	1	4

To determine that our control group mothers had not used cocaine, and to ascertain what other drugs were used by both control and experimental groups, we used three methods of verification: urine screens on mother and infant, meconium testing of infants, and drug histories on the mothers. Infants were placed in the experimental group if they were positive on any of the three methods of verification. The unreliability of using only one of the verification methods is demonstrated by this study. One mother chosen as a control was subsequently placed in the experimental group from her self-history of cocaine use during pregnancy although she was not selected for urine screening by the hospital. One mother in the experimental group from self-history and positive urine assay had a negative meconium test for cocaine.

Measures

The initial measures were done within the first week after birth. In most of the subjects, the measurements were taken in the first 2 days post-birth when the neonate and mother were still in the hospital. In those subjects who were not in an alert state during the first 2 days, the mother or foster mother returned with the neonate within the first week after birth. Ages of the neonates and infants at the time of the two observations are presented in Table 3.

The protocol was the same for experimental and control group neonates. It was conducted as follows: The nurses in the well-baby nursery alerted the physician-investigator or the nurse-investigator when a neonate in the nursery tested positive for cocaine or whose mother tested positive for cocaine through urine assay. The nurse-investigator explained the procedure, presented the Informed Consent Form to the mother and filled out the Substance Questionnaire (see Appendix) by interviewing the mother. The nurse-investigator collected a stool specimen and sent it to be tested through Damon Clinical Laboratories at the Detroit Medical Center. Ostrea, Parks, and Brady (1990) reported their radioimmunoassay to detect the metabolites of heroin, cocaine, amphetamines, and cannabinoids is reliable for meconium collected up to 3 days of age. The nurse-investigator took the alert infant to the designated site for videotaping. The mother could observe the procedures if she wished.

Stimulus Levels

1. Eye contact only. The neonate was placed in a reclining position in a newborn infant seat. The investigator turned on the Olympus VS403 Camcorder videocamera placed on a tripod behind her shoulder and focused on the baby's face. With her face approximately 12 inches from the neonate's face she attempted to make eye contact and hold the neonate's gaze within a 3-minute period. To gain the neonate's attention, she spoke softly, but after the neonate was looking at her, she did not talk. There was no attempt to follow the neonate's eyes to require interaction when the neonate looked away.

Table 3. Ages of Subjects for Gaze Interaction Videotaping

	Cocaine Exposed	**Nonexposed**
Mean Age at Observation 1	7 days	6 days
Range	0–24 days	2–15 days
Mean Age at Observation 2	2 mo. 27 days	2 mo. 17 days
Range	1 mo. 28 days–3 mo. 4 days	1 mo 27 days–4 mo. 14 days

2. Eye contact plus soothing speech. The investigator used the same procedure as done for "eye contact only," except the investigator employed soothing speech through-out the 3-minute period.

3. Eye contact plus soothing speech plus touch. The investigator used the same procedure as done for "eye contact plus soothing speech," except that the neonate was stroked on the arms, legs, and body.

After each of the first two procedures, the neonate had a 1-minute rest period. The neonate was given a pacifier and placed in an infant swing without music and rocked vertically. There was no interaction with the investigator during the time-out. In a few instances, neonates or infants were fed by their mothers during the time-out procedure. When the infants returned for their follow-up visits at 2 months, procedures were repeated.

It should be noted that the three procedures consist of occurrences that are normal and natural in interactions of neonates and infants with adults. Undue stress was not employed on the neonates or on the 2-month-old infants. The nature of the procedure was such that soothing speech and touch can be done in a standard manner. As with all interactions, it could not be exactly the same with each subject because of the part that the neonate or infant plays in that interaction. A rest period of 1 minute for both neonates and 2-month-olds seems reasonable to abbrogate the effect of carryover from one treatment to another (Baillargeon, 1987; Haith, Hazen, & Goodman, 1988; Mandler, 1990).

Data Analysis

The variable to be measured was length of time that each infant maintained mutual gaze with the investigator at each of the three levels of stimuli. All videotapes were analyzed at Western Michigan University's Charles Van Riper Speech and Hearing Center. Two observers (speech pathology graduate students) who were unaware of the neonate's group designation, viewed the taped segments independently. Interobserver reliability was computed by analysis of variance at the .05 level of significance ($p = 0.2371$) indicating no significant difference between the observer's recordings from the videotaped samples. A custom software computer program called "Time Recorder" was written for this project at Western Michigan University's Department of Speech Pathology and Audiology Laboratory. Each time the observer judged that the neonate or infant made eye contact with the investigator, that observer depressed a key on the Zenith PC/XT compatible computer. When the observer judged that the eye contact was broken, the observer depressed another key. The time recordings were saved in a file. The smallest value that could be stored was 0.55 seconds. If an observation fell between 0.55 seconds and the next value of 0.110 seconds, the computer counted the value as 0.110 seconds if the value was half or more of the interval between the two values. The computer automatically totaled the time samples and printed a hard copy of the results coded to the infant's file number. The mean of the two observer measurements was the data point for that child per observation.

A repeated measures experimental design was employed. The analysis includes both crossed and repeated factors. The repeated factors are stimulus (eye contact only; eye contact plus soothing speech; and mutual gaze plus soothing speech plus touch) and age (neonate and 2-months old) and the crossed factor is cocaine exposure and no exposure. Data were analyzed using a repeated measures ANOVA. First, analysis were completed for each of the two age groups separately by two factor repeated measures ANOVA (three levels of stimuli and exposure to cocaine). In addition, an overall analysis consisting of a three factor ANOVA for repeated measures was done.

Several infants had missing values for certain observations due to the mothers not bringing in the infants for follow-up visits, the infants sleeping through the testing, or the infants avoiding the observer's gaze completely. The analysis of variance computing procedure only uses a subject's observations if the complete set of variables, both the dependent variable as well as all the independent variables, are present. This, in addition to the small sample size, further limited the numbers of observations used in the modelling procedure.

Results

Self-reported substance use is summarized in Table 4. The percentage of experimental group mothers who reported using a substance at any time during their pregnancy is reported. In addition, to track changing

Table 4. Summary of Experimental Group Mothers' Self-Report of Substance Use

	1st Trimester %	2nd Trimester %	3rd Trimester %
Smoking 100%			
1 pack per day or more	63	45	45
Fewer than 1 pack per day	27	45	54
No smoking	9	9	0
Coffee 54%			
2 cups per day or more	27	18	27
Fewer than 2 cups per day	18	9	0
No coffee	9	27	27
Beer 63%			
1 per day or more	27	27	18
Fewer than 1 per day	27	27	18
No beer	9	9	27
Liquor 27%			
1 oz per day or more	0	9	9
Less than 1 oz per day	9	9	18
No liquor	18	9	0
Primos (cocaine in marijuana) 63%			
1 per week or more	18	36	45
Fewer than 1 per week	0	9	18
No primos	45	18	0
Crack Cocaine 54%			
1 pack per week or more	18	18	18
Fewer than 1 per week	9	9	18
No crack	27	27	18
Cocaine Powder 36%			
1 pack per week or more	18	9	9
Fewer than 1 per week	0	9	9
No cocaine powder	18	9	9

(continued)

Table 4. (continued)

	1st Trimester %	2nd Trimester %	3rd Trimester %
Marijuana 27%			
1 per day or more	9	9	9
Fewer than 1 per day	18	9	9
No marijuana smoking	0	9	9

habits during the pregnancy, only those mothers who report any use of a substance are also reported under that substance for no use at some time during the pregnancy. For example, 63% of the subjects reported using primos (a rock of cocaine imbedded in marijuana and smoked). Forty-five percent of the subjects who used primos at any time did not use them in the first trimester; by the third trimester, all of the 63% were using primos.

Smoking

All of the experimental group mothers smoked cigarettes at some time during the pregnancy. Some who smoked one or more packs per day had cut their consumption to less than one pack by the second trimester, but by the third trimester, all were smoking.

Coffee and Alcohol

Coffee was included on the form to encourage accurate reporting, not because it is considered to have adverse effects on the fetus. Alcohol use was reported to be light. Liquor consumption increased by the third trimester by those women who reported drinking liquor.

Illegal Drugs

Primos (defined previously) was the preferred method of cocaine administration by the experimental group mothers. The marijuana is said to reduce the "let down" after the euphoric feeling of a crack "rush." Primo administration increased from the first trimester to the third. Forty-five percent of the women who used primos in the third trimester had not used them in the first trimester. Increased use is also evident in the use of crack cocaine (a rock or crystal of cocaine smoked in a pipe), cocaine powder (smoked or sniffed), and marijuana. One mother reported using 10 rocks of crack once per week in the first and second trimesters, increasing her use to 15 rocks but dropping the frequency to 3 times per month in the third trimester.

None of the mothers reported using more than two of the four methods of administration: primos, crack, marijuana, and cocaine powder. One mother used primos exclusively, and all the others used only two. Sixty-six percent of those who used crack also used primos, whereas 50% of those who used cocaine powder also smoked marijuana.

Univariate statistics for both groups is presented in Table 5. Although mean gaze time is shorter in the cocaine-exposed neonates than in the control neonates, mean gaze times reverse at the 2-month level: the cocaine-exposed 2-month-olds had longer mean gaze times than the nonexposed group. Interestingly, all but one group had one to three subjects who did not lock gaze with the examiner at all during the 3-minute period, and that group was the cocaine-exposed 2-month-olds at level three. Six of the 10 control subjects at stimulus level three did not lock gaze with the examiner for any

Table 5. Gaze Behavior by Age and Level of Stimulus

	Cocaine Exposed			Nonexposed		
	n	Mean (Range)	SD	n	Mean (Range)	SD
Newborn						
Level 1	8	6.40. (0–22.85)	8.13	9	9.74. (0–59.80)	19.41
Level 2	7	2.55. (0–8.68)	3.35	9	5.58. (0–27.88)	8.71
Level 3	5	2.48. (0–4.64)	2.27	9	6.91. (0–47.52)	15.41
2 Months Old						
Level 1	10	47.28. (0–118.81)	40.59	10	20.71. (0–81.37)	29.79
Level 2	10	58.20. (0–113.54)	42.03	10	21.16. (0–77.06)	30.81
Level 3	10	41.28. (0.96–157.19)	53.15	10	15.09. (0–50.71)	17.94

Level 1: gaze alone; Level 2: gaze + voice; Level 3: gaze + voice + touch.

measureable length of time. The mean was computed from the other four, with three of those measures at 4 to 5 seconds and one at 47.5 seconds. In the following results, treatment refers to cocaine exposure or no exposure. Interaction means that the effects of the factors together differ from the effects of either factor alone.

1. There is a significant difference in total gaze time between the cocaine-exposed group and the control group ($p = 0.0486$). This finding is irrespective of age as both ages were combined for treatment and control groups.
2. There is a significant age by treatment effect ($p = 0.0071$). Not only were the treatment groups different, when age was considered there was a significant interaction between age and treatment group. Cocaine-exposed neonates' gaze time was significantly different from the nonexposed neonates' gaze time. The gaze times for the exposed infants was likewise significantly different from the nonexposed group.
3. There is no significant stimulus by treatment group interaction ($p = 0.5952$).

Therefore, cocaine exposure did not affect the neonates' or infants' responses to gaze alone; gaze plus speech; or gaze, speech, and touch together.

Discussion

Research on a drug's subsequent effects on children is challenging because drug-dependent women rarely use just one drug. Illegal drugs, such as cocaine, methamphetamines, PCP, and marijuana, are commonly combined with alcohol and cigarettes. This pattern of polydrug use, coupled with the fact that the illegal substances ingested are seldom pure, makes it difficult to determine which drugs a pregnant woman has used, or when during pregnancy, and how much she has taken. In addition, drug-dependent, pregnant women often have poor nutrition, increased infections, other medical complications, and little or no prenatal care. All of these factors can cause problems for infants, making it difficult to sort out the effects of drugs from the effects of a generally unhealthy prenatal environment or maternal lifestyle. Furthermore, none of the three methods of verification of drug use—urine toxicology screen, meconium testing, and mothers' drug histories—is a completely objective and reliable measure.

Urine screens measure a concentration in the urine of the cocaine metabolite that remains in the mother's body for approximately 48 hours after use. However, if the mother drinks enough water to dilute her urine, the concentration of the metabolite in her urine may fall below the laboratory threshold for a positive report. Newborn urine is relatively dilute in the first 24 hours, hence the concentration of the metabolite may fall below the standard threshold for the baby as well. More sensitive meconium testing was employed as an additional objective measure. Meconium is formed in the fetus at approximately 20 weeks gestation, and metabolites of cocaine, heroin, marijuana, and amphetamines remain in the meconium throughout fetal development. The threshold for detection of the metabolite in urine is set by federal standards (National Institute of Drug Abuse) at 300 ng/ml; if the concentration is below 300 ng/ml, the laboratory will report it as negative (Chasnoff, 1992). Meconium may not be sampled correctly; the sample may not be adequate to contain enough of the drug or metabolite of the drug to show up in the test results.

We also took careful histories of drug use: amount, method of administration, and timing, all of which have room for error. The increasing use of cocaine during pregnancy was unexpected and unexplained.

The surprise in this process was the relative ease of obtaining consent from the cocaine-positive mothers, compared to the extreme difficulty in obtaining controls. As stated previously, we approached cocaine-positive mothers after the hospital's urine toxicology test came back positive and the mother had been so informed; at that point her drug use was known. The fact that we would then take a stool specimen from the baby for drug analysis was only confirmatory. The positive effect of remuneration ($25) on response rate (Bryant, Kovar, & Miller, 1975) appears to be substantiated for the experimental group mothers in this project. They all returned for follow-up. However, the control infants were chosen from those newborns in the nursery who matched the experimental group newborns, who had not had a urine screen, or who had a negative screen. When those mothers were approached, they were told the purpose of the study and that if they chose to participate, a stool specimen would be taken for laboratory analysis. The laboratory would report if the mother had used cocaine anytime after the first trimester of pregnancy. Time after time mothers of potential control subjects seemed interested until we asked for a stool specimen and drug history. Some of these mothers said no immediately. Others made an appointment for a time after they left the hospital and then did not appear.

Based on conversations with these mothers, the reasons for nonparticipation seemed to be: (a) they had used cocaine during the pregnancy and they feared detection, and (b) they feared reprisal for use of other drugs. Although we offered monetary incentives the disincentives were too high. Even though anonymity was explained by the use of code numbers instead of names, the mothers feared detection, which could mean removal of the baby by Social Services.

Conclusions

Results of this study support the conventional wisdom that cocaine-exposed neonates lock their interactive gaze less often than do nonexposed infants. The range of gaze time at the newborn level suggests that nonexposed neonates are more variable in their responses than are cocaine-exposed neonates. There appears to be a suppressor effect of cocaine on gaze behavior which is evident in the early neonatal period, but recovery of gaze behavior is present at 2 months of age. The reversed pattern in the 2-month-olds suggests that some of the cocaine-exposed infants are quite able to maintain interactive gaze even longer than nonexposed infants. This longer lock-on time may itself be an aberration; it is consistent with reports that cocaine-exposed infants "stare" (Struthers & Hansen, 1992).

An unexpected result was that the level of stimuli did not make a difference in gaze time to neonates or infants. Although we might say intuitively that stimuli from more than one sense should have an effect on gaze time, the lack of significance in our data set is explained by the high variability within infant and within treatment group for stimulus. This finding may not be true in a large data set.

Caregivers and healthcare providers should be cautious in their interactions with cocaine-exposed neonates by allowing the neonates to set the limits of interactive gaze time. By 2 months, however, exposed infants may be quite ready to engage in interactive gaze. The caution that cocaine-exposed infants can handle only one stimulus at a time (eye contact, voice, touch) to avoid gaze aversion is not supported by this study for all cocaine-exposed infants by 2 months of age.

Acknowledgments

The authors wish to thank the following people for their invaluable assistance: Radha Prathikanti for statistical analysis; Joan Pierce the nurse-investigator; John Brown for designing the software program; Charles Howard for preparation of the proposal and comments on the manuscript; and Michelle Meyer and Krista Klein, observers and data coders.

This work was supported by a Grant from the Faculty Research and Creative Activities Support Fund, Western Michigan University

References

Adler, T. (1989). Cocaine babies face behavior deficits. *APA Monitor, 20*(7), 14.

Ambrose, A. (1963). The concept of a critical period for the development of social responsiveness in early human infancy. In B. Foss (Ed.). *Determinants of infant behavior II* (pp. 201–225) London: Methuen.

Baillargeon, R. (1987). Object permanence in 3.5 and 4.5-month-old infants. *Developmental Psychology, 23*, 655–64.

Bates, E. (1976). *Language and context: The acquisition of pragmatics.* New York: Academic Press.

Bee, H. L., Barnard, K. E., Eyres, S. J., Gray, C. A., Hammond, M. A., Spietz, A. L., Snyder, C., & Clark, B. (1982). Prediction of IQ and language skill from perinatal status, child performance, family charactistics, and mother-infant interaction. *Child Development, 53*, 1134–1156.

Brazelton, T. B. (1984). *Neonatal behavior assessment scale* (2nd ed.). Philadelphia: J. B. Lippincott.

Bryant, E. E.., Kovar, M. G., & Miller, H. (1975). A study of the effect of remuneration upon response in the health and nutrition examination survey. In U.S. Department of Health, Education, and Welfare Publication No. (HRA) 76-1341, Series 2, Number 67, 1–18.

Chasnoff, I. J. (1992, May). *Drugs, alcohol, pregnancy and the child.* Paper presented at Drug Use in Pregnancy: Impact on Families and the Growing Child. National Association for Perinatal Addiction Research and Education (NAPARE) Conference, San Francisco.

Chasnoff, I. J., Burns, W. J., Schnoll, S. H., & Burns, K. A. (1985). Cocaine use in pregnancy. *The New England Journal of Medicine, 313*(11), 666–669.

Chasnoff, I. J., Lewis, D. E., Griffith, D. R., & Wiley, S. (1989). Cocaine and pregnancy: Clinical and toxicological implications for the neonate. *Clinical Chemistry, 35*(7), 1276–8.

Chouteau, M., Namerow, P. B., & Leppert, P. (1988). The effect of cocaine abuse on birth weight and gestational age. *Obstetrics and Gynecology, 72*(3), 351–4.

Dore, J. (1975). Holophrases, speech acts and language universals. *Journal of Child Language, 2*, 21–40.

Griffith, D. R. (1988). The effects of perinatal cocaine exposure on infant neurobehavior and early maternal-infant interactions. In I. Chasnoff (Fd.), *Drugs, alcohol, pregnancy and parenting* (pp. 105–113). Boston: Kluwer Academic Publishers.

Hadeed, A. J., & Siegel, S. R. (1989). Maternal cocaine use during pregnancy: Effect on the newborn infant. *Pediatrics, 84*(2), 205–10.

Haith M. M., Hazen C., & Goodman J. (1988). Expectation and anticipation of dynamic visual events by 3.5-month-old babies. *Child Development, 59*, 469–479.

Howard, J. (1989). Cocaine and its effects on the newborn. *Devopmental Medicine and Child Neurology, 31*(2), 255–257.

Hume, R. F., & O'Donnell, K. J., Stanger, C. L., Killam, A. P., & Gingras, J. L. (1989). In utero cocaine exposure: Observations of fetal behavioral state may predict neonatal outcome. *American Journal of Obstetrics and Gynecology, 161*(3), 685–90.

Hutt, C., & Ounsted, C. (1966). The biological significance of gaze aversion with particular reference to the syndrome of infantile autism. *Behavioral Science, II*, 346–353.

Klaus, M., & Kennel, J. (1976). *Maternal-infant bonding.* St. Louis: C.V. Mosby.

Lewis, M., & Feiring, C. (1989). Infant, mother, and mother-infant interaction behavior and subsequent attachment. *Child Development, 60*, 831–837.

Lewis, M., & Rosenblum, L. (1974). *Effects of the infant on its caregiver.* New York: Wiley.

Little, B. B., Snell, L. M., Klein, V. R., & Gilstrap, L. C. (1989). Cocaine abuse during pregnancy: Maternal and fetal implications. *Obstetrics and Gynecology, 73*(2), 157–60.

Mandler, J. M. (1990). A new perspective on cognitive development in infancy. *American Scientist, 78*, 236–243.

Moerk, E. (1977). *Pragmatic and semantic aspects of early language development.* Baltimore: University Park Press.

Ostrea, E. M., Parks, P., & Brady, M. (1989). The detection of heroin, cocaine, and cannabinoid metabolites in meconium of infants of drug dependent mothers. *Annals of the New York Academy of Sciences, 562*, 373–374.

Robson, K. S. (1967). The role of eye contact in maternal-infant attachment. *Journal of Child Psychology and Psychiatry, 8*, 13–25.

Robson, K. S., & Moss, H. A. (1970). Patterns and determinants of maternal attachment. *Journal of Pediatrics, 77*, 976–985.

Snow, C. (1972). Mother's speech to children learning language. *Child Development, 43*, 549–565.

Struthers, J. M., & Hansen R. L. (1992). Visual recognition memory in drug-exposed infants. *Journal of Developmental and Behavioral Pediatrics, 13*, 108–111.

Wolff, P. H. (1963). Observations on the early development of smiling. In B. M. Foss (Ed.), *Determinanats of infant behavior II* (pp. 113–138) London: Methuen.

Address correspondence to:
Shirley N. Sparks, CCC-SLP
1560 Sand Hill Road, #204
Palo Alto, CA 94304

Appendix

Code Number_____

Substance Questionnaire

We are interested in substances that you smoked or drank during your pregnancy. Your answers will not be identified by your name and will be kept completely confidential.

	1st 3 months	middle 3 months	last 3 months
Cigarettes	_____	_____	_____
Coffee	_____	_____	_____
Beer	_____	_____	_____
Wine	_____	_____	_____
Liquor (gin, bourbon, vodka)	_____	_____	_____
Marijuana (Pot)	_____	_____	_____
Cocaine	_____	_____	_____
Crack	_____	_____	_____
Primos	_____	_____	_____
Heroin	_____	_____	_____
Amphetemines	_____	_____	_____
Prescription	_____	_____	_____
Other	_____	_____	_____

Frequency (and Quantity)   How used

0 – No use in 3 mos.   A – oral
1 – once per month   B – smoking
2 – once per week   C – Inhale
3 – 2–3 times per week   D – I.M.
4 – more than 3 times per week   E – I.V.
5 – once daily
6 – 2–3 times daily
7 – more than 3 times daily

Service Patterns and Educational Experiences Between Two Groups Who Work With Young Children Prenatally Exposed to Cocaine: A Study Across Four States

J. Keith Chapman, Ph.D.
Phyllis K. Mayfield, Ph.D.
Martha J. Cook, Ed.D.
Brad S. Chissom, Ed.D.
The University of Alabama
Tuscaloosa, Alabama

A sample of early childhood special educators and pediatric professionals in the states of Alabama, Florida, Georgia, and Mississippi were surveyed to determine service patterns and preservice/inservice preparation experiences regarding working with and addressing the needs of young children prenatally exposed to cocaine. Of the 240 surveys distributed, 162 responded, for a return rate of 67.5%. Across the two professional groups, findings suggested differences in service delivery pattern, with maternal self-report identified as the primary identification procedure. In addition, a lack of perceived meaningful educational preparation in working with young children exposed to cocaine and their families was indicated. Needed additional educational experiences and competency areas were identified.

Over the past decade, a major concern has emerged regarding the use of illicit drugs by women of childbearing age as reflected in recent medical and governmental reports. For example, the National Institute of Drug Abuse [NIDA] (1989) reported that approximately 15% of women (14 to 44 years of age) are current users of illicit drugs. Another recent report estimated that 4.8 million women of childbearing age have used some form of illicit substance(s) during any given month (Khalsa & Gfroerer, 1991). Commensurate with the above data, an especially problematic issue is the use of cocaine by women in this age range. Specifically, the NIDA (1991) reported that overall the prevalence of cocaine use in the United States is declining (in 1990 an estimated 6.6 million individuals reported use in the preceding year compared with 12 million in 1988); however, this report indicated that one group that continues to use cocaine at high rates were women of childbearing age. Likewise, increases in the number of infants exposed to cocaine are anticipated as well (Office of the Inspector General [OIG], 1990).

Alarming statistics have been reported that substantiate the likelihood that multiservice agencies will become increasingly involved in assisting both these children and their families in the near future. Some reports (Bays, 1990; Besharov, 1989) have estimated that approximately 60,000 to 70,000 infants who are prenatally exposed to cocaine are born each year in this country. These estimates, however, may be conservative, as other reports have suggested that each year as many as 200,000 to 375,000 infants are cocaine-exposed (Gittler, 1990; OIG, 1990; Smith, 1988).

Although there continues to be disagreement regarding the extent and duration of distinct physiological, behavioral, and/or environmental manifestations that are developmentally specific for infants and young children prenatally exposed to cocaine (Chapman, Worthington, Cook, & Mayfield, 1992), medical research has indicated that these young children are potentially *at risk* for a cluster of developmental anomalies (Chasnoff, Griffith, Freier, & Murray, 1992; Eisen, Field, Bandstra, Roberts, Morrow, Larson, & Steele, 1991; Schneider & Chasnoff, 1992; van de Bor, Walthes, & Sims, 1990). Beyond the potential effects of cocaine exposure on infant development, some investigators have indicated that the imprint of this substance may persist into toddlerhood. It has been suggested that these young children may be prone to exhibit developmental delays in cognitive and language development, social interaction, and emotional regulation (Rodning, Beckwith, & Howard, 1989; Trad, 1992). In addition, risk factors associated with postnatal environmental variables such as poverty, poor housing, lead poisoning, malnutrition, and poor parenting skills, may subject young children to serious developmental consequences (Griffith, 1992; Zuckerman & Bresnahan, 1991).

Currently, there are no state or national guidelines for screening newborns and/or their mothers for suspected cocaine/illicit substance exposure. Maternal self-reports, one of the most widely reported methods of identification (Shriver & Piersel, 1994), may not be a reliable option because many mothers are hesitant to report their drug use for fear of prosecution and other legal/personal ramifications (MacDonald, 1992; Schutter & Brinker, 1992). Without a systematic and accurate identification process, the magnitude and scope of the problem may remain relatively unknown. This is disheartening when one considers the wide range of estimates regarding the numbers of infants prenatally exposed to illicit substances each year.

In addition, the potential varied needs of these young children and their families could transcend those provided by the medical field and may impact greatly on education and various service agencies. The well-documented shortage of early intervention personnel under PL 99-457 (Meisels, 1989; Meisels, Harbin, Modigiliani, & Olsen, 1988), the projected costs of medical/preventive care, the present acute shortage of trained foster care providers, and diverse legal issues, are variables that may interact to limit collaboration and coordinated delivery of services. According to the U. S. General Accounting Office [GAO] (1990), a tremendous diversity exists among county, state, and federal agencies in attempting to identify and serve this emerging population of young children.

Presently, there has been relatively little research attempting to *determine* the extent to which educational and related service professionals are addressing the needs of this population, and to *describe* the types of preservice/inservice development these professionals have received in providing services to young children prenatally exposed to cocaine and their families. Therefore, the major objective of this study was to seek descriptive information within two professional groups, (early childhood special educators and pediatric professionals) in the states of Alabama, Florida, Georgia, and Mississippi in order to:

1. Determine if these children are being served, the number of children being served, the primary procedure(s) employed in identification, and sources of referral.
2. Determine the types *and* the effectiveness of educational preparation and experiences these two groups have received regarding young children prenatally exposed to cocaine.
3. Identify educational and competency areas these two groups of professionals consider to be important in effectively meeting the needs of this population.

Method

Subjects

Participation in the study involved two professional groups ($N = 240$) in the states of Alabama, Florida, Georgia, and Mississippi. Early childhood special education (ECSE) professionals ($n = 120$) were randomly selected from the *1993 Alabama, Florida, Georgia, and Mississippi DEC Directories*. Pediatricians ($n = 120$) were randomly selected from *The 1992 Medical Association of the State Pictorial Membership Roster* for each of the above states. Located in urban, suburban, and rural settings, these ECSE programs and pediatric practices employed a variety of intervention and medical services, and they varied in size and scope.

Instrument and Procedural Verification

The authors designed a 30-item instrument used for data collection purposes (see the Appendix at the end of this article). Two major objectives were considered in constructing the instrument. The first objective was to develop a brief questionnaire that could be subdivided into logical categories as identified in the literature. Second, an attempt was made to incorporate language and format that was concise and unambiguous. The initial draft of the questionnaire was independently reviewed by six educational and medical professionals who were knowledgeable about early intervention and illicit substance use. These professionals evaluated for clarity of instructions, the adequacy of response options, and the appropriateness of items. As a result of this review, minor modifications were made to the questionnaire. To further verify instrument and survey procedures, the questionnaire was also piloted with 20 individuals who were similarly situated to the subjects of the study and who were providing services to young children. Feedback from pilot respondents resulted in no suggested revisions regarding the organization or format of the questionnaire.

Part I of the survey consisted of demographic data in which respondents provided information about their educational level, degree emphasis, description of their program/practice, and the population density in which they were located. Part II of the survey requested information regarding service patterns to young children prenatally exposed to cocaine. Part III of the survey asked respondents to relate the types of preparation they had received in providing services to children prenatally exposed to cocaine and their families, and then to rate on a 5-point Likert-type scale the effectiveness of these training experiences. The second section of Part III consisted of an open-ended question that asked respondents if there were other areas in which they believed additional preparation was needed. Part IV of the survey asked respondents to circle those responses (1 through 15) on a 5-point Likert-type scale that best described the importance of competency areas in providing services to these infants/children and their families. The respondents were also asked to rank order the five competencies they perceived as the most important in providing services to this population.

Procedures

Coded surveys were mailed to ECSE educators and practicing pediatricians in the states of Alabama, Florida, Georgia, and Mississippi. Follow-up letters, surveys, and stamped return materials were sent to those who did not respond after 4 weeks and again after 7 weeks. Of the 240 surveys mailed, 162 were returned, for a response rate of 67.5%. Two surveys were returned stating that their program/practice was not service-oriented. In this case, those data supplied were not included in the analysis.

Data Analysis

Descriptive statistics procedures and content analysis were conducted on the data obtained from the survey. Descriptive statistics, from hand-coded raw data on the survey, were obtained by running statistical computer package procedures (SAS Institute, 1989). Content analysis was applied to organize data from the open-ended questions by bracketing, categorizing, and sorting the data according to the primary theme or idea exhibited (Johnson & LaMontagne, 1993)

Results

Subject Demographics

Sixty-four or 53% of early childhood special educators (female = 89%; male = 11%) and 98 (82%) of pediatric professionals (female = 16%; male = 84%) sampled participated in this study. Table 1 presents a breakdown of the demographic data obtained from participants. All ECSE possessed college-level degrees; however, this group also exhibited a wide range of degree area/concentrations associated with level of degree. When asked to describe their current position, 100% of the respondents reported ECSE teacher or coordinator. The majority of ECSE programs were center-based in focus and were also primarily located in rural to small town/city areas.

All pediatric professionals were board certified and fully licensed to practice in their perspective states. The majority of these pediatricians were involved in private single or group center-based practices located in rural to small town/city areas.

Service Patterns

This section of the survey focused on each of the two groups' response to four questions regarding (a) whether young children identified as prenatally exposed to cocaine are being served and if yes, (b) how many, (c) the procedures employed in the identification process, and (d) their sources of referral

Table 1. Demographic Data Regarding Respondents

		Percentage of Responses N = 162	
		ECSE (n = 64)	Pediatrician (n = 98)
1. Gender	Male	11%	84%
	Female	89%	16%
2. Highest Degree	High School	—	—
	BS/BA	79%	—
	MS/MA	16%	—
	Ed.S.	05%	—
	PhD/EdD	—	—
	MD	—	100%
3. Degree Area	None	—	—
	Elementary Education	23%	—
	ECSE	32%	—
	Early Childhood Education	17%	—
	Mental Retardation	08%	—
	Hearing Impaired	—	—
	Learning Disabilities	10%	—
	OH/OHI	—	—
	Speech Pathology	—	—
	Multihandicapped	03%	—
	Behavioral Disorders	07%	—
	Pediatrics	—	100%
4. Title of Current Position	ECSE Teacher (84%) ECSE Coordinator (16%)		Pediatrician (100%)
5. Program Description	Center-based (91%) Home-based (03%) Combination (06%)		Private Practice (88%) State Health Dept (02%) Medical Center (10%)
6. Location of Program			
	Rural (below 20,000)	36%	49%
	Small Town/City (20,000–100,000)	45%	31%
	Large Metropolitan Area (over 100,000)	19%	20%

for services for this population of children. As Table 2 indicates, approximately 28% of ECSE programs and over 40% of pediatric professionals reported providing services to young children prenatally exposed to cocaine. Furthermore, 18 ECSE educators reported providing services ranging from 1–3 children as opposed to 42 pediatric practices who were providing services ranging from 1–6 children exposed to cocaine.

Table 2. Service Patterns Regarding Children Exposed to Cocaine

Question and Response	Percent of Professional Category Responding	
	ECSE (n = 64)	Pediatrics (n = 98)
1. Does your program/practice serve prenatally cocaine exposed children?		
Yes	28.1%	42.8%
No	50.0	45.9
Unknown	21.8	11.2
	ECSE (n = 18)	Pediatrics (n = 42)
2. If yes, how many?		
One	83.3%	57.1%
Two	11.1	28.5
Three	5.6	4.7
Four	0.0	2.4
Five	0.0	4.7
Six	0.0	2.4
	ECSE (n = 18)	Pediatrics (n = 42)
3. If known, what procedure(s) was employed to identify theses young children?		
Maternal Report	44.4	35.7
Urine Screens	0.0	19.0
Combination	0.0	07.01
Unknown	55.6	38.1
	ECSE (n = 18)	Pediatrics (n = 42)
4. Please indicate your sources for referral for these children.		
Dept of Human Resources	27.7	35.7
Public Health	16.7	23.8
Child Care Centers	5.6	4.7
Public Hospital	0.0	4.7
Neonatologist	0.0	4.7
Unknown	50.0	26.2

When asked to report the procedures employed to identify these children, a significant number of ECSE (55.6%) educators and a moderate number of pediatricians (38.1%) presently providing services stated the method was unknown. However, of those who responded, maternal report was the predominant method (ECSE 44.4%; Pediatricians 35.7%). Moreover, urine screening (19.0%) and a combination (7.1%) of urine screens and maternal report were additional identification procedures reported by the pediatric group. Finally, when asked the primary sources of referral for these children, 30 pediatricians reported a diverse range of referral sources with The Department of Human Resources (35.7%) and public health (23.8%) being the primary referral avenues. On the other hand, only 9 ECSE educators, or 50.0% of those presently providing services, reported sources of referral. However, this educational-based group also identified The Department of Human Resources and public health as primary referral sources.

Types and Effectiveness of Educational Experiences

This section of the survey was designed to examine the types of educational experiences regarding young children prenatally exposed to cocaine these two groups have received in their professional development. Additionally, each respondent was asked to rate the effectiveness of those educational experiences. Means, standard deviations, frequency of response, and percentages for all respondents reporting an educational preparation item, and rating responses regarding the effectiveness of that educational experience, were calculated.

As Table 3 indicates, ECSE opportunities for educational development focused on conferences/seminars (90.6%), journals (87.5%), and printed materials (e.g., government publications) (62.5%). However, when asked to rate these educational experiences, the majority of ECSE respondents rated these experiences as somewhat effective, and none reported any inservice or workshop opportunities related to providing services to young children prenatally exposed to cocaine. Pediatric respondents also exhibited similar types and ratings of educational experiences; however, these professionals employed journals as a major educational approach (94.9%), and rated this preparation opportunity as *somewhat effective/effective* predominantly. Also, over 40% of pediatric professionals reported that they relied on personal experience as an educational focus.

The last part of this section consisted of an open-ended question regarding areas in which respondents believed additional preparation was needed. Twenty-three (35%) of the ECSE educators and thirty-two (32%) of pediatric professionals responded to the open-ended question. The types of additional preparation, frequency, and percentage of those responses according to group are tabulated in Table 4.

A vast majority of ECSE (69.5%) who responded to the open-ended question identified inservice/workshop activities as their needed preparation area. In addition, pediatricians who responded identified knowledge regarding referral sources (87.5%) as their primary additional preparation need.

Educational Competencies

The purpose of this section was to examine those educational competency areas that subjects rated as important in providing services to young children prenatally exposed to cocaine. Subjects rated the 15 items in the section on a 5-point scale (1 = not important; 2 = not very important; 3 = somewhat important; 4 = important; 5 = very im-

Table 3. Types and Effectiveness of Educational Experiences

Professional Category	Type of Educational Experience	Mean, Standard, Deviation and Percent of Professional Group Responding			Percentage of Professional Discipline Responding to the Effectiveness of Educational Experiences*					
		M	SD	%	NR	NE	NVE	SWE	EFF	VE
ECSE (n = 64)	Conference/Seminars	.93	.26	90.6	9.4	—	6.2	65.5	15.6	3.1
	Inservice Activities	—	—	—	100.0	—	—	—	—	—
	Workshops	—	—	—	100.0	—	—	—	—	—
	Journals	3.74	1.37	87.5	12.5	—	1.6	78.1	6.2	1.6
	Personal Experience	.69	1.94	10.9	89.1	—	4.6	1.6	1.6	3.1
	Printed Materials	3.41	2.79	62.5	37.5	3.1	4.6	50.0	3.1	1.6
Pediatrics (n = 98)	Conference/Seminars	.36	.47	36.7	63.3	—	10.2	12.2	14.3	—
	Inservice Activities	.37	.76	17.4	82.6	—	4.1	8.2	5.1	—
	Workshops	.32	1.01	13.3	86.7	—	3.0	5.1	5.1	—
	Journals	3.82	.94	94.9	5.1	3.1	6.1	51.0	31.6	3.1
	Personal Experience	2.75	2.60	44.9	55.1	4.1	17.3	12.2	9.2	2.0
	Printed Materials	2.56	3.07	40.9	59.1	—	12.2	23.5	5.1	—

*Effectiveness Scoring Scale: NR = No Response, NE = Not Effective, NVE = Not Very Effective, SWE = Somewhat Effective, EFF = Effective, VE = Very Effective

Table 4. Percent of Professional Groups Responding to the Open-Ended Question Regarding Additional Preparation Needs

Additional Educational Need Area	ECSE (n = 23)		Pediatrics (n = 32)	
	n	%	n	%
Inservice training/workshops	16	69.5	4	12.5
Summer course work	5	21.8	0	0.0
Hands-on activities	1	4.3	0	0.0
Strategies in working with both child and parents	0	0.0	0	0.0
Knowledge regarding referral service	1	4.3	28	87.5
Total	23	99.9	32	100.0

portant). The range of overall means as shown on Table 5 was 3.15 to 4.86; overall M = 4.04, and SD = .87.

As Table 5 indicates, professionals across the two groups had similar perceptions regarding needed educational-based competencies. Overall, competencies such as characteristics of young children prenatally exposed to cocaine (M = 4.86), state and federal laws (M = 4.38), infant/child assessment (M = 4.34), and knowledge of resources (M = 4.34) were consistently rated as *important* by respondents. However, when competencies are considered across groups, ECSE educators tended to rate competency items related to intervention models and approaches, assessment, and technology/curriculum development more highly than pediatric professionals. Additionally, both groups consistently rated items that addressed family dynamics (e.g., characteristics of ethnic and cultural groups) in the *somewhat important* range.

Finally, the subjects were asked to rank (1–5) the five competencies they perceived as the most important in providing services to young children prenatally exposed to cocaine. Again, both groups exhibited similar feelings regarding educational competencies. Table 6 illustrates the rank order and percentage of responses of those competencies identified by both professional groups. Both groups ranked characteristics of young children prenatally exposed to cocaine as their top competency with infant/child assessment and knowledge of research/physiological effects consistently ranked across groups. Pediatric professionals placed major emphasis on state and federal laws and knowledge related to resources.

Discussion

The primary purpose of this investigation was to examine service patterns and educational experiences of two professional groups who work potentially with young children prenatally exposed to cocaine. This investigation was guided by three primary objectives. The first objective was to determine the extent to which young children prenatally exposed to cocaine are being served and the primary procedure(s) em-

Table 5. Descriptive Results of Group Perceptions of Educational Need Areas

Need Area Item Statement*	Overall (n = 162)		ECSE (n = 64)		Pediatrics (n = 98)	
	M	SD	M	SD	M	SD
Characteristics of infants/children prenatally exposed to cocaine	4.86	.32	4.96	.21	4.76	.44
State/federal laws	4.38	.94	4.09	.99	4.66	.89
Infant/child assessment	4.34	.69	4.56	.79	4.12	.60
Knowledge and availability of resources	4.34	.84	4.39	.99	4.29	.68
Research and physiological effects of cocaine	4.34	.94	4.56	.66	4.12	1.22
Knowledge of intervention models/approaches	4.27	.75	4.65	.57	3.88	.93
Typical/atypical infant/child development	4.25	.80	4.74	.45	3.76	1.15
Service delivery options	4.12	.66	4.30	.76	3.94	.55
Assessment of family strengths and needs	4.00	.92	4.30	.87	3.70	.98
Knowledge of service coordination	3.92	1.02	4.08	.90	3.76	1.15
Consultation/collaboration	3.92	1.04	4.08	.99	3.76	1.09
Technology/curriculum development	3.77	.93	4.13	.92	3.41	.94
Family beliefs, values, and biases	3.63	1.31	3.78	1.67	3.47	.94
The impact of socioeconomic status	3.25	.93	3.26	1.13	3.23	.83
Characteristics of ethnic and cultural groups	3.15	1.02	3.30	1.18	3.00	.87

*Note. Items are rank ordered by overall mean importance (1 = not important, 2 = not very important, 3 = somewhat important, 4 = important, 5 = very important).

ployed in identifying these children. Eighteen ECSE educators and 42 pediatric professionals reported providing services to these children. Respondents indicated that 22 young children were presently receiving services in 18 ECSE classrooms, and 74 young children were being served in the pediatric sector. Although ECSE programs do not initially identify these children, there seems to be a disparity in the numbers being identified in pediatric practices and those receiving services in early intervention programs. Chapman and Elliott (in press) argue that many young children prenatally exposed to cocaine

Table 6. The Five Highest Ranking Competencies and Percentage of Response.

Competency Item	Early Childhood Special Educators (n = 64)	
	Rank	%
Characteristics of children prenatally exposed to cocaine	1	96.8
Typical/atypical infant/child development	2	75.0
Infant/child assessment	3	68.7
Knowledge of intervention models and approaches	4	62.5
Research and physiological effects of cocaine	5	57.8
	Pediatric Professionals (n = 98)	
Characteristics of children prenatally exposed to cocaine	1	95.9
State and federal laws	2	82.6
Knowledge and availability of resources	3	78.5
Research and physiological effects of cocaine	4	66.3
Infant/child assessment	5	46.9

often exhibit symptoms that do not fit state categorical definitions for disabilities that are necessary to meet eligibility requirements for early intervention and related services. Within this context, these children are often ineligible to receive intervention services they may need.

One of the primary avenues for estimating the magnitude of the cocaine problem is identifying these children. The two groups in this study reported that maternal report was the primary identification process, which may be most unreliable as an identification option (MacDonald, 1992). Identification can occur in two stages: During the mother's pregnancy *or* at birth. Smith (1988) reported that more often than not, individuals who use cocaine during pregnancy do not usually receive or seek prenatal care. In this case, the child may be identified at birth through the mother's self-report during problem deliveries (e.g., preterm) or screening of suspected drug usage. However, research has suggested that 70% of infants prenatally exposed to cocaine are full term, appear healthy, are discharged within normal time frames, and are not identified (State of New York, 1989). In addition, the potential biological and/or environmental effects of cocaine exposure may not appear until later in the child's development (Trad, 1992).

Findings in this study corroborate above-mentioned concerns, as a majority of the respondents reported maternal report was the primary identification process employed to identify this population of young children in their program or practice. One explanation for the reliance on maternal report may be that identification policies are not uniformly applied. A OIG report (1990) suggested that identification procedures may occur in a uneven fashion across socioeconomic groups as many pediatricians serving low-income women, who receive subsidized medical insurance, are more likely to be tested for cocaine use than those serving private pay or insured individuals. Shannon, Lacouture, Roa, and Woolf (1989) reported that with the potential rise in the numbers of children potentially exposed to cocaine, the implementation of routine toxicologic screening/identification procedures appear to be justified, and the coordination of these procedures is essential, especially in the pediatric population.

Sources for referral identified across both groups were diversified, with child welfare/public health services being the predominant referral sources. Although this finding suggests that many of these children are referred to welfare/health services, it also indicates that they are not receiving the coordinated intervention and/or related services they may require. Perhaps the identification-to-initial referral process, while helpful in displaying identification points and initial referral sources, does not represent actual referral lines between programs (Chapman & Elliott, in press). In addition, Feig (1990) reported that often child welfare agencies, by default, are typically the first point at which children prenatally exposed to cocaine enter the system, and what happens to these infants and young children from this point is still open to conjecture. This rather inadequate collaboration among agencies may result in a weakened formal referral system, which suggests that there is a distinct possibility that a significant number of these children may be "slipping through the cracks," and, if needed, are not receiving essential early intervention services.

Another explanation for the lack of collaboration between agencies regarding this population might be the provision of Part H, PL 99-457 (U.S. Department of Education, 1989) in that individual states have the option of expanding the definition of the target population to include all high-risk infants and young children who may be in need of early intervention services (Shonkoff & Meisels, 1991). Additionally, policy relative to societal perceptions of the cocaine problem is a major factor in determining whether options under the law regarding this population are enacted. Although at this time the states of Alabama, Florida, Georgia, and Mississippi are providing or are in the process of developing Part H services, they have not embraced early intervention legislation with *at-risk* populations, including prenatal drug exposure, as an option.

Finally, although some children prenatally exposed to cocaine may be receiving services, the approach to providing these services can vary greatly depending on the orientation of the agency. Each discipline may operate according to its own standards, area of expertise, and purview. For example, the pediatric sector is often bound by confidentiality requirements that may limit collaboration with key agencies and educational professionals. In this instance, client records and treatment regimes may not be shared among service agencies and could impose significant obstacles to developing coordinated referral lines and a continuum of services for these children and their families.

The second objective of the study was to examine the types and the effectiveness of educational experiences these two professional disciplines have received regarding young children prenatally exposed to cocaine. The two identified educational opportunities for ECSE educators were conferences/seminars and journals. Pediatric professionals placed major emphasis on journals. A majority of both groups rated these educational experiences as primarily *somewhat effective*. Professionals were also asked to identify needed additional educational experiences. A majority of pediatric professionals (87.5%) responding identified further knowledge regarding sources of referral as essential. A consensus of ECSE (69.5%) responding to the question identified inservice/workshop activities as their preferred choice for future professional development.

One possible explanation for these perceptions may center on the technical nature of journal articles focusing on prenatal cocaine exposure. Currently, the majority of journals and conferences/seminars regarding cocaine exposure are based on medical research findings. Additionally, one primary vehicle for rapid utilization of information in this area is through inservice/workshop education. Unfortunately, there has been little medical or educational-based longitudinal research regarding this population (Williams & Howard, 1993), and, consequently, the complexity of existing studies may make it difficult for educators and related service professionals to transfer this knowledge into meaningful information. At this time, research in this area continues to be tentative and inconclusive; therefore, it is not uncommon that conflicting findings, results, and strategies be presented to service professionals.

The last objective focused on the relative importance of identified competencies these two groups of professionals perceive to be most critical for effectively meeting the needs of young children prenatally exposed to cocaine and their families. As illustrated in Tables 5 and 6, there were common competency ratings and rankings with characteristics, assessment, and research/physiological effects uniformly identified across groups. Noteworthy, pediatric professionals placed significant emphasis on legality; however, when one considers the present legal climate concerning litigation and the medical profession in the United States, it is not surprising that this professional group expressed concern regarding its legal responsibilities as it relates to this emerging population of young children and their families. Also, when considering the family-centered focus of early intervention, it is of interest that a majority of respondents did not put as much emphasis in this area as would be expected. One reason may be that the focus on families is a relatively new feature of service delivery, and, as such, many of these professionals may be providing services centralized to issues involving the infant or young child, rather than addressing the needs of the child within the context of the family.

Interestingly, preparation and competency areas reported by the ECSE group seem to be no more than a partial representation of the overall conceptual and functional foundation that these professionals should have received as a preservice/inservice preparation experiences. Another explanation may be related to demographic data as only 32% of ECSE educators reported that ECSE was there primary degree emphasis. These findings may suggest that many frontline service providers who work with infants and young children lack preparation within the family-centered focus of early intervention. As Lesar (1992) suggested, the medical, education, developmental, and social needs of children prenatally exposed to cocaine often require a full range of comprehensive services that are often interrelated with functioning of the entire family.

Competencies reflect *content* area needs. That is, coursework, conferences, and journals alone, although vital for orientation and conceptualization, will not completely impart appropriate skill areas in working with this population. According to Lesar (1992), many frontline service providers lack opportunities for supervised experiences with children prenatally exposed to cocaine and their families. These opportunities could facilitate confidence and enhance the service provider's ability to plan for individual differences, apply essential instructional/management strategies, and bridge collaborative gaps between related service professionals and agencies.

Conclusions

The overall results of this study regarding professional educational development and service provisions to young children prenatally exposed to cocaine and their families is consistent with a previous study (Chapman & Elliott, in press) which reported that service providers perceived a lack of a conceptual and/or functional orientation in providing services to this population. However, the majority of educational need areas identified in these studies are no more than intact components that should already be in place in ECSE and related professional preservice/inservice programming. This, in concert with the present lack of mandated identification procedures, generalizable research, and a consensus regarding the subsequent short- and long-term effects of prenatal cocaine exposure, suggests that we may need to rethink how this population is presently conceptualized. Because of the lack of substantive knowledge regarding these children, we suggest that these children be conceptualized as a diverse and heterogeneous group who are *at increased risk* for an array of developmental, behavioral, and/or societal difficulties. Within this context, we possibly already know enough to begin preparing educators and related service professionals to work with these children and their families, as there are a number of successful early intervention programs providing services to diverse, heterogeneous groupings of young children (Kronstadt, 1991).

The logical extension of a study of this nature would be to collect information from within other specific disciplines and with a broader array of service providers. Moreover, descriptive and analytical information needs to be collected at diverse regional and national levels to ascertain the impact of cocaine exposure on education and other early intervention service providers. This data will provide an empirical foundation on which to develop or refine preservice and/or functional/practical inservice opportunities for those who must provide these services to this and other *at-risk* populations.

References

Alabama DEC Directory. (1993). Unpublished manuscript.

Bays, J. (1990). Substance abuse and child abuse: Impact of addiction on the child. *Pediatric Clinics of North America, 37*, 881–904.

Besharov, D. J. (1989, Fall). The children of crack: Will we protect them? *Public Welfare*, pp. 7–11.

Chapman, J. K., & Elliott, R. N. (in press). Preschool children exposed to cocaine: A regional study of early childhood special education and head start preparation experiences. *Journal of Early Intervention*.

Chapman, J. K., Worthington, L. A., Cook, M. J. & Mayfield, P. (1992). Cocaine-exposed infants: A potential generation of at-risk and vulnerable children. *Infant-Toddler Intervention: The Transdisciplinary Journal, 2*(3), 223–237.

Chasnoff, I. J., Griffith, D. R., Freier, C., & Murray, J. (1992). Cocaine/polydrug use in pregnancy: Two-year follow-up. *Pediatrics, 89*, 284–289.

Eisen, L. M., Field, T. M., Bandstra, E. S., Roberts, J., Morrow, C., Larson, S. K., & Steele, B. M. (1991). Perinatal cocaine effects on neonatal stress behavior and performance on the Brazelton Scale. *Pediatrics, 88*, 477–480.

Feig, L. (1990). *Drug exposed infants and children: Service needs and policy questions.* Washington, DC: U.S. Department of Health and Human Services, Office of Social Services Policy, Division of Children and Youth Policy.

Florida DEC Directory. (1993). Unpublished manuscript.

Georgia DEC Directory. (1993). Unpublished manuscript.

Gittler, J. (1990). Infants born exposed to drugs: A problem growing at alarming rates. *Early Childhood Reporter, 1,* 1–6.

Griffith, D. R. (1992, September). Prenatal exposure to cocaine and other drugs: Developmental and educational prognoses. *Phi Delta Kappan,* 30–34.

Johnson, L. J., & LaMontagne, M. J. (1993). Using content analysis to examine the verbal or written communication of stakeholders within early intervention. *Journal of Early Intervention, 17,* 73–79.

Khalsa, J. H., & Gfroerer, J. (1991). Epidemiology and health consequences of drug abuse among pregnant women. *Seminars in Perinatology, 15,* 265–270.

Kronstadt, D. (1991, Spring). Complex developmental issues of prenatal drug exposure. *The Future of Children,* 36–49.

Lesar, S. (1992). Prenatal cocaine exposure: A challenge to education. *Infant-Toddler Intervention: The Transdisciplinary Journal, 2*(1), 37–52.

MacDonald, C. C. (1992). Perinatal cocaine exposure: Predictor of an endangered generation. *Infant-Toddler Intervention: The Transcisciplinary Journal, 2*(1), 1–12.

Meisels, S. (1989). Meeting the mandate of Public Law 99-457: Early childhood intervention in the nineties. *American Journal of Orthopsychiatry, 55,* 451–460.

Meisels, S., Harbin, G., Modigiliani, K., & Olsen. (1988). Formulating optimal state early intervention policies. *Exceptional Children, 55,* 159–165.

Mississippi DEC Directory. (1993). Unpublished manuscript.

National Institutes of Drug Abuse Report. (1989, September). Infants exposed in utero to acids, alcohol, and drugs. *NIDA Seminar,* 1–4.

National Institute of Drug Abuse. (1991). National household survey of drug abuse for 1990. Bethsda MD: NIDA.

Office of the Inspector General. (1990). *Crack babies* (OEI-03-89-01540). Washington, DC: U. S. Department of Health and Human Services.

Rodning, V., Beckwith, L., & Howard, J. (1989). Characteristics of attachment organization and play organization in prenatally drug-exposed toddlers. *Development and Psychopathology, 1,* 277–189.

SAS Institute, Inc. (1989). *SAS statistical software: Version 6.07 edition.* Cary, NC: Author.

Schneider, J. W., & Chasnoff, I. J. (1992). Motor assessment of cocaine/polydrug exposed infants at age 4 months. *Neurotoxicology and Teratology, 11,* 477–491.

Schutter, L. S., & Brinker, R. P. (1992). Conjuring a new category of disability from prenatal cocaine exposure: Are the infants unique biological or caretaking casualties? *Topics in Early Childhood Special Education, 11,* 84–111.

Shannon, M., Lacouture, P. G., Roa, J., & Wolf, A. (1989). Cocaine exposure among children seen at a pediatric hospital. *Pediatrics, 83,* 337–342.

Shonkoff, J. P., & Meisels, S. J. (1991). Defining eligibility for services under P.L. 99-457. *Journal of Early Intervention, 15,* 21–25.

Shriver, M. D., & Piersel, W. (1994). The long-term effects of intrauterine drug exposure: Review of recent research and implications for early childhood special education. *Topics in Early Childhood Special Education, 14,* 161–183.

Smith, J. (1988). The dangers of prenatal cocaine use. *The American Journal of Maternal/Child Nursing, 13,* 174–179.

State of New York. (1989). *Crack babies: The shame of New York.* Committee on Investigation, Taxation, and Government Operations Report, p. 5.

The Medical Association of the State of Alabama: Pictorial Membership Roaster. (1992). Burna Park, CA: Universal Publishing Co.

The Medical Association of the State of Florida: Pictorial Membership Roaster. (1992). Burrna Park, CA: Universal Publishing Co.

The Medical Association of the State of Georgia: Pictorial Membership Roaster. (1992). Burna Park, CA: Universal Publishing Co.

The Medical Association of the State of Mississippi: Pictorial Membership Roaster. (1992). Burna Park, CA: Universal Publishing Co.

Trad, P. V. (1992). Toddlers with prenatal cocaine exposure: Principles of assessment Part I. *Infant-Toddler Intervention: The Transdisciplinary Journal, 2*(4), 285–305.

U. S. General Accounting Office. (1990). *Drug-exposed infants; A generation at risk* (GAO/HRD–90–138). Washington, DC: U. S. Department of Health and Human Services.

U. S. Department of Education. (1989, June 22). Early intervention program for infants and toddlers with handicaps: Final regulations. *Federal Register* (Document CPR 34, Part 303). Washington, DC: Government Printing Office.

van de Bor, M., Walthes, F. J., & Sims, M. E. (1990). Increased cerebral blood flow velocity in infants of mother who abuse cocaine. *Pediatrics, 85*, 733–736.

Williams, B. F., & Howard, V. F. (1993). Children exposed to cocaine: Characteristics and implications for research and intervention. *Journal of Early Intervention, 17*, 61–72.

Zuckerman, B., & Bresnahan, K. (1991). Developmental and behavioral consequences of prenatal drug and alcohol exposure. *Pediatric Clinics of North America, 83*, 1387–1407.

Address Correspondence to:
J. Keith Chapman, Ph.D.,
P.O. Box 870231,
College of Education,
The University of Alabama,
Tuscaloosa, AL 35487-0231

Appendix

Prenatal Cocaine Exposure Survey: Early Childhood Special Educators/Pediatric Professionals

Please respond to each of the following questions.

I. DEMOGRAPHIC INFORMATION

1. Gender: ECSE   Pediatricians

   Male   _____   _____
   Female   _____   _____

2. Please indicate your highest degree area.

   Type of Degree: ECSE   Pediatricians

   High School   _____   _____
   B.A./B.S.   _____   _____
   M.A./M.S.   _____   _____
   Ed.S.   _____   _____
   Ed.D./Ph.D.   _____   _____
   MD (Pediatrics)   _____   _____

3. Please indicate your primary degree area or medical certification.
   ECSE _____
   Pediatrics _____

4. What is the primary title of your current position?
   ECSE _____
   Pediatrics _____

5. Please describe your present place of employment (e.g., center-based).
   _____
   _____

6. Which best describes the area in which your program/practice is located?

                       ECSE   Pediatricians
   Rural   _____   _____
   Small Town/City   _____   _____
   Large Metropolitan _____   _____

II. SERVICE PATTERNS

1. To your knowledge does your program/practice currently serve young children prenatally exposed to cocains?

   ECSE   Yes_____   No_____
   Pediatricians Yes_____   No_____

2. If yes, how many?   ECSE_____   Pediatricians_____

3. If known, what procedure(s) was employed to identify these children (e.g., thin-layer urine screening)?

   ECSE _____

   Pediatrics _____

4. Please indicate your primary source(s) for referral regarding these young children.

   ECSE _____

   Pediatrics _____

III. TYPE OF PREPARATION AND ADDITIONAL NEED AREAS

A. Please check the types of preparation you have received in regard to working with young children prenatally exposed to cocaine, their families, and how effective these experiences were.

Preparation Area	Not Effective		Somewhat Effective		Very Effective
____Conferences/seminars	1	2	3	4	5
____Course work	1	2	3	4	5
____Inservice activities	1	2	3	4	5
____Workshops	1	2	3	4	5
____Printed materials	1	2	3	4	5
____Personal experience	1	2	3	4	5

B. Are there any other areas in which you believe you need additional preparation in appropriately providing services to this population of young children and their families? (Please specify below)

IV. COMPETENCY AREAS FOR WORKING WITH YOUNG CHILDREN PRENATALLY EXPOSED TO COCAINE AND THEIR FAMILIES

Please circle the responses that best describe the relative importance areas in working with this population. Also, please **rank order (1 through 5)** the five competencies you perceive as the most important.

A. To work **effectively** with these young children and their families, it is important to have knowledge and skills in the following areas:

Rank Order (5)		Not Effective		Somewhat Effective		Very Effective
1. ____	Characteristics of ethnic and cultural groups.	1	2	3	4	5
2. ____	The impact of socio-economic status.	1	2	3	4	5
3. ____	Research and physiological effects of cocaine.	1	2	3	4	5
4. ____	Characteristics of cocaine exposed children.	1	2	3	4	5
5. ____	Typical/atypical infant and toddler development.	1	2	3	4	5
6. ____	Family beliefs, values, and biases.	1	2	3	4	5
7. ____	Assessment of family strengths and needs.	1	2	3	4	5
8. ____	Infant/toddler screening and assessment.	1	2	3	4	5
9. ____	State and federal laws and mandates.	1	2	3	4	5
10. ____	Technology/Curriculum development.	1	2	3	4	5
11. ____	Knowledge of service coordination.	1	2	3	4	5
12. ____	Knowledge and availability of resources.	1	2	3	4	5
13. ____	Service delivery options.	1	2	3	4	5
14. ____	Knowledge of intervention models/approaches.	1	2	3	4	5
15. ____	Consultation/collaboration.	1	2	3	4	5

Cognitive Performance of Prenatally Drug-Exposed Infants

Delmont Morrison, Ph.D.
Sylvia Villarreal, M.D.
University of California
San Francisco, California

Previous research using the Bayley Infant Scales, a measure providing one summary score of infant cognitive development, has consistently demonstrated that prenatally drug-exposed (PDE) infants perform in the average range. This study evaluated 55 PDE infants (mean CA 17 months) with the Infant Mullens Scale of Early Learning, a multidimensional scale measuring development in five domains. Using clinical criteria of a month or more below age level and a T-score of 42 or less, the following percent were delayed in each of the five domains: Gross Motor 35–40%; Visual Reception, 39–43%; Visual Expression, 50–52%; Language Reception, 52–59%; Language Expression, 35–40%. The results indicate that PDE children perform less well on a multidimensional measure of intelligence than on a measure providing one summary score.

Children who were exposed in utero to illicit drugs, especially crack cocaine, may experience a wide range of neurologic and cognitive abnormalities (Handler, Kistin, Davis, & Ferre, 1991). Prenatal cocaine exposure is associated with prematurity, intrauterine growth retardation, and microcephaly (Lutiger, Graham, Einarson, & Koren, 1991). Teratogenic effects of cocaine have been proposed to alter brain development (Volpe, 1992). Although limited generalizations to human subjects is recognized, animal data in rats, pigs, and lambs have demonstrated defects in learning and memory (Sobrain et al., 1990). Teratogenic and structural vascular damage of ischemia and hemorrhage may in combination produce both short- and long-term neurodevelopmental changes (Hoyme et al., 1990). Newborn cocaine-induced neurologic syndrome of tremors, irritability, poor feeding and sleep patterns, and seizures is well described, usually short-lasting, and perhaps not predictive of long-term outcome (Dow-Eduard, 1991; Kramer, Locke, Ogunyemi, & Nelson, 1990). Few prospective longitudinal studies have established neurodevelopmental outcomes for chemically exposed children (Chasnoff, Griffith, & Azuma, 1992; Howard, Beckwith, Rodning, & Kropenske, 1989). Longitudinal studies of the effects of prenatal drug exposure on cognitive development also are relatively rare. However, the studies that do exist are consistent in demonstrating that generally prenatally drug-exposed infants perform at age level and often at the same level as controls. These results have implications for the delivery of services for these children as well as research on prenatal drug exposure and cognitive development. There is evidence that the cognitive performance of drug-exposed infants may vary as a function of the particular evaluation procedure being used.

Previous research has used the Bayley Scale of Infant Development (Bayley, 1969), providing general measures of gross motor and cognitive development that are summarized in the Mental Development Index (MDI) and the Motor Development Index (PDI). Children born to non-drug-dependent women from comparable socioeconomic and racial backgrounds are used for comparison groups. Strauss, Starr, Ostrea, Chavaz, and Stryker (1976) found that both narcotic-exposed and comparison infants scored within the normal range on the Bayley PDI and MDI. The infants were evaluated at 3, 6, and 12 months, and the PDI scores of the exposed infants declined with age and were significantly lower than comparison infants at 12 months of age. However, it should be noted that the mean PDI of the exposed sample at 12 months was 102.8 (SD = 11.00), well within normal range, while the mean for the comparison group was 110.4 (SD = 9.80). Rosen and Johnson (1982) found no differences between drug-exposed and control groups on MDI and PDI scores at 6 months, but found narcotic-exposed infants to have lower MDI and PDI scores at 12 and 18 months of age. The mean PDI scores of the drug-exposed sample fell from 101 to 92.6 over the interval of the study, while the mean PDI scores for the comparison group remained the same. In contrast, the mean MDI scores for the drug-exposed sample essentially remained the same, (mean = 95) while the mean of the comparison group increased from 100.7 to 106.4. The statistical difference between the MDI means of the two groups appears to be due to the increase in the scores of the comparison group.

In a longitudinal study evaluating drug-exposed and comparison children at 3, 6, 12, and 24 months, Chasnoff, Schnoll, Burns, and Burns (1984) found that both groups performed in the average range and that there was no difference in mean MDI or PDI scores between the two groups over the interval of the study. Lodge (1977) also failed to find differences between drug-exposed and comparison groups on either the MDI or PDI at 6 and 12 months of age. Griffith (1991) found that infants prenatally exposed to crack had normal scores on the Bayley but had less ability to modulate their own behavior and were less persistent than controls. In a summary of the research to date, Kronstadt (1989) concluded that there was little evidence that prenatal substance exposure of either cocaine, marijuana, opiates, or tobacco is linked with significant deficits on standardized tests.

Environmental factors such as low socioeconomic status, poor housing, and stress have been shown to have as great an effect on development as does prenatal drug exposure (Kaltenbach & Finnegan, 1989). Control group studies must have quantitative measures in both the drug-exposed and non-drug-exposed samples of study variables such as family organization, stressful life events, and caregiver-child interaction. A recent review of previous research indicates that these environmental variables have not been adequately measured or controlled for (Tronick & Beeghly, 1992).

Another problem with previous studies of the effect of prenatal drug exposure on cognitive development is the use of the Bayley as an outcome measure. The Bayley Scales of Infant Development (Bayley, 1969) originally were standardized over 20 years ago on 1,262 infants stratified according to sex, race, and education of the head of household. Used in a number of research studies, the Bayley has satisfactory test-retest reliability, interexaminer reliability, and split-half reliabilities, and it does not appear to be influenced by repeated use. The motor scale (PDI) includes normed gross motor tasks such as the child's ability to balance, walk on a straight line, and walk up and down stairs. Examination of the items making up the mental scale (MDI) indicates that a variety of interrelated yet relatively independent skills such as visual-motor integration, language reception, and language expression are being measured. These different components contribute to an overall general measure that is expressed by the MDI.

The Bayley MDI score reflects the view that cognitive development can be described as a unified capacity for acquiring knowledge, reasoning, and solving problems. The use of such a general measure as an MDI relates to the theories of Alfred Binet and Theodore Simon, the developers of one of the first useful mental tests, the Stanford Binet (McCandless, 1967). Both Binet and Simon saw intelligence as a fundamental capacity contributing to the individual's ability to adapt to the environment. Charles Spearman also concluded that all people have a general intelligence factor. He argued that, as a rule, people who do well or poorly on some intellectual tasks also do well or poorly on a variety of intellectual tasks. Historically, a theory of general intelligence has been the primary justification for using a single index of intelligence such as the IQ (intelligence quotient) as a meaningful summary of an individual's performance. The same logic is obvious in the use of the MDI for the mental scale of the Bayley.

An alternative theoretical approach is seen in the views of Thurstone and Gulford who hold that intelligence is composed of separate mental abilities that operate more or less independently (McCandless, 1967). This theoretical approach rejects the view of intelligence as a single factor as well as the exclusive use of an IQ as a useful measure of an individual's capacity to learn and perform. Gardner (1985) has argued for a theory of multiple independent intelligences which follow somewhat different developmental paths. For example, manual intelligence, one of at least seven intelligences that Gardner has proposed, appears early in development, whereas linguistic skills intelligence occurring later requires a period of apprenticeship and imitation.

Beyond theoretical considerations, the use of the MDI as an index of infant intelligence may result in a child appearing to be functioning in the average range, whereas significant delays may be occurring in specific areas of intelligence such as receptive or expressive language. These children would be classified as not in need of services, because of reference to the MDI, yet have specific cognitive delays in need of intervention. These children would eventually be classified as false negatives: screened as not needing services but later on demonstrating specific delays. A number of the prenatally drug-exposed children who were the subjects of the research previously reviewed may have been false negatives. Although at risk, they were assessed as being in the average range on the Bayley MDI.

Studies of infant ability indicate that intelligence in young children is not a unitary trait but a composite of abilities which do not necessarily co-vary with one another. Reviews of infant and preschool scales emphasize the need for a test of intelligence which assesses separate domains and provides guidelines for psychoeducational interventions (Sheehan & Klein, 1989). The use of such a test with prenatally drug-exposed infants could provide researchers with needed data regarding the possible effects of such exposure to specific cognitive domains that are more difficult to examine with an instrument such as the Bayley. A test measuring multiple and separate domains of cognitive development would be useful to educators as guidelines for interventions for this population.

An appropriate measure addressing the issue of the multiple dimensions of infant intelligence is the Infant Mullen Scale of Early Learning (MSEL) (Mullen, 1989). The MSEL provides assessments of the following: gross motor, visual reception, visual expression, language reception, and language expression. Research has shown that the MSEL has acceptable concurrent validity (Mullen, 1989). In a study of 103 normal children 7 to 14 months of age, scores from the four cognitive scales of the MSEL were correlated with the Bayley MDI. The correlations ranged from a low of .53 for the visual expression scale to a high at .60 for the language expression scale, demonstrating that although related to the MDI the subscales are measuring abilities that are different from those expressed in the MDI score. Using the same sample and a composite score from the four MSEL cognitive subscales, a correlation of .97 was established between the MSEL and the Bayley MDI. This confirms the strength of the MSEL when considered a G-Factor measure of intelligence.

Although the MSEL has demonstrated test-retest reliability and satisfactory psychometric characteristics (Mullen, 1989), it has not been used extensively to evaluate prenatally drug-exposed infants. In a preliminary study with a sample of 30 prenatally drug-exposed infants, Morrison (1991) found that 32 to 40% were functioning below age norms on the five scales of the MSEL. This suggests that when evaluated on a scale providing discreet rather than global measures of intelligence, prenatally drug-exposed infants do not perform as well.

The purpose of this study was to use the MSEL to evaluate two separate samples of prenatally drug-exposed infants and toddlers. Mean age and T-scores for each sample were obtained for the gross-motor scale and each of the four mental scales. Clinically valid scoring criteria were used to establish those children who were performing significantly below the level expected for their age on each of the scales. This provided the number and percentage of the two samples that were significantly delayed.

Method

Subjects

Easter Seal Sample

Thirty-two consecutive referrals of prenatally drug-exposed infants were made to the Infant Development Services (KIDS) of the Easter Seal Program in Marin County, California. The sample consisted of 14 (44%) females and 18 (56%) males, with an average age of 14.93 months (SD = 8.79). Of this group, 20 (63%) were of African-American background, 10 (31%) were Caucasian, and two (6%) were of mixed heritage. In terms of birth history, 26 (81%) were full-term, and 6 (19%) were premature.

Early Childhood Evaluation Clinic Sample (ECEC)

Twenty-three consecutive referrals of prenatally drug-exposed infants were made to the ECEC, Department of Psychiatry, University of California, San Francisco. These infants were referred from the Pediatric Department, San Francisco General Hospital, for developmental evaluation. There were 14 males (61%) and 9 females (39%), with an average age of 18.34 months (SD = 8.98). All were African-American. At birth, 15 (65%) were full-term and 8 (35%) were premature.

All children were under pediatric care and none had diagnosed physical handicaps such as cerebral palsy or loss of hearing that would interfere with performance on the developmental evaluation. In the total sample, 44 (80%) lived in a foster home, 8 (15%) lived with a parent, and 3 (5%) were in residential care.

The problems of establishing and controlling for what drug or drugs were used prenatally and at what time during the pregnancy have been discussed and are common to all quasiexperimental designs with this population (Tronick & Beeghly, 1992). Drug use was established in this study by toxicity screen and review of mother and child's medical records. The most common drug reported was cocaine.

Infant Mullen Scale of Early Learning (MSEL)

The MSEL (Mullen, 1989) was standardized on 1,231 children ranging from 1 month to 37 months, approximating the population demographics of the U.S. population in 1989. Males composed 51% of the sample, and 49% of the sample were females. The MSEL consists of five subscales, a gross-motor scale, and four scales measuring cognitive abilities. Visual Receptive Organizational abilities are evaluated on the VRO scale. Tasks on this scale measure visual discrimination, spatial organization, sequencing, short-term memory, ability to organize simple and complex visual information, and visual-spatial concepts. Visual-expressive organizational abilities are evaluated on the VEO scale. Fine motor development, perceptual planning, and motor control are assessed by tasks requiring manipulative skills involving bilateral and unilateral motor patterns. Adaptive arm-hand functions are evaluated by tasks requiring graded reach and grasp, release, wrist-arm rotation, and horizontal and vertical movements. Receptive language development is evaluated by the Language Reception Organization (LRO) scale. Items on the LRO scale involve auditory and auditory-visual information requiring the child to listen to verbal input, comprehend questions, follow simple and more complex directions, and solve problems involving verbal-spatial concepts. Overall verbal expressive ability is evaluated on the VEO scale. Auditory memory and comprehension are assessed on all VEO tasks, while spontaneous language, ability to respond to structured input, short-term verbal memory, and abstract reasoning are evaluated on specific tasks.

In research using the Cronbach Alpha coefficient, the internal consistency coefficients for the MSEL were .95 for the motor scale and .97 for each of the four cognitive scales. Test-retest reliability estimates for a 2-week interval ranged from .70 to .99 for the five scales for four different age ranges: 10–12 months, 14 months, 16–25 months, and 28–36 months. Interscorer reliability estimates were obtained by pairing evaluators. One evaluator administered the test to a child and each evaluator scored the test independently. The sample consisted of 175 children divided into the following age groups: 1–2 months, 3–4 months, 6–8 months, 10 months, 12 months, 14 months, 16–19 months, 22–25 months, 28–31 months, and 36 months. Interscorer estimates for all age groups ranged from .78 to 1.00, indicating that directions for administration and scoring are clear, and results across examiners are comparable.

In one of a series of studies of concurrent validity, the MSEL LRO and LEO scales were administered to 25 children at 18 months and 20 children at 24 months of age who had been evaluated independently on the

Preschool Language Assessment, auditory comprehension and verbal ability scales (Zimmerman, Steiner, & Evatt, 1979). The coefficient of correlations between the MSEL scales and the two Preschool Language Assessment scales ranged from .78 to .93, indicating acceptable concurrent validity.

All the evaluations in the current study were completed by experienced individuals appropriately trained in evaluating infants and toddlers with the MSEL. The evaluations were done individually in a room appropriately equipped for testing. Each tester scored his or her own test and knew the clinical status of the child. The MSEL provides age and T-scores for each subscale. The mean T-Score is 50 and the SD is 10.

Results

Easter Seal Sample

The data from this sample are summarized in Table 1. The children were at age level (14.93 months) in gross-motor development and were approximately 1½ months delayed in Visual Reception. The children were delayed by approximately 2 months in Visual Expression and Language Reception and by 3 months in Language Expression. Examination to the corresponding T-scores indicates that the group was performing at the lower limits of the average range in the Gross Motor, Visual Expression, and Language Expression Scales, and were one standard deviation or more below average on the Visual Reception and Language Reception Scales.

The MSEL scores also can be examined in terms of individual scores that are below average on each of the subscales. The criteria applied with this sample for being below average were performance that resulted in a score that was one month or more below chronological age *and* a T-score that was equal to or less than 42. The results of this analysis are summarized in Table 3. Of the total sample, the number performing below average was 13 (40%) in Gross Motor performance, 14 (43%) in Visual Reception, 16 (50%) in Visual Expression, 19 (59%) in Language Reception, and 13 (40%) in Language Expression.

Early Childhood Evaluation Clinic Sample (ECEC)

Examination of the data from this group in Table 2 indicates that the children were performing at age level (18.34 months) on the Gross Motor and Visual Reception scales. The group was approximately 1½ months below chronological age on the remaining scales. Examination of the T-scores indicates that children were performing at low average in Gross Motor, Visual Reception, and Language Reception performance, and at

Table 1. Summary of MSEL Performance: Prenatally Drug-Exposed Infants Referred to the Easter Seal KIDS Program

	MSEL Scales				
	Gross Motor	Visual Reception	Visual Expression	Language Reception	Language Expression
Mean Age Score	14.40	13.40	12.60	12.59	11.87
Standard Deviation	9.17	7.55	7.96	7.42	8.50
Mean T-Score	43.00	40.5	41.60	38.12	43.43
Standard Deviation	10.26	12.33	9.87	10.61	12.40

Table 2. Summary of MSEL Performance: Prenatally Drug-Exposed Infants Referred to the Early Childhood Evaluation Clinic

	MSEL Scales				
	Gross Motor	Visual Reception	Visual Expression	Language Reception	Language Expression
Mean Age Score	18.54	18.04	16.65	16.80	16.73
Standard Deviation	9.64	8.89	10.21	9.84	10.31
Mean T-Score	45.05	44.91	42.39	44.52	43.21
Standard Deviation	10.66	9.44	9.96	8.31	9.31

the lower level of the average range in Visual Expression and Language Expression. Applying the earlier-described criteria and analysis of individual scores that fell below average demonstrated that the number meeting these criteria was 8 (35%) for Gross Motor performance, 9 (39%) for Visual Reception, 12 (52%) for Visual Expression, 11 (48%) for Language Reception, and 8 (35%) for Language Expression. These data are presented in Table 3.

Discussion

Contrasting the results of this study with previous studies using the Bayley to evaluate prenatally drug-exposed children indicates that a significant number of these children perform below age expectancy when a multidimensional measure of intelligence is used. When group performance is examined, the MSEL scores were in the average to low average range. This result is similar to previous studies using the Bayley where prenatally drug-exposed children were found to be performing in a similar range (Kaltenbach & Finnegan, 1989). However, if individual scores on each of the subscales are examined, 35 to 59% of the children are found to be performing below clinical criteria.

The use of subscales to measure separate domains of intelligence allows for a more discrete analysis of intellectual performance than is possible when a single dimension measure is employed. Multidimensional test

Table 3. Number and Percent of Children Considered Delayed on the MSEL by Referral Source[1]

Referral Source	MSEL Scales				
	Gross Motor	Visual Reception	Visual Expression	Language Reception	Language Expression
Easter Seal KIDS Program					
Number	13	14	16	19	13
Percent	40	43	50	59	40
Early Childhood Evaluation Clinic					
Number	8	9	12	11	8
Percent	35	39	52	48	35

[1]One month behind chronological age *and* T-score ≤ 42

construction also allows for the development of an objective intervention program based on a child's intellectual strengths and weaknesses.

The fact that consistent results occurred in two independent samples supports the generalization of these results. The KIDS samples were referred for evaluation from a number of sources, while the ECEC sample were all referred from a pediatric service. The results may be influenced by the fact that a large percentage of the children (80%) were being raised in foster homes. Comparison of children being raised in foster homes and contrasting conditions such as children raised with biological parents receiving varying levels of social support may establish the environmental factors that contribute significantly to the prenatally drug-exposed child's growth and development. The fact that the clinical status of the children was known to the evaluators may have influenced the results of the study. This limitation in design can be addressed in future studies by having the evaluations completed without knowledge of clinical status.

The relative utility of the MSEL and Bayley in evaluating prenatally drug-exposed infants specifically or infants in general needs to be explored by a direct comparison of the two scales with the same sample. The results of this study do suggest that the MSEL identifies more delays in this age range than does the Bayley. The particular design of the current study does not provide an opportunity to explore whether there is a particular pattern of cognitive delays unique to prenatally drug-exposed infants. However, examination of Table 3 suggests that there were more problems in visual expression and language reception than in the three remaining evaluated domains. In a longitudinal study of prenatally drug-exposed infants who were evaluated with the Bayley, Griffith (1991) found that they had normal intelligence, but on independent assessments 30 to 40% had problems with attention and delays in language.

The early application of the MSEL to evaluate prenatally drug-exposed infants may establish that the problems in attention are related to the child's early delays in visual-motor integration that result in the child's lack of motivation to attend and concentrate. Sensory-motor integration is basic to many problem-solving skills in infancy (Morrison, 1985). Since 50% of drug-exposed children may have these delays, a high percentage also will have problems in attention and concentration. Problems in various language functions also can contribute to problems in attention and concentration (Cunningham & Barkley, 1978). The early evaluation of either receptive or expressive language delays with the MSEL would be important to the establishment of an early intervention program focused on these delays.

There is a major need to retest the sample in this study with the MSEL. This would establish how stable the performance of this sample of prenatally drug-exposed infants is over time. There is evidence that prenatally drug-exposed infants do demonstrate consistent cognitive development over time (Poulsen, 1991), and it is important to establish that the MSEL is a consistent evaluative procedure with these children. It is also important to demonstrate that the delays evaluated at one point in time with the MSEL continue with development and, therefore, may be deficiencies and are not transitory delays. Children who met the criteria in this study for delays during the first evaluation should continue to meet these criteria when reevaluated after a 1-year interval. This can apply only if no significant intervention has occurred. For a variety of reasons, no intervention has been provided to most of this sample, and repeat evaluations with the MSEL are in progress.

References

Bayley, N. (1969). *Manual for the Bayley Scales of Infant Development.* New York: The Psychological Corporation.

Chasnoff, I., Griffith, D., & Azuma, S. (1992). Intrauterine cocaine/polydrug exposure: Three-year outcome. *Pediatric Research, 31,* 9A.

Chasnoff, I. J., Schnoll, S. H., Burns, W. J., & Burns, K. (1984). Maternal non-narcotic substance abuse during pregnancy: Effects on infant development. *Neurobehavioral Toxicology and Teratology, 6*(4), 277-280.

Cunningham, C. E., & Barkley, R. A. (1978). The role of academic failure in hyperactive behavior. *Journal of Learning Disabilities, 11,* 15-21.

Dow-Eduard, D. (1991). Cocaine effects on fetal development: A comparison of clinical and animal research findings. *Neurotoxicology and Teratology, 13,* 347-52.

Gardner, H. (1985). *Frames of mind.* New York: Basic Books.

Griffith, D. (1991). Intervention needs of children prenatally exposed to drugs. *Congressional Testimony Before the House Select Committee on Special Education,* Washington, DC.

Handler, A., Kistin, N., Davis, F., & Ferre, C. (1991). Cocaine use during pregnancy: Perinatal outcomes. *American Journal of Epidemiology, 133,* 818-825.

Howard, J., Beckwith, L., Rodning, C., & Kropenske, V. (1989). The development of young children of substance-abusing parents: Insights from seven years of intervention and research. *Zero to Three, 9,* 8-12.

Hoyme, H. E., Jones, K. L., Dixon, S. D., Jewett, T., Hanson, J. W., Robinson, L. K., Masall, M. E., & Allanson, P. (1990). Prenatal cocaine exposure and fetal vascular disruption. *Pediatrics, 85,* 743-747.

Kaltenbach, K., & Finnegan, L. A. (1989). Prenatal narcotic exposure: Perinatal and developmental effects. *Neuro-Toxicology, 10,* 597-604.

Kramer, L., Locke, G., Ogunyemi, A., & Nelson, L. (1990). Neonatal cocaine-related seizures. *Journal of Child Neurology, 5,* 60-64.

Kronstadt, D. (1989). *Pregnancy and cocaine addiction: An overview and impact of treatment.* San Francisco: Far West Laboratory for Education Resource and Development.

Lodge, A. (1977). A developmental finding with infants born to mothers on methadone maintenance: A preliminary report. In G. Beshner & R. B. Rotman (Eds.), *Symposium on comprehensive health care for addicted families and their children.* Washington, DC: Government Printing Office.

Lutiger, B., Graham, K., Einarson, T., & Koren, G. (1991). Relationship between gestational cocaine use and pregnancy outcome: A meta-analysis. *Teratology, 44,* 405-414.

McCandless, B. (1967). *Children: Behavior and development.* New York: Holt, Rinehart, and Winston.

Morrison, D. (1985). *Neurobehavioral and perceptual dysfunction in learning disabled children.* Toronto, Canada: C. J. Hogrefe Inc.

Morrison, D. (May 1991). The intelligence of prenatally drug-exposed infants. *Annual Meeting of Council for Exceptional Children,* New Orleans, LA.

Mullen, E. (1989). *Infant MSEL manual.* Cranston, RI: T.O.T.A.L. Child Inc.

Poulsen, M. (1991). *Schools meet the challenge: Educational needs of children at risk due to substance exposure.* Sacramento: Resources in Special Education.

Rosen, T. S., & Johnson, N. L. (1982). Children of methadone maintained mothers: Follow-up to 18 months of age. *Journal of Pediatrics, 101,* 192-196.

Sheehan, R., & Klein, N. (1989). Infant assessment. In R. Wang, D. Reynold, & N. Walb (Eds.), *Handbook of special education: Research and practice* (Vol. 3). New York: Pergamon.

Sobrian, S. K., Burton, L. E., Robinson, N. L., Ashe, W. K., James, N. Stokes, O. L., & Turner, L. W. (1990). Neurobehavioral and immunological effects of prenatal cocaine exposure in rats. *Pharmacologic Biochemical Behavioral, 35,* 617-629.

Strauss, M. E., Starr, R. H., Ostrea, E. M., Chavaz, C. J., & Stryker, J. C. (1976). Behavioral concomitants of prenatal addiction to narcotics. *Journal of Pediatrics, 89,* 842-846.

Tronick, E. Z., & Beeghly, J. (1992). Effect of prenatal exposure to cocaine on newborn behavior and development: A critical review. *OSAP Monograph, 11*, 25–48.

Volpe, J. (1992). Effect of cocaine use on the fetus. *The New England Journal of Medicine, 327*(6), 399–407.

Zimmerman, I. L., Steiner, V. G., & Evatt, R. L. (1979). *Manual for preschool language assessment*. Columbus, OH: Charles E. Merrill.

Address correspondence to:
Delmont Morrison, Ph.D.,
Department of Psychiatry,
Box CAS-0984, University of California,
San Francisco, CA 94143-0984

Part IV:
Tracheostomy, Vocalizations, and Communicative Intentions

The Role of Vocalizations on Social Behaviors of a Tracheostomized Toddler

*Laura A. Fus, M.A.**
University of Iowa
Iowa City, Iowa

David P. Wacker, Ph.D.
University of Iowa
Iowa City, Iowa

The authors of this study investigated the social interactive behaviors of an aphonic tracheostomized toddler who was given the ability to vocalize via a speaking valve. Tracy, tracheostomized since 3 months of age, was socially withdrawn and noninteractive prior to speech and language intervention. Adaptation to the speaking valve required 3 months of direct therapy, after which time Tracy became increasingly communicative, using both verbal and nonverbal socially interactive behaviors. Over time, Tracy interacted at an increasingly higher level when the speaking valve was in place versus when it was off, as was displayed during consecutive alternating sessions.

With rapid advances in medical technology, many infants with respiratory disorders of various etiologies are surviving more often than in the past. A common medical course for these infants often includes a tracheostomy. Over the past two decades, there has been a significant increase in the duration of tracheostomies, due to the increased survival rate of children with tracheostomies during their developmental years (Singer, Wood, & Lambert, 1985; Wetmore, Handler, & Potsic, 1982). For example, the mean duration of tracheostomy in one large sample of children doubled over the 10-year period between 1970 and 1980 (Wetmore et al., 1982). Children with long-term tracheostomies are a new and unique segment of the population who were not present a generation ago, as it was not until the mid-1960s that neonatal critical care units and the use of assisted ventilation were developed for children with severe respiratory disorders. Therefore, re-

*Currently at Children's Seashore House, Philadelphia, Pennsylvania.

search regarding the developmental sequelae and outcomes of these children is minimal. There is, however, growing evidence that a long-term tracheostomy has a negative effect on development, independent of concomitant medical and social factors (Singer, Hill, Orlowski, & Doershuk, 1991; Singer et al., 1989). Singer et al. (1991) studied 32 children who had been tracheostomized for at least 3 months and found low average intelligence scores (mean = 92.1, SD = 14.5), low mean percentile of weight for age (36.8%), high incidence of behavioral problems (>98th percentile), and low degrees of social competence (<2nd percentile), compared to same-age peers.

It is becoming increasingly apparent that tracheostomies have a significant effect on communication. Past research has found consistent delays in receptive and expressive language skills in children who had long-term tracheostomies, with expressive language more delayed than receptive (Hill & Singer, 1990; Kaslon & Stein, 1985; Ross, 1982; Singer et al., 1991). Singer et al. (1991) showed that seven subjects without other medical or social factors all demonstrated a negative effect of the tracheostomy on language outcome, independent of medical and social risk variables. A possible interpretation of these results is that inhibited vocalizations had a negative effect on the ability to use language expressively and contributed to a lack of language experiences in general.

Locke and Pearson (1990) claim that aphonia prevents tracheostomized children from discovering the referential value of voicing and discourages the development of a phonetic repertoire. As a child is tracheostomized into his or her developmental years, there is greater phonological impairment and lack of learned association between oral motor movements and sounds. Further, because the aphonic child has no means to discover that the voice can be used practically and communicatively, children with tracheostomies are orally passive and do not strive to make their voice work.

Recently, speaking valves have been used with tracheostomized children as an assistive device to help them produce voicing. The speaking valve is a one-way valve which directs the airflow through the oral cavity upon exhalation, allowing air to flow across the vocal folds. It has been shown to improve vocal skills and maximize communication skills (Ward, 1991).

This article investigates the role of vocalizations on the social interactions of a tracheostomized toddler. It is hypothesized that vocalizations have a positive effect on social interactive behaviors, and thus, contribute to the toddler's overall speech and language development. Because vocalizations enable tracheostomized toddlers to interact with their environment, it is also hypothesized that these children will be less passive communicators once given the ability to voice.

Methods

Subject

Tracy, the child with a tracheostomy who was the subject in this study, was 2 years old at the time of the investigation. She received a tracheostomy at 3 months of age due to severe bronchopulmonary dysplasia (BPD). At the time of the investigation, she was fitted with a Shiley tracheal tube, pediatrics size 2. She required direct oxygen input 24 hours a day and was on the ventilator at night and as needed for respiratory difficulties. Brainstem auditory evoked response assessment indicated that Tracy had normal auditory function bilaterally; she also wore corrective lenses. She had behavioral feeding problems that included food and drink refusal and received her nutrition through a gastrointestinal tube. She was on a behavior management feeding protocol to increase food and drink acceptance and overall oral intake. Tracy's family was not involved in her care and foster home placement was in process during this investigation.

Prior to intervention, Tracy was characterized as noninteractive by her primary caretakers. Favored activities included isolated play with toys, listening to music, and stereotypic/self-stimulating behaviors (e.g., rocking). Tracy did not vocalize around her tracheostomy, but an air leak around the tracheostomy was present, as evident by sounds heard during crying. Prior to intervention, it was estimated that Tracy was developmentally delayed approximately 12–15 months, based on infant development scales. She did not receive speech-language or education services prior to this investigation.

Equipment

Based on a recommendation by Tracy's allergy/pulmonary pediatric nurse practitioner and consultation with the speech pathologist, a speaking valve was introduced to facilitate vocalizations. An Airlife™ "T" adapter with 15 mm I.D. base, both arms 22 mm O.D., an open oxygen stem, internal inhalation valve, and internal exhalation valve was adapted to be used as a speaking valve. The exhalation valve was inverted so that it served as a one-way valve (inhalation only). This device was chosen for use because it allowed for attachment of the oxygen input line for constant oxygen flow, which was necessary for Tracy's medical condition. The speaking valve allowed air to enter the trachea through the tracheal tube, then upon exhalation, the valve closed off, forcing air to be redirected through the normal airway, vibrating the vocal folds and creating the potential for voicing. This device required a breathing pattern that was initially more strenuous because the patient had to exhale through the normal airway. Therefore, this device had to be introduced slowly and with close supervision by the medical and respiratory staff.

Data Collection

It required approximately 3 months to orient Tracy to the speaking valve. During this time, she was seen for speech therapy 3–5 times a week for a half hour of direct service and was on a daily speech stimulation program with her nursing staff. The goals of speech therapy at this time were to tolerate the speaking valve for at least 10 minutes, produce open vowel sounds with the speaking valve on, and imitate oral motor movement (i.e., "raspberries," lip smacking) with the speaking valve off. All therapy was conducted at the bedside or in the playpen.

Data collection was initiated when Tracy tolerated the speaking valve for at least 10 minutes. Data were collected approximately once a week during probes of speech therapy sessions conducted with the first author for 12 weeks. Independent observers trained in behavioral psychology collected the data. Each probe session was 5 minutes in duration and included therapy when the speaking valve was on as well as when it was off. The probe sessions were randomly alternated between sessions when the speaking valve was used and when it was not used. This design controlled for order effect when consecutive probe sessions were conducted within one visit.

Data were collected using a 6-second partial interval event recording system. Target behaviors that were recorded are listed in Table 1. The communicative behaviors that indicated social exchange included prompted and independent vocalizations, such as glottal sounds or open vowel sounds; prompted and independent prespeech oral movements, such as "raspberries" or lip smacking; direct eye contact with the therapist; and

Table 1. Social Communicative Behaviors

Vocalizations
  prompted or independent
  glottal sounds
  open vowel sounds

Prespeech Oral Movements
  prompted or independent
  repeated labial closures (lip smacking)
  labial sputters (raspberries)

Other Social Interactions with Therapist
  direct eye contact
  smiling

smiling at the therapist. The categories of social communicative behaviors were not mutually exclusive, so more than one could occur within each interval.

Reliability

A second observer simultaneously, but independently, collected reliability data on approximately 20% of the sessions. Interobserver agreement was calculated on an interval-by-interval basis (Kazdin, 1982) for occurrence of target behaviors. An agreement occurred when both observers recorded the same behaviors within the same intervals. Agreement was computed for the partial interval recording system by dividing the number of agreements by the number of agreements plus disagreements and multiplying by 100. Interobserver agreement averaged 88.8% and ranged from 85% to 90%.

Data Analysis

Raw data were analyzed for each session individually. The frequency of occurrence of positive communicative behaviors was calculated by dividing the number of intervals in which at least one target behavior occurred by the total number of intervals for the session and multiplying by 100 to derive a percent occurrence.

To calculate the difference in positive behaviors between consecutive alternating sessions, the percent of occurrence of positive behaviors during sessions without the speaking valve was subtracted from the percent occurrence of positive behaviors during the session with the speaking valve that immediately preceded or followed the session conducted without the speaking valve. This derived the difference in positive behaviors between consecutive alternating sessions.

Results

The data of positive communicative behaviors for all probe sessions are presented in Figure 1. Although there are initial inconsistencies within the two types of sessions, with the speaking valve and without the speaking valve, the trends were evident by the fourth and fifth sessions. Tracy's positive communicative behaviors generally occurred at a higher rate when the speaking valve was in place. In other words, Tracy was overall more communicative and interactive with the therapist when the speaking valve was on.

The data illustrating the difference in positive behaviors between consecutive alternating sessions are shown in Figure 2. The figure illustrates data collected on those dates in which two consecutive probe sessions were conducted, systematically alternated between sessions with the speaking valve on and with the speaking valve off. The difference between the occurrence of positive behaviors when it was on and when it was off increased over time. Tracy's positive behaviors became more discriminant between alternating sessions over time. In other words, Tracy's overall positive behaviors were increasingly differentiated between the two conditions.

Although the major focus of this study was social interactions, informal notes were made of speech. Unfortunately, speech sound anal-

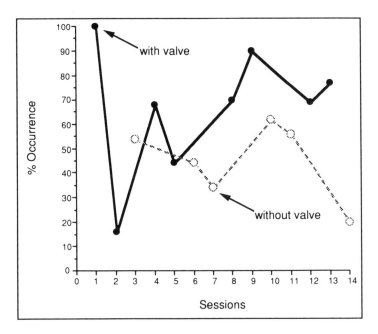

Figure 1. Positive communicative behaviors.

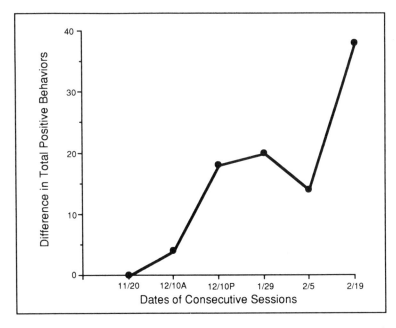

Figure 2. Difference in positive behaviors between consecutive alternating sessions.

ysis was not undertaken, so it is not possible to report the changes in the variety of speech sounds used. However, it was apparent that Tracy acquired a large repertoire of vocalizations and babbling behaviors which were used when the speaking valve was in place. She used numerous open vowel sounds and combinations, as well as a variety of /b (vowel)/ combinations. Tracy used vocalizations spontaneously, in imitation, and to obtain desired reinforcements (i.e., tickles, bouncing on lap). Vocalizations became significant components of Tracy's positive behaviors and interactions.

Discussion

Bruner (1975) suggested that there exist "inseparable bonds among language, social interaction, and learning from the very start of life" (p. 256). The child's first use of language, promoting joint and shared interactions with a caregiver, has a social basis, and language continues to occupy the key role in socialization and learning throughout a child's development (Halliday, 1975). Social interaction and language illustrate a reciprocal relationship: A child acquires language through his or her interactions with persons in the environment and uses language to interact socially. Thus, socialization is a key basis to language acquisition. Tracy is an example of a child who was noninteractive and preferred to be engaged in independent play with toys, music, or self-stimulating behaviors. Vocalizations were nonexistent due to the tracheostomy, so a means for her to use her voice was devised in the hope that it would improve her overall social interactions. The introduction of a speaking valve that could facilitate vocalization was initially resisted, but was accepted for 10-minute segments after 3 months of training. As a result of using the speaking valve, Tracy's social communicative behaviors increased when the device was on, compared to those sessions conducted while it was off. Not only did vocalizations and babbling increase, but so did pre-speech oral movements and nonverbal communication, such as eye contact and smiling. Tracy's vocalizations can be classified as primitive speech acts, as they consisted of single vocal patterns used to convey intention (i.e., labeling, requesting, practicing) and serve as precursors to subsequent speech acquisition (Dore, 1975). Most importantly, Tracy's differentiated positive behaviors in consecutive sessions (when the valve was on vs. when it was off) illustrated that she responded differently to her environment when the vocal component was available to her.

Because children with long-term tracheostomies have an increased probability of behavior problems and social isolation (Simon & McGowan, 1989; Singer et al., 1991; Singer et al., 1989; Singer et al., 1985; Ward, 1991), it is important to provide them with the opportunity to interact positively and more actively. The ability to vocalize had a positive effect on Tracy's overall behavior, and sessions conducted with the speaking valve on showed a marked increase in interactions. Tracy was a more active communicator with the speaking valve such that she used vocalizations spontaneously, to request reinforcers, and to initiate interactions.

Over time, the speaking valve became a discriminative stimulus to Tracy. When the valve was on, she knew she could attain reinforcement by responding to the presence of the speaking valve in the form of voicing and other interactions. When the speaking valve was removed, there was subsequently no responding, that is, no vocalizations. The presence of the ability to voice gave Tracy control over her environment that she never had before, since she could be the initiator of interactions as well as the respondent.

Successful use of the speaking valve did not occur immediately. Just as a high-technology computer is useless to the naive person without training, so was the speaking valve to Tracy. The use of this device was approached carefully. Tracy became accustomed to the alternate breathing method and then learned that she would be reinforced for making sounds. It was necessary to approach sound acquisition as a game rather than a demand. The successful acquisition of vocalizations can be attributed to the careful therapy provided by the speech therapist and nursing staff, as well as the use of the device itself.

This case study has substantial application for professionals and caretakers who work with tracheostomized children. Because these children have a tracheostomy, it is possible that fewer linguistic demands are placed on them during their development. However, this study indicates that vocalizations are an important component to overall social development. Thus, speech pathologists should implement therapy goals that target sound production. Once the speech pathologist is comfortable with the child's safety in using a device to facilitate vocalizations, other therapists and caregivers should also incorporate socialization through sound play in the course of their interactions. For example, the occupational therapist can include imitative babbling during sensory play; the early intervention specialist can encourage voicing during games such as peek-a-boo, patty-cake, and "so big"; and parents or nursing staff can socialize with voicing during daily care activities, such as feeding, bathing, and dressing. Success in the acquisition of vocalization relies not only on the speech pathologist, but also on every person who participates in the tracheostomized child's development.

It is natural to wonder what happened to Tracy after the investigation was concluded. Tracy was taken as a foster child by a caring and dedicated family. Close contact was kept between the researcher and Tracy's family after the study was concluded. Tracy continues to use the speaking valve a great deal and continues to receive speech therapy. The valve is on approximately 7 hours a day, taken off only to eat and sleep. Tracy lifts her chin when she wants the speaking valve put on. Her mother reports that she babbles and vocalizes so much with the speaking valve on that they "can't keep her quiet." Tracy is using a variety of consonant-vowel combinations, including *mama, mo/more, baba, da,* and other open vowel sounds. She is also interacting with her environment with increasing variety. Tracy has been receptive to using signs, as well as vocalizations, and is now chaining two and three signs together. By providing Tracy with an instrument for vocalizing, she has made substantial gains in overall social behaviors in 1 year, and has blossomed into an interactive toddler.

In summary, these results support the assertion that the aphonia imposed by long-term tracheostomies has an adverse effect on phonemic development and expressive language development (Handler, Simon, & Fowler, 1983; Kaslon & Stein, 1985; Locke & Pearson, 1990; Singer et al., 1991; Singer et al., 1989; Singer et al., 1985). Tracy thus serves as an example of tracheostomized children whose prognosis for speech sound development and expressive language development improves greatly with the ability to vocalize and with consistent speech-language intervention to further facilitate this development. Tracy also exemplifies the need to consider vocal communication as a key component for overall social development of tracheostomized toddlers.

Acknowledgments

I would like to extend sincere appreciation to Ken Bleile, Ph.D., for his assistance in composing this manuscript. I would also like to thank Shari Miller for her assistance in editing.

References

Bruner, J. S. (1975). From communication to language — A psychological perspective. *Cognition, 3*, 255-287.

Dore, J. (1975). Holophrases, speech acts and language universals. *Journal of Child Language, 2*, 21-40.

Halliday, M. A. K. (1975). *Learning how to mean: Explorations in the development of language.* London: Edward Arnold.

Handler, S., Simon, B., & Fowler, S. (1983). Speech and the child with a long-term tracheostomy — The problem and the otolaryngologist's role. *Journal of Pediatric Otolaryngology, 36*, 67-71.

Hill, B., & Singer, L. (1990). Speech and language development after infant tracheostomy. *Journal of Speech and Hearing Disorders, 55*, 15-20.

Kaslon, K., & Stein, R. (1985). Chronic pediatric tracheostomy: Assessment and implications for habilitation of voice, speech, and language in young children. *International Journal of Pediatric Otorhinolaryngology, 9*, 165-171.

Kazdin, A. E. (1982). *Single-case research designs: Methods for clinical and applied settings.* New York: Oxford University Press.

Locke, J., & Pearson, D. (1990). Linguistic significance of babbling: Evidence from a tracheostomized infant. *Journal of Child Language, 17*, 1-16.

Ross, G. (1982). Language functioning and speech development of six children receiving tracheostomy in infancy. *Journal of Communication Disorders, 15*, 95-111.

Simon, B., & McGowan, J. (1989). Tracheostomy in young children: Implications for assessment and treatment of communication and feeding disorders. *Infant and Young Children, 1*, 1-9.

Singer, L., Hill, B., Orlowski, J., & Doershuk, C. (1991). Medical and social factors as predictors of outcome in infant tracheostomy. *Pediatric Pulmonology, 11*, 243-248.

Singer, L., Kercsmar, C., Legris, G., Orlowski, J., Hill, B., & Doershuk, C. (1989). Developmental sequelae of long-term infant tracheostomy. *Developmental Medicine and Child Neurology, 31*, 224-230.

Singer, L., Wood, R., & Lambert, S. (1985). Developmental follow-up of long-term infant tracheostomy: A preliminary report. *Developmental and Behavioral Pediatrics, 6*, 132-136.

Ward, P. (1991, November). *Use of Passy-Muir valve in the pediatric tracheostomized population.* Paper presented at American Speech-Language-Hearing Association Annual Convention, Atlanta.

Wetmore, R., Handler, S., & Potsic, W. (1982). Pediatric tracheostomy: Experience during the past decade. *Annals of Otolaryngology, 91*, 628-632.

Address correspondence to:
Laura A. Fus, M.A.,
Department of Communication Disorders,
Children's Seashore House,
3405 Civic Center Boulevard,
Philadelphia, PA 19104.

Communicative Intentions of Three Prelinguistic Children with a History of Long-term Tracheostomy

Marilyn K. Kertoy, Ph.D.
Robert J. Waters, M.Cl.Sc.
University of Western Ontario
London, Ontario, Canada

This study examined early communication in three children ranging in age from 20 to 27 months who had been tracheostomized during the first year of life and who remained cannulated at the time of this study. The communicative intentions and means as well as rate of communication were examined. The study documents the early communication patterns in children who are at risk for language as well as cognitive and social skills and who communicate through gestures when most children typically progress to vocalization and word use. The study of early communication patterns may help to identify those children most at risk for future language delay as well as to understand the potential contributions of social, cognitive, and language skills to the onset of early words. The results of the study showed that all three children exhibited slightly more than one communicative intention per minute on average. All children exhibited communicative intentions in the three major categories of behavior regulation, social interaction, and joint attention, but intentions categorized as behavior regulation were most frequent. The percentage of communicative intentions categorized as behavior regulation were more frequent and those categorized as joint attention were less frequent, compared to percentages of communicative intentions reported for normal and late-talking children of similar age.

The focus of numerous language studies with tracheostomized children has been the impact of their inability to vocalize during the prelinguistic period (prior to the onset of first words) on later language development (Hill & Singer, 1990; Kaslon & Stein, 1985; Ross, 1982; Simon, Fowler, & Handler, 1983). Little attention has been given to the early communication of children with tracheostomy including mother-child interaction, development of gestures and sounds, and/or onset of intentional communication (Adamson & Dunbar, 1991). The study of intentional communication is of interest to clinicians, as identifying patterns of intentional communication at an early age will help to determine patterns that could place children at risk for future language difficulties (Prizant & Wetherby, 1990; Wetherby, Cain, Yonclas, & Walker, 1988). Theoretically, the study of early communication has gained importance as researchers search for overlapping developments in social, cognitive, and linguistic skills to better understand the factors influencing language development (as well as delay) (Thal & Tobias, 1994). Children with a history of tracheostomy during the prelinguistic period are at double risk for language delay, as their restricted environments and lack of opportunities to communicate may influence not only language but cognitive and social development as well. Further, children with tracheostomy appear to remain at the gestural stage of communication during a period from birth to 18 months when children normally progress through stages of vocalization (reflexive, reactive, sound making, instrumental, interactional, and heuristic) for a variety of communicative functions (Stark, Bernstein, & Demorest, 1993).

Development of Communicative Intentions

From 9 to 12 months, most children engage in intentional communication. These intentions are expressed through nonverbal and verbal means (Coggins & Carpenter, 1978; Greenfield & Smith, 1976). Bruner (1981) described three major categories of communicative intention that are exhibited by children by the end of the first year of life. These categories include behavior regulation (requests or protests regarding objects and actions), social interaction (showing off objects, greetings, social routines) and joint attention (seeking information, commenting). Prizant and Wetherby (1990) suggested that children progress through a continuum of communicative intentions, moving from behavior regulation to social interaction and then to joint attention. This continuum reflects greater social relatedness on the part of the child as well as the child's growing socioemotional competence. Although the full clinical implications of this continuum have not been established, it appears important to later language development that children communicate for a variety of communicative intentions.

Influence of Tracheostomy on the Development of Intentional Communication

The development of intentional communication takes place in early interactions between parent and child (Bruner, 1975; Schaffer, Collis, & Parson, 1977). A child attempts to signal needs and feelings and in turn receives feedback from his or her parents about the adequacy of those signals (Moerk, 1977; Stern, 1977). The child with a tracheostomy may be limited in his or her ability to vocalize, and parents may misinterpret the child's signals. Children are hospitalized while undergoing tracheostomy or respiratory care, and normal opportunities for parent-child interaction are interrupted. Some tracheostomized children experience frequent or prolonged hospitalizations, and extended hospitalizations may limit further opportunities for communication for a variety of functions (Browne, 1993; Simon & McGowan, 1989). Approximately 24 to 50% of total cases with tracheostomy are reported to be due to bronchopulmonary dysplasia (Arcand & Granger, 1988; Hill & Singer, 1990; Line, Hawkins, Kahlstrom, McLaughlin, & Ensley, 1986). Nearly 50% of children with long-term tracheostomy are born prematurely (Singer et al., 1989). These premature babies may overreact or underreact to stimuli, and this can make the interpretation of early signals extremely difficult (Als, et al., 1986). Despite the difficulty, mothers may still attribute intent to their babies' infrequent or unclear communication attempts (Yoder & Feagans, 1988).

In addition to limited opportunities for parent-child interaction and their potential impact on early language learning, the tracheostomized child may have limited experiences with objects and people. The neonatal intensive care unit (NICU) provides limited opportunities to interact with caregivers for social reasons. Caregivers interact most frequently to provide medical or physical care (Jacobsen & Wendler, 1988). Excessive handling by different caretakers or poor positioning can influence the quality of the interactions as well as the child's readiness for interactions (Frank, Maurer, & Shepard, 1991). Further, the NICU may offer excessive light and noise, yet provide few stimulating toys (Campbell, 1986). Little is known about the availability of objects for children to manipulate while hospitalized, yet manipulation of objects has a vital role in the child's involvement of others with objects of interest (Bates, Camaioni, & Volterra, 1976). In turn, families may have fewer opportunities to follow the child's lead or to jointly attend to objects. Episodes of joint attention have been shown to influence language learning (Tomasello & Farrar, 1986). Although recent programming advances increase the probability that children will have play activities whenever feasible, tracheostomized children likely have fewer opportunities to mutually attend to objects or to engage in social action games in the hospital than they would experience at home (McCue, Wagner, Hansen, & Rigler, 1986; Platt & Coggins, 1990).

Finally, sometimes the life-threatening nature of the tracheostomized child's condition influences opportunities for the child to regulate the behaviors of self and others. These children may have needs met for them immediately to avoid stress or unwanted medical emergencies (Leander & Pettet, 1986). Families of tracheostomized children report disciplining the tracheostomized sibling less than other siblings (Wills, 1983). Therefore, the tracheostomized child may not develop the ability to cope with stressful situations, to understand the consequences of his or her behavior, or to develop positive self-esteem (Friday & Lemanck, 1993). Social and language skills develop in parallel in the young child, and socioemotional competence may have a potential impact on language development (Prizant & Meyer, 1993).

Recently, several investigators have studied the rate and pattern of use of communicative intentions in normally-developing and late-talking children in the prelinguistic period to determine their role in predicting later language outcome (Paul & Shiffer, 1991; Wetherby et al., 1988). However, the communicative intentions of children who have undergone tracheostomy have not been examined. This study documents the use of communicative intentions in children who have undergone long-term tracheostomy and who remain cannulated to (a) determine if the rate and types of communicative intentions are similar to those previously reported for normally developing children and (b) to determine the means used to express the communicative intentions. Most children with tracheostomy make slow language gains, but reach expected language levels by age 5. It is not known why some 13 to 17% of children who undergo tracheostomy continue to have speech and language difficulties several years after decannulation (Bleile, 1993). The identification of early communication patterns may help to determine those tracheostomized children at greatest risk for communication delay.

Method

Subjects

Subjects were three African American toddlers, 2 boys and 1 girl, ranging in age from 20 to 27 months who had undergone tracheostomy prior to 8 months of age at a children's hospital in Michigan. The children remained cannulated at the time of the study. The parents of each child voluntarily agreed to participate in the study when contacted by an airway management nurse from the hospital. These children were selected on the basis of showing no complicated medical conditions in addition to the one necessitating the tracheostomy and of having normal cognitive and motor skills based on the nurses' and parents' reports. Children for whom the onset of cannulation had occurred in the prelinguistic period and who were undergoing a lengthy cannulation were also selected. Each child's hearing had been tested at the hospital and was reported to be within normal limits. Based on parent interviews, all children showed receptive language skills within 3 months of their chronological age on the *Receptive-Emergent Language Scale-2* (Bzoch & League, 1991). (See Table 1 for the subjects' demographics.)

Procedures

Children were videotaped at home engaging in activities with structured and unstructured contexts to ensure sampling of a full range of communicative intentions (Coggins, Olswang, & Guthrie, 1987). A General Elec-

Table 1. Subject Demographics

	Subject 1	Subject 2	Subject 3
Gender	male	female	male
Term of gestation	7 months	9 months	9 months
Age at testing	27 months	24 months	20 months
Age at cannulation	8 months	1 month	1.5 months
Length of cannulation	19 months	23 months	18.5 months
Reason for cannulation	narrow airway	paralysed vocal folds	narrow airway
Total length of time in hospital	17 months	12 months	10 months
Reasons for hospitalizations	respiratory distress	respiratory distress, pneumonia, laryngoscopic evaluation, tracheal surgery	respiratory distress

tric camera (Model 9-9806) was placed at a standard distance of 2 to 3 feet to capture a full view of the child, toys, and examiner. Interactions were also audiotaped to provide a back-up for the audio portion of the interactions using a Marantz cassette recorder (Model PMD-420) and a Crown PZM microphone. The microphone was placed on a table near each child. Two observers worked as a team with each family. One observer interviewed the parents and ensured the camera and microphone were functioning while the other observer served as the examiner for the structured interactions.

The sampling procedures for the structured context consisted of the communicative temptations and sharing books procedures from the *Communication and Symbolic Behaviour Scales (CSBS)* (Wetherby & Prizant, 1993). The sampling procedure for the unstructured context was a 10-minute parent-child play interaction.

The standardized procedures and standardized materials for the communication temptations and book sharing from the *CSBS* were used. During the communicative temptation procedure, each child was presented with a series of eight temptations. For example, bubbles were blown in front of the child and then the child was handed the bubble jar with the lid tightly closed. During sharing books, each child was given the opportunity to comment on four picture books. One parent of each child was present during the structured contexts and given the opportunity to interact with the child in a typical way. Children were seated in high chairs or at tables and chairs that encouraged their full attention on the temptations. The structured interactions ranged in length from $24\frac{1}{2}$ to $25\frac{1}{2}$ minutes.

During play, the parent and child interacted as they usually did. The mother-child dyads played with a doll, a plastic plate, mixing bowl, spoon, knife, fork, spatula, a baby bottle, a washcloth, and a Little Tykes doll house. Each child-parent dyad was seated at a table or on a blanket on the floor. The play interactions varied in length; eight consecutive minutes from each play interaction (selected from the 1-minute point of each interaction) were used to code communicative intentions.

Analysis of Communicative Intentions

The videotaped samples of each child's communication from the structured and unstructured contexts were analyzed in the following way. First, the occurrence of each communicative intention was noted by marking the counter number shown on a Sony Video Editing Controller (Model RM-E300) attached to a Sony VHS Digital Picture Recorder (Model SLV-R5UC). All segments were viewed by all observers using this equipment, as segments could be framed and replayed in slow motion. Videotapes also contained a time code generated at recording. The counter number on the editing controller was matched to the time code on the videotape to align the segments and to ensure consistency across observations by several observers. The first observer viewed each interaction continuously in time and noted the occurrence of each communicative intention.

Each communicative intention had to meet the criteria prescribed by Wetherby and Prizant (1993): (a) the intention was a gesture, vocalization, or verbalization; (b) the intention was directed toward the adult; and (c) the intention served a communicative function. After the observer was comfortable that a communicative intention had occurred, it was categorized according to one of four types: behavior regulation, social interaction, joint attention, or unclear (see the Appendix for definitions of the categories of communicative intentions) (Wetherby & Prizant, 1993).

The communicative means used by the children to express the communicative intentions were also coded. Communicative means consisted of the categories of gestural, vocal, verbal, and combinations of gestural/vocal and gestural/verbal. Refer to the Appendix for the definitions of the categories for communicative means based on definitions provided by Wetherby et al. (1988).

Interobserver Agreement

Interobserver point-by-point agreement was determined for the identification as well as the categorization of communicative intentions for three observers for greater than 33% of the interactions for each child. One observer viewed and coded the entire structured and unstructured activities for each family, and these codes served as the gold standard. Two additional observers, who were unfamiliar with the children prior to viewing the taped interactions, were trained to identify and categorize communicative intentions and communicative means. Prior to coding any videotaped interactions, the observers reviewed the procedures for identifying communicative intentions and for scoring intentions and means according to category. They viewed the first few minutes of each interaction for each tracheostomized child and identified and categorized each intention, checking their responses against a score sheet. Disagreements on scoring were resolved by reviewing the videotape and by referring to the definitions and procedures provided with the CSBS.

The two additional observers scored 20 segments from each videotape, for a total of 60 segments from all three videotapes. The segments had been randomly selected from the original interactions, but occurred sequentially in time. None of the segments had been viewed during training. The segments to be scored were designated on a score sheet by counter numbers from the Sony Editing Controller and may or may not have contained communicative intentions. The observers independently identified each potential communicative intention by marking a plus or a minus sign beside each counter number. Each communicative intention was then categorized as belonging to behavior regulation, social interaction, joint attention or unclear categories. The means used to express the communicative intentions were also coded. Tallies were made of the communicative intentions and means occurring for the structured and unstructured contexts separately.

Interobserver point-by-point agreement for identification of communicative intentions by three observers ranged from 91 to 95% in the structured context for all three subjects and was 100% in the unstructured context for all three subjects. The interobserver agreement for assignment of a category in the structured context was 96% for behavior regulation, 100% for social interaction, and 75% for joint attention. The interobserver agreement for joint attention jumped to 86% when agreement for only two of the observers was calculated. In the unstructured context, the interobserver point-by-point agreement for assignment of a category by all three observers was 96% for behavior regulation, 90% for social interaction, and 100% for joint attention. Interobserver agreement for the communicative means ranged from 87 to 100% across the means categories.

Results

Types of Communicative Intentions

The children exhibited a significantly greater percentage of communication intentions in the category of behavior regulation than in the other categories ($F (2,6) = 148.08$, $p < .001$). Communicative intentions in the category of social interaction were the next most frequently occurring. The percentage of communicative intentions in the social interaction category was higher in the structured than in the unstructured context, while the percentage of communicative intentions in the joint attention category was higher in the unstructured than in the structured context. The differences across contexts were not significant (see Table 2).

Communication Rate

Communication rates were calculated by dividing the total number of communication intentions by the number of minutes in each communication context for each child. The communication rates in the structured context ranged from 1.12 communicative intentions per minute (Subject 2) to 1.22 communicative intentions per minute (Subject 1). The communication rates in the unstructured context ranged from .25 communicative intentions per minute (Subject 2) to 1.13 communicative intentions per minute (Subject 3). The communication rates for each child for the two contexts are shown in Table 3.

Means of Expressing Communicative Intentions

The communicative means used to express the communicative intentions were also calculated. The children used a significantly greater percentage of gestures to express communicative intentions than other means of communication ($F(2,6) = 14.07, p < .01$.). From 68.9 to 81.3% of their communicative

Table 2. Percentage of Communicative Intentions (and Sds) in the Categories of Behavior Regulation, Social Interaction, and Joint Attention for Structured and Unstructured Contexts

	Structured	**Unstructured**
Behavior regulation	75.7 (.09)	84.7 (.16)
Social interaction	18.7 (.09)	7.4 (.12)
Joint attention	5.6 (.05)	7.9 (.06)

Table 3. The Communication Rate for Each Subject in the Structured and Unstructured Contexts

	Subject 1	**Subject 2**	**Subject 3**
Structured	1.22	1.12	1.14
Unstructured	1.0	.25	1.13

intentions were expressed with gestures. Ninety percent of these gestures were conventional (pointing, giving, showing). The children also expressed from 17.5 to 27.3% of their communicative intentions with a combination of gestures and vocalizations, depending on the context. Vocalizations alone were an infrequent means of communication (1.2 to 3.7%). See Table 4 for the categories of communicative means exhibited.

Discussion

The results of this study showed that three tracheostomized children used a greater percentage of communicative intentions categorized as behavior regulation and a lesser percentage of communicative intentions categorized as joint attention than previously reported percentages for normally developing and late-talking children. All three tracheostomized children exhibited the highest percentage of communicative intentions in the category of behavior regulation and the lowest percentage in joint attention. This pattern is the reverse of a pattern shown by normally developing and late-talking children studied by Paul and Shiffer (1991) and by normally developing children studied by Wetherby et al. (1988). Children in the prelinguistic and one-word stages in the Wetherby et al. (1988) study exhibited communicative intentions categorized as behavior regulation 36 to 42% of the time compared to 75.7 to 84.7% of the time by children in the current study. Children in the prelinguistic stage studied by Wetherby et al. also exhibited communicative intentions in the category of joint attention from 39 to 49% of the time compared to 5.6 to 7.9% of the time by children in the present study (Wetherby et al., 1988).

Specific communicative intentions occurring within the major categories of behavior regulation, social interaction, and joint attention were not reported here. However, commenting on objects, a communicative intention categorized as joint attention was used infrequently. Requests for objects and protests, in the category of behavior regulation, were frequent. It has been hypothesized that commenting may occur less frequently as comments are more difficult for adults to interpret and reinforce than other intentions (Warren, Yoder, Gazdag, Kim, & Jones, 1993). If commenting occurs infrequently in subsequent studies of prelinguistic communication with larger numbers of tracheostomized children, it would be important to determine factors that influence the occurrence of commenting. Is commenting exhibited by tracheostomized children but not acknowledged by the parent or caretaker? Or are there few opportunities for tra-

Table 4. Percentage of Communication Means (and Ranges) in Each Category Used To Express Communicative Intentions in Structured and Unstructured Contexts

Context	Category of Means	Percentage (Range)
Structured	Gestural	81.3 (58.1–100)
	Vocal	1.2 (0–3.6)
	Gestural and vocal	17.5 (0–41.9)
Unstructured	Gestural	68.9 (44.4–100)
	Vocal	3.7 (0–11.1)
	Gestural and vocal	27.3 (0–44.4)

cheostomized children to comment on objects or activities in the NICU?

The three tracheostomized children also exhibited a communication rate similar to the rates shown by younger, normally developing children. The children expressed an average of just over one communicative intention per minute. This rate is similar to the rate reported by Wetherby et al. (1988) for children in the prelinguistic stage, 11 to 15 months old. Multiple samplings of communication behaviors would ensure that these rates were not influenced by the children's unfamiliarity with the examiner and the context.

Finally, an examination of the communicative means the children used to express the communicative intentions showed a strong reliance on gestures. Vocalizations combined with gestures were also emerging as a means of expressing intent. Compared to the children studied by Wetherby et al. (1988) in either the prelinguistic or one-word stage, children in the current study used gestures with greater frequency and combined gestures with vocalizations less of the time.

The conclusions drawn in this study are limited due to the sample size and because the children were selected from one cultural group who experienced long-term tracheostomy. The small sample size could have contributed to the profiles of communicative intentions observed. However, children used all categories of intentions, and their percentage of use was considerably different from the results reported from normal children under similar sampling conditions. Children from other cultural and socioeconomic backgrounds may express different proportions of communicative intentions and communicate at different rates. This study provides the first quantification of prelinguistic communication in children experiencing long-term tracheostomy.

The study of early communication in children undergoing long-term tracheostomy should be broadened. Analysis of parent-child discourse patterns may provide additional information about children's use of intentions in the joint attention and social interaction categories. Children in this study seemed to increase their use of intentions in the joint attention category during free play with their mothers. An analysis of the number of episodes of joint attention that occur between mother and child may be a better reflection of the frequency with which children engage in joint attention. By studying episodes of joint attention, those factors that support the child's effective showing of objects, requesting actions and commenting on ongoing activities will be better understood (Tomasello & Farrar, 1986).

Longitudinal study of the development of communication means in children during and following tracheostomy should also be undertaken. Of interest is whether the child's use of gestures at a stage when children would normally be progressing to use of combinations of gestures with vocalizations or words hinders language or social communication. Do these children exhibit the full range of intentions through gesture that children normally exhibit through gesture and/or vocalizations from birth to 18 months? Earlier studies have shown that children with tracheostomy rebound remarkably in language development once decannulation occurs. Wetherby et al. (1988) found that normally developing children continue to use predominantly vocalizations and gestures in both the prelinguistic and one-word stages. Not until the multiple word stage did the children studied by Wetherby et al. (1988) show a substantial increase in word use. It may be that these tracheostomized children will show normal and rapid progress in the use of communicative means (greater reliance on gestures and vocalizations as well as words) once they are decannulated and no longer restricted in their ability to vocalize. However, the potential impact of the extended use of gestures as a communicative means during the first year of life and into the second on the development of expressive and receptive vocabulary has not been studied. It is also possible that children with tracheostomy show vocabulary comprehension difficulties that contribute to their pattern of use of communicative means (Thal & Tobias, 1994).

Clinical Implications

Based on the initial findings that the rate and type of communication intentions may be influenced by long-term tracheostomy in the prelinguistic period, professionals should ensure that tracheostomized children have opportunities to communicate for a variety of functions in the hospital and at home. Particular emphasis should be placed on having caregivers model communicating for a variety of reasons with children, particularly for joint attention and social interaction.

References

Als, H., Lawhorn, G., Brown, E. Gibes, R., Duffy, F., McAnulty, G., & Blickman, J. (1986). Individualized behavioral and environmental care for the very low birth weight preterm infant at high risk for bronchopulmonary dysplasia: Neonatal intensive care unit and developmental outcome. *Pediatrics, 78*, 1123–1132.

Adamson, L.B., & Dunbar, B. (1991). Communication development of young children with tracheostomies. *Augmentative and Alternative Communication, 7*, 275–283.

Arcand, P., & Granger, J. (1988). Pediatric tracheostomy: Changing trends. *The Journal of Otolaryngology, 17*, 121–124.

Bates, E., Camaioni, L., & Volterra, V. (1976). Sensorimotor performatives. In E. Bates (Ed.), *Language and context: The acquisition of pragmatics* (pp. 49–71). New York: Academic Press.

Bleile, K. (1993). Children with long-term tracheostomies. In K. Bleile (Ed.) *The care of children with long-term tracheostomies* (pp. 3–20). San Diego: Singular Publishing Group.

Browne, J. V. (1993, June). *Growing up in the hospital: Meeting the needs of long-term hospitalized infants.* Paper presented at the First Interdisciplinary Symposium, High Risk Infants, Henry Ford Hospital, Warren, Michigan.

Bruner, J. (1975) The ontogenesis of speech acts. *Journal of Child Language, 2*, 1–19.

Bruner, J. (1981). The social context of language acquisition. *Language and Communication, 1*, 155–178.

Bzoch, K., & League, R. (1991). *Receptive-Expressive Emergent Language Scale (2nd ed.)* Austin, TX: Pro-Ed.

Campbell, S. K. (1986). Organizational and educational considerations in creating an environment to promote development of higher-risk infants. *Physical and Occupational Therapy in Pediatrics, 6*(3), 191–204.

Coggins, T. E., & Carpenter, R. (1978). *Categories for coding pre-speech intentional communication.* Unpublished manuscript, University of Washington, Seattle.

Coggins, T. E., Olswang, L. B., & Guthrie, J. (1987). Assessing communicative intents in young children: Low structured observation or elicitation tasks? *Journal of Speech and Hearing Disorders, 52*, 44–49.

Frank, A., Maurer, P., & Shepard, J. (1991). Light and sound environment: A survey of neonatal intensive care units. *Physical and Occupational Therapy in Pediatrics, 11*(2), 27–45.

Fridy, J., & Lemanek, K. (1993). Developmental and behavioral issues. In Ken Bleile (Ed.), *The care of children with long-term tracheostomies* (pp. 141-166). San Diego: Singular Publishing Group.

Greenfield, P., & Smith, J. (1976). *The structure of communication in early language development.* New York: Academic Press.

Hill, B. P., & Singer, L. T. (1990). Speech and language development after infant tracheostomy. *Journal of Speech and Hearing Disorders, 55*, 15–20.

Jacobsen, C. H., & Wendler, S. S. (1988). Language stimulation in the neonatal intensive care unit. *Human Communications Canada, 12*, 48–51.

Kaslon, K. W., & Stein, R. E. (1985). Chronic pediatric tracheostomy: Assessment and implication for habilitation of voice, speech, and language in young children. *International Journal of Pediatric Otorhinolaryngology, 9*, 165–171.

Leander, D., & Pettet, G. (1986). Parental response to the birth of a high-risk neonate: Dynamics and management. *Journal of Children in Contemporary Society, 17*(4), 205–216.

Line, W. S., Hawkins, D. B., Kahlstrom, E. J., MacLaughlin, E. F., & Ensley, J. L. (1986). Tracheostomy in infants and young children: The changing perspective 1970–1985. *Laryngoscope, 96*, 510–515.

McCue, K., Wagner, M., Hansen, H., & Rigler, D. (1986). A survey of a developing health care profession: Hospital "play" programs. *Child life: An overview* (pp. 16–22). Washington, DC: Association for the Care of Children's Health.

Moerk, E. (1977). *Pragmatic and semantic aspects of early language development*. Baltimore: University Park Press.

Paul, R., & Shiffer, M. E. (1991). Communicative initiations in normal and late-talking toddlers. *Applied Psycholinguistics, 12*, 419–431.

Platt, J., & Coggins, T. E. (1990). Comprehension of social-action games in prelinguistic children: Levels of participation and effect of adult structure. *Journal of Speech and Hearing Disorders, 55*, 315–326.

Prizant, B., & Meyer, E. (1993). Socioemotional aspects of language and social-communication disorders in young children and their families. *American Journal of Speech Language Pathology, 3*(3), 56–71.

Prizant, B., & Wetherby, A. (1990). Assessing the communication of infants and toddlers: Integrating a socioemotional perspective. *Zero to Three. Bulletin of the National Center for Clinical Infant Programs, 11*(1), 1–12.

Ross, G. S. (1982). Language functioning and speech development of six children receiving tracheostomy in infancy. *Journal of Communication Disorders, 15*, 95–111.

Schaffer, H., Collis, G., & Parson, G. (1977). Vocal interchange and visual regard in verbal and pre-verbal children. In H. Schaffer (Ed.), *Studies in mother-child interaction* (pp. 291–324). New York: Academic Press.

Simon, B. M., Fowler, S. M. & Handler, S. D. (1983). Communication development in children with long-term tracheostomies: Preliminary report. *International Journal of Pediatric Otorhinolaryngology, 6*, 37–50.

Simon, B. M., & McGowan, J. S. (1989). Tracheostomy in young children: Implications for assessment and treatment of communication and feeding disorders. *Infants and Young Children, 1*, 1–9.

Singer, L. T., Kercsmar, C., Legris, G., Orlowski, J. P., Hill, B. P., & Doershuk, C. (1989). Developmental sequelae of long-term infant tracheostomy. *Developmental Medicine and Child Neurology, 31*, 224–230.

Stark, R. E., Bernstein, L. E., & Demorest, M. E. (1993). Vocal communication in the first 18 months of life. *Journal of Speech and Hearing Research, 36*, 548–558.

Stern, D. (1977). *The first relationship*. Cambridge, MA: Harvard University Press.

Tomasello, M., & Farrar, M. J. (1986). Joint attention and early language. *Child Development, 57*, 1454–1463.

Thal, D., & Tobias, S. (1994). Relationships between language and gesture in normally developing and late-talking toddlers. *Journal of Speech and Hearing Research, 37*(1), 157–170.

Warren, S. F., Yoder, P., Gazdag, G. E., Kim, K., & Jones, H. A. (1993). Facilitating prelinguistic communication skills in young children with developmental delay. *Journal of Speech and Hearing Research, 36*(1), 83–97.

Wetherby, A., Cain, D., Yonclas, D., & Walker, V. (1988). Analysis of intentional communication of normal children from the prelinguistic to the multiword stage. *Journal of Speech and Hearing Research, 31*, 240–252.

Wetherby, A., & Prizant, B. (1993). *Communication and Symbolic Behavior Scales*. Normed Edition. Manual. Chicago: Riverside Publishing.

Wills, J. M. (1983). Concerns and needs of mothers providing home care for children with tracheostomies. *Maternal-Child Nursing Journal, 12*(2), 89–107.

Yoder, P. J., & Feagans, L. (1988). Mothers' attributions of communication to prelinguistic behavior of developmentally delayed and mentally retarded infants. *American Journal on Mental Retardation, 93*(1), 36–43.

Address correspondence to:
Marilyn K. Kertoy, Ph.D.
University of Western Ontario
Department of Communicative Disorders
1510 Elborn College
London, Ontario N6G 1H1
Canada

APPENDIX

Categories of Communicative Intentions (Wetherby & Prizant, 1993)

Behavior Regulation

Acts used to regulate the behavior of another person to obtain a specific result. Child's goal is to get the adult to do something or stop doing something. Examples include:

Request Object/Action Acts: Used to direct another to give a desired object or to carry out an action.

Protest Object/Action Acts: Used to refuse an object that is not desired or to direct another to cease an action that is not desired.

Social Interaction

Acts used to attract or maintain another's attention to oneself. Child's goal is to get adult to look at or notice him or her. Examples include:

Request Social Routine Acts: Used to direct another to begin or continue carrying out a game-like social interaction.

Request Comfort Acts: Used to seek another's attention to comfort from wariness, distress, or frustration.

Call Acts: Used to gain the attention of another to indicate that a communicative act is to follow.

Greet Acts: Used to indicate notice of a person or object's presence or to signal the initiation or termination of an interaction.

Show-Off Acts: Used to attract another's attention to oneself by displaying a performance.

Request Permission Acts: Used to seek another's consent to carry out an action; involves carrying out or wanting to carry out an action.

Joint Attention

Acts used to direct another's attention to an object, event, or topic of a communicative act. Child's goal is to get adult to look at or notice an entity or event. Examples include:

Comment on Object/Action Acts: Used to direct another's attention to an entity or event.

Request Information Acts: Used to seek information, explanations, or clarifications about an entity or previous utterance; includes *wh*-questions and other utterances with a rising intonation contour.

Unclear

Acts used for a communicative purpose but for which there is insufficient information to determine the category of function that it most appropriately fits. That is, it cannot be determined whether the child's goal is to communicate for behavior regulation, social interaction, or joint attention.

Categories of Communicative Means (Wetherby et al., 1988)

Gestural

The child used only his or her body or body part (excluding structures of the oral cavity).

Vocal

The child produced an utterance, including transcribable vocalizations and nontranscribable sounds.

Verbal

The child used conventional/referential words, as determined by the context, containing at least 50% of the target phonemes.

Gestural/Vocal

The child used both gestural and vocal communicative means simultaneously.

Gestural/Verbal

The child used both gestural and verbal communicative means simultaneously.

Part V: Development of Premature and Low Birthweight Children

Effects of Prematurity on the Language Development of Hispanic Infants

Gary Montgomery, Ph.D.
University of Texas-Pan American
Edinburg, Texas

Donald Fucci, Ph.D.
Maria Diana Gonzales, M.Ed.
Ramesh Bettagere, M.S.
Mary E. Reynolds, M.A.
Ohio University
Athens, Ohio

Linda Petrosino, Ph.D.
Bowling Green State University
Bowling Green, Ohio

Limited research is available on the language development of premature versus full-term infants of different ethnic groups. The present study compared the language development of premature and full-term Hispanic (Mexican-American) infants. Receptive and expressive language and mean length of response were the outcome measures used to compare the two groups. The subjects consisted of 12 premature (evaluated at 22 months corrected chronological age) and 12 full-term (evaluated at 22 months chronological age) Hispanic infants. The Sequenced Inventory of Communication Development-Revised (SICD-R) was used to determine the Receptive and Expressive Communication Ages and Mean Length of Response for each subject. The Spanish translation of the SICD-R was used with bilingual infants whose dominant language was Spanish and with monolingual Spanish speakers. The results suggest that premature Hispanic infants may acquire language at a slower rate than full-term Hispanic infants. Expressive language skills were more affected than receptive language skills. Implications of the findings and the need for further research are discussed.

Numerous studies have found a difference in the receptive and expressive language development between full-term and premature infants. The studies revealed that premature infants were delayed in language acquisition compared to full-term infants (Casiro et al., 1990; Crnic, Ragozin, Greenberg, Robinson, & Basham, 1983; Forslund & Bjerre, 1990; Grunau, Kearney, & Whitfield, 1990; Hubatch, Johnson, Kistler, Burns, & Moneka, 1985; Kenworthy, Bess, Stahlman, & Lindstrom, 1987; Siegel, 1982; Wright, Thislethwaite, Elton, Wilkinson, & Forfar, 1983; Ungerer & Sigman, 1983). A study by Menyuk, Liebergott, Schultz, Chesnick, and Ferrier (1991), however, did not find significant differences between the linguistic and cognitive development of premature and full-term English-speaking infants. Differences were found only between the very low birthweight infants and the full-term infants.

Some investigators found that while very low birthweight infants had language skills with means within the normal range, their language abilities were still significantly lower than the full-term infants (Casiro et al., 1990; Grunau et al., 1990). Casiro et al. (1990) revealed that 39% of the very low birthweight subjects they investigated exhibited significant language delays. Wright et al. (1983) also found significant differences between the receptive and expressive language skills of very low birthweight infants and full-term infants, but no differences were found in articulatory or hearing skills. McAllister et al. (1993) found the reverse to be true. Upon tracking the outcome of 118 neonatal intensive care graduates at 3 years of age, they found differences in articulation skills but no differences in comprehension and production.

When comparing full-term infants with premature infants who also exhibited respiratory distress syndrome, Hubatch et al. (1985) found significant differences on the receptive and expressive measures of both groups. Kenworthy et al. (1987) investigated 395 very low birthweight infants of which 15% exhibited respiratory distress syndrome. Their findings revealed an overall prevalence of hearing loss in this population ranging from 12 to 30%. They also concluded that one-third of the subjects exhibited speech and language delays.

While some of the studies mentioned previously included a limited number of Hispanic subjects (Ungerer & Sigman, 1983) and African-American subjects (Hubatch et al., 1985; Resnick et al., 1992), most of the research investigating the effects of prematurity on cognitive and language development has been performed on white (of non-Hispanic origin) infants. Research about this topic, focusing primarily on infants of different ethnic backgrounds (Cohen, Parmelee, Beckwith, & Sigman, 1986; Escalona, 1982; Pena, Teberg, & Hoppenbrouwers, 1987), is limited.

Review of the literature revealed three studies that have investigated different factors impacting on the development of premature Hispanic infants (Cohen et al., 1986; Escalona, 1982; Pena et al., 1987). Escalona (1982) studied 114 infants for 3½ years from birth to 40 months of age and their families. The infants were selected on the basis of prematurity and came from poor urban families. The major purpose of their study was to investigate how biologic and social factors impinged on the cognitive development of low birthweight premature infants. Fifty percent of the subjects were African-Americans, 25% were Hispanic (primarily Puerto Rican), and 25% were white Americans. The Bayley Scales of Infant Development were used to assess cognitive development up to 15 months of age. Afterwards, the Stanford-Binet was used to assess cognition. The results revealed that the infants demonstrated normal cognitive development up to 15 months of age. A severe decline in cognition was noted by 28 months, which was associated with lower social class. Escalona concluded that apparently both full-term and premature infants are vulnerable to environmental deficits and stressors, but premature infants appear to be even more susceptible.

Cohen et al. (1986) investigated the eventual outcome of premature infants at 8 years of age. All subjects were followed from birth to 8 years of age. Cohen et al. studied how the environment and the infant's abilities determined the eventual cognitive development. Several different assessments were administered by pediatricians and psychologists at certain developmental stages of the infants' lives. A subset of their subjects were Spanish-speaking who were found to have different outcomes than the English-speaking subjects. Reportedly, when the infants were analyzed at 2 and 5 years of age, the Hispanic infants appeared to score much lower on standardized tests. The investigators thought the lower scores were due to delays in language development. When followed up at 8 years of age, 30% of the Spanish-speaking subjects were enrolled in special education, whereas only 20% of the English-speaking children were. According to Cohen et al. (1986), they found that biological factors exhibited greater association with the 8 year olds' outcome in the Spanish-speaking group than social factors. In comparison, social factors were found to have greater association after 8 years in the English-speaking group regardless of the biologic factors.

Pena et al. (1987) investigated the effectiveness of using the Gesell Developmental Schedule with low birthweight Hispanic infants. The premature infants were evaluated at 20 and 40 weeks corrected chronological age by the same Hispanic pediatrician. They were assigned a Developmental Age which is an average of the scores on the following five areas: adaptive, gross motor, fine motor, language, and personal social. The investigators found that the overall Developmental Quotient declined in addition to the Language and Fine Motor Quotients between 20 and 40 weeks of age. More than 90% of the infants had a decrease in the Language Quotient when evaluated at 40 weeks. The investigators concluded that the Hispanic infants did not follow the white middle-class norms of the Gesell Developmental Schedule (Pena et al., 1987).

Escalona (1982), Cohen et al. (1986), and Pena et al. (1987) have investigated how prematurity, environment, and other factors may impact on cognition and overall development of premature infants. Cohen et al. and Pena et al. reported delayed language development in premature Hispanic infants; yet, neither study compared the language development of premature Hispanic infants to full-term Hispanic infants. They also reported general language findings but did not mention any details about specific language outcome measures. Cohen et al. (1986) recommended that in order to understand the development of infants from different ethnic and language groups, separate investigations should be performed on those groups.

The purpose of this present study was to compare the language development of premature and full-term Hispanic (Mexican-American) infants. Receptive and expressive language and mean length of response were the outcome measures used to compare the two groups.

Method

Subjects

The subjects in this study were 12 premature and 12 full-term infants participating in a longitudinal study. The premature subjects were selected from newborns in a neonatal intensive care unit in a hospital that services a large Hispanic population in the most southern tip of Texas. The criteria for selection of the premature infants consisted of admission and dismissal from a neonatal intensive care unit, gestational age at or below 37 weeks, birthweight equal to or less than 2700 grams, and Hispanic ethnic background. The criteria for selection of the full-term infants included a gestational age of 38 to 40 weeks, birthweight greater than 2700 grams (one full-term infant weighed 2494 grams), and Hispanic ethnic background. None of the premature or full-term infants had any obvious physical limitations. The full-term infants were selected from four community programs. The parents of the infants participating in the study were paid $10.00 upon completion of the evaluation.

The premature subjects were selected and matched with the full-term subjects on the basis of corrected age (determined by subtracting the gestational age from 40 weeks to obtain a corrected chronological age and then subtracting that number from the day on which testing occurred), socioeconomic status, ethnic background, and dominant language.

The premature subjects consisted of eight males and four females, whereas the full-term subjects consisted of five males and seven females. The premature mean gestational age was 31.6 weeks, and the full-term mean gestational age was 39.8 weeks. The gestational ages of the premature subjects ranged from 24 to 35 weeks. The premature group had a mean birthweight of 1676 grams compared to a mean birthweight of 3314 grams found in the full-term group. The premature group's birthweights ranged from a low of 878 to a high of 2693 grams. The mean maternal age of the full-term group was 22 years ranging from 15 to 31 years. The maternal ages for the premature group ranged from a low of 22 years to a high of 38 years. The mean age was 29 years. Ninety-two percent of the premature infants resided in a two-parent home, whereas 50% of the full-term infants resided in a single-parent home (see Table 1).

The Two Factor Index of Social Position, which utilizes occupation and education to determine a family's social position, was used to classify the families of all the subjects (Hollingshead, 1957). The subjects were matched and classified into the following socioeconomic classes (ranging from upper to lower class): two from Social Class II with scores ranging from 18 to 27; one from Social Class III with a score of 40; seven from Social Class IV with scores ranging from 44 to 60; 14 from Social Class V with scores ranging from 61 to 77. The mean socioeconomic score of the premature group was 57.5 compared to 58.5 for the full-term group. The mean maternal and paternal educational levels for the full-term group were 12 years and 11 years, respectively. The premature group had a mean maternal and paternal educational level of 11 years (see Table 1).

All of the subjects were Hispanic Americans of Mexican descent. The subjects from each group were also matched according to their dominant language. The dominant language was informally determined by asking the parents questions as to the languages spoken within the home. The questions consisted of determining the language spoken most often in the home and the language the parent felt the infant comprehended and produced best within the home setting. Three subjects each from the premature and full-term group had Spanish as the dominant language. Six subjects from each group had English as the dominant language, and three subjects from each group were exposed to both English and Spanish but a dominant language was not established (see Table 1).

Procedures

The subjects were scheduled for a complete language evaluation at the University of Texas-Pan American Speech and Hearing

Table 1. Sample Characteristics of the Premature and Full-term Hispanic Infants

Characteristics		Premature	Full-Term
Socioeconomic status	Class II	1	1
	Class III	0	1
	Class IV	4	3
	Class V	7	7
Gender	Male	8	5
	Female	4	7
Birthweight	Mean	1676 grams	3314 grams
Gestational age	Mean	31.6 weeks	39.8 weeks
Dominant language	Spanish	3	3
	English	6	6
	English & Spanish	3	3
Maternal age	Mean	29 years	22 years
Maternal educational level	Mean	11 years	12 years
Paternal educational level	Mean	11 years	11 years
Marital status of parents	Single	1	6
	Married	11	6

Center. Each infant was scheduled to be evaluated at plus or minus 20 days of his or her birthday. The premature infants were evaluated at 22 months corrected chronological age and the full-term infants at 22 months chronological age.

The parents signed consent forms and completed case history questionnaires before any testing was initiated. After completion of the case history forms, the information was reviewed and discussed with the parents for further clarification and elaboration. The infants were scheduled for 2-hour sessions. If testing was not completed and/or a representative language sample was not obtained within that time frame, then the infant was rescheduled later that same week for completion of the assessment. The infants were evaluated in unfurnished therapy rooms, and the only materials present were age-appropriate toys, a cassette recorder, and testing items. The child-size furniture was removed from the therapy rooms so that the infant and the examiners could sit on the floor. This allowed for a more unstructured assessment. The parents/caregivers were always encouraged to be present during all aspects of the speech and language evaluation, and they were given the option of sitting on the floor or on a chair. They were an integral part of the evaluation process, as they were required to respond to some of the test items. They were also asked to provide additional information about their infant's receptive and expressive language skills within the home setting as opposed to the therapeutic setting. Parents were also asked if the language sample obtained was representative of the infant's utterances in a more naturalistic setting.

The speech and language evaluations were administered by groups of two graduate speech-language pathology student clinicians under the supervision of certified speech-language pathologists. Participation in the study was not allowed until the student clinicians demonstrated proficiency in administering the Sequenced Inventory of Communication Development-Revised (SICD-R) (Hedrick, Prather, & Tobin, 1975). Proficiency was determined by having the students administer the test to the certified speech-language pathologist. The student clinicians then had to administer the test to each other while one role-played the examiner and the other role-played an infant. Only bilingual student clinicians were assigned to evaluate bilingual and monolingual Spanish-speaking infants. The graduate clinicians were assigned to each evaluation in groups of two as recommended by the test. This allowed for the minimization of scoring difficulties of the SICD-R. The supervisor also reviewed the SICD-R scores.

Before the evaluations were begun, parental approval for videotaping of the sessions was obtained. The video cameras were mounted on the wall to minimize distractions. The student clinicians established rapport with the infant before engaging in any testing. When it was deemed that rapport had been established, the student clinicians collected a spontaneous language sample. The student clinicians engaged in play with the child for approximately 20 to 30 minutes to obtain the language samples. At times, only a limited number of utterances were obtained, as some of the infants had a very limited vocabulary. Attempts were always made to collect 50 utterances from each child whenever possible. The analysis of the spontaneous language sample yielded a Mean Length of Response which was one output measure used to score the expressive portion of the SICD-R. Each evaluation was also audio recorded for later transcription. The second clinician transcribed what was said during the evaluation to guard against loss of information from the audio recording. After the spontaneous language sample was obtained, the receptive and expressive components of the SICD-R were administered to obtain Receptive and Expressive Communication Ages on each infant.

Adaptations of the SICD-R were necessary to minimize cultural biases toward infants from a population who exhibited linguistic and cultural diversity. One adaptation employed was the use of the Spanish translation of the SICD-R. The Spanish translation was used with bilingual infants and monolingual Spanish speakers. According to Hedrick et al. (1975), the Spanish translation of the SICD-R has not been standardized with Spanish-speaking subjects. The Spanish lexicon used by the Hispanic individuals from the Rio Grande Valley, Texas, varied from the Spanish translation proposed by the SICD-R. Spanish lexicon appropriate to the population was used instead. The supervisors and the majority of the student clinicians evaluating the infants were bilingual and native to the area so that adaptation of the Spanish translation did not pose a problem. The parents were asked to verify whether the Spanish lexicon used with their infant during testing was familiar to the infant. If the parent reported the use of other Spanish lexicons, then those terms were used for that particular infant. These adaptations were employed so as not to penalize monolingual Spanish-speaking or bilingual infants. Informal observations, parental report, and the spontaneous language sample were used to assist the supervisors and the student clinicians in determining the validity of the SICD-R results. In cases where a dominant language was not established, all of the test items were presented in Spanish and then English to give the infant every opportunity to respond. The SICD-R was administered in English to infants whose dominant language was English.

An oral motor mechanism examination of each infant was attempted during each evaluation. At times the examination was cursory due to noncompliance of the infant. All of the oral motor mechanism examinations revealed structures adequate for speech production. Parental report revealed that 7 of 9 full-term and 5 of 11 premature infants had a prior history of middle ear infections. Information was not available on the remaining 4 subjects. Most of the subjects could not tolerate headphones so sound field hearing screenings were performed when possible. Appropriate referrals were made when a hearing screening was failed for any reason. Of the 12 premature infants, 4 had received audiological evaluations, and hearing was reported to be within normal limits. Hearing screenings were performed on the remaining 8 premature infants. The screenings were performed by the graduate student clinicians supervised by certified speech-language pathologists. Because these infants had never received an audiological evaluation, the supervisors were very cautious in interpreting hearing screening results. All of the remaining 8 subjects passed a hearing screening. Of the 12 full-term infants, 6 passed a hearing screening. Two of the infants failed the screening and were referred for an audiological evaluation. Hearing screenings on 4 of the full-term infants were not completed due to an inability to condition the infants; they were referred for audiological evaluations. Informal observation and speech-language testing revealed that the 6 infants who failed the hearing screening exhibited normal speech and language development, with the exception of one. The full-term infant who did exhibit a delay had normal receptive language skills with a mild to moderate expressive language delay.

Results

A one-way multivariate analysis of variance (MANOVA) was performed on the data to determine if a significant difference existed between the premature and full-term infants on language comprehension and production. Receptive Communication Age, Expressive Communication Age, and Mean Length of Response were the three outcome measures compared between groups. A significant difference ($p = .0123$) was found between the premature and full-term groups on the language comprehension outcome measure. The full-term group scored a mean of 24 months, with a standard deviation of 3.814 (see Table 2), whereas the premature group scored a mean of 20.333 months, with a standard deviation of 2.674. A significant difference ($p = .0007$) was also found between both groups on the expressive outcome measure of the SICD-R. The full-term group scored a mean of 23 months, with a standard deviation of 3.015; the premature group scored a mean of 19 months, with a standard deviation of 1.809 (see Figure 1).

A one-way analysis of variance (ANOVA) was performed on the Mean Length of Response even though this outcome measure was used in scoring the expressive component of the SICD-R. Since Mean Length of Response data were not obtained on 7 of

Table 2. Means and Standard Deviations of Receptive Language Age, Expressive Language Age, and Mean Length of Response for the Premature and Full-Term Infants

Subjects	Receptive Language Age		Expressive Language Age		Mean Length of Response	
	M	SD	M	SD	M	SD
Full-term infants	24 months	3.814	23 months	3.015	1.309 words	.773
Premature infants	20.333 months	2.674	19 months	1.809	.412 words	.250

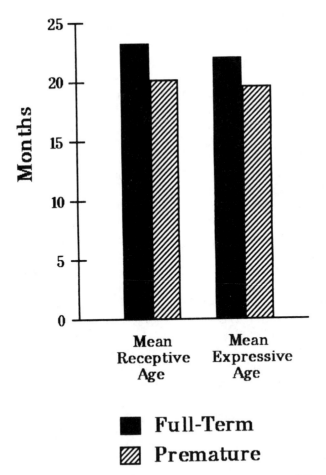

Figure 1. Mean receptive and expressive communication ages of the full-term ($n = 12$) and premature ($n = 12$) Hispanic infants.

the subjects, this analysis was performed on only 17 (11 full-term, 6 premature) subjects. A significant difference ($p = .0154$) was found between both groups (see Figure 2). The standard deviation of the full-term group was .773 and .250 for the premature group. The results of the expressive component of the SICD-R were further substantiated by the Mean Length of Response. The full-term group had an average Mean Length of Response of 1.309 words, whereas the premature group had an average Mean Length of Response of .412 words (see Table 2). The speech-language pathologists relied more heavily on the spontaneous language samples and parental reports than the results of the SICD-R to determine if an expressive language delay existed. Determining whether a language delay existed was based on chronological age and not corrected age. Since the SICD-R was adapted, the scores were rendered invalid. Therefore, the speech pathologists relied on a combination of information obtained from formal testing,

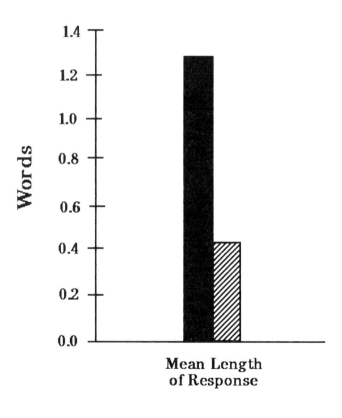

Figure 2. Average mean length of response of the full-term ($n = 11$) and premature ($n = 6$) Hispanic infants.

informal testing, spontaneous language samples, and parental report to determine the presence of a language delay.

Discussion

The present study suggests that premature Hispanic infants acquire language at a slower rate than full-term Hispanic infants. This study revealed significant differences between the Receptive and Expressive Communication Ages of the premature versus the full-term Hispanic infants. The receptive language scores were slightly higher than the expressive language scores in both groups. All of the full-term infants had normal receptive language abilities, whereas 7 of the premature subjects had receptive language abilities within normal limits. Only 5 of the premature infants exhibited mild receptive language delays. If an infant appeared to exhibit an overall receptive and/or expressive language delay of approximately 4 to 6 months on all the formal and informal testing obtained, the delay was considered to be mild. Delays of greater than 6 months were considered to be moderate.

Eleven of the full-term infants exhibited normal expressive abilities while only 1 exhibited a mild to moderate expressive language delay. Only 3 of the premature subjects exhibited normal expressive skills, whereas 8 exhibited mild expressive delays, and 1 exhibited a mild to moderate expressive language delay (see Table 3). As can be seen, expressive language skills appeared to be more delayed than receptive language skills.

The assessments of the premature infants revealed less frequent vocalizations as noted by the spontaneous language samples obtained during the evaluation sessions. In general, the full-term infants appeared to initiate social interactions on a more frequent basis than the premature infants. Some of the premature Hispanic infants were capable of imitating sounds and words, but as a group they had greater difficulty with spontaneous utterances. It was consistently observed that the premature group had a smaller expressive lexicon than the full-term group. The parents of the premature subjects consistently indicated limited single-word usage within the home setting. Six of the 12 parents reported that their premature infants had expressive vocabularies of 15 words or less within the home setting. Three parents indicated that their infants used 20 to 30 single words, whereas another 3 parents stated the emergence of two-word utterances in their premature infants. These findings were in direct contrast to what the parents of the full-term infants reported. Eleven of the parents indicated that their full-term infants were demonstrating the emergence of or use of two- and three-word utterances. Only one parent of a full-term infant

Table 3. Number of Full-term and Premature Hispanic Infants Exhibiting Language Delays

Receptive/Expressive Diagnoses	Full-Term	Premature
Normal receptive language skills	12	7
Mild receptive language delay	0	5
Normal expressive language skills	11	3
Mild expressive language delay	0	8
Mild/moderate expressive language delay	1	1

reported that the infant had an expressive lexicon of only 25 words.

Research by Jackson-Maldonado, Thal, Marchman, Bates, and Gutierrez-Clellen (1993) revealed that Spanish-speaking full-term infants develop vocabulary comprehension and production like English-speaking children. Both receptive and expressive skills develop in a linear fashion across age, with receptive skills advancing more rapidly than expressive skills. The findings of this study demonstrated that the premature infants appeared to be following the same linear pattern, as their expressive language skills were more delayed than their receptive skills.

Jackson-Maldonado et al. (1993) also found that Spanish-speaking toddlers whose expressive vocabulary consisted of less than 72 words were more likely to use single utterances comprised of common nouns with fewer predicates and closed class items such as pronouns, questions, locatives, and quantifiers. After informally analyzing the spontaneous language samples of the premature infants, it was found that nine of the subjects had expressive vocabularies of less than 30 words. The spontaneous language samples and parental reports revealed that the types of single words uttered by the infants also consisted primarily of common nouns. The majority of the communication intents exhibited by the premature infants consisted of comments.

Although the sample size was limited, these findings allow more insight into the knowledge of language development in premature Mexican-American infants up to 22 months corrected age (24 months chronological age). The majority of the previous studies investigating cognitive and language development in premature infants limited their research to English-speaking white American infants (Crnic et al., 1983; Siegel, 1982). The present study lends support to the suggestion that premature Hispanic infants, like premature white (of non-Hispanic origin) American infants, acquire language at a slower rate than full-term infants.

Six of the full-term infants who came from single-parent households in the present study were recruited from a community program that provided daycare for the infants so the parent could continue attending school. Attendance at the daycare facility may account for additional language stimulation, which may have impacted on their overall linguistic achievement when tested.

Since the majority of the subjects from the present study were from the lower socioeconomic strata, further research is warranted to determine how much of an impact social/environmental factors have on the language development of Hispanic infants. It is important to establish whether these factors have a more negative impact on infants when coupled with prematurity as indicated by Siegel (1982) or whether the biological factors alone are more predictive of outcome as hypothesized by Cohen et al. (1986).

The implications of these findings are far-reaching, as this study revealed that at 22 months corrected age the majority of these premature Mexican-American infants still had not attained age-appropriate language development. Ungerer and Sigman (1983) reported that any differences between language skills of premature versus full-term infants may still be present at 22 months, but will not be maintained by the end of the third year. Continued testing of premature Hispanic infants at ages 3 and 4 is warranted to determine if Hispanic infants also overcome linguistic delays by age 3. Early childhood interventionists realize the importance of intervening as early as possible and, until further research is available to demonstrate that premature Hispanic infants do overcome linguistic delays by age 3, it is recommended that intervention be instituted with these "at risk" infants as soon as they are dismissed from the neonatal intensive care unit. A family-centered approach is strongly recommended, and any intervention, parent training, and/or home programs should be sensitive to individual family linguistic, cultural, and socioeconomic needs.

Some form of intervention, whether direct intervention (especially with low birthweight premature infants) or regular follow-up, is recommended, as linguistic delays, if continued beyond ages 3 and 4, may negatively affect later developmental processes and academic learning (Bishop & Adams, 1990; Scarborough, 1991).

Acknowledgments

The research reported here was supported by the NIGMS MBRS Grant S06GM08038-22. The investigators thank Teri Mata-Pistokache and Dr. Barbara Johnson for their assistance in data collection. Sincere gratitude is extended to the Psychology students and the Speech-Language Pathology graduate student clinicians who participated in the study and assisted in the collection of the data.

References

Bishop, D. V. M., & Adams, C. (1990). A prospective study of the relationship between specific language impairment, phonological disorders and reading retardation. *Journal of Child Psychology and Psychiatry, 32*(7), 1027–1050.

Casiro, O. G., Moddemann, D. M., Stanwick, R. S., Pannikkar-Thiessen, V. K., Cowan, H., & Cheang, M. S. (1990). Language development of very low birth weight infants and full-term controls at 12 months of age. *Early Human Development, 24*, 65–77.

Cohen, S. E., Parmelee, A. H., Beckwith, L., & Sigman, M. (1986). Cognitive development in preterm infants: Birth to 8 years. *Developmental and Behavioral Pediatrics, 7*(2), 102–110.

Crnic, K. A., Ragozin, A. S., Greenberg, M. T., Robinson, N. M., & Basham, R. B.(1983). Social interaction and developmental competence of preterm and full-term infants during the first year of life. *Child Development, 54*, 1199–1210.

Escalona, S. K. (1982). Babies at double hazard: Early development of infants at biologic and social risk. *Pediatrics, 70*(5), 670–676.

Forslund, M., & Bjerre, I. (1990). Follow-up of preterm children: II. Growth and development at four years of age. *Early Human Development, 24*, 107–118.

Grunau, R. V. E., Kearney, S. M., & Whitfield, M. F. (1990). Language development at 3 years in pre-term children of birthweight below 1000g. *British Journal of Disorders of Communication, 25*, 173–182.

Hedrick, D., Prather, E., & Tobin, A. (1975). *Sequenced inventory of communication development*. Seattle: University of Washington Press.

Hollingshead, A. B. (1957). *Two factor index of social position*. New Haven, CT: Author.

Hubatch, L. M., Johnson, C. J., Kistler, D. J., Burns, W. J., & Moneka, W. (1985). Early language abilities of high-risk infants. *Journal of Speech and Hearing Disorders, 50*, 195–207.

Jackson-Maldonado, D., Thal, D., Marchman, V., Bates, E., & Gutierrez-Clellan, V. (1993). Early lexical development in spanish-speaking infants and toddlers. *Journal of Child Language, 20*, 523–549.

Kenworthy, O. T., Bess, F. H., Stahlman, M. T., & Lindstrom, D. P. (1987). Hearing, speech, and language outcome in infants with extreme immaturity. *The American Journal of Otology, 8*(5), 419–425.

McAllister, L., Masel, C., Tudehope, D., O'Callaghan, M., Mohay, H., & Rogers, Y. (1993). Speech and language outcomes 3 years after neonatal intensive care. *European Journal of Disorders of Communication, 28*, 369–382.

Menyuk, P., Liebergott, J., Schultz, M., Chesnick, M., & Ferrier, L. (1991). Patterns of early lexical and cognitive development in premature and full-term infants. *Journal of Speech and Hearing Research, 34*, 88–94.

Pena, I. C., Teberg, A. J., & Hoppenbrouwers, T. (1987). The Gesell developmental schedule in Hispanic low-birth weight infants during the first year of life. *Infant Behavior and Development, 10*, 199–216.

Resnick, M. B., Roth, J., Ariet, M., Carter, R. L., Emerson, J. C., Hendrickson, J. M., Packer, A. B., Larsen, J. J., Wolking, W. D., Lucas, M., Schenck, B. J., Fearnside, B., & Bucciarelli, R. L. (1992). Educational outcome of neonatal intensive care graduates. *Pediatrics, 89*(3), 373–378.

Scarborough, H. S. (1991). Early syntactic development of dyslexic children. Annals of *Dyslexia. 41*, 207–218.

Siegel, L. S. (1982). Reproductive, perinatal, and environmental factors as predictors of the cognitive and language development of preterm and full-term infants. *Child Development, 53*, 963–973.

Wright, N. E., Thislethwaite, D., Elton, R. A., Wilkinson, E. M., & Forfar, J. O. (1983). The speech and language development of low birth weight infants. *British Journal of Disorders of Communication, 18*(3), 187–196.

Ungerer, J. A., & Sigman, M. (1983). Developmental lags in preterm infants from one to three years of age. *Child Development, 54*, 1217–1228.

Address correspondence to:
Donald Fucci, Ph.D.
School of Hearing & Speech Sciences
Lindley Hall 219
Ohio University
Athens, OH 45701

Differences in the Early Social Interaction Between Jaundiced Neonates Treated with Phototherapy and Their Nonjaundiced Counterparts

Shahrokh M. Shafaie, Ph.D.
Southeast Missouri State University
Cape Girardeau, Missouri

Patricia A. Self, Ph.D.
Oklahoma State University
Stillwater, Oklahoma

Previous work on jaundiced infants suggests that hyperbilirubinemia may affect neonatal performance on neurobehavioral assessments (e.g., the Brazelton Neonatal Behavioral Assessment Scale). However, it is not known whether elevated bilirubin during the early days of life disturbs the social interaction of neonates and their responsiveness toward their mothers. The present study explored the patterns of the early social interaction of full-term jaundiced and nonjaundiced neonates with their mothers during the first few days after birth. Significant differences were found between the jaundiced and nonjaundiced neonates' behaviors across observations and according to their health status. Jaundiced neonates terminated ongoing visual contact with their mothers more frequently, had shorter eye contact with them, were irritable more frequently, and ended their tactile interactions with their mothers more often than nonjaundiced neonates. These findings indicate that jaundiced neonates, treated with phototherapy, behave differently from their nonjaundiced counterparts in early interaction with their mothers.

One of the common illnesses among neonates is hyperbilirubinemia or neonatal jaundice. It is a well-recognized complication that might be experienced by many full-term and preterm neonates during the first few days after birth (Maisels, 1975). The neurotoxic effects of hyperbilirubinemia have been documented, and the relationship between a high bilirubin concentration and the risk of brain damage in neonates has been stressed by many investigators (e.g., Brodersen, 1980; Johnson & Boggs, 1974; Levine, Fredericks, & Rapoport, 1982; Maisels, 1987).

Several studies have investigated the correlation between the maximum neonatal serum bilirubin concentration and infants' performance in the neurological, developmental, and mental examinations (Boggs, Hardy, & Frazier, 1967; Crichton, Dunn, & McBurney, 1972; Hodgman, 1976; Lenhardt, 1983; Naeye, 1978; Odell, Storey, & Rosenberg, 1970; Rubin, Balow, & Fisch, 1979). The results of these long-term and short-term longitudinal studies examining the behavioral sequela of perinatal and early childhood conditions of jaundiced infants suggest that a high level of serum bilirubin concentration during the neonatal period is related to a neurological abnormality, a developmental deficit, and a delayed mental performance of infants at least during the first year of their lives. With regard to the effects of hyperbilirubinemia during the later years of the affected subjects' lives, findings from the longer follow-up studies are not consistent.

Jaundiced neonates have been studied from neurobehavioral perspectives by several investigators. In a study by Telzrow, Snyder, Tronicks, Als, and Brazelton (1980), the Brazelton Neonatal Behavioral Assessment Scale (BNBAS) was administered to jaundiced and nonjaundiced newborns before the phototherapy treatment, during the treatment (days 3–6), and on the 10th day of the infants' lives. The results revealed that the jaundiced infants who had been treated with phototherapy scored lower than nonjaundiced infants on state control/interaction dimensions of the BNBAS. Differences between jaundiced and nonjaundiced infants were also found on the orienting items (response to specific animate and inanimate visual and auditory stimuli; e.g., a visual following of the face, etc.) of the BNBAS. These differences were noted at the onset of the treatment (phototherapy) and were evident throughout the study. However, the differences were greater during the treatment period (phototherapy and separation from the mother): Jaundiced infants scored lower than their nonjaundiced counterparts on most of the items such as alertness, muscle tone, pull-to-sit, and cuddliness. Jaundiced infants also had lower scores on orienting items and self-quieting three days after the treatment.

In another study, Paludetto, Mansi, Rinaldi, Curtis, and Ciccimarra (1983) replicated the Telzrow et al.'s (1980) study using a larger sample and making sure that the testers were blind to the infants' health conditions (treated vs. comparison subjects). Paludetto et al. (1983) also included in their sample a group of neonates who were clinically jaundiced but were not treated with phototherapy due to a lower serum bilirubin concentration than that of the treatment group. The BNBAS was administered to all the subjects on the 3rd, 4th, and 30th days after birth. The results were consistent with Telzrow et al.'s (1980) findings, revealing higher scores for the jaundiced-treated group in the orientation cluster (visual and auditory orientation to animate and inanimate stimuli), the motor performance cluster (pull-to-sit), and the regulation of state cluster (cuddliness, alertness). The jaundiced infants who were treated with phototherapy showed a significantly poorer performance in these clusters on the 4th day and continued to score lower in the orientation items on the BNBAS than their jaundiced-but-not-treated peers and their healthy counterparts. This suggests that in addition to the elevated bilirubin, phototherapy treatment may contribute to the poor performance of jaundiced babies on the BNBAS.

In a similar study by Nelson and Horowitz (1982) the BNBAS-K was administered immediately preceding treatment, immediately following treatment, and at the end of 2 weeks. Item-by-item analysis of BNBAS-K revealed that the infants in the jaundiced group were more irritable, showed less state control, were less responsive to the tester and to other animate stimuli, and performed poorer than nonjaundiced infants on orienting items of BNBAS. Based on these behavioral differences between the two groups obtained under experimental conditions, Nelson and Horowitz have speculated that treated jaundiced infants may tend to behave in the same fashion during early interaction with their mothers.

In summary, the results of these short-term longitudinal studies have consistently revealed detailed sets of behavioral deficits of photo-treated jaundiced infants during the first few weeks after birth as assessed by measures such as the BNBAS. Overall, under experimental conditions, jaundiced infants have shown a poorer ability to orient animate and inanimate visual and auditory stimuli, have been less responsive to the tester(s), have been more irritable, have shown poorer state control (greater sleepiness), and low alertness and self-quieting ability and cuddliness, and, finally, have shown poorer motor performance (muscle tone and pull-to-sit) than their nonjaundiced peers. Considering these neurobehavioral changes in jaundiced infants, it has been speculated (e.g., Nelson & Horowitz, 1982) that jaundiced infants might be less responsive and less reinforcing to their caregivers in a natural social setting than nonjaundiced infants and, therefore, their early interaction with their mothers may characterize the social interactive deficits which have been assessed by BNBAS in previous studies.

Since there has been no systematic study of this topic, the present study investigated this speculation by examining the early interaction of neonates with their mothers before they develop jaundice or require phototherapy, during the phototherapy treatment, and after the termination of phototherapy.

Method

Subjects

Forty mothers and their newborns were the subjects of this study. The criteria for the selection of the mothers were as follows: (1) a vaginal delivery of the baby and a lack of complications during pregnancy and delivery, (2) a primiparous first-time mother, (3) a normal, healthy, and full-term infant as assessed by the pediatrician, and (4) the mother's plan to bottle-feed her infant. Because some pediatricians tend to encourage mothers to terminate breastfeeding when neonates develop jaundice, the fourth criterion was included to ascertain that the feeding procedure was consistent across our groups. A total of 73 mothers who met the criteria were approached and were told that the purpose of this study was to describe early mother-infant interaction. Forty-nine mothers agreed to participate in the study; however, data could not be completed on 9 subjects due to various medical and technical problems. Specifically, 3 dyads were lost because neonates developed further medical complications; 2 mothers withdrew their consent and refused to continue their participation in the study due to their concern for their jaundiced infants; and the remaining 4 subjects were lost because their early discharge from the hospital did not allow the experimenters to complete the last phase of the data collection. As a result, the final sample consisted of 40 infants (20 jaundiced and 20 nonjaundiced) and their mothers. The infants of each sex were evenly distributed between jaundiced and nonjaundiced groups.

The mothers ranged in age from 19 to 28 years ($M = 21.6$) with an average of 11.9 years of education (range 9–16 years). Fifteen of the mothers were black (7 in the jaundiced group and 8 in the nonjaundiced group), and 25 mothers were Caucasian. None of the mothers had any major medical complications during pregnancy, delivery, or in the immediate postpartum period. There were no significant group differences among the mothers of jaundiced and nonjaundiced infants with respect to race, age, and education.

The major criteria for the selection of the infants were: (1) a birth weight of over 3000 grams, (2) a gestational age between 39 and 41 weeks, (3) APGAR scores over 6 at 1 minute and over 8 at 5 minutes, and (4) a lack of identifiable abnormalities and/or postnatal complications other than hyperbilirubinemia, that is, not caused by ABO or Rh incompatibility.

Given these criteria, all of the neonates in this study were full-term, vaginally delivered, and healthy, with no postnatal complications at the onset of the study, except those who developed jaundice later. The demographic characteristics are listed in Table 1. The description of the subjects' assignments to each group is presented in the procedure section.

Procedure

The setting for the data collection was a two-bed or a one-bed hospital room on the postpartum unit. Each newborn was brought to his or her mother's room from the newborn nursery for each data collection session. The general directions to the mothers were: "We'd like you to interact and play with your baby in your natural way, just like when you are alone together. Try to hold your baby in a position in which she or he can see your face if he or she wishes, and do not worry if your baby cries." No other specific instructions were given to the mothers regarding the nature of the interaction.

The infants' interaction with their mothers was observed and videotaped during three time periods, and the first 5 minutes of the videotaped interaction were used for data analysis; no written notations were made during the videotaping.

The first observation (Session 1) for all babies was conducted during the first 24 hours after birth. Obviously, at this point it was not known to us which baby would develop clinical jaundice. The medical staff monitored changes in the bilirubin concentration of all neonates, and routine blood tests were carried out by taking a blood sample from one of the babies' heels. As some of the healthy babies developed a medium or a high level of hyperbilirubinemia after the first observation (Session 1) and required phototherapy

Table 1. Demographic Data for the Jaundice and Nonjaundice Groups

Health Status	Gestational Age in Weeks		Weight in Grams		APGAR Scores at 5 Minutes		Race	
	Mean	Range	Mean	Range	Mean	Range	Black	Caucasian
Jaundice ($n = 20$)	40	39–40	3410	3080–4500	8.9	8–10	7	13
Nonjaundice ($n = 20$)	40	39–41	3434	3010–4060	8.9	8–10	8	12

treatment, they were assigned to the jaundice group; otherwise they remained in our "nonjaundice" or "control" group. It is important to note that the assignment of the subjects to the "jaundice" group was determined only by a clinical "need" for phototherapy, based on the specific medical criterion used by the incharge physicians and the medical staff at the hospital. As a rule of thumb, the general criterion to initiate phototherapy treatment for physiologic jaundice among full-term newborns is a serum bilirubin concentration of 7–8 mg/100 ml during the first 24 hours after birth, a rise of more than 5 mg/100 ml in 24 hours, or a rise in the bilirubin level to 12 mg/100 ml any time after birth (Kivlahan & James, 1984).

The second observation (Session 2) of the jaundiced babies' interaction with their mothers was completed when the phototherapy treatment had begun for several hours, whereas the healthy babies' second observation was made sometime during the second day after birth. The final observation (Session 3) of jaundiced dyads was conducted after the termination of the phototherapy treatment and on the day the jaundiced infants were discharged. The last observation of the healthy infants was completed before they were discharged from the hospital, too.

According to the hospital policy, all jaundiced infants received phototherapy treatment in a neonatal special-care nursery. Mothers were permitted unlimited visiting privileges, but they were encouraged not to interrupt the phototherapy treatment by removing the jaundiced babies from the incubator. Jaundiced babies could be held by mothers or staff during the feeding time; however, after feeding and a visiting period, infants had to be returned to the special care nursery to continue their phototherapy treatment.

Measures

Infants' behavioral measures were obtained from the videotaped observations of the infants' interaction with their mothers on the three observation sessions during the first few days after birth. Each 5-minute videotape was scored through a version of the microanalytic techniques developed by DeMeis, Francis, Arco, and Self (1985), which provide multiple measures of neonatal behavior in visual, vocal, and tactile modalities. These behavioral categories are described in the Appendix at the end of this article. The frequency and duration of the infants' behaviors were scored by trained coders for the individual behavior of the infants within each modality. All scoring was done anonymously, using subject code numbers, and the coders were not aware of the subjects' health status (jaundiced vs. nonjaundiced). The Observational System Event Recorder, Model OS3, was used for a continuous scoring of neonatal behavioral changes. This Event Recorder not only permits a rapid, continuous scoring of interaction and events but also provides raw data and summary statistics for the duration and frequency of each target behavior.

Infants' behaviors were scored by independent coders, and the agreement/disagreement method was used to evaluate the interceder reliability. For the duration of neonatal behavioral measures, the reliability of the observers was computed by dividing the total number of seconds of agreement by the number of seconds of agreement plus disagreement. To compute the observers reliability for the frequency of behavioral measures, the lesser frequency of occurrence of a behavior noted by some observers was divided by the frequency of occurrence noted by the other observers. The average reliability for infants' behaviors in visual, vocal, and tactile modalities was .89, .96, .87, respectively.

The duration and frequency measures were used as dependent variables in a series of multivariate, repeated measure analyses of variance to examine possible significant differences in infants' behaviors as a function of neonatal jaundice. Further description of these analyses is presented in the results section.

Results

The first step of analyses for behavioral measures included tests of gender differences in neonatal behavior. Six multivariate repeated measure analyses of variance, Session (3 Levels) by Health Status (2 Levels) by Gender (2 Levels) were performed to examine the effects of infant gender on neonatal visual, vocal, and tactile behavior. These analyses were conducted within each modality separately, and dependent variables in each of these independent analyses were the frequency and duration of neonatal behaviors described in behavioral categories. Since analyses of duration and frequency measures showed no gender differences, gender was not included in the subsequent analyses.

To test for differences in neonates' behavior across sessions (three observations) and according to their health status, a series of Session-by-Health status (3 × 2) multivariate repeated measure analyses were conducted. Session can be defined as a within-subject variable, whereas health status is a between-subject variable. There were three independent analyses for each modality (visual, vocal, and tactile), which will be presented in the following sections. All of the F statistics for the MANOVAs are according to Wilk's Lambda criterion.

Neonatal Visual Behavior

Two 3(session) × 2(health status) MANOVAs, one for the frequency and one for the duration measures, were computed.

Analysis of the frequency measures revealed a significant multivariate F for session $F(10, 56) = 3.91, p < 0.001$. The significant univariate Fs for session were: The frequency of visual TERMINATE $F(2, 81) = 3.93, p < 0.02$, the frequency of visual ON OTHER $F(2, 81) = 3.62, p < 0.03$, and the frequency of visual OTHER $F(2, 81) = 8.22, p < 0.006$.

Subsequent examination of the means (Table 2) and the results of post hoc comparisons of the means for these dependent variables revealed that the frequency of visual TERMINATE (ending an ongoing visual behavior with the mother) and visual OTHER behaviors (visual contact with something other than the mother) increased significantly in the jaundiced group during Session 2 (while phototherapy was used) and Session 3 (after therapy was completed). Although the frequency of visual ON OTHER behavior (visual engagement — though not face to face — with the mother) declined in neonates who experienced jaundice, this decline was not statistically significant.

Findings from the analysis of duration measures of visual behavior revealed a significant multivariate F due to Session, $F(8, 56) = 7.22, p < 0.001$ for the duration of visual MONITOR $F(2, 81) = 24.21, p < 0.001$ and the duration of visual OTHER $F(2, 81) = 26.78, p < 0.001$.

The means of duration measures representing neonatal visual behavior were compared, and it was found that during Sessions 2 and 3 jaundiced neonates had significantly shorter visual eye contact with their mothers than with anything else in the hospital room.

Also, the multivariate F for the Health Status factor was significant, $F(4, 9) = 7.88, p < 0.006$, and it influenced three dependent measures: The duration of visual MONITOR $F(1, 12) = 16.36, p < 0.002$, the duration of visual ON OTHER $F(1,12) = 5.29, p < 0.04$, and the duration of visual OTHER $F(1, 12) = 29.91, p < 0.001$.

Examination of the means (Table 3) showed that neonates in the jaundiced group had less eye contact with their mothers than with anything else in the room compared to the infants in the nonjaundiced group.

Table 2. Means for the Frequency of Neonatal Visual Behaviors — Session Effect

Health Status	TERMINATE (M)	ON OTHER (M)	OTHER (M)
Jaundice (n = 20)			
Session 1	10.90	6.40	6.70
2	16.30	3.00	14.00
3	16.55	4.30	13.50
Nonjaundice (n = 20)			
Session 1	10.50	4.30	5.55
2	10.55	4.50	6.80
3	9.40	3.75	4.90

Terminate: Ending an ongoing visual contact with the mother's face. **On Other:** Visual engagement with the mother, excluding eye or face-to-face visual contact. **Other:** Visual contact with something other than the mother.

Table 3. Means for the Duration of Neonatal Visual Behaviors in Seconds — Health Status Effect

Health Status	MONITOR (M)	OTHER (M)	ON OTHER (M)
Jaundice (n = 20)			
Session 1	203.64	39.66	20.19
2	80.14	153.03	12.74
3	107.47	116.03	20.35
Nonjaundice (n = 20)			
Session 1	198.91	42.58	20.35
2	193.64	37.64	21.99
3	204.65	38.85	14.83

Monitor: Maintaining visual contact with the mother's eyes or face.

However, a significant multivariate F due to interaction of Session and Health Status was obtained, $F(8, 18) = 2.49, p < .05$, for the duration of visual MONITOR, $F(2, 12) = 8.41, p < .005$, and for the duration of visual OTHER behaviors, $F(2, 12) = 12.54, p < .001$.

Neonatal Vocal Behaviors

The frequency and duration of the neonatal vocal behaviors were used as dependent variables in two independent 3(session) × 2(health status) repeated measure MANOVAs. No main effect or interaction effects were found in these multivariate analyses. Further examination of the univariates for the dependent measures of neonatal vocal behaviors showed significant univariate Fs for the frequency, $F(1, 12) = 7.31), p < .01$, and the duration, $F(1,12) = 6.59, p < .02$, of neonates' vocal OTHER (e.g., irritability, crying, and fussiness) as a function of the infants' Health Status. The group means of this dependent variable (Table 4) suggested that neonates in the jaundiced group were irritable and fussy more frequently and for a longer duration than their nonjaundiced counterparts.

Neonatal Tactile Behaviors

The frequency and duration measures of neonates' tactile behaviors were analyzed using two independent multivariate 3(session) × 2(health status) analyses of variance repeated measures. The analysis of frequency measures revealed a marginally significant effect due to Health Status $F(4, 9) = 3.49, p < .056$. Further examinations of univariate Fs for the frequency measures of neonates' tactile behaviors indicated that the frequency of neonates' tactile TERMINATE, $F(1, 12) = 5.26, p < .04$, was influenced by neonates' Health Status. Examination of the means (Table 5) suggested that the average number of tactile TERMINATE (ending a tactile interaction with the mother) increased in the jaundiced group during Sessions 2 and 3.

The analysis MONAOVA of the duration measures of neonatal tactile behaviors did not reveal any significant effects due to session, health status, or the interaction of these variables.

In summary, the purpose of this study was to explore the behavior of neonates who experienced jaundice and were treated with phototherapy by observing their social interaction with their mothers. The interaction of 20 jaundiced neonates with their mothers as well as 20 healthy mother-neonate pairs were videotaped on three different occasions. The first data collection occurred prior to the diagnosis of jaundice; the second assessment

Table 4. Neonatal Behaviors: VOCAL OTHER Means of Frequency and Duration Measures*— Health Status Effect

| | Frequency | | | Duration (in sec) | | |
| | Session | | | Session | | |
Health Status	1	2	3	1	2	3
Jaundice (n = 20)	0.70	2.30	2.1	3.57	8.29	6.89
Nonjaundice (n = 20)	0.10	0.85	0.85	0.195	2.44	1.49

*Means of the duration measure in seconds. **Vocal other:** Infant's fussiness and crying.

Table 5. Neonatal Tactile Behaviors Means of Frequency Measure: TERMINATE — Health Status Effect

| | Session | | |
Health Status	1	2	3
Jaundice (n = 20)	3.1	4.90	6.20
Nonjaundice (n = 20)	3.05	2.65	5.55

Terminate: Ending and interrupting an ongoing tactile contact with the mother.

was within 24 hours after treatment had begun; and the final phase of the data collection took place on the last day before the infants were discharged from the hospital.

In the following section, our findings are discussed, and their practical implications for jaundiced infants' subsequent development are examined.

Discussion

Visual Behaviors

The most impressive differences between the jaundiced and nonjaundiced groups of infants were noticed in visual behavior. Specifically, subjects with jaundice were significantly less engaged visually with their mothers than the nonjaundiced subjects, terminated their ongoing visual contact with their mothers more frequently, had much shorter visual contact with their mothers, and spent more time looking at something other than their mothers in the room. Since no significant differences were revealed about Visual OFF behavior (infants' eyes closed, sleepiness), it was inferred that, overall, this sample of jaundiced neonates were alert but were visually disengaged from their mothers.

The changes in the jaundiced neonates' visual behavior were evident during the treatment (phototherapy) and were maintained even after the treatment was over although no significant differences were initially found between the jaundiced and nonjaundiced infants on day one, before jaundice was diagnosed. These significant changes in the neonates' visual interactive behavior on Sessions 2 and 3 suggested that hyperbilirubinemia, phototherapy, shielding the infants' eyes (e.g. babies' deprivation of visual experience during phototherapy), separation from the mother and maternal behavior, or a combination of these factors may have provoked these visual disengagement patterns in the jaundiced infants.

These findings regarding jaundiced neonates' visual behavior are consistent with the results of studies that have examined jaundiced neonates' performance from a neurobehavioral perspective. As the discussion of these studies has revealed, jaundiced infants score lower than their nonjaundiced counterparts on the state control/interaction dimensions of BNBAS, show lower responsiveness to visual stimuli (e.g., a visual following of the face), and have less frequent eye contact with the tester (Nelson & Horowitz, 1982; Telzrow et al., 1980). These investigators have speculated that jaundiced infants might exhibit the same pattern of low visual responsiveness in a natural interactive social setting. Our study has confirmed this notion for the first time.

On the basis of the literature with "at risk" infants, (Field, 1977, 1980a, 1980b; Goldberg, 1978) these patterns of low visual responsiveness in jaundiced neonates have significant clinical implications. For instance, the lack of proper eye contact with the mother and the low visual responsiveness of infants during the neonatal period have been associated with a poor bonding process and subsequent attachment disorders (Klaus & Kennell, 1976; Robson, 1967; Waters, Vaughn, & Egeland, 1980). Therefore, from "maternal-infant bonding" and "attachment" perspectives, the jaundiced infants' low visual engagement with the mother, along with the separation from her, places them at risk if their visual disengagement with the caregiver (e.g., mother) persists. Unfortunately, there is no empirical evidence regarding the long-term stability or changes in their social visual inattentiveness. However, under experimental conditions, it is known that jaundiced infants do maintain their low responsiveness to social and nonsocial visual stimuli up to the age of 6 weeks (Friedman, Waxler,

& Werthman, 1983). Whether this period of 6 weeks is long enough to disturb the early mother-neonate relationship and lead to future personality problems in the jaundiced infant needs to be investigated. Among the long-term follow-up studies of jaundiced infants, only one study has investigated their personality characteristics, and its findings support this concern (Stewart, Walker, & Savage, 1970). These researchers used the Junior Eysenck Personality Inventory to assess the personality of 150 children, ages 7 to 14 years, who had been jaundiced during the neonatal period. Their findings revealed that personality characteristics, such as minimal behavioral dysfunction and nervous tension, were evident in these children. Moreover, these personality traits were associated with the intensity of hyperbilirubinemia and the extent of its treatment during the neonatal period.

In the examination of the role of early mother-infant visual contact in the infant's subsequent development, other studies have indicated that it is associated with later language and communication development (e.g., Collis & Schaffer, 1975; Milenkovic & Uzgiris, 1979; Stern, Spieker, & Mackain, 1982). From this perspective, then, it can be reasoned that if jaundiced infants' low visual responsiveness to their mothers continues, their communication and linguistic skills might be delayed. The risk in this area is greater in the context of jaundiced neonates' low responsiveness to auditory stimuli. Indeed, the findings from other studies have reported an impaired auditory sensitivity and perception of children and infants who had jaundice during the neonatal period. For example, in a study by Nakamura, Skimabuku, and Negishi (1985) evidence of the impaired auditory nerve and the abnormal auditory brainstem responses was found in neonates with mild jaundice. Also, Lenhardt (1983) examined the immediate auditory memory of 100 6-year-old children who had been jaundiced as infants. Lenhardt's findings revealed that photo-treated jaundiced subjects scored significantly lower than their nontreated jaundiced counterparts, suggesting the long-term negative contribution of phototherapy to the process of short-term auditory memory even several years later. In addition, the 3-year follow-up report of children who had been jaundiced as infants revealed a relationship between total serum bilirubin concentration and difficulties in expressive and receptive language as well as abnormal speech production, hearing impairment, and visual-perceptual deficiencies (Naeye, 1978). Johnson and Boggs (1974) reported similar findings regarding the relationship between the intensity of neonatal jaundice and language difficulties displayed by many children at the age of four. The findings of these investigations point to the need for further study to focus on the communication and language development of infants and children who were jaundiced during the neonatal period and were treated with phototherapy.

The above speculations and concerns are proposed based on maternal-bonding, attachment, and communication-language literature and are conditional, assuming that jaundiced infants' low visual responsiveness and inadequate mutual visual contact with the caregiver and their poor responsiveness to social auditory stimuli persist. If such stability in jaundiced infants' visual inattentiveness becomes documented, it enhances the concerns for possible developmental complications for the jaundiced neonates in subsequent years after birth.

Vocal and Tactile Behaviors

The jaundiced infants in our sample were more often irritable and terminated tactile stimulations that were directed toward them more frequently than the nonjaundiced infants. It is possible that the high irritability of jaundiced infants may have contributed to their limited eye contact. The increase in the rate of tactile disengagement with the mother was more evident in Session 2 when they were receiving phototherapy. In conjunction with jaundiced neonates' visual disengagement behaviors toward their mothers, the pattern of tactile disengagement in these infants is an important finding that requires further discussion.

The jaundiced neonates in this sample tended to be less engaged tactilely and terminated maternal efforts to establish physical contact more frequently than nonjaundiced neonates. This finding is consistent with reports of neurobehavioral examinations of jaundiced infants in previous studies (e.g., Paludetto et al., 1983; Telzrow et al., 1980). These reports have characterized jaundiced infants as uncuddly, with poorer scores than their nonjaundiced counterparts on the BNBAS items measuring muscle tone, pull-to-sit, and tremulousness during the first few weeks of the infants' lives. Jaundiced neonates also displayed — according to Friedman et al. (1983) — quicker tactile habituation patterns than their nonjaundiced counterparts. It can be inferred that hyperbilirubinemia and/or phototherapy may introduce some changes in the neonates' sensory threshold that elicit oversensitivity to maternal tactile and vocal stimulations. Since it has been shown that infants with a poor muscle tone and motor maturity are handled by their mothers more often than normal children are (e.g., Brazelton, Tronick, Adamson, Als, & Wise 1975; Osofsky, 1976), the oversensitivity of jaundiced neonates to tactile stimulation may elicit more irritability and avoidance of tactile engagement with the mothers.

Moreover, since holding the infant firmly as well as talking to him or her generally tends to reduce crying and fussing (Hirshman, Meland, & Oliver, 1982), jaundiced infants who are characterized by irritability, uncuddliness, and low responsiveness to social and nonsocial auditory stimuli leave limited behavioral options for their mothers to use for their soothability. The possibility for the stability of such difficult temperamental qualities (e.g., undistractability, uncuddliness, and negative mood) suggests that taking care of a jaundiced infant might become a frustrating and disappointing experience. Given the negative relationship of these infants' temperamental attributes and later emotional behavioral problems (Chess & Thomas, 1977), we can speculate that if these negative temperamental characteristics of jaundiced neonates continue, both mother and infant will be at risk for a prolonged disturbed relationship, and other undesirable developmental outcomes may emerge thereafter.

In summary, this study is the first to report data about the early social interaction of full-term jaundiced babies with their mothers. Our findings from this naturalistic observational study are consistent with the reported results of previous studies which examined jaundiced neonates' performance on neurobehavioral assessments (e.g., the BNBAS) under experimental conditions. Our data have shown that jaundiced babies also behave differently from their nonjaundiced peers in their early interaction with their mothers and support the speculation that the jaundiced babies early interaction with their mothers characterizes the social interactive deficits which have been assessed by the BNBAS in previous studies.

It is important to note, however, that our results and conclusions should not be interpreted to mean that we are talking about the effects of jaundice per se. Although it appears that the observed changes in jaundiced infants' behaviors are influenced by the toxic effect of elevated bilirubin, its documented potential effects could be confounded with the impact of other factors. For example, as previous investigators have emphasized, the changes in infants' responses and behaviors after experiencing jaundice could be explained by the possible contribution of variables such as phototherapy, shielding the infants' eyes during treatment, prolonged separation from the mother at the hospital, the behavior of the mother who is encountering a lethargic and a low responsive baby after several hours of separation, or a combination of these factors along with jaundice.

Nevertheless, the implications of our findings could prove crucial in helping practitioners whose aim is to facilitate a more effective early interaction between mother and jaundiced infant and researchers who are interested in describing and charting the developmental course of jaundiced neonates during the subsequent months and years of life. Studies have shown that neonatal risk factors such as health complications may reduce the baby's responsiveness to the mother and hinder his or her ability to send proper readable signals to the caregiver (e.g., Divitto & Goldberg, 1980; Field, 1977, 1978, 1980b). In addition, neonatal risk factors (e.g., low birth weight, gestational age, medical problems) may elicit feelings of failure, depression, and incompetence in mothers and alter their perceptions of their infants (e.g., McGrath, Pucker, Boukydis, & Lester, 1988; Seashore, 1983). Such negative feelings might interfere with a mother's ability to interpret her baby's signals accurately and to be an effective, flexible, and responsive partner in dealing with the infant's disorganized rhythms (e.g., Brown & Bakeman, 1978; Field, 1977, 1978, 1980b, 1987).

While there is no empirical evidence in the literature as to the level of stress experienced by the parents of jaundiced neonates, especially in first-time mothers, there is consensus that considerable difficulties are present. For instance, Klaus (1974) has expressed his concern regarding the possible negative contributions of the use of eye patches during phototherapy, of hospital routines, and of early separation of baby from mother in the attachment process. According to Klaus (1974):

> There is a second patient that we all take care of, and this is the mother. Blue lights are extremely frightening and disturbing to the mother.... Blue bilirubin lights can be extremely upsetting since they make the infant appear dead. Mothers who have sick or pre-mature infants quickly believe the infants will die even with bilirubin lights and start anticipatory grief — the process of giving up the infant. (p. 186)

Frequently, health complications after birth (e.g., jaundice) require special treatment which may lead to separation of mother and newborn. This is another factor that can enhance mothers' concerns about their babies and influence their feelings as well as the quality of their relationships with their infants. Some mothers perceive separation as a punishment (Richards, 1978). According to Seashore (1981, 1983), separation after birth reduces the mother's opportunity to reassure herself about the infant's existence as well as a chance to establish a reciprocal relationship with the newborn. Mothers of jaundiced neonates lack this opportunity to be with their infants, since phototherapy requires separation of mothers and newborns for several days or weeks. The opportunity for physical contact is further reduced since breast milk may elevate bilirubin levels (e.g., Maisels, 1987).

The studies reviewed in this section are valuable by indicating the importance of early contact as a desirable facilitator of subsequent optimal mother-infant interactions and the role of the infant's postnatal health problems as risk factors for developing emotional bonds and interaction problems. Although no documented evidence is available about mothers' feelings or perceptions when their newborns develop jaundice, the above-mentioned studies suggest that mothers of jaundiced neonates may not experience positive feelings or perceptions when their babies become jaundiced. Therefore, it is important that practitioners and early interventionists monitor mothers' feelings and perceptions when their newborns develop jaundice and take necessary steps to promote mother-newborn interaction during treatment and after infants are dismissed from the hospital.

The findings of the present research have clearly demonstrated the impaired nature of jaundiced neonates' interactive behaviors. However, since these findings are limited to the neonatal period and no follow-up was provided for jaundiced infants after being dismissed from the hospital, the extent and possible stability of these behavioral deficits and their contribution to the jaundiced infants' subsequent development must be examined in future studies.

References

Boggs, T. R., Jr., Hardy, J. B., & Frazier, T. M. (1967). Correlation of neonatal serum total bilirubin concentrations and developmental status at age eight months. *Journal of Pediatrics, 71,* 533.

Brazelton, T. B., Tronick, E., Adamson, L., Als, H., & Wise, S. (1975). Early mother-infant reciprocity. In *Parent-infant interaction, The Ciba Foundation Symposium* (Vol. 33, p. 137). Amsterdam: Elsevier.

Brodersen, R. (1980). Bilirubin transport in the newborn infant, reviewed with relation to kernicterus. *The Journal of Pediatrics, 96*(3), 349-356.

Brown, J., & Bakeman, R. (1978). Relationships of human mothers with their infants during the first year of life. In R. W. Bell & W. P. Smotherman (Eds.), *Maternal influences and early behavior* (pp. 283-290). Holliswood, NY: Spectrum.

Chess, S., & Thomas, A. (1977). Differences in outcome with early intervention in children with behavior disorders. In M. Roff (Ed.), *Life history research in psychopathology* (Vol. II). Minneapolis: University of Minnesota Press.

Collis, G. M., & Schaffer, F. R. (1975). Synchronization of visual attention in mother-infant pairs. *Journal of Child Psychology and Psychiatry, 16,* 215-320.

Crichton, J. U., Dunn, H. G., & McBurney, A. K. (1972). Long term effects of neonatal jaundice on brain function in children of low birthweight. *Pediatrics, 49,* 656-670.

DeMeis, D. K., Francis, P. L., Arco, C. M. B., & Self, P. A. (1985). *Theoretical and methodological perspectives in early social interaction.* Unpublished manuscript.

Divitto, B., & Goldberg, S. (1980). The effects of newborn medical status on early parent-infant interaction. In T. Field, A. Sostek, S. Goldberg, & H. H. Shuman (Eds.), *Infants born at risk: Behavior and development* (pp. 352-361). Jamaica, NY: Spectrum Publications.

Field, T. M. (1977). Effects of early separation, interactive deficits, and experimental manipulations on infant-mother face-to-face interaction. *Child Development, 48,* 763-771.

Field, T. M. (1978). The three Rs of infant-adult interactions: Rhythms, repertoires, and responsivity. *Journal of Pediatric Psychology, 3,* 131-136.

Field, T. M. (1980a). Supplemental stimulation of preterm neonates. *Early Human Development, 413,* 301-314.

Field, T. M. (1980b). Interaction patterns of preterm and term infants. In T. Field, A. Sostek, S. Goldberg, & H. H. Shuman (Eds.), *Infants born at risk: Behavior and development* (pp. 561-573). Jamaica, NY: Spectrum.

Field, T. M. (1987). Affective and interactive disturbances in infants. In J. D. Osofsky, (Ed.), *Handbook of infant development* (pp. 972-1005). New York: Wiley & Sons.

Friedman, S. L., Waxler, M., & Werthman, M. W. (1983, July/August). *Physiologic jaundice as a predictor of sensory, neurological and affective function in low risk preterm infants.* Paper presented at the 7th Biennial Meeting of ISSBD, Munich, West Germany.

Goldberg, S. (1978). Prematurity: Effects on parent-infant interaction. *Journal of Pediatric Psychology, 3,* 137-144.

Hirshman, R., Meland, L., & Oliver, C. (1982). The psychophysiology of infancy. In B. Wolman (Ed.), *Handbook of developmental psychology* (pp. 230-241). Englewood Cliffs, NJ: Prentice-Hall.

Hodgman, J. E. (1976). Clinical application of phototherapy in neonatal jaundice. In D. Bergman & S. H. Blondheim (Eds.), *Bilirubin me-*

tabolism in the newborn (II) (pp. 3-10). New York: American Elsevier.

Johnson, L., & Boggs, T. R. (1974). Bilirubin-dependent brain damage: Incidence and indications for treatment. In G. B. Odell, R. Shcaffner, & A. P. Simopoulus (Eds.), *Phototherapy in the newborn: An overview* (pp. 122-149). Washington, DC: National Academy of Science.

Kivlahan, C., & James, E. J. P. (1984). The natural history of neonatal jaundice. *Pediatrics, 74*, 364-370.

Klaus, M. (1974). Important considerations in the clinical management of infants with hyperbilirubinemia. In G.B. Odell, R. Schaffer, & A. P. Simopoulos (Eds.), *Phototherapy in the newborn: An overview* (pp. 181-189). Washington, DC: National Academy of Sciences.

Klaus, M. H., & Kennell, J. H. (1976). *Maternal-infant bonding*. St. Louis: C. V. Mosby.

Lenhardt, M. L., (1983). Effects of neonatal hyperbilirubinemia on token test performance of six-year-old children. *The Journal of Auditory Research, 23*, 195-204.

Levine, R. L., Fredericks, A. B., & Rapoport, M. D. (1982). Entry of bilirubin into the brain due to opening of the blood-brain barrier. *Pediatric, 69*, 255-259.

Maisels, M. J. (1975). Neonatal jaundice. In G. B. Avery (Ed.), *Neonatology: Pathophysiology and management of the newborn* (pp. 782-795). Philadelphia: J. B. Lippincott.

Maisels, M. J. (1987). Neonatal jaundice. In G. B. Avery (Ed.), *Neonatology: Pathaphysiology and management of the newborn* (3rd ed., pp. 865-879). Philadelphia: J. B. Lippincott.

McGrath, M., Pucker, M., Boukydis, C. Z., & Lester, B. M. (1988). *Maternal self-esteem, maternal perception and infant risk status*. Paper presented at the 6th International Conference on Infant studies, Washington DC.

Milenkovic, M. F., & Uzgiris, I. C. (1979). The mother-infant communication system. In I. C. Uzgiris (Ed.), *Social interaction and communication during infancy* (pp. 441-456). San Francisco: Jossey-Bass.

Naeye, R. L. (1978). The role of congenital bacteria infections in low serum bilirubin brain damage. *Pediatrics, 62*, 497.

Nakamura, H. R., Shimabuku, R., & Negishi, H. (1985). Auditory nerve and brainstem responses in newborn infants with hyperbilirubinemia. *Pediatric Research, 18*(4), 337.

Nelson, C. A., & Horowitz, F. D. (1982). The short-term behavioral sequelae of neonatal jaundice treated with phototherapy. *Infants Behavior and Development, 5*, 165.

Odell, G. B., Storey, G., & Rosenberg, L. (1970). Studies in kernicterus, III. The saturation of serum proteins with bilirubin during neonatal life and its relationship to brain damage at five years. *Journal of Pediatrics, 76*, 12.

Osofsky, J. D. (1976). Neonatal characteristics and mother-infant interaction in two observational studies. *Child Development, 47*, 1138-1147.

Paludetto, R., Mansi, G., Rinaldi, P., Curtis, M. D., & Ciccimarra, F. (1983, April). *The behavior of jaundiced infants treated with phototherapy*. Paper presented at the Meeting of Society for Research in Child Development, Detroit, Michigan.

Richards, M. P. M. (1978). Possible effects of early separation on later development in children. In F. S. W. Brimblecombe, M. P. M. Richards, & N. R. C. Roberton (Eds.), *Early separation of special care baby units*. Clinics in Developmental Medicine. London: SIMP/Heinemann Medical Books.

Robson, K. S. (1967). The role of eye-to-eye contact in maternal-infant attachment. *Journal of Child Psychology and Psychiatry, 8*, 13-25.

Rubin, R. A., Balow, B., & Fisch, O. (1979). Neonatal serum bilirubin levels related to cognitive development at ages four through seven years. *Journal of Pediatrics, 94*, 601-604.

Seashore, M. J. (1981). Mother-infant separation: Outcome assessment. In V. L. Smeriglio (Ed.), *Newborns and parents: Parent-infant contact and newborn sensory stimulation* (pp. 75-87). Baltimore, MD: Johns Hopkins University.

Seashore, J. H., Leifer, A. D., Barnett, C. R., & Leiderman, P. H. (1983). The effects of denial of early mother-infant interaction on maternal self-confidence. *Journal of Personality and Social Psychology, 26*, 369-378.

Stern, D. N., Spieker, S., & MacKain, K. (1982). Intonation contours as signals in maternal speech to prelinguistic infants. *Developmental Psychology, 18*, 727-735.

Stewart, R. R., Walker, W., & Savage, R. D. (1970). A developmental study of cognitive and personality characteristics associated with hemolytic disease of the newborn. *Developmental Medicine and Child Neurology, 12*, 16–26.

Telzrow, R. W., Snyder, D. M., Tronick, E., Als, H., & Brazelton, T. B. (1980). The behavior of jaundiced infants undergoing phototherapy. *Developmental Medicine and Child Neurology, 22*, 317–326.

Waters, E., Vaughn, B. E., & Egeland, B. R. (1980). Individual differences in infant-mother attachment relationships at age one: Antecedents in neonatal behavior in an urban, economically disadvantaged sample. *Child Development, 51*, 208–216.

Address correspondence to:
Shahrokh M. Shafaie, Ph.D.
Southeast Missouri State University,
Department of Human
Environmental Studies,
Child Development Program,
Cape Girardeau, MO 63701

Appendix

Behavioral Categories Coded for Newborns by Modality

The following behavioral measures were identified and scored within each modality. In a given modality, neonatal behaviors were segmented into analytic units; a unit ended and a new unit began when there was a change or pause in the infant's behavior.

Visual Modality

Initiate: The infant begins or sets the stage for visual interaction and looks at the mother's eyes or face.

Monitor: The infant engages in visual behaviors designed to maintain an initiated visual interaction or maintains a visual behavior with the mother's eyes or face.

Terminate: The infant ends an ongoing visual behavior that is directed towards the mother's face. Terminate is not coded when the mother's behavior causes the infant to end visual contact (e.g., changing infant's position).

Off: The infant's eyes are closed either because they are blocked in some way or because the infant is sleepy.

On Other: Initiating and maintaining visual contact with the mother's body excluding eye or face-to-face visual contact.

Other: The infant is visually engaged with something other than the mother (e.g., something in the environment).

Vocal Modality

Initiate: This refers to any verbal speech and nonspeech sounds emitted by the infant (e.g., sneeze, hiccoughs, etc.) except crying, fussing, or anything that represents the infant's discomfort or irritability.

Monitor: The infant maintains an initiated verbal behavior (e.g., duration of crying, fussing, etc.).

Other: This refers to fussing, crying, or any verbal sounds that represent the infant's irritability, discomfort, and distress.

Tactile Modality

Initiate: The infant emits a tactile behavior which can be regarded as beginning or setting the stage for an interaction with the mother (e.g., the infant's hand touches the mother's arm or chest).

Monitor: The infant maintains an initiated tactile behavior or one which occurred in response to a behavior emitted by the mother.)

Terminate: The neonate engages in a behavior which ends tactile contact (e.g., the infant pulls his or her hand away when the mother puts her finger in the palm of the neonate's hand). Terminate is not coded in cases where the mother's behavior ended or caused the end of tactile contact.

Off: No active tactile contact with the mother. Being held by mother is not a tactile behavior to be coded.

Action: The infant engages in a tactile behavior which is clearly in response to a tactile behavior emitted by the mother. Example: The infant grabs the mother's finger (action) when the palm of his or her hand is being tactilely stimulated by the mother's extended finger. This behavior is in response to the mother's tactile stimulation.

Preverbal Communicative Abilities of High-Risk Infants

Marcia J. Brown, Ph.D., CCC-SLP
Southeast Missouri State University
Cape Girardeau, Missouri

Kenneth F. Ruder, Ph.D., CCC-SLP
Southern Illinois University at Carbondale
Carbondale, Illinois

The purpose of this study was to specify the differences (if any) between the preverbal communicative behaviors of premature and full-term infants at 4 and 7 months of age. The communicative behaviors of their mothers were also examined. Six randomly selected minutes of each dyad were analyzed for occurrences of preverbal communicative behaviors in the categories of kinesics (facial expression), gestures, ocular behaviors, tactile-kinesics (touching), and vocalizations. Mother behaviors analyzed included kinesics, gestures, tactile-kinesics, and vocalizations.

The results of the study support the hypotheses that there would be differences in the preverbal communicative abilities of premature infants compared to those of full-term infants. These data add to the existing data base regarding preverbal interactions of premature infants, with specific information about the differences in the preverbal communicative skills of premature infants. The results of this study indicate that further research is necessary to determine whether early intervention targeting of these preverbal skills is effective in averting subsequent verbal language delays.

The incidence of speech and language problems in the premature population is well-documented. As early as 1958, Kastein and Fowler reported "retardation of speech and language" for 58% of their 66 premature subjects. O'Leary, Coster, and Dorantes (1986) found in their first year of operating a clinic for premature and respiratory distress syndrome (RDS) infants that speech and language problems were one of the two most frequently reported problems (the other being nutrition).

Most research studies of speech and language development in premature infants have reported incidences of speech and language delay and/or qualitative differences of communication when comparing premature infants to full-term controls (DeHirsch, Jansky, & Langford, 1964; Hubatch, Johnson, Kistles, Burns, & Moneka, 1985; Lassman, Fisch,

Vetter, & LaBenz, 1980). It would seem that, if the possibility exists that a child is at risk for delays in the development of his or her verbal language, the possibility also exists that there are differences in the child's preverbal communicative abilities as well.

Comparisons of mother-infant interactions involving high-risk infants to those of normal gestational age and birthweight suggest that mothers of high-risk infants interact differently with them than do mothers of normal infants. Possible reasons suggested by various authors include prolonged periods of minimal sensory experiences in the first few weeks of life (which contributes to the disruption of the sensorimotor and mental growth of the infant); the disruption of the parent-infant relationship that occurs due to prolonged hospitalization of the high-risk infant; difficulties associated with the physical care of the high-risk infant; and the small size and frail appearance of the high-risk infant (Barnett, Leiderman, Grobstein, & Klaus, 1970; Klaus & Kennell, 1970; Leifer, Leiderman, Barnett, & Williams, 1972; Seashore, Leifer, Barnett, & Leiderman, 1973).

There are a number of variables that may account for a difference in preverbal communicative abilities of premature infants. These variables are often concomitant with prematurity, so it is difficult to separate the effect that prematurity has on the development of communicative behavior from the effects of these other variables. The variables include maternal age, race, marital status, parity (birth order), past obstetric history, medical and/or obstetric illness, reproductive tract abnormalities, maternal nutrition, maternal smoking habits during pregnancy, maternal education, family income and socioeconomic status (Aubry & Pennington, 1973; Keller, 1981; Parmelee, Kopp, & Sigman, 1976; Seigel, 1982). The contribution of any one of these variables to the differences noted during preverbal interaction in premature infants is difficult to quantify.

Dyadic interactions involving premature infants and their mothers appear to be qualitatively different from those involving full-term infants. One of the most striking differences noted in early mother/preterm infant interactions is the apparent absence of "fun" in the dyad. Observed interactions between the premature infant and his or her mother appear to be characterized by greater activity and stimulation by the mother, less responsiveness and communicative competence by the infant, and less apparent enjoyment and positive affect by both members of the dyad (Crnic, Ragozin, Greenberg, Robinson, & Basham, 1983; Field, 1979, 1983; Goldberg, Brachfield, & DiVitto, 1980; Lasky, Tyson, Rosenfeld, Priest, Krasinski, Heartwell, & Gant, 1983; Masi & Scott, 1983).

The purpose of this investigation was to determine if there are differences between the preverbal communicative abilities of premature and full-term infants at 4 and 7 months adjusted age, and if differences between the communicative behaviors used by the mothers of both groups exist. The preverbal communicative behaviors that were observed include kinesics, gestures, ocular movements, tactile-kinesics, and vocalizations (adapted from Ziajka, 1981). The communicative behaviors observed for the mothers included kinesics, gestures, tactile-kinesics, and vocalizations.

Method

Subjects

The subjects for this study were 40 infants divided into two groups; premature (N = 20) and full-term (N = 20). Subjects in the premature group had a birthweight of less than 2500 grams and a gestation period of 37 weeks or less. Subjects in the full-term group had a birthweight of greater than 2500 grams and a gestation period between 37 and 42 weeks. Birthweight (BW) and gestational age (GA) for all subjects are summarized in Table 1. No subjects were included

Table 1. Birthweight (BW) and Gestational Age (GA) for Premature and Full Term Infants

	Premature Group	
Subject	**Birthweight**	**Gestational Age**
1	1470 grams	31 weeks
2	1800 grams	32 weeks
3	2000 grams	33 weeks
4	960 grams	27 weeks
5	2400 grams	34 weeks
6	1200 grams	29 weeks
7	680 grams	26 weeks
8	2000 grams	32 weeks
9	680 grams	24 weeks
10	1800 grams	33 weeks
11	2200 grams	33 weeks
12	2000 grams	32 weeks
13	1850 grams	34 weeks
14	960 grams	26 weeks
15	2250 grams	33 weeks
16	820 grams	28 weeks
17	2000 grams	33 weeks
18	1000 grams	31 weeks
19	1800 grams	30 weeks
20	700 grams	24 weeks
	Full-Term Group	
Subject	**Birthweight**	**Gestational Age**
1	3350 grams	41 weeks
2	3035 grams	40 weeks
3	3400 grams	40 weeks
4	4135 grams	40 weeks
5	3700 grams	42 weeks
6	3650 grams	40 weeks
7	3300 grams	42 weeks
8	3100 grams	39 weeks
9	3500 grams	39 weeks
10	3550 grams	41 weeks
11	3900 grams	40 weeks
12	3600 grams	40 weeks
13	2890 grams	40 weeks
14	3550 grams	38 weeks
15	3750 grams	40 weeks
16	3490 grams	42 weeks
17	4025 grams	40 weeks
18	2850 grams	40 weeks
19	3700 grams	42 weeks
20	2950 grams	40 weeks

in either group who were the product of multiple births, had known or suspected sensory deficits, central nervous system dysfunctions (including cerebral hemorrhage) or other physically and/or mentally debilitating conditions (including hydrocephalus, Down syndrome, venereal disease, fetal alcohol syndrome, drug addiction, acquired immune deficiency syndrome, or any other known or suspected deficiencies or syndromes).

Procedure

The subjects were videotaped in their homes on two separate occasions, at the gestational ages of 4 and 7 months. The mother was instructed to play with her baby as she normally would if the investigator were not present. The mother-infant interaction was videotaped for 30 minutes. The videotapes collected in the home were later analyzed by the investigator and occurrences of preverbal communicative behaviors were tabulated. To establish intra-examiner reliability, the investigator rescored one tape in its entirety, as well as 10% of the remaining tapes, selected at random. To establish inter-examiner reliability, a second investigator scored one tape from each group in its entirety, as well as 10% of the remaining tapes selected randomly. The method of analysis was adapted from a procedure described by Ziajka (1981). Ziajka's model was designed for use with older infants and toddlers, and, therefore, was not compatible for use with infants at 4 and 7 months of age in its original form.

Kinesic measures in the adapted scale included smiles and other facial expressions of the infant and the mother. Gestures included reaching for the communicative partner, reaching for objects, pointing, waving of the arms and legs, and conventional gestures such as beckoning and waving "bye-bye." Ocular behavior included instances of the infant looking at the mother. Tactile-kinesic behaviors involved instances of purposive touching between the mother and infant, as well as object or body-part manipulation. Credit was not given for accidental body contact, which occurred as a result of proximity or by virtue of being held. Vocalizations of the infants included crying, cooing, gurgling, squealing, growling, grunting, laughing, giggling, screaming, and babbling. Mother vocalizations included prelinguistic sounds, laughing, giggling, and real word vocalizations.

The videotapes were analyzed by selecting three 2-minute segments of the 30-minute interaction at random, and completing a frame-by-frame analysis of each segment. Data were tabulated by counting the number of occurrences in each behavioral category that occurred during each of the 2-minute segments.

Statistical Analyses

The infants' data derived from the analyses of the videotapes were submitted to a 2×2 multivariate analysis of variance (MANOVA), with repeated measures on one effect. The main effects were group (premature and full-term infants) and time (4 months and 7 months). Contingent univariate analysis of variance (ANOVA) procedures were performed to determine differences between the preverbal communicative abilities used by the infants in the premature and full-term groups.

The mothers' data were submitted to an identical 2×2 multivariate analysis of variance (MANOVA) with repeated measures on one effect. As with the infants, the main effects were group (premature and full-term) and time (4 and 7 months). Contingent univariate analyses of variance (ANOVA) were performed to determine differences between the communicative behaviors used by the mothers of the full-term and premature infants.

Infants

The mean number of occurrences of kinesic behaviors, gestures, ocular contacts, tactile-kinesic behaviors, and vocalizations observed during the 30-minute interaction for both the premature and full-term groups are shown in Table 2. The results of the MANOVA procedure, as depicted in Table 3, indicated a significant time-by-group interaction effect; that is, the difference between the 4- and 7-month-old infants' performances was different for the premature and full-term groups. This interaction of time by group confounded the main effects of time and group.

The time-by-group interaction, which was significant at the multivariate level, was not significant at the univariate level for the category of kinesics, as depicted in Figure 1. Both the full-term and premature infants experienced a slight decrease in the mean number of facial expressions used between the 4- and 7-month-old infants' sessions. In the category of gestures, the mean use of gestures for the full-term group decreased from the 4-month-old infants' visit to the 7-month-old infants' visit, while the mean use of gestures for the premature group increased from the 4-month-old infants' visit to the 7-month old infants' visit, as depicted in Figure 2. In the ocular category, the mean of ocular contacts with mother in the full-term group decreased from the 4-months of age session to the 7-months of age session. The mean of ocular behavior in the premature group increased from the 4-months of age session to the 7-months of age visit, as depicted in Figure 3. In the tactile-kinesic category, the mean of tactile-kinesic behaviors for the full-term group increased from the 4-months of age visit to the 7-months of age session. There was a decrease in the mean number of tactile-kinesic behaviors displayed by the infants in the premature group at 4 months of age compared to their performance at 7 months of age, as depicted in Figure 4. In the vocal category, the mean for the infants in the full-term group decreased from the 4- to the 7-months of

Table 2. Group Means and Range of Communicative Behaviors Utilized in Three Randomly Selected 2-Minute Segments of a 30-Minute Interaction

		Means				
Group	Age	Kinesics	Gestures	Ocular	Tactile-Kinesics	Vocalizations
Premature	4 mo.	2.40	10.35	4.65	13.95	6.90
Premature	7 mo.	7.75	16.45	8.90	8.95	12.50
Full Term	4 mo.	10.45	22.75	14.45	11.45	19.90
Full Term	7 mo.	12.05	18.25	9.00	24.95	8.40
		Ranges				
Group	Age	Kinesics	Gestures	Ocular	Tactile-Kinesics	Vocalizations
Premature	4 mo.	0–11	1–18	0–21	0–26	1–10
Premature	7 mo.	4–12	8–23	4–24	0–18	1–19
Full Term	4 mo.	1–27	5–32	3–29	4–26	9–33
Full Term	7 mo.	5–32	9–28	4–20	20–32	2–31

Table 3. Doubly Multivariate Repeated Measures Analysis of Variance for Infants

Source	Multivariate			Univariate					
	F	Df	p	Var.	SS(h)	SS(e)	Df	F	p
Group	9.54	5,34	.00001	Kin	756.45	1832.75	1,38	15.68	.0003
				Ges	1008.20	2178.60	1,38	17.59	.0002
				Ocu	490.05	2105.95	1,38	8.84	.0051
				Tac	911.25	2211.30	1,38	15.66	.0003
				Voc	451.25	1135.70	1,38	15.10	.0004
Time	10.90	5,34	.00001	Kin	245.00	445.55	1,38	20.90	.0001
				Ges	12.80	720.40	1,38	0.68	.4164
				Ocu	7.20	771.35	1,38	0.35	.5550
				Tac	361.25	796.50	1,38	17.23	.0002
				Voc	140.45	998.10	1,38	5.35	.0263
Time by Group	28.96	5,34	.00001	Kin	68.45	445.55	1,38	5.84	.0206
				Ges	561.80	720.40	1,38	29.63	.00001
				Ocu	470.45	771.35	1,38	23.18	.00001
				Tac	1711.25	796.50	1,38	81.64	.00001
				Voc	1566.45	998.10	1,38	59.64	.00001

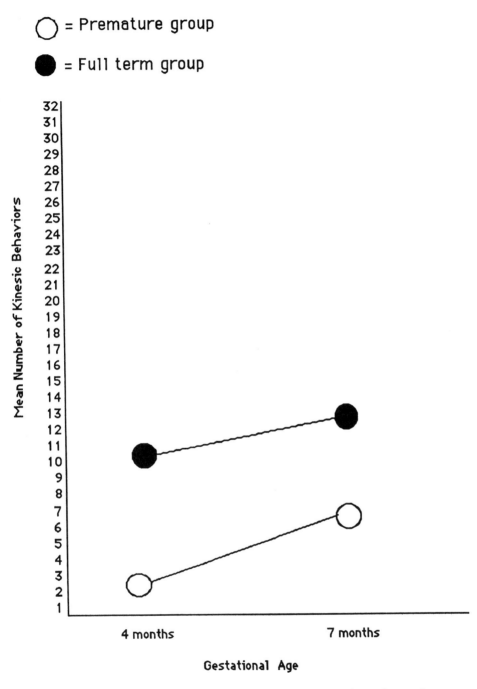

Figure 1. Mean number of kinesic behaviors utilized by infants during three randomly selected 2-minute segments of a 30-minute interaction.

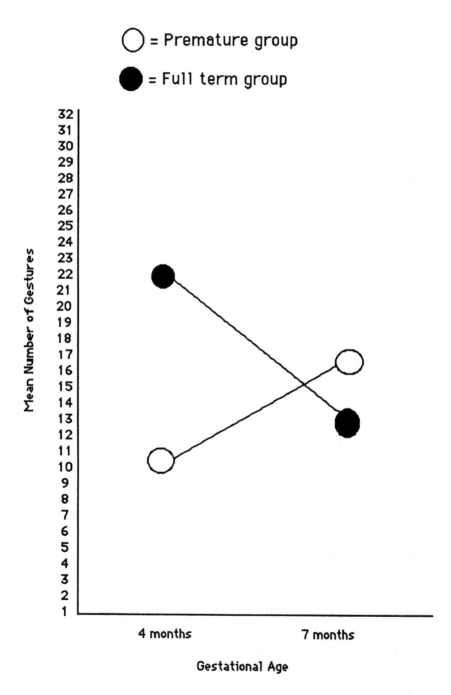

Figure 2. Mean number of gestures utilized by infants during three randomly selected 2-minute segments of a 30-minute interaction.

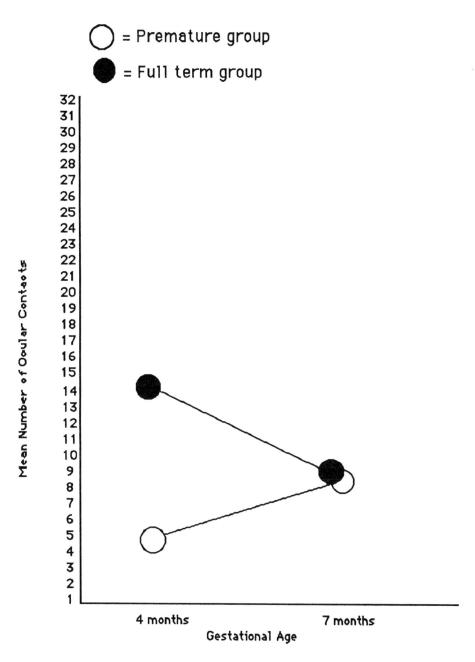

Figure 3. Mean number of ocular contacts utilized by infants during three randomly selected 2-minute segments of a 30-minute interaction.

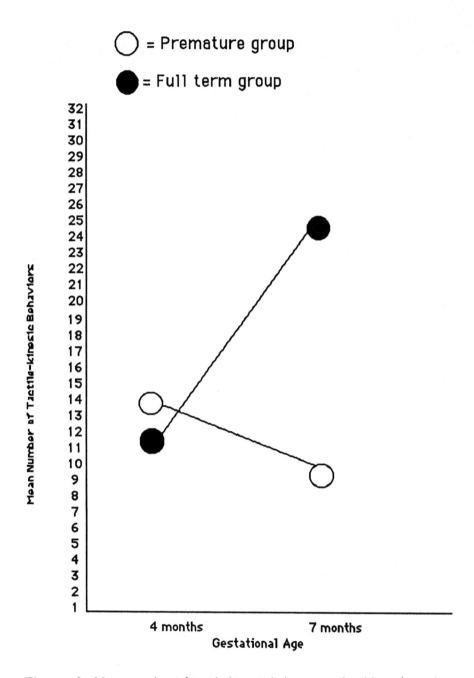

Figure 4. Mean number of tactile-kinesic behaviors utilized by infants during three randomly selected 2-minute segments of a 30-minute interaction.

age sessions, while the mean for the infants in the premature group increased from the 4-months of age visit to the 7-months of age visit, as depicted in Figure 5.

The group effect was also found to be statistically significant. That is, there were significant differences between the two groups' preverbal communicative abilities, although this difference was confounded by the time-by-group interaction. Contingent ANOVA procedures indicated that the specific behaviors that differed by group included kinesics, gestures, ocular behaviors, tactile-kinesics, and vocalizations.

There was also a significant overall multivariate time (or age) effect; that is, there were significant differences between the performances of the infants at 4 and 7 months of age, which was confounded by the time-by-group interaction. The ANOVA procedures indicated univariate differences from 4 to 7 months of age occurred in the categories of kinesics and tactile-kinesics.

Mothers

The data derived from the analysis of the mothers' behaviors were submitted to a multivariate analysis of variance with contingent univariate analyses of variance. The mean number of occurrences of communicative behaviors displayed by the mothers appear in Table 4. The results of the MANOVA procedure indicated that the main effects of time and group were confounded by the significant interaction of time by group, as depicted in Figures 6–9. This significant interaction effect indicates that the difference in mothers' behaviors from the 4- to 7-months of age sessions was different for the premature and full-term groups. While statistical significance was achieved at the multivariate level, the contingent univariate tests were not significant, as depicted in Table 5.

The results of the MANOVA procedure indicated that there was an overall group effect; that is, there were significant differences between the communicative behaviors of the mothers in the premature group compared to the mothers of the full-term group, which was confounded by the time-by-group interaction. The contingent ANOVA procedures indicated that the significant differences between the two groups occurred in the categories of gestures and vocalizations.

The time effect (change in performance from 4 to 7 months of age) was not significant for mother behaviors. Since the multivariate test was not significant, the univariate tests were not interpreted.

Discussion

The results of this investigation indicated that there were differences between the preverbal communicative abilities of the premature group and the full-term group as a whole, as well as differences between the 4-month-old infants and the 7-month-old infants. This overall difference between the two groups supports findings from previous research that have indicated that the preverbal interactions of premature infants are different from those of full-term infants (Crnic et al., 1983; Field, 1979, 1980, 1983; Lasky et al., 1983; Masi & Scott, 1983). The specific communicative abilities that appear to be different in infants are gestures, eye contact, tactile-kinesic behaviors, and vocalizations. The mothers of the premature infants in this investigation used more gestures and fewer vocalizations than the mothers of full-term infants.

The results of this study add to the existing data base regarding the preverbal interactions of premature infants and their mothers with information regarding specific differences in preverbal communicative skills. Longitudinal data from previous research demonstrate correlations between

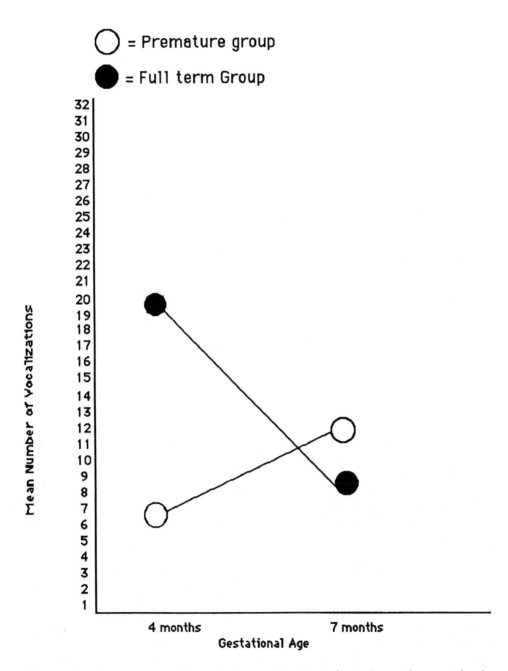

Figure 5. Mean number of vocalizations utilized by infants during three randomly selected 2-minute segments of a 30-minute interaction.

Table 4. Group Means of Communicative Behaviors Utilized by Mothers in Three Randomly Selected 2-Minute Segments of a 30-Minute Interaction

Group	Session	Kinesics	Gestures	Tactile-Kinesics	Vocalizations
Premature	4 mo.	4.30	20.85	24.70	26.05
Premature	7 mo.	4.70	21.30	23.60	25.75
Full Term	4 mo.	4.05	11.40	25.40	30.30
Full Term	7 mo.	2.85	13.40	26.40	33.50
Ranges					
Group	Age	Kinesics	Gestures	Tactile-Kinesics	Vocalizations
Premature	4 mo.	0–21	2–34	5–35	5–35
Premature	7 mo.	0–18	5–35	6–35	8–35
Full Term	4 mo.	0–11	0–24	1–35	19–35
Full Term	7 mo.	0–10	0–25	13–33	31–35

performance during preverbal interactions and later verbal language skills (Cohen & Beckwith, 1979; Field, 1978, 1980; Largo, Molinari, Comenale-Pinto, Weber, & Duc, 1986). Research has also demonstrated that premature infants may be at risk for delayed development of verbal language (DeHirsch et al., 1964; Hubatch et al., 1985; Kastein & Fowler, 1959; Lassman et al., 1980; O'Leary et al., 1986). Since there appears to be a relationship between these early delays in preverbal performance and later developmental testing, early intervention would appear to be an appropriate choice for these infants.

The first consideration to be investigated in terms of early intervention with this population is whether the process of training parents how to interact with their infants changes behavior in the infant, or whether the apparent improvements in the parent-infant interaction result from improvements in ability of the parent to communicate with the infant. To provide useful information regarding the efficacy of early intervention targeting preverbal communication skills, longitudinal investigations will have to be undertaken.

Implications

The data from this study support results from previous research that have indicated differences between mother-infant interactions of premature and full-term infants. These data should be of assistance to professionals working with premature infants and their families. Since specific behaviors have been identified as being different, they can be utilized as "red flag" items (i.e., skills or behaviors to be looking for) in the observation or assessment of the mother-infant dyad. In the observation of premature infants, red flag items include gestures, vocalizations, eye contact, and tactile-kinesics (touching). Red flags for the mothers of premature infants include gestures and vocalizations.

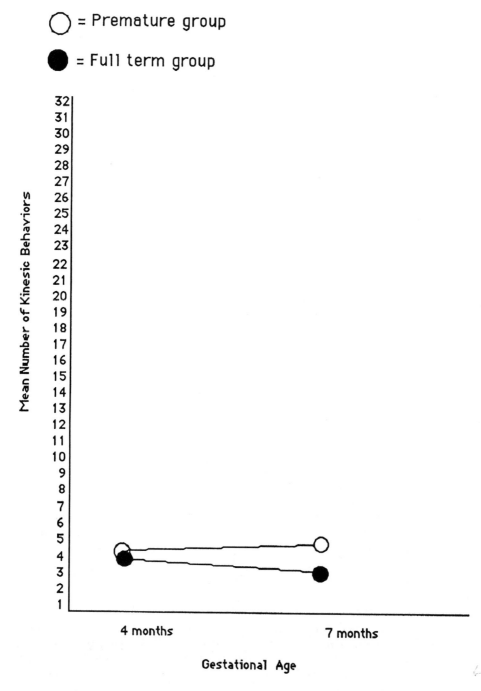

Figure 6. Mean number of kinesic behaviors utilized by mothers during three randomly selected 2-minute segments of a 30-minute interaction.

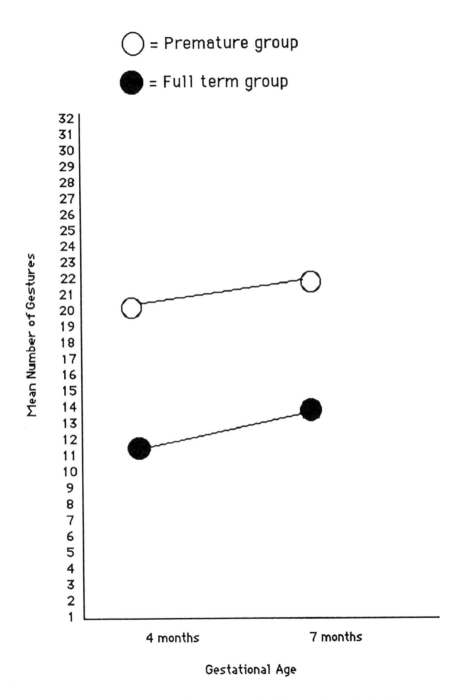

Figure 7. Mean number of gestures utilized by mothers during three randomly selected 2-minute segments of a 30-minute interaction.

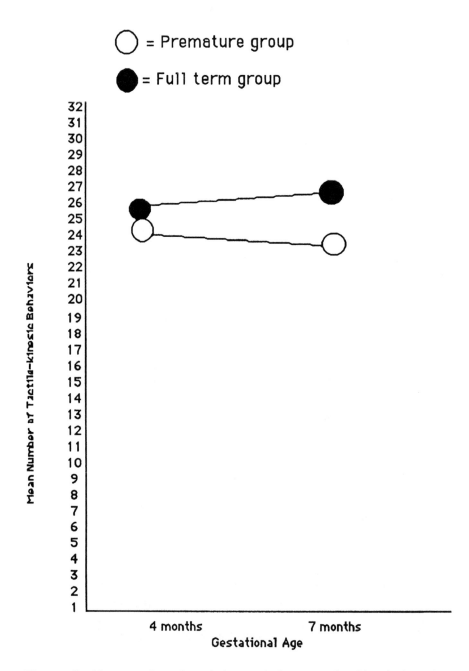

Figure 8. Mean number of tactile-kinesic behaviors utilized by mothers during three randomly selected 2-minute segments of a 30-minute interaction.

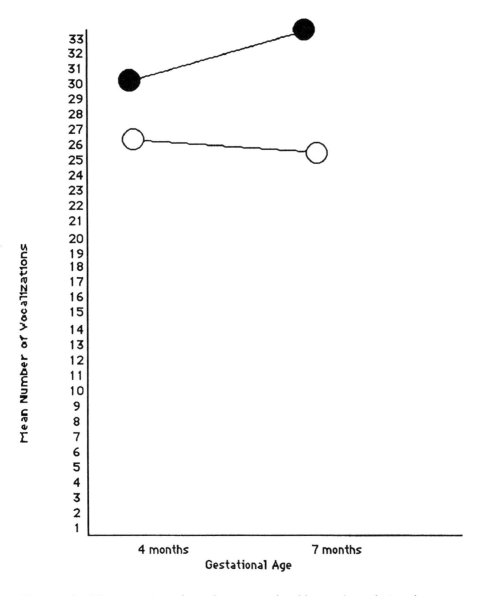

Figure 9. Mean number of vocalizations utilized by mothers during three randomly selected 2-minute segments of a 30-minute interaction.

Table 5. Doubly Multivariate Repeated Measures Analysis of Variance for Mothers

	Multivariate				Univariate				
Source	F	Df	p	Var.	SS(h)	SS(e)	Df	F	p
Group	6.41	4,35	.0006	Kin	22.05	1350.90	1,38	0.62	.4358
				Ges	1505.11	4221.88	1,38	13.55	.0007
				Tac	61.25	673070	1,38	0.35	.5600
				Voc	720.00	2331.20	1,38	11.74	.0015
Time	2.39	4,35	.0694	Kin	3.20	153.00	1,38	.79	.3783
				Ges	30.01	154.48	1,38	7.38	.0099
				Tac	.05	709.90	1,38	.00	.9590
				Voc	42.05	438.70	1,38	3.64	.0639
Time by Group	2.73	4,35	.0446	Kin	12.80	153.00	1,38	3.18	.0826
				Ges	12.01	154.48	1,38	2.96	.0937
				Tac	22.05	709.90	1,38	1.18	.2841
				Voc	61.25	438.70	1,38	5.31	.0268

Specific implications of these data for intervention in this population are unclear, as no intervention was attempted in this investigation. However, it would appear that these behaviors could be used as guidelines for improving the interaction between the premature infant and his or her mother in an intervention setting. For example, since the data from this study suggest that mothers of premature infants talk less to their babies, intervention may include assisting the mother in increasing the amount of time spent talking to her baby in an attempt to improve the quality of the interaction. The data from this study also indicate that premature infants spent less time looking at their mothers; therefore, intervention may include demonstrating strategies to the mother to encourage eye contact with her baby. These suggestions for intervention, while based on the results of the current investigation, should be considered tentative at best, since the data reported in this investigation were **not** collected in an intervention setting, but rather only from observing the mother-infant dyad. The suggestions mentioned should not be considered as an inclusive list, but simply as examples gleaned from the data in this study. Further research should be undertaken to investigate whether intervention can bring about changes in the behaviors described in this investigation.

Acknowledgments

The authors gratefully acknowledge the assistance of Dr. John Mouw, Dr. Suzanne Hungerford, the staff at Cardinal Glennon Memorial Hospital for Children in St. Louis, Missouri, and the parents and infants who served as subjects for this investigation.

References

Aubry, R., & Pennington, J. (1973). Identification and evaluation of high-risk pregnancy: The perinatal concept. *Clinical Obstetrics and Gynecology, 16*, 3–27.

Barnett, C., Leiderman, P., Grobstein, R., & Klaus, M. (1970). Neonatal separation: The maternal side of interactional deprivation. *Pediatrics, 45*, 197–205.

Cohen, S., & Beckwith, L. (1979). Preterm infant interaction with the caregiver in the first year of life and competence at age two. *Child Development, 50*, 767–776.

Crnic, K., Ragozin, A., Greenberg, M., Robinson, N., & Basham, R. (1983). Social interaction and developmental competence of preterm and full-term infants during the first year of life. *Child Development, 54*, 1199–1210.

DeHirsch, K., Jansky, J., & Langford, W. (1964). The oral language performance of premature children and controls. *Journal of Speech and Hearing Disorders, 29*, 60–69.

Field, T. (1979). Games parents play with normal and high-risk infants. *Child Psychiatry and Human Development, 10*, 41–48.

Field, T. (1980). Interactions of high-risk infants: Quantitative and qualitative differences. In D. Sawin, R. Hawkins, II, L. Walker, & J. Penticuff (Eds.), *Exceptional infant volume 4: Psychosocial risks in infant-environment transactions* (pp. 120–143). New York: Brunner/Mazel, Inc.

Field, T. (1983). High-risk infants "have less fun" during early interactions. *Topics in Early Childhood Education, 3*, 77–87.

Goldberg, S., Brachfield, S., & DiVitto, B. (1980). Feeding, fussing and play: Parent-infant interaction in the first year of life as a function of prematurity and perinatal medical problems. In T. Field, S. Goldberg, D. Stern, & A. Sostek (Eds.), *High-risk infants and children: Adult and peer interactions* (pp. 133–151). New York: Academic Press.

Hubatch, L., Johnson, C., Kistles, D., Burns, W., & Moneka, W. (1985). Early language abilities of high-risk infants. *Journal of Speech and Hearing Disorders, 50*, 195–207.

Kastein, S., & Fowler, E. (1958). Language development among survivors of premature birth. *Archives of Otolaryngology, 69*, 131–135.

Keller, C. (1981). Epidemiological characteristics of preterm births. In S. Friedman & M. Sigman (Eds.), *Preterm birth and psycholog-*

ical development (pp. 3–15). New York: Academic Press.

Klaus, M., & Kennell, J. (1970). Mothers separated from their newborn infants. *Pediatric Clinics of North America, 17*, 1015–1037.

Largo, R., Molinari, L., Comenale-Pinto, L., Weber, M., & Duc, G. (1986). Language development of term and preterm children during the first five years of life. *Developmental Medicine and Child Neurology, 28*, 333–350.

Lasky, R., Tyson, J., Rosenfeld, C., Priest, M., Krasinski, D., Heartwell, S., & Gant, N. (1983). Differences on Bayley's infant behavior record for a sample of high-risk infants and their controls. *Child Development, 54*, 1211–1216.

Lassman, F., Fisch, R., Vetter, D., & LaBenz, E. (1980). *Early correlates of speech, language and hearing: The collaborative perinatal project of the national institute of neurological and communicative disorders and stroke*. Littleton, MA: PSG Publishing.

Leifer, A., Leiderman, P., Barnett, C., & Williams, J. (1972). Effects of mother-infants separation on maternal attachment behavior. *Child Development, 43*, 1203–1218.

Masi, W., & Scott, K. (1983). Preterm and full-term infants' visual responses to mothers' and strangers' faces. In T. Field & A. Sostek (Eds.), *Infants born at risk: Physiological, perceptual and cognitive processes* (pp. 54–67). New York: Grune & Stratton.

O'Leary, K., Coster, J., & Dorantes, D. (1986, November). *High risk infants and children: Developmental assessment and follow-up*. Poster session presented to the American Speech, Language and Hearing Association, Detroit, MI.

Parmelee, A., Kopp, C., & Sigman, M. (1976). Selection of developmental assessment techniques for infants at risk. *Merrill-Palmer Quarterly, 22*, 177–199.

Seashore, M., Leifer, A., Barnett, C., & Leiderman, P. (1973). The effects of denial of early mother-infant interactions on maternal self-confidence. *Journal of Personality and Social Psychology, 26*, 369–378.

Seigel, L. (1982). Reproductive, perinatal and environmental factors as predictors of the cognitive and language development of preterm and full-term infants. *Child Development, 53*, 963–973.

Ziajka, A. (1981). *Prelinguistic communication in infancy*. New York: Praeger Publishers.

Address Correspondence to:
Marcia J. Brown, Ph.D., CCC/SLP
Southeast Missouri State University,
One University Plaza,
Cape Girardeau, MO 63701

Index

A

Acoustic reflex testing, 60, 63
Acoustics, speech
  dimensions, 113–115
  duration, 114–115
  frequency, 114
  intensity, 113–114
  loudness, 113–114
Advisory Group on the Early Identification of Children with Hearing Impairments, 9
Alcohol. *See also* Beer; Liquor
  mothers' use report, 187, 188, 189, 193
ALGO-1 Plus™, 14
American Academy of Audiology (AAA), hearing loss statistics, 6–7
American Speech-Language-Hearing Association (ASHA)
  "Guidelines for Audiologic Screening of Newborn Infants Who Are At Risk for Hearing Impairment," 56
  "Guidelines for the Audiologic Assessment of Children From Birth Through Thirty-Six Months of Age," 57
  infant hearing impairment identification program (IHIIP) survey, 9–10
  joint committee with Council on Education of the Deaf, Individuals with Disabilities Education Act (IDEA), Part H, 35–36
  sensorineural hearing loss (SNHL) definition, 6
Aminoglycosides, 12, 56
Amplification. *See also* Hearing aid
  goal of, 94–95
  Individualized Family Service Plan (IFSP), 93
  interference, 94–905
  and lighting, poor, 95
  long-term average speech spectrum (LTASS), 94, 103
  and sight deficits, 95
Apnea, 101
Asphyxia, 12
Aspiration, meconium, 101

Assessment
  audiologic. *See also* Screening, hearing.
    acoustic immittance testing, 59–60
    acoustic reflex testing, 63
    auditory brainstem response (ABR), 64–65, 67, 69, 70
    behavioral techniques, 58–59
    conditioned play audiometry (CPA), 58–59, 63, 67, 68
    conductive hearing loss (CHL), 63
    electrophysiologic, 57–58
      auditory brainstem response (ABR), 58. *See also* Screening, hearing.
    follow-up, 72–73
    frequencies testable per session, 60
    informal
      speech audibility, 62
    interpretation, 60–62. *See* Interpretation, audiologic.
    Northwestern University Children's Perception of Speech (NU-CHIPS) test, 59
    pure tone air conduction threshold average (PTA), 59, 63, 67
    pure tone audiogram, speech perception, 60, 62, 93
    speech audiometry, 59
    speech awareness threshold (SAT), 59, 63
    speech detection threshold (SDT), 59
    speech perception, and pure tone audiogram, 60, 62
    speech recognition threshold (SRT), 59
    tangible reinforcement operant conditioning audiometry (TROCA), 59
    typanometry, 60, 63, 71
    visual reinforcement audiometry (VRA), 58, 64, 66, 71
    visual reinforcement operant conditioning audiometry (VROCA), 59
    Word Intelligibility by Picture Identification (WIPI) test, 59, 67–68
    word recognition, 59

Assessment *(continued)*
  hearing aid, conductive hearing loss (CHL), 63–64
Assistive technology, powered mobility, 134–136
Atresia
  choanal, 66
  congenital, 94
Audiometry. *See also* Behavioral observation audiometry (BOA); Crib-O-Gram (COG); Screening, hearing; Visual reinforcement audiometry (VRA)
  auditory brainstem response (ABR), 13–14, 56
  automated auditory brainstem response (AABR), 13, 14
  behavioral observation audiometry (BOA), 10–11
  brainstem auditory evoked response (BAER), 14, 228
  conditioned play audiometry (CPA), 58–59, 63, 67, 68
  tangible reinforcement operant conditioning audiometry (TROCA), 59
  visual reinforcement audiometry (VRA), 11–12, 58, 64, 66, 71, 81
  visual reinforcement operant conditioning audiometry (VROCA), 59
Auditory brainstem response (ABR), 6, 56, 81, 101, 104
  assessment, audiologic, 58, 64–65
  automated auditory brainstem response (AABR), 4, 13, 14, 16, 19, 32, 43
  brainstem auditory evoked response (BAER), 14, 228
  limitations, 58
  screening, 13–14
  sensorineural hearing loss (SNHL), 64–65, 67, 69, 70
Auditory deprivation, first 3 years, 5
Auditory function
  and mild hearing impairment, 77–88
  normal development, 79–81, 92
Auditory trainer, 67, 99, 104
Augmentative communication, 93–94, 135, 156
Automated auditory brainstem response (AABR), 4, 13, 14, 16, 19, 32, 43. *See also* Auditory brainstem response (ABR)
  ALGO-1 Plus™, 14

B

Bayley Infant Scales, 215, 216–217
Beer. *See also* Alcohol; Liquor
  mothers' use report, 187, 193
Beginnings (parent-infant hearing impairment training), 72
Behavioral categories, neonate, 279–280
Behavioral observation audiometry (BOA), 10–11
Bigfoot powered cart, 138
Birthweight
  low, 56
    high-risk registries (HRR), 12
  very low, and language development, 252
Brainstem auditory evoked response (BAER), 14, 228
  neonatal screening, 14
Brazelton Neonatal Behavioral Assessment Scale (BNBAS), 266–267
Bronchopulmonary dysplasia (BPD), 102–103, 104–105, 228, 236–237

C

Caregivers, and neonate gaze attachment, 181–182, 191
Cerebral palsy (CP), 135, 141–158, 145–149
  communication intervention, 163–164, 173–175
  communicative intent development, 161–176
    overview, 161–162
  defined, 141–142
  early motor development, 142
  handicapping conditions influence, 162–163
  occupational therapist (OT), 145–149, 156–158
physical therapist (PT), 145–149
  speech-language therapist (SLP), 145–149
CHARGE associated syndrome, 66–67
Cigarette smoking, mothers' use report, 187, 188, 193
Cleft lip, 103–104
Cleft palate, 12
Cocaine
  crack
    cognitive performance, 215
    mothers' use report, 187, 188–189, 193
  powder, mothers' use report, 187, 188–189, 193

Index

prenatal exposure. *See also* Drug exposure, prenatal; High-risk infants.
  caregiver attachment, 182
  children
    education, 195–210
    service patterns, 195–210
  cognitive performance, 215–222
  collaboration, multidisciplinary, lack, agency, 206
  data collection, 197–213
  education
    competencies, professional, 201, 203, 204, 207–208
    effectiveness, 201, 202, 203, 206–207
    types, 201, 202, 203
  family/provider interrelationship, 207
  gaze interaction, 181–191
  Infant Mullen Scale of Early Learning (MSEL), 218–222
  legal responsibilities, professional, 206
  neonate, gaze, eye contact stimuli, 185–186, 190–191
  overview, 195–196
  physical characteristics, 182–183
  Prenatal Cocaine Exposure Survey: Early Childhood Special Educators/Pediatric Professionals, 211–213
  Public Law (PL) 99-457, 196
  questionnaire
    early intervention professional, 197–213
    Prenatal Cocaine Exposure Survey: Early Childhood Special Educators/Pediatric Professionals, 211–213
    Substance Questionnaire (maternal self-report), 185, 187–188, 193
  referral sources, 206
  screening, 196–197
  self-reports, maternal, 185, 187–188, 193, 196, 206
  service patterns, 198–201
  statistics, 196, 205
    need for, 208
  primos (cocaine in marijuana), mothers' use report, 187, 188–189, 193
Cochlear implants, 71–72, 100
Coffee, mothers' use report, 187, 188, 193
Collaboration, 101
  multidisciplinary
    across agencies, 44–45

Joint Committee on Infant Hearing (JCIH), 42, 44
  neonatal hearing screening, 16–20
  screening, hearing, 42, 44
Colorado Home Intervention Program (CHIP), 39
Commission on Education of the Deaf to the President and Congress of the United States, 8
Communication
  augmentative, 93–94, 135, 156. *See also* Augmentative communication.
  effect of hearing loss on, 92–94
  oral/aural, 93
  total, 93
Communication and Symbolic Behaviour Scales (CSBS), 239
Communicative intent development, 141–158
  behavior regulation, defined, 247
  cerebral palsy (CP), 161–176. *See under* Cerebral palsy (CP).
  "choose or request" use training, 146
  handicapping conditions influence, 162–163
  joint attention, defined, 247
  looking at object and adult teaching, 146–147
  social interaction, defined, 247
  taxonomy, 167–168, 175–176
  tracheostomy, toddler, 235–248
  unclear, defined, 247
Communicative means
  gestural, defined, 247
  gestural/verbal, defined, 248
  vocal, defined, 247
Communicative signal taxonomy, 148
Conditioned play audiometry (CPA), 58–59, 63, 67, 68
Conductive hearing loss (CHL)
  assessment, audiologic, 63
  hearing aid assessment, 63–64
  overview, 61
  screening, 13
Cooper Car, 137–138
Cortical atrophy, 102
Co-treatment. *See also* Intervention; Therapy; Treatment
  speech-language therapist (SLP)/physical therapist (PT)/occupational therapist (OT), 145–149, 156–158

Council on Education of the Deaf, joint committee with American Speech-Language-Hearing Association (ASHA), Individuals with Disabilities Education Act (IDEA), Part H, 35–36
Craniofacial anomalies, 56
Crib-O-Gram (COG), 10
  neonatal intensive care unit (NICU), 11
Cytomegalovirus (CMV), 12, 13

D

Deafness. *See also* Hearing loss; Sensorineural hearing loss (SNHL)
  and electrocardiogram (ECG), 57
  Individualized Family Service Plan (IFSP), 69
Development
  and hearing, 5
  language/communication importance, 4–5
Diagnosis, and screening, hearing, 19
Diagnostic Early Intervention Project (DEIP), 72
Diuretics, loop, 12, 56
Drug exposure, prenatal. *See also* Cocaine, prenatal exposure
  cognitive performance, 215–222
  Infant Mullen Scale of Early Learning (MSEL), 218–222

E

Early learning, powered mobility, 133–139
Education, costs
  and identification, early, 40–42
  sensorineural hearing loss (SNHL), 41
Educational Audiology Association, Executive Board of (EBEAA), screening costs, 40–41
Electric Mobility Corp, 139
Electrocardiogram (ECG), 57
Electrophysiologic assessment, audiologic, 57–58
Evoked otoacoustic emissions (EOAEs), 5, 6.
  See also otoacoustic emissions (OAEs)
Extracorporeal membrane oxygenation (ECMO) therapy, 101–102

F

Family. *See also* Individualized Family Service Plan (IFSP)
  amplification management, 93
  audiology counseling, 67
  Beginnings (parent-infant hearing impairment training), 72
  cerebral palsy (CP), 145–149, 157–158
  cocaine, prenatal exposure, 207
  deafness, 69
  hearing screening, 17–18
  and Hispanic premature infants, 261–262
  Individualized Family Service Plan (IFSP), auditory skills, 93
  Infant Hearing Resources, 72
  John Tracy Clinic, 72
  parent-child power struggles, 97
  prematurity, 282
  tracheostomy, communicative intention development, 243, 244
  universal newborn hearing screening (UNHS) follow-up, 35–37
FM auditory trainer, 67, 99
FM system, 99, 100–101, 116

G

Gastrostomy tube, 66, 101, 104
Gaze, neonate
  and caregiver attachment, 182
  cocaine, prenatal exposure, and caregiver attachment, 181–182
  stimuli
    auditory/tactile, 182
    level of, 191
    suppressor effect, 191
Genetics, 57
"Guidelines for Audiologic Screening of Newborn Infants Who Are At Risk for Hearing Impairment," ASHA, 56
"Guidelines for the Audiologic Assessment of children From Birth Through Thirty-Six Months of Age," ASHA, 57

H

Haemophilus influenzae, 12, 56
Healthy People 2000: National Health Promotion and Disease Prevention Objectives, 5, 9
Hearing, developmental important, 5

Index

Hearing aids, 94–105. *See also* Amplification; Vibrotactile aids
  alternatives to, 99–100
  amplification goal, 94–95
  assessment, conductive hearing loss (CHL), 63–64
  behavioral tests, 96
  behind-the-ear (BTE), 94, 97
  body type, 94
  bone conduction (BC), 94
  case presentations, 100–105
  components, basic, 94
  daily listening check, 98–99
  dehumidifier, 99
  dependency, 97
  desired sensation level (DSL), 95, 100, 101, 103
  and developmental delay, 98
  earmold fit, 98
  electroacoustic analysis, 95
  feedback, 97–98
  hearing normalcy, 96
  Huggie Aids™, 97
  initial use, 97–98
  interference, 94–905
  in-the-canal (ITC), 94
  in-the-ear (ITE), 94
  and lighting, poor, 95
  long-term average speech spectrum (LTASS), 94, 103
  misconceptions, 96–97
  MT (microphone plus telecoil), 99
  Northwestern University Children's Perception of Speech (NU-CHIPS) test, 96
  parent-child power struggles, 97
  PB-K (phonetically balanced-kindergarten) word list, 96
  performance check, 68–69
  real-ear probe-tube microphone measures, 96, 102–103
  real-ear saturated response (RESR), 96, 103
  selection, 95–96
  sensorineural hearing loss (SNHL), 68–69
  and sight deficits, 95
  and spoken intelligibility, 115
  testing, 95–96
  troubleshooting, 99
  T (telecoil), 99
  Word Intelligibility by Picture Identification (WIPI) test, 96
  word recognition ability, 96
Hearing Health Institute (HHI) hearing screening information management software package, 35
Hearing impairment. *See also* Hearing loss
  auditory deprivation, first 3 years, 5
  mild, 77–88
    defined, 78–79
    modeling effects of, 83–86
    and phonetic discrimination, 82–83
    and speech perception, 81–83
    and World Health Organization (WHO) definition, 86
Hearing loss. *See also* Deafness; Hearing impairment; Intervention, early (hearing)
  age of identification, 92
  classification, 61–62
  conductive, modeling effects of, 83, 84
  conductive hearing loss (CHL), 13, 63–64. *See also* Conductive hearing loss (CHL).
    overview, 61
  conversational development strategies, 116–118
  early identification, 4–20. *See also* Screening, hearing.
  and educational overview, 56–57
  effect on communication, 92–94
  and health, total, 56–57
  identification delay consequences, 7–8
  Individualized Family Service Plan (IFSP), 69
  intelligibility learning, 109–126
  mixed, 62
  ossicular defects, congenital, 63
  risk factors, 56
  screening. *See* Screening, hearing.
    overview, 5–6
  sensorineural hearing loss (SNHL), 37. *See also* Deafness; Sensorineural hearing loss (SNHL).
    defined, 6
    educational costs, 41
    high-risk registries (HRR), 12
    intelligibility learning, 110–112
    mild-to-moderate, 64–66
    moderate, 66–69
    overview, 61
    risk factors, 56
    severe, 69–72, 110–112
    severe-to-profound, 69

Hearing loss *(continued)*
  severe, 100–101
  statistics, 6–7
HELP, 102
Herpes, 12
High-risk infants. *See also* Cocaine, prenatal exposure; Prematurity
  preverbal communicative abilities, 281–299
Hispanic infants
  language development, and prematurity, 251–263
  prematurity, and language development, 251–263
Home health visitors, 10, 11
Huggie Aids™, 97
Hyper-ABLEDATA, 135
Hyperbilirubinemia, 12, 265–277. *See also* Jaundice
  phototherapy, 266–277
Hyperthyroidism, 66
Hypotonia, 104

I

Individualized Family Service Plan (IFSP), 34
  amplification management, 93
  auditory skills, 93
  deafness, 69
Infant hearing impairment identification program (IHIIP), 9–10
Infant Hearing Resources, 72
Infant Mullen Scale of Early Learning (MSEL), 218–222
Influenzae, Haemophilus, 12, 56
Intelligibility with hearing loss, 109–126
  acquisition of spoken language
    awareness development, 118–119
    clear speech development, 121–122
    and hearing ability, 122–123
    responding considerations, 119–121
    sensitivity development, 118–119
  conversational development strategies, 116–118
  everyday opportunities, 110–112
  examples, 110–112
  expectation, 111
  FM system, 116
  hearing aids, 115
  language development, 110
  and learning level, 110
  listening development, 110
  residual hearing stimulation, 113–118
  speech acoustics, 113–115. *See also* Acoustics, speech.
  speech learning
    consonants, 124–125
    prosodic features control, 124
    vocalizing abundance, 123–124
    vocal quality control, 124
    vowels, 124–125
Interpretation, audiologic
  audiograms
    information plotted, 60–61
    minimal response levels (MRLs), 60, 66, 71
  classification, hearing loss, 61–62
Intervention. *See also* Co-treatment; Play therapy; Therapy
  "choose or request" use training, 146
  early (hearing)
    benefits, 37–40
      individual, 38–39
      societal, 39–40
    collaboration, multidisciplinary, 42–45
    Colorado Home Intervention Program (CHIP), 39
    versus "late" intervention, 38–39
    Minnesota Child Development Inventory (MCDI), 39
  looking at object and adult teaching, 146–147
  personnel shortage, 196
Intrauterine growth retardation, 215
Invacare Corporation, 138

J

Jaguar XC powered wheelchair, 138
Jaundice
  phototherapy, 266–277
  social interaction, 266–277
  tactile behavior, 272–273, 274–277
  visual behavior, 270–271, 273–274
  vocal behavior, 271–272, 274–277
John Tracy Clinic, 72
Joint Committee on Infant Hearing (JCIH)
  collaboration, multidisciplinary, 42, 44
  risk factors for hearing loss, 56
  screening, hearing, 12–13, 16–17, 32–33, 40, 56

L

Learning problems, and otitis media, early, 78
Liquor. *See also* Alcohol; Beer
   mothers' use report, 187, 188, 193
   substance abuse, mothers' use report, 187, 188, 193
Long-term average speech spectrum (LTASS), 94, 103

M

MacArthur Communicative Development Inventory, 102
Marijuana, mothers' use report, 187, 188, 193
Measles, 12
Meconium aspiration, 101
Medication
   aminoglycosides, 12, 56
   diuretics, loop, 12, 56
   ototoxic, 12, 56, 105
Meningitis, 12, 56
Methamphetamines, 189
Meyra Inc., 139
Meyra 2472 powered wheelchair, 138–139
Microcephaly, 215
Minnesota Child Development Inventory (MCDI), 39
Mobility, powered
   assistive technology, 134–136
   early learning, 133–139
   negative aspects, 134
Motor disability. *See also* Cerebral palsy (CP)
   communicative signal treatment, target signal selection, 156
Motorized Scooter Board, 137
Multidisciplinary collaboration. *See* Collaboration, multidisciplinary.
Mumps, 12
Muscular dystrophy (MD), 100–101

N

National Center for Hearing Identification and Management (NCHIM), 34
National Institute of Drug Abuse (NIDA), 96
National Institute on Disabilities and Rehabilitative Research, 135
National Institutes of Health (NIH) Consensus Development Conference on Identification of Hearing Impairments in Infants and Young Children, 5–6, 9, 17, 18
Neonatal intensive care unit (NICU)
   auditory brainstem response (ABR), 66
   caregiver interaction limitation, 237
   Crib-O-Gram (COG), 11
   lighting, 237
   noise, 237
   toys, 237
Neonate behavioral categories, 279–280
Neurodegenerative disorder, 12, 13
Neurofibromatosis Type II, 13
NICD Directory of National Organizations and Centers of and for Deaf and Hard of Hearing People, 73
Northwestern University Children's Perception of Speech (NU-CHIPS) test, 59, 96

O

Occupational therapist (OT), 100, 101, 102, 105
   cerebral palsy (CP), 145–149, 156–158
   conductive hearing loss (CHL), 63
   co-treatment, speech-language therapist (SLP)/physical therapist (PT), 145–149, 156–158
Oral/aural communication, 93
Otitis media, 101
   binaural function, 80
   with effusion, 77–78
   language problems, 78
   learning problems, 78
   tympanostomy tubes, 66
Otoacoustic emissions (OAEs), 81
   evoked otoacoustic emissions (EOAEs), 5, 6
   overview, 14–15
   transient evoked otoacoustic emissions (TEOAEs), 4, 14–16, 16, 19, 32, 43
Ototoxic medication, 12, 56, 105

P

Parent-Infant Communication Scales, 102
PB-K (phonetically balanced-kindergarten) word list, 96

PCP, 189
Phototherapy, jaundice, 266–277
Physical therapist (PT), 100, 101, 102
  cerebral palsy (CP), 145–149
  conductive hearing loss (CHL), 63
  co-treatment, speech-language therapist (SLP)/occupational therapist (OT), 145–149
Play audiometry. *See* Conditioned play audiometry (CPA).
Play therapy, 142. *See also* Intervention; Therapy
  cerebral palsy (CP), 165–166
  "choose or request" use training. *See also* Therapy.
  materials, 147, 166
    probe session, 147–148
Powered mobility
  assistive technology, 134–136
  and early learning, 133–139
  negative aspects, 134
Power 900 powered wheelchair, 138
Prelinguistic development, 142
Prematurity, 215. *See also* High-risk infants
  birthweight very low, and language development, 252
  family, 282
  Hispanic infants, 251–263
  and language development, 281–299
  mother-infant interactions, 282
  respiratory distress syndrome (RDS), and language development, 252, 281
Prenatal Cocaine Exposure Survey: Early Childhood Special Educators/Pediatric Professionals, 211–213
Prenatal substance abuse, marijuana, mothers' use report, 187, 188, 193
Preverbal communicative abilities, high-risk infants, 281–299
Primos (cocaine in marijuana), mothers' use report, 187, 188–189, 193
Public Law (PL) 99-457, 196
  Part H, 55, 206
Pure tone air conduction threshold average (PTA), 59, 63, 67

R

R. J. Cooper & Associates, 138
Renal failure, 102–103
Report of the National Conference on Education of the Deaf, 8
Research, transient evoked otoacoustic emissions (TEOAEs), 15–16
Residual hearing stimulation, 113–118
Respiratory distress syndrome (RDS), and language development, 252, 281
Rhode Island Hearing Assessment Program (RIHAP), 15–16
Rubella, 12, 13

S

Screening
  "distraction test." *See* Behavioral observation audiometry (BOA).
  hearing. *See also* Assessment, audiologic; Universal newborn hearing screening (UNHS).
    advocacy, 42–43
    age of testing, 56
    ALGO-1 Plus™, 14
    approaches, 10–14
    auditory brainstem response (ABR), 13–14, 56
    automated auditory brainstem response (AABR), 16, 19, 32, 43
    behavioral observation audiometry (BOA), 10–11
    behavioral screening, 10–12
    brainstem auditory evoked response (BAER), 14
    collaborative model, 16–20
    components, critical, 43
    cost analysis, 40–42
    Crib-O-Gram (COG), 10
    delay consequences, 7–8
    and diagnostic goals, 19
    family, 17–18
    and follow-up care, 10, 18, 33–37, 72–73
    goals, 43–44
    high-risk registries (HRR), 12–13, 14
    history, early screening, 8–10
    infant hearing impairment identification program (IHIIP), 9–10
    Joint Committee on Infant Hearing (JCIH), 12–13, 16–17, 32–33, 40, 56
    National Institutes of Health (NIH) Consensus Development Conference on Identification

Index

of Hearing Impairments in Infants and Young Children, 5–6, 9, 17, 18
overview, 5–6
public awareness campaign approach, 10
Rhode Island Hearing Assessment Program (RIHAP), 15–16
task forces, 42–43
technology. *See* Otoacoustic emissions (OAEs); individual methods.
transient evoked otoacoustic emissions (TEOAEs), 14–16, 16, 19, 32, 43. *See also* Transient evoked otoacoustic emissions (TEOAEs).
universal newborn hearing screening (UNHS), 6, 16–20. *See also* Universal newborn hearing screening (UNHS).
visual reinforcement audiometry (VRA), 11–12. *See also* Assessment, audiologic.

Sensorineural hearing loss (SNHL)
auditory brainstem response (ABR), 64–65, 67
bilateral
high-risk criteria, 12–13
identification delay consequences, 7
defined, 6
educational costs, 41
hearing loss statistics, 6–7
high-risk registries (HRR), 12
intelligibility learning, 110–112
intervention, overview, 37
mild-to-moderate, 64–66
moderate, 66–69
overview, 61
risk factors, 56
screening, universal, 6
severe, 69–72, 110–112
severe-to-profound, 69
unilateral, identification delay consequences, 7–8

Sensory development, neonatal, 79–80
Sequenced Inventory of Communication Development-Revised (SICD-R), Spanish, 251, 256–262
lexicon selection, 256–257
Signals, communicative, 142
Smoking. *See* Cigarette smoking.
Software, Hearing Health Institute (HHI) hearing screening information management package, 35

Speech audiometry, 59
Speech awareness threshold (SAT), 59, 63
Speech detection threshold (SDT), 59
Speech-language therapist (SLP)
aural rehabilitation, 100–101
cerebral palsy (CP), 145–149
conductive hearing loss (CHL), 63
co-treatment, physical therapist (PT)/occupational therapist (OT), 145–149
Speech perception, 60, 62
and language learning, 93
neonatal, 81–83
importance of, 87
phonetic discrimination, 82–83, 87
and production, 93
Speech recognition threshold (SRT), 59
Stigmata, 12, 46
Substance abuse, prenatal
cigarette smoking, mothers' use report, 187, 188, 193
coffee, mothers' use report, 187, 188, 193
liquor, mothers' use report, 187, 188, 193
Substance Questionnaire (self-report), 185, 187–188, 193
Surgery, ear, 64
Syphilis, 12

T

Tangible reinforcement operant conditioning audiometry (TROCA), 59
Tay-Sach's disease, 12
Technology, assistive, powered mobility, 134–136
Technology: The Future Is Today, 135
Tests
HELP, 102
MacArthur Communicative Development Inventory, 102
Northwestern University Children's Perception of Speech (NU-CHIPS) test, 59, 96
Parent-Infant Communication Scales, 102
PB-K (phonetically balanced-kindergarten) word list, 96
Word Intelligibility by Picture Identification (WIPI) test, 59, 67–68, 96
Therapy. *See also* Play therapy
cerebral palsy (CP), 141–158
communicative intent development, 141–158

Therapy. *(continued)*
  co-treatment, 145–149
  play, 142
T M Innovative Products Inc., 138
Tobacco. *See* Cigarette smoking.
Total communication, 93
Toxoplasmosis, 12
Toys. *See* Play therapy.
Toys for Special Children, 137
Tracheostomy
  bronchopulmonary dysplasia (BPD), 236–237
  communicative intentions
    behavior regulation, 232, 242
    gesture reliance, 243–244
    joint attention, 242
    parent-child interaction, 235–236
    toddler, 235–248
  coping mechanism development, 237
  expressive language development, 233
  hospitalization limiting family communication, 236–237
  neonatal intensive care unit (NICU), caregiver interaction limitation, 237
  phonemic development, 233
  social behaviors, and vocalization, 227–233
  speaking valve orientation, 229, 232–233
  toddler, communicative intentions, 235–248
  vocalization, inability, prelinguistic, 235
Tracheotomy tube, 66
Transient evoked otoacoustic emissions (TEOAEs), 4, 14–16, 16, 19, 32, 43. *See also* Otoacoustic emissions (OAEs)
  Rhode Island Hearing Assessment Program (RIHAP), 15–16
Trauma, head, 56
Treatment. *See also* Co-treatment
  order of training, 158
Turbo powered wheelchair, 139
Tympanometry, 60, 63, 71
Tympanostomy tubes, 66, 100, 101

U

United Cerebral Palsy Association, 135
Universal newborn hearing screening (UNHS), 6, 16–20. *See also* Screening, hearing
  advocacy, 42–43
  "aggregate burden," 40
  collaboration, multidisciplinary, 42, 44–45
  components, critical, 43
  cost analysis, 40–42
  Educational Audiology Association, Executive Board of (EBEAA), 40–41
  follow-up, 33–37, 72–73
    data management, 34–35
    National Center for Hearing Identification and Management (NCHIM), 34
    parents/guardians, 35–37
    questionnaire-based, 33–34
  goals, 43–44
  societal benefits, 39–40
  task forces, 42–43

V

Ventilation, assisted, 101
Vibrotactile aids, 71–72, 99
Visual reinforcement audiometry (VRA), 11–12, 58, 64, 66, 71, 81
Visual reinforcement operant conditioning audiometry (VROCA), 59

W

Word Intelligibility by Picture Identification (WIPI) test, 59, 67–68, 96

Y

Youthmobile Jaguar, 138